W9-AFO-355

*An Introduction to Indian Thought*

DATE DUE

| | | | |
|---|---|---|---|
| DEC 21 197[illegible] | | | |
| NOV 28 19[illegible] | | | |

30 508 JOSTEN'S

# *An Introduction to Indian Thought*

**A. L. HERMAN**
*University of Wisconsin*
*Stevens Point*

Prentice-Hall, Inc., *Englewood Cliffs, New Jersey*

*Library of Congress Cataloging in Publication Data*

HERMAN, A L

An introduction to Indian thought.

Bibliography: p.
Includes index.

1. Philosophy, Indic. I. Title.

B131.H464 181′.4 75–31587

ISBN 0-13-484477-7

© 1976 by Prentice-Hall, Inc., Englewood Cliffs, New Jersey.

All rights reserved. No part of this book may be reproduced in any form or by any means without permission in writing from the publisher.

Printed in the United States of America.

10 9 8 7 6 5 4 3 2 1

Prentice-Hall International, Inc., *London*
Prentice-Hall of Australia, Pty. Limited, *Sydney*
Prentice-Hall of Canada. Ltd., *Toronto*
Prentice-Hall of India Private Limited, *New Delhi*
Prentice-Hall of Japan, Inc., *Tokyo*
Prentice-Hall of Southeast Asia Pte. Ltd., *Singapore*

B
131
H464

***For Bay and Di Di***

10673

# *Contents*

# *Preface*

The purpose of this book is really twofold: First, to introduce the reader to the subject of philosophy, and, second, to introduce the reader to Indian thought. Both purposes are combined in this work by using Indian thought to illustrate the various activities and subfields of philosophy. Philosophy should always involve the pursuit of intellectual problems and puzzles, and this book attempts to pursue those problems in the context of the history of Indian thought. However, there's more to such a pursuit than merely the flushing out and the chase, joyful as those endeavors may be. Philosophical pursuit of a problem also involves the careful statement of and the clear explication of the problem as well—while the philosopher chases problems, he also knows very well what he's chasing. The pursuit thus involves stating the problem as clearly as possible, explaining how or why it is significant in the context in which it lies, whether that context be metaphysical or theological or moral, and then showing why it is a problem, why it is a puzzle or a paradox at all. Further, the pursuit of an intellectual problem also involves wrestling with solutions or attempted solutions to the problem. The philosophic hunter, once the game has been run to ground, examined and analyzed, revives and reinforces it, puts it back on its feet, redirects its path, releases it, and then goes off once again, chasing after the now strengthened quarry. Finally, the pursuit of philosophic game does something to the philsopher who engages in the chase, who identifies the game, who captures and then releases and repursues the revivified prey. The pursuit teaches one something not only about the world in which one lives, but also about oneself. For it is an ancient belief of both the classical philosophers of Greece as well as the classical philosophies of India, that philosophy, the exercise of reason and intelligence, is a good and ennobling enterprise, one of the highest callings and achievements of which man is capable; and, that philosophic pursuit can show man the way to happiness for the species and liberation and freedom for the individual.

The book begins with an introduction to philosophy as an historical discipline by describing the two major kinds of philosophy, critical and speculative, and by outlining several of the subfields of philosophy. It moves to early Indian thought, proceeding chronologically, beginning with the Indus Valley civilization. It then turns to the sacred and philosophical texts of India, the *Vedas*, the *Upaniṣads*, and the *Bhagavad Gītā*. The aim in examining these compositions is twofold: First, to search out the central themes running through these works, themes in religion, metaphysics, epistemology, and ethics, in order to give the student of philosophy and comparative religion a glimpse into the historical and orderly workings of Indian thought and its development; and second, to pursue the various intellectual problems that arise in these texts and that come to the surface in presenting the history of that thought. The presentation of these problems, as the philosophic pursuit continues, will be accompanied by attempts at solutions, together with a defense and critique of the attempted solutions. The acceptance or rejection of solutions to problems is left to the reader on several occasions where he or she is invited to construct his or her own defense or critique. Thus the final thrust of the book is to make the reader familiar with both the nature of philosophy and the nature of Indian thought.

There are a number of persons that have helped in the critical preparation of this book and to whom I am deeply indebted. First of all, Russell T. Blackwood, Barbara Herman, and David B. White read the manuscript in its near entirity and made valuable comments on the whole work. To the following people I owe a great debt as well for their readings and comments on parts of the work, and for general help over the months that it was in preparation: John D. Bailiff, J. Baird Callicott, Daniel H. H. Ingalls, Karl H. Potter, Joseph L. Schuler, and John P. Zawadsky. Finally, to Sandra DiSomma of Prentice-Hall who worked closely with me on the final preparation of the manuscript and proofs, and to Judi Opiola who typed the original manuscript and its various penultimate versions, I am especially grateful. Whatever merit the work prossesses is due to the collective kindness and attention of all of these very generous people.

A. L. HERMAN
*Stevens Point, Wisconsin*

# *Pronunciation of Sanskrit Terms*

Sanskrit is written in an ancient and elegant script called *devanagārī*. For those who don't read *devanāgarī* this script must be transliterated into English and the English pronounced according to the phonetic rules of Sanskrit. Below are some general pronunciation guidelines for the transliterated *devanāgarī* letters:

The vowels with macrons, e.g., *ā*, *ī*, *ū*, are long vowels and are pronounced as in *father*, *machine*, and *rude*. The same vowels without macrons are short vowels and equivalent in sound to *but*, *tin*, and *full*. Vowel *ṛ* is sounded as in *rill* and is lightly trilled. The vowels *e*, *ai*, *o*, and *au*, are pronounced as in *grey*, *aisle*, *open*, and *cow*.

All consonants with *h* after them are aspirated consonants and the breath should be slightly released when pronouncing them. Thus *kh*, *gh*, *ch*, *jh*, *ph*, and so on sound like *rockhouse*, *doghouse*, *churchhouse*, *fudgehouse*, *tophouse*, and so on. Other consonants that one must watch out for are *c* as in *cheese*, *ś* and *ṣ* both as in *ship*, *s* as in *sip*, and *jñ* as in *gyāna*.

*An Introduction to Indian Thought*

# A.
# *Introduction*

## 1. CRITICAL PHILOSOPHY AND SPECULATIVE PHILOSOPHY

The subject of this book is Indian thought—the philosophic and religious thoughts of the men and women who lived in the Asian subcontinent of India from about 2500 B.C.E. (Before the Christian Era) to about 200 B.C.E. Some of these thoughts are mutely expressed in the artistic and archeological traditions that have survived the ravages of climate and man, while others survive in the oral and written literary traditions that have similarly come down to us. Our task will be to investigate these thoughts by getting clear on what they were and then critically examining what they mean. In other words, our task will be to state, by example or translation, what these Indian materials were stating or saying and what these statements and sayings may have meant. I say that ours will be a "critical examination," for part of our task will be to bring the powers of analysis and reason to bear on the materials that we have chosen for study. There will be a certain pleasure in carrying out this activity, I promise you, for man delights generally in the exercise of his reason, as Plato and Aristotle long ago pointed out, and man similarly delights in discovering how other men have managed to survive in what must often seem a dangerous and hostile world.

Thus, thinking and survival constitute two of the chief occupations of man, and each, as we shall see, forms part of the task of philosophy. For, on the one hand, philosophy is an intellectual discipline which looks rationally and critically at judgments and pronouncements that are made about the world, and man, and life. It seeks, through intelligent scrutiny of these judgments, to arrive at clarity and precision in our understanding of them, and, aside from a certain delight that accompanies such an exercise of reason, it has no other goal than making the crooked judgment as straight as possible. This kind of philosophy we might simply label "critical philosophy." The critical philosopher sees life as a spectacle rather than a predicament. He is primarily concerned about the judgments people make about the spectacle and assume to be true about the spectacle. He seeks to render those judgments and those assumptions as clear and as precise as possible. A well-known contemporary British philosopher, C. D. Broad, has caught the spirit of critical philosophy extremely well when he says that it involves ". . . the analysis and definition of our fundamental concepts, and the clear statement and resolute criticism of our fundamental beliefs."

On the other hand, philosophy has been thought of as that activity which will lead man to happiness and liberation *in* the world or *from* the world. Philosophy in this second sense sees life as a predicament rather than a spectacle. This kind of philosophy we might simply label "speculative philosophy." The speculative philosopher feels the anguish of his existential predicament and, driven by that anguish, he seeks to ameliorate it or to end it. The speculative philosopher speculates in order to survive, to save his soul, to become liberated from pain and suffering, to achieve accommodation to or happiness in this world. But those speculations involve him in the development, oftentimes, of labyrinthine systems of thought, vast and complex metaphysical and theological structures, through which he attempts to see the world, explain life, and relieve his temporal suffering. Speculative philosophy, then, is the attempt to answer the riddle of life, to frame a vision of existence, to reveal the hidden and the mysterious. Alfred North Whitehead, the famous twentieth-century mathematician and philosopher, has well defined speculative philosophy as " . . . the endeavor to frame a coherent, logical, necessary system of general ideas in terms of which every element of our experience can be interpreted."

But critical philosophy and speculative philosophy do not exist isolated and separated one from the other. The critical philosopher has a kind of parasitical relationship with speculative philosophy in the sense that if the latter did not exist, then neither would he. And the speculative philosopher, of course, does not speculate in a philosophic vacuum, letting his anguished imagination run free while erecting fortresses of icy ontology. He, too, has a kind of parasitical relationship, but upon the discipline and techniques of critical philosophy, which prevents his speculations from turning into nightmares on the one hand or philosophic fantasies on the other. Hence, critical philosophy is dependent on the subject matter that speculative philosophy presents in its synthesis of thought, and speculative philosophy, in turn, is dependent on the tools that critical philosophy uses in its analysis of thought. For example, when speculative Indian philosophers claim that they know that happiness and liberation are reached by either ritual sacrifice, or knowledge of Ātman, or by yoga, or through the will of God, then the critical philosopher steps forward demanding to know what the terms mean that are used in these speculative judgments; he proceeds by asking for clarification about basic concepts such as "liberation" or "Ātman" or "yoga"; he requests precision in meaning in any discussion about the justification for the belief that yoga leads to true happiness; he seeks to critically evaluate the various philosophical problems and solutions that arise out of the speculative Indian tradition. We shall be concerned to play critical philosopher in precisely this sense in our examination of Indian speculative philosophy.

The present work attempts to bring both critical and speculative philosophy together in the investigation of Indian thought. An American philosopher, Josiah Royce, in *The Spirit of Modern Philosophy*, has captured the spirit of this joining of critical philosophy with speculative philosophy, and Royce's characterization of philosophy as a discipline committed to both life's spectacle and its predicament epitomizes the approach to philosophy that this book will take. Royce says:

> You philosophize when you reflect critically upon what you are actually doing in your world. What you are doing is, of course, in the first place, living. And life involves passions, faiths, doubts, and courage. The critical inquiry into what all these things mean and imply is philosophy.

As far as Indian thought is concerned, we shall be examining it both as critical philosophers concerned with matters of clarity, truth, knowledge, evidence, and the manifold problems that these concepts engender, and as speculative philosophers concerned about the human predicament, the confrontation between the self and the world, the existential condition of pain, anxiety, and suffering, and the attempts to find escape, happiness, or liberation under such conditions.

Since we shall be dealing with Indian thought within the context of several rather well-defined and traditional fields of philosophy, let me say a brief word about those fields.

## 2. THE FIELDS OF PHILOSOPHY

The word "philosophy" (from the Greek *philein*, to love, and *sophos*, wisdom; hence "the love of wisdom") is a Greek invention, though philosophy, as an activity of critical and speculative thought, is not. And since "philosophy" is a Greek invention, it is not surprising that the names of the chief subdivisions or fields of philosophy are Greek as well. There are four such fields: metaphysics, epistemology, ethics, and logic. Let me say something rather briefly about each and then conclude this introduction with a remark about religion, which we shall be treating as a field of speculative philosophy in this book.

### a. *Metaphysics*

"Metaphysics" was originally the title given to a collection of Aristotle's writings by one Andronicus in the first century B.C.E. Andronicus, in cataloging this group of manuscripts, placed them after another set of writings which Aristotle himself had called *Physis* or "Physics." The word *physis* means "nature" in Greek, so *metaphysis* or "metaphysics" meant "beyond or after nature." But while this story gives us the word "metaphysics," it does not explain the meaning that the word has come to have: for the ancient Greeks engaged in metaphysics even before Andronicus gave a name to their activity. Such activity, traditionally implied by "metaphysics," is simply an investigation into the nature of ultimate reality. The metaphysician is concerned with asking and then answering questions about the ultimately real, and for the Greeks only that which was independent, unchanging, uncreated, and eternal could be called "real" or "ultimately real."

There are four subfields of metaphysics, each concerned with the ultimate nature of one particular area of reality: (1) being in general, (2) the cosmos, (3) man, and (4) the Gods. The four subfields of metaphysics that look into these areas are called "ontology," "cosmology," "rational psychology," and "rational theology," respectively.

### b. *Epistemology*

Epistemology, the second field of philosophy, will form an extremely important part of any investigation into the nature of Indian thought. "Epistemology" is a compound Greek word formed from two simpler parts, *epistemē* which means "knowledge," and *logos* which means "thought" or "discourse." Hence, "epistemology" means "a discourse on the nature of knowledge." The epistemologist is interested in questions such as: What are the criteria of knowledge? How does one know or come to know anything at all? and, most importantly: How does one know that one knows anything? This last question gets the philosopher into a discussion of the grounds of knowledge—the means or ways or *pramāṇas* to knowledge—and it is in discussions of these ways and their validity or efficacy that epistemology has been most exciting.

### c. *Ethics*

The word "ethics" comes from the Greek word for "character." Ethics is simply that field of philosophy that studies or investigates the nature of rightness and goodness and obligation as those concepts apply to human conduct. There are, to be sure, nonmoral uses of "right" and "good" and "obligation" in which the ethetician is not interested. Thus when someone says, "What you just said was right (true or correct)," or "That's a good (well-made) vase," or "You ought (if you want to laugh) to see the funny pictures," then he is exhibiting the nonmoral uses of "right," "good," and "obligation." But when these terms appear in moral contexts, then they are of primary concern to the philosopher interested in ethics. Thus when I say, "Honoring your parents is always right," or "Telling the truth is never wrong," or "Producing the greatest amount of pleasure is the highest good," or "Whatever action is right is always obligatory," the ethetician is interested in both the meanings of the moral terms involved and the criteria for their correct employment in these contexts.

### *d. Logic*

The word "logic" comes from the Greek *logos*, which means, among other things, "word," "thought," and "discourse." Logic itself is, quite simply, the study of the nature of inference. It raises and examines questions concerned with the legitimacy of drawing conclusions from one set of statements to another statement or set of statements. Thus if I already know that all Hindus accept the authority of the *Vedas*, can I legitimately infer that this particular Hindu will accept the authority of the *Vedas*?; or, if this Hindu accepts the *Vedas* as authoritative, and that Hindu accepts the *Vedas* as authoritative, and so on for many other *Vedas*-accepting Hindus, can I then legitimately (validly) infer that all Hindus will accept the authority of the *Vedas*?—and, if so, why and on what grounds? We shall refer to logic and inference only indirectly in our discussions of Indian thought.

### *e. Conclusion*

In addition to being concerned about the metaphysics, epistemology, and ethics of Indian thought, we shall also be concerned about the role of religion. Together with the three above-mentioned fields of philosophy, religion will form a fourth division in our discussion of the Indian texts: the *Vedas*, the *Upaniṣads*, and the *Bhagavad Gītā*. The word "religion" is a Latin, rather than a Greek, word, and it means "to bind back." It has come to have the sense of "disciplining" or "rigorous training" and is synonymous with certain meanings of the word "yoga." But rather than trying to state all the meanings that "religion" will have or could have in the historical periods and texts we shall be examining, let me merely indicate here that as speculative philosophy it will be an area of chief concern to us in what follows.

Without any further preliminaries, we turn now to the early history of man in India, and to the beginnings of philosophic stirrings in the subcontinent's earliest civilization, the Indus Valley civilization.

# *B.*
# *Pre-Āryan Civilization*

## 1. STONE-AGE MAN

The first signs of primitive man in India occur during the period from 400,000 to 200,000 B.C.E. This paleolithic ("old stone age") man has left behind chipped pebble tools in the area of the Punjab in Northeastern India (see Map 1). He is called "pithecanthropus" or "ape man" by the anthropologist, and his remains are found during this long geologic period at other sites, usually by or near inland rivers—for example, in Indonesia near Trinil, where he is known as Java man, and at other sites in China as well. He is most closely related, judging by the skull and jaw fragments we possess, to European Neanderthal man, that popular and famous precursor of modern man who dwelt in caves in the Neander Valley in Germany. Evidence from Indian digs would also seem to point to the existence of some kind of early *homo sapiens* in and around the region of Madras along the southeastern coast of India (see Map 1) during this same period. These early men used stone tools and probably developed the first stone axe ever used by man.

The next significant occurrence of primitive man in India occurs during the neolithic ("new stone age") period from 10,000 to 6000 B.C.E. in the northwest of India and in the Deccan, the south-central area of India (see Map 1). Neolithic man seems to have taken a more aggressive attitude toward his surroundings, endeavoring to actively tame it and bend it to suit his needs and comforts. Neolithic man no longer chips and chops his stone tools but is noted instead for his attempts to smooth and polish these working implements. He turns from the less controllable and more chancy hunting and fishing of his previous existence to farming and grazing; thereby giving up the wandering, nomadic existence that the former ways of food-gathering seemed to necessitate for the more permanent and secure methods of agricul-

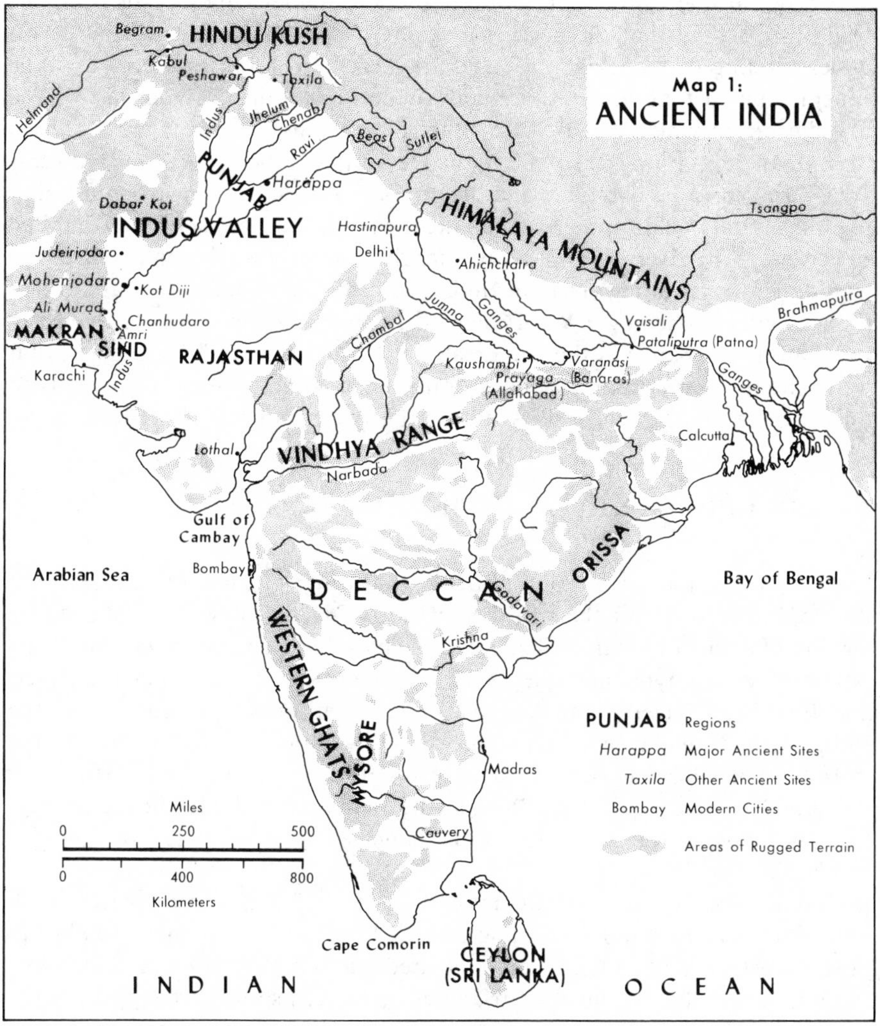


Map 1. Ancient India.
(Map by Robert C. Hyde, Cartographic Laboratory, Department of Geography, University of Minnesota, Minneapolis.)

ture and animal husbandry. The cessation of the wandering life and the adoption of the settled life must have meant that neolithic man also accepted some form of communal existence, perhaps including community defense and civil government, along with rules for acceptable behavior within as well as outside that community. But what these institutions may have been like is moot and subject only to conjecture.

Neither paleolithic nor neolithic Indian man left any records or viable traditions behind that the modern Indologist can seize upon to enlarge his understanding of stone-age man in India. We can, however, come to some general conclusions about this great subcontinent that provide us with a foundation on which to base our future discussions. First, the areas chosen for human habitation—the Punjab, the Deccan, and the southeastern Madras area—proved to be habitable and hospitable to man. This meant, quite simply, that India could support human life. Second, since many of the inhabited sites were along rivers, perhaps any later developments of human civilization would also occur along rivers in India. Both of these conclusions are in fact true, as later archeological work has borne out: Human culture survived in India along the banks of the two great rivers, the Indus and the Ganges, that drain the northern mountainous regions of the country (see Map 1). It is to one of these great rivers and its culture that we turn next.

## 2. THE GEOGRAPHY OF ANCIENT INDIA

At about the same time in history that other great river cultures were developing throughout the world, the Indus River Valley also spawned its version of ancient human civilization. Side by side with the civilizations of the Nile valley in Egypt, and the Mesopotamian Kingdoms along the Tigris and Euphrates Rivers, and the Yellow River culture of ancient China, the Indus River Valley provided a comfortable livelihood to early civilized man in India. If civilization occurs whenever man learns to live in cities (from the Latin *civis* which means "city"), then the Indus River Valley in the twenty-fifth and twenty-fourth centuries B.C.E. gave India its first domicile for civilization.

The subcontinent that we are calling "India" was approximately 1500 miles wide and 2000 miles long and included the modern country of Pakistan in the West, as well as the recently created state of Bangla Desh in the East. India is shaped like an inverted triangle; its eastern shores are lapped by the waters of the Bay of Bengal, and its western boundary is marked by the Arabian Sea. To the north is the base of the triangle, the gigantic chain of mountains, the great Himālayas, which provides a nearly impenetrable barrier to Siberian winds and hostile Mongol invaders. The southernmost tip of India, the point of the triangle that forms the Cape of Comorin, juts out into the Indian Ocean and stands some 200 miles from the island of Ceylon (now called "Sri Lanka"). In the north, where our philosophical story of India begins, three great rivers and their tributaries drain the snow-clad heights of the Himālayas. From the north-central part of India, the river Ganges with its major tributary, the Jumna River, drains the plain of the

Ganges and the eastern part of the Himālayas into the Bay of Bengal. From the extreme eastern extension of the Himālayas the mighty Brahmaputra River carries off the melting snows of the eastern chain of mountains and joins its torrents with the Ganges for a final plunge into the Bay of Bengal.

On the Western slopes of the Himālayas five rivers flow into the plain of the Indus Valley. These five rivers form the region of the Punjab (which means "five rivers") in the northwest corner of our continental triangle. The Indus River gathers up these five smaller rivers of melting Himālayic snows and carries the waters into the western Arabian Sea. Along the banks of this river and its tributaries Indian culture began, and that culture is referred to as the *Indus Valley civilization.*

## 3. INDUS VALLEY CITIES

The Indus River was called *sindhu* by the Indians of an earlier day. But invading Persians who entered the country found it difficult to pronounce the initial sibilant 's' sound by which the local inhabitants referred to their river. Hence, to the Persians the river became known as the *Indu* or *Hindu*, and it was by this name that the later invading Greeks also came to know the river. And so, as a consequence of a speech-impediment of the ancient Persians, the Sindhu River became the Indu and, later, the Indus River.

Two principal sites in the Indus Valley have become, since Sir John Marshal began his excavations in 1924, of paramount interest to the archeologist. These two sites are known as Harappā and Mohenjo-daro. Harappā (see Map 1) lies to the north along the Ravi River, one of five rivers which, with the Indus, compose the single and wider Indus River farther to the south. Mohenjo-daro lies along that larger and more southern body of the Indus that flows as a single mighty body into the Arabian sea near Karachi in modern Pakistan. The whole of the Indus valley plain no longer exists in India proper, but, since the partition of India into Pakistan and the Republic of India in 1947, that plain is now part of Pakistan. So we are talking about a portion of the geography of ancient India that is today no longer a part of India.

From the excavations of these ancient sites of Harappā and Mohenjo-daro, a number of highly interesting conclusions can be drawn that have significant bearing on later Indian religion, art, and philosophy.

The people who first inhabited these cities we shall refer to as "*Harappāns*," a people whose descendents still occupy parts of South India to this day. We can tell something of the appearance of these Harappāns by the works of art that were left behind when the cities either expired or were abandoned. I say "expired or abandoned" for no one is certain as to what did happen to these once flourishing and apparently rather beautiful cities. It remains something of a mystery as to whether they fell from internal or external causes, or even a combination of both.

The Harappāns lived in the cities built upon the sites of Harappā and Mohenjo-daro and elsewhere, and the general name given by archeologists to this collection of Indus cities and people is *the Harappān culture.* From Mohenjo-daro, which lay about 250 miles above the mouth of the Indus, to Harappā itself on the Ravi River some 400 miles farther to the north, the Harappān culture flourished for nearly a thousand years during the third millennium B.C.E. Let me say something very briefly about the cities of the Harappān culture, one city in particular, and then describe the people of these cities and their culture insofar as they relate to Indian thought.

The two cities of Harappā and Mohenjo-daro were similar in general appearance. The towns proper lay at the foot of fortified hills or citadels which lay to the west of the cities.[1]

On this acropolis, not unlike the famous upper citadel of Athens, all the public buildings of the two cities were erected. Below the acropolis lay the city itself, each city being approximately three miles in circumference.

The cities were well planned and well laid out in a grid pattern. Recent excavations at the deepest levels (at Mohenjo-daro alone, nine levels have been found) indicate that the streets were approximately 30 feet wide, thereby separating the city into large blocks with wide lanes criss-crossing at right angles within. A twentieth-century city planner would be both envious and gratified at the civic sense and aesthetic foresight demonstrated by the city engineers of the Harappān culture. For example, a modern covered sewer system of baked clay bricks connected the one-, two-, and more-storied brick dwellings that lined the streets. Magnificent courtyards surrounded by living quarters complete with indoor baths and toilets would indicate an aesthetic and hygienic concern well beyond any comparable civilization of the third or second millennium B.C.E.; its sewer system alone would rival that of the city of Rome during its imperial period some 2500 years later.

The acropolis at Mohenjo-daro was built upon a man-made mound about 240,000 square feet in area and fortified by a baked red brick wall approximately 50 feet high, mounted with brick watch towers that guarded the walls. Within this fortified hill city, among other luxuries, was a large bath measuring 29 by 33 feet, complete with waterproofed bitumen walls and handsome steps leading into the bath. Near it lay a granary of timber and brick for the storage of grains with a runway and loading dock for grain wagons. In addition to the great bath and the well-planned granary (which

[1]For a more complete discussion of all the points that follow see A. L. Basham, *The Wonder That Was India* (New York: Grove Press, Inc., 1954); Stuart Piggott, *Prehistoric India* (Baltimore: Penguin Books, 1961); and Sir Mortimer Wheeler, *Civilizations of the Indus Valley and Beyond* (New York: McGraw-Hill, 1966).

practically and wisely allowed for the proper ventilation of its contents) there were two great pillared halls. One contained a number of rooms with smaller baths in them; the other, a longer building mẹasuring 230 by 78 feet, was possibly used for state or ritual purposes. The overall effect produced on the viewer by this acropolis and the city is described by Sir Mortimer Wheeler: "The general indication of combined kingly and priestly rule fits the habit of the third millennium"; and "In its prime, the whole city bespeaks middle-class prosperity with zealous municipal controls."[2] But whether or not the city was ruled by priests or kings, and whether or not it is fair to import "middle class" into a description of the early prosperity of the city or cities, is highly debatable. What we know of the governance and the control of the city or cities is meager enough, as we shall see.

## 4. THE ARTS OF THE INDUS

The language spoken by these people of the Harappān culture is unknown to us. The written script that is known contains about 270 characters, but it has not been deciphered, even though over 2000 stone seals produced from soft steatite by the Harappāns have been discovered. These seals, about one inch square, when pressed into wet clay then left behind the raised impression engraved on the original seal. It is from the pictures of animals, grotesque beasts, curious shapes and designs, and the images of the men on these seals and tablets, together with the stone and bronze art objects left intact through the centuries, that our knowledge of this mysterious Harappān people comes.

Of the thousands of intact artifacts and significant sherds only three are of particular interest to us: two objects of magnificent artistic merit and one singularly handsome stone seal. The first object is a steatite bust of a bearded man, eyes half closed as if in meditation (see Figure 1, p. 13). The eyes are long, wide, heavy-lidded slits, each approximately as wide as the large, full lips. A beard covers the entire face except for the clean-shaven upper lip. The beard is well trimmed, as we can see by close scrutiny of the series of clean vertical lines that define its limits at the upper face and the upper neck. The nose, though chipped badly at its tip, appears to be flat and broad. The statural proportions indicate a relatively short, powerfully built, broad-chested person. The expression suggests a certain austere, aristocratic hautiness. Above the middle of the forehead stands the small circle of a headband, almost like a third eye peering out from a broad expanse of bare skull. A similar band is worn on the upper right forearm. The other arm is hidden beneath a cloak or shirt, worn so that the upper one-third of the torso

[2] *Op. cit.*, pp. 18, 21.

is exposed, and this diagonally draped garment is decorated with a pattern of trefoils or *fleur-de-lis*. The hair, worn long and apparently tied at the back, exposes the well-shaped but lobeless ears.

This small statue from Mohenjo-daro can tell us a number of things about the people of the Harappān culture. It tells us that the Harappāns may have been people with Australoid, Mongoloid, and Negroid features. The short stature, the long eyes, the flat nose, the thick lips, and, from later accounts, the dark skin, have given anthropologists no end of clues in typing or racially cataloging these people of the third millennium. And later Āryan accounts of the indigenous people they met when they invaded India in the second millinnium B.C.E. would seem to confirm that the figure represented in the clay of Mohenjo-daro was a typical man of the Harappān culture.

The second artifact that is worth some attention here, though not for anthropological reasons, is a beautiful bronze work, again from Mohenjo-daro. The statue shows a thin and angular naked girl with small breasts and medium-length hair, her head lifted slightly, one hand resting gracefully on her hip. The other hand holds a small bowl, and the arm is covered with bracelets from armpit to wrist. A necklace with three baubles graces her throat. One leg is bent at the knee, throwing the buttocks back at an abrupt teasing angle. The totally "feminine" pose, provocative and sensuous, has led some Indologists to believe that she represents a dancing girl, a temple prostitute, or personal household slave. There is no evidence to support any of these guesses. Like the male figure previously mentioned she has full and wide lips, a high forehead, and a broad, flat nose, together with a possibly short stature (see Figure 2, p. 13).

The figure achieves a level of artistic realism and sophistication, aesthetic charm and beauty, that must mark it as one of the most significant archeological finds from the ancient world. She stands in such stark secular opposition to the rather abundant squat, wide-hipped mother-fertility goddesses and the erect stone *liṅga* (phalluses) of the Harappān religious culture, that she is always worth noting in any work on the art of Mohenjo-daro. Heinrich Zimmer has well said of this figure, "The statuette is notable particularly for its treatment of the slim back and long legs, and for its alert resiliency and refined force. The body of the graceful, slender girl is full of the dynamism of life, the same hidden energy welling from within that constitutes one of the most characteristic features of classic Indian art."[3]

In mysterious contrast to these two statues of Harappān man and woman, and to Harappān secular life in general, stands a more chthonic work also from Mohenjo-daro (Figure 3). Of the thousands of pots, plates, clay toys, pieces of jewelry, statues and figurines, and significant chunks, bits,

[3]Heinrich Zimmer, *The Art of Indian Asia*, Two Volumes (New York: Pantheon Books, 1955), Vol. I, p. 35.

Figure 1. Bearded man (Mohenjo-daro).

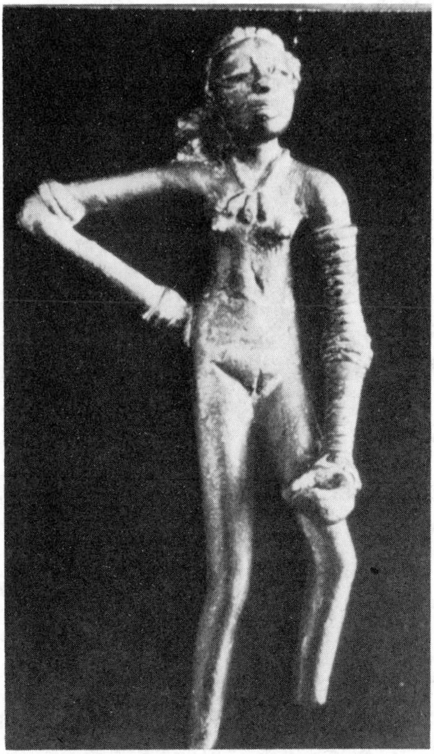

Figure 2. Bronze girl (Mohenjo-daro).

Figure 3. Proto-Śiva seal (Indus Valley).

pieces and parts that the Harappān digs have yielded, this third work must come as a pleasant but disturbing surprise to the casual observer. It is a small stone seal about one inch square showing a figure seated in a cross-legged pose, typical of that used by yogis in a later period. The figure seems to wear a large horned headdress, and he is seated on a raised, adorned platform. His left hand rests on his left knee (the other hand is obliterated by an unfortunate chipping, so that the entire left corner of the seal is missing), and the fingers seem to be pointing to the ground. An animal mask, possibly that of a lion or tiger, seems to cover the face of this mysterious being, and the entire figure is surrounded by smaller representations of animals—an elephant, a tiger, a buffalo, a rhinoceros, and what appears to be some horned creature, probably an antelope. Some Harappān glyphs across the top and above the horned headdress of the figure are quite plain but remain undeciphered. Just above the crossed heels of the figure an erect penis can be seen, indicating that the being is probably associated with a fertility cult; indeed, he may be one of the Gods of the cult itself.

A later Indian tradition has come to associate this Harappān figure with the God Śiva. There are five reasons for the association and they are worth mentioning here. First, Śiva, in that later tradition, is identified with the *liṅga*, the erect penis of the Indus seal. These *liṅga* can be seen in India today, reaching heights of 6 feet and more, and they are found in temples and other holy places sacred to Lord Śiva. Śiva in modern Hinduism is also associated with one of the three aspects of *Brahman*, the holy Power in the universe. These three aspects or powers of *Brahman* are called the *trimūrti*, the united triple form consisting of Brahmā, the creator, Viṣṇu, the preserver and savior of the world, and Śiva, the destroyer or dissolver of the world. It is interesting that in addition to his function as destroyer—that aspect of the trinity that brings universal creation and maintenance to an end—we also have Śiva's fecund, fertilizing, and vitalizing function represented as well by the erect phallus. At any rate the presence of the *liṅga* in this Indus seal would seem to establish an early connection between this figure and the Hindu God Śiva.

Second, the Hindu Śiva is the Lord of yoga and the patron saint of *yogis*. The Indus Valley figure, seated as he is in the typical cross-legged lotus posture of the traditional *yogi*, hands resting (presumably) on knees, and heels together would, again, seem to indicate some strong connection with that later Hindu Lord Śiva. Third, the Hindu Śiva is constantly referred to as *vānaspati*, Lord of the Forest, or *paśupati*, Lord of Wild Animals. The Indus Valley figure is surrounded by wild animals, and in particular he is associated here with the tiger, an animal with whom Śiva later becomes identified. Since the yogi practiced his austerities in solitude, the forest (*vāna*) became his home, so there is a connection between the second and third reasons for associating the Indus figure with the Hindu Śiva. Fourth, the horned antelope is also one of the later totem symbols of Śiva, and the Indus figure wears his horned mask most prominently.

Fifth, and finally, Lord Śiva is not one of the Āryan deities brought into India by those northern invaders from the Caucasus. There is no mention of Śiva in any of the Āryan texts or *Vedas* and yet he appears in India, suddenly and inexplicably, about the time of the rise of Buddhism. Where did he come from, suddenly and mysteriously? The best guess would seem to be that Śiva was always there: he was one of the indigenous Gods of the aboriginal natives of the Indus Valley who was associated with the *liṅga*, the fertility rites, the tiger and horned antelopes and wild desolate places where he consoled and directed his worshippers and his devotees in *yoga* meditation and ritual sacrifice. The hypothesis is conjectural, as all hypotheses are, but the evidence to support it seems strong.

In conclusion we might say that it is from the arts of the Indus Valley, its bronzes, stone and clay figures and seals, its pots and toys, its tools and implements of manufacture, that we come to know the people of the Harappān culture. These artifacts are all that remain to us of this once mighty and magnificent culture. Save for its later influence on the religion of the Āryans and the still later Hindu religious practices, the Indus Valley civilization is dead dust and now lost forever to generations of philosophers, theologians, and historians. What was it that brought this once flourishing culture to an end? What forces proved to be so strong that even these people could not stand against them? To these questions we now turn our attention.

## 5. THUS ARE THE MIGHTY BROUGHT LOW

It is not known what brought about the demise of the Indus Valley civilization. A number of hypotheses have been advanced to account for the destruction of the once magnificent cities of Harappā and Mohenjo-daro, but all of them seem to be wanting in some regard or other. Three hypotheses, however, stand out from the many to account for the fall of the Harappān culture, and these are worth considering. They are, first, that the culture was destroyed by external human forces, in particular the Āryan invasions from the northwest, with which it could not cope. Second, that the culture was set upon by external natural forces to which it could not properly respond. Third and finally, that the culture died from specific internal human forces, urban pollution and overpopulation, that it could not contain. Let us take these three causal possibilities in order in hopes of discovering how the mighty fell so low.

First, the Harappān culture was destroyed, it is supposed, because it was crushed and obliterated by the invading nomadic tribes of Āryan warriors from the northwest. One of the early champions of this position was the contemporary archeologist and Indologist, Sir Mortimer Wheeler. Wheeler had strongly suggested that the Āryan invaders from the northwest might have been the "ultimate agents of destruction." In support of this contention, which he has subsequently rescinded, Wheeler referred to the massive defensive towers and walls of the ancient Indus cities. The Harappāns were afraid of something and the walls were merely a sign of that fear. What was it they feared so much? The later *Vedas*, the sacred texts of the Āryan invaders, speak at many places of the conquest of the people in the walled cities, the wars against the people of dark skins, and the overthrowing of this enemy people by the Āryan war-god Indra. This conclusion was supported, in part, by the findings from the upper levels of the more recent archeological period at Mohenjo-daro. At these recent and upper layers of the ancient city human skeletons were discovered sprawled about in grotesque attitudes of violent death. Of one particular area at the site Wheeler states:

> In a room of "H.R. Area" fourteen skeletons of men, women and a child, some of them wearing ornaments of the Indus period, were found in attitudes suggesting simultaneous and violent death; two of the skulls showed cuts by axe or sword.[4]

These and other later remains at Mohenjo-daro would seem to support the conclusion that much of the community was indeed violently and unexpectedly slain by invaders, and quite possibly by those very same invaders for which the community had much earlier built its high towers and its seemingly impregnable walls. That which they feared most finally broke through and overwhelmed them.

This conclusion does not explain, however, why it was that the internal military defenses of the community proved useless or inoperable at the very time of these attacks. That is to say, the mortal blow to the Harappān culture could possibly have come about only through the operation of other factors. We turn, consequently, to the second possible explanation for the fall of the great Indus Valley civilization.

The second hypothesis states that the Harappān culture collapsed because it was set upon by disastrous natural forces to which it could not properly respond. Recent excavations of the multiple levels at the Indus Valley sites indicate that the rivers themselves, alternating between stages of flood and drought, may have driven the inhabitants, whose lives depended on the close proximity, as well as the proper level, of the rivers, out of the stricken cities and into more habitable areas. The probable causes of these violent alterations in the rivers are found in the theory that cataclysmic geomorphological upheavals occurred during the latter days of the culture's existence. This would mean that if we bracket the Indus culture sometime

[4]*Op. cit.*, p. 80.

between 2500 and 1800 B.C.E., we would have to expect important geological changes during the last five centuries or so of this period. Since the Indus culture occupied such a wide expanse of territory—from the foothills of the northwestern Himālayas to the shores of the Arabian Sea, a distance of nearly 1000 miles—we cannot reasonably expect uniform changes throughout this wide expanse. We must look instead for signs of local geologic change: and recent evidence would seem to support the contention that rather startling changes in the river levels did in fact occur at the lower end of the Indus River, south of Mohenjo-daro. At these southern Indus river sites it has been noted that there was a startling and persistent occurrence of sedimentary silting along with other identifiable marine deposits. In particular, large deposits of marine zoological material are found about 150 miles upriver from the mouth of the Indus and approximately 100 miles from Mohenjo-daro itself, farther to the north, and they have been identified as a species of salt-water marine mollusc. This might indicate a gigantic backing up of the salt sea water from the Arabian Sea (see Map 1) into the fresh-water Indus, making certain sites of the culture uninhabitable. Whether the salt-water contamination affected Mohenjo-daro and even Harappā still farther to the north (some 400 miles), and whether it was late enough (that is, during the period 2000 to 1800 B.C.E.) to fit the declining years of the Indus Valley culture, is still open to further research and debate.

Recent evidence points to a series of geologic uplifts along the northern flank of the Arabian Sea. These uplifts may explain the backing up of both the fresh floodwaters of the Indus and the salty estuarine waters of the sea, which ultimately produced enormous inland ponds together with the abnormal swamping found, for example, at Mohenjo-daro. It has been conjectured that the low river areas around Mohenjo-daro did in fact fill with brackish swamp water and that the result would have been malaria and polluted drinking water, together with the general salination of the soil. Further, these events could have occurred within the critical time period we are discussing, with the deplorable results for the Harappān people that one would anticipate from such occurrences:

> From whatever cause, the intermittent floods at Mohenjo-daro (and at Chanhu-daro) [about 100 miles down-river from Mohenjo-daro] no doubt helped, by a process of attrition, to wear down the morale of the inhabitants, and may well have contributed to the progressive deterioration which has long been recognized in their civic standards. For one thing is clear about the end of Mohenjo-daro: the city was already slowly dying before its ultimate end.[5]

It is to these civic standards, and the third cause of the death of Harappān culture, that we now turn.

[5] *Ibid.*, p. 76.

The third hypothesis states that the Harappān culture died because of certain internal human forces: urban pollution and overpopulation. There is a striking difference between the earlier (older) and the later (more recent) archeological levels of excavation at Mohenjo-daro. At the earlier levels we find all of the characteristics mentioned previously of a well-planned, well-developed, and well-run municipality. The streets were wide, spacious, and attractive; the houses were large, open, and beautiful; the sewer system, the grain-storage, and building and trade facilities bespeak a growing, healthy, and handsome city inhabited by an industrious, energetic, and beautiful people. Thus things remained for several hundred years. Then, as time passed, the population swelled and spilled out and over the older established limits; new houses were hastily built on the ruins of older ones; the older houses were divided and then divided again into smaller and smaller spaces—apartments and tenements to accommodate the burgeoning population; trees and forests, cut to fuel the brick kilns and ovens that must have worked overtime for decades to supply the baked clay bricks to build new houses, slowly disappeared as the landscape around the city was stripped bare; poorer-quality houses were constructed to meet the booming demands of the engulfing populace; overgrazing by cattle and stock on the treeless environs eventually followed; and suddently, from the evidence of this recent period, economic decline and cultural stagnation were everywhere. Trade with Mesopotomia, which had been high in the earlier period, also mysteriously declined during this later time. It would seem that Mohenjo-daro, and with it probably the whole Harappān culture in general, died of that civic disease which is becoming all too common in the twentieth century: the inability of the populace to handle their various internal problems, pollution, slums, the plundering of the resources available to the cities, together with the lack of proper management over both the uncontrollable vagaries of nature and the booming population of the cities. All this in Harappān times made the culture ripe for invasion and conquest—if, indeed, there was anything left for the Āryan invaders to conquer.

The three causes of the decline and fall of the Indus Valley civilization probably run together and are mutually related. The picture that emerges is that of a once energetic, ambitious, conscientious, and dedicated people, finally overcome, conquered, and overthrown, not by foreign invaders, but by themselves. The Āryans were not responsible, the river was not responsible, but the major cause of the decline and death of the Harappān culture which made the two previous causes operable lay with that culture's own people. For, ironically enough, they seem to have possessed the technology as well as the wisdom to solve their external problems as long as those problems were external and identifiable. But some strange myopia prohibited them from recognizing that their own decline and death, without resurrection, lay within the city walls, among the inhabitants, in the hearts of the citizens themselves. The Indus Valley civilization, its magnificent cities, its art and crafts, its language and government, its technology and its collective wisdom, passed suddently and terribly from the pages of history. But its religious heritage[6] lived on in the later traditions of that culture that took its place. The people of that culture are called *Āryans*, and we turn next to the Āryan influence on Hinduism, India, and the world.

[6]The pre-Āryan religious heritage in general probably includes such diverse concepts and practices as meditational yoga, worship of the Great Goddess, cults of trees, waters, and animals, phallic worship, bhaktism, *saṁsāra*, *mokṣa*, *puja*, and a host of village deities, demons, ghosts, and spirits.

# *C.*
# *Āryan Civilization and the Origins of Hinduism*

## 1. THE COMING OF THE ĀRYANS

Sometime during the period 1800 to 1500 B.C.E. a series of disorganized and discrete invasions occurred in northwest India. These incursions were mounted and directed by a tribe of nomadic wanderers known collectively as the Āryans ("noble ones" in Sanskrit). The early trickle of these Āryans into India in the 1800s turned into a torrent by the middle of the second millennium. They swept before them what remained of the Indus Valley civilization as they moved from out of present-day Afghanistan into the Punjab and the plains south and west of the Himālaya mountains (see Map, page 7).

It is believed that these people came from an area that lies in the modern Soviet Union along the eastern shores of the Caspian sea. The Āryan movements to the Himālayas and the subcontinent of India coincided in the second millennium with a vast movement of the same people into northern Europe, Iran, the Middle East, and the Greek Peninsula. These people all migrated simultaneously from the great steppes of Central Asia, an area stretching from the Caspian sea northwards, and they became, consequently, the ancestors of the Celts and Teutons in northern Europe, the Greeks and Latins in the south, and the Hittites and the Kassites in the eastern Mediterranean. The Āryans are, as a result, the ancestors of practically all present-day Europeans, not only in physical appearance, as we shall see, but also in religion, philosophy, social and political structure, and language. The language of the Āryans is called *Sanskrit* (which means "elegant" or "well formed"), and Sanskrit stands as a close cousin to almost all modern European languages. As a comparison consider the cognitive and phonetic similarity between Sanskrit and Sanskrit roots and several other Indo-European languages with respect to the following English words and their synonyms (Table 1).

TABLE 1. A COMPARISON OF INDO-EUROPEAN WORDS

| *English* | *Sanskrit* | *Greek* | *German* | *Latin* | *Anglo-Saxon* |
|---|---|---|---|---|---|
| father | pitṛ | patēr | vater | pater | faeder |
| mother | mātṛ | mētēr | mutter | mater | mōder |
| {divinity<br>{divine | divas<br>deva | Zeus<br>dios | — | Jou-is | Tiwes |
| not | na | nē, mē | nein/nicht | ne | ne |
| {wizard<br>{witch | √vid<br>(know) | oida<br>(to see is<br>to know) | wissen<br>(know) | videre<br>(see) | witan<br>(see) |
| serpent | √sṛp<br>(creep) | herpō<br>(creep, go) | — | serp-ere<br>(creep) | — |
| star | √stṛ | astēr | stern | stella | steorra |
| sweat | √svid | hidiō | schweiss | sūdā-re | swāt |
| {measure<br>{make | √mā | metron | masz<br>machen | mă-nu-s | — |
| mouse | √mus<br>(rob) | mus | maus<br>mausen<br>(to/steal) | mūs | mūs |
| murder | √mṛ<br>mṛta<br>(dead)<br>amṛta<br>(immortal) | mortos | mord | mor-i<br>(die) | mordor |

Unlike the Harappāns, who were short, dark, thick-lipped, flat-nosed, and short-headed, the Āryans were quite the opposite: tall, light-skinned, straight-nosed, and long-headed. They brought with them in their wanderings superior weapons as well as ingenious martial strategems. Among their weapons was the bow, a weapon dearly loved by the Āryans, and the two-wheeled two-horse chariot. Here is a passage from the *Ṛg Veda*, one of the sacred texts of the Āryans, describing the bow in a most enchanting fashion:

> With Bow let us win cattle; with Bow in battle let us win victories in our hot encounters.
> The Bow brings grief and sorrow to our foes: armed with Bow let us conquer all regions.
>
> Close to the ear as if she would speak she presses, holding her dear-beloved friend in her embrace.
> Strained on Bow, she whispers like a woman—this Bow-string that saves us all in the fight.[1]

[1] *Ṛg Veda*, VI. 75. Unless otherwise indicated, the translations are based on Ralph T. W. Griffith, *The Hymns of the Ṛg Veda*, Two Volumes (Benares: E. J. Lazarus & Co., 3d ed., 1920–1926). Hereafter called "Griffith" or "after Griffith."

Armed with the bow, standing in his chariot driven by a trusted companion and drawn by two fearless horses, the Āryan warrior was a formidible and fearsome spectacle indeed.

But these horse-tamers and conquering warriors brought something even more important than the bow, the chariot, and heroic courage into the Punjab. They carried with them a religion and a way of life that was to influence the subcontinent and the world for centuries to come. What we know of that religion and the philosophy that accompanied it are found in their sacred texts, known collectively as the *Vedas*.

## 2. THE VEDAS

The *Vedas* (the word *veda* is from the Sanskrit root $\sqrt{vid}$, "to know") probably existed, in part at least, as early as the beginning of the second millennium B.C.E. and were part of the ancient oral tradition of myths, legends, poems, and hymns of the Āryan nomads. The poems-legends-hymns that make up the early *Vedas*, however, while partially composed at that early date, were probably not brought together as a collection until some time between 1200 to 800 B.C.E., after the tribe had settled in the north of India. This compilation, however, does not mean that the poems were written down at that time. That writing did not occur until sometime late in the first millennium B.C.E. Thus the earliest parts of the *Vedas* may well have been composed around 1800 B.C.E., compiled, organized, and completed about 1000 B.C.E., and then committed to writing probably some time after the sixth century B.C.E.

The *Vedas* as we know them today are divided into four major texts. The oldest is called the *Ṛg Veda* (from the root $\sqrt{ṛc}$, which means "a hymn," "to praise," and "to shine"). The *Ṛg Veda* is simply a collection of the earliest Āryan hymns, many of them probably recited by the so-called "*hotṛ* priest," who invoked the Gods during the rather elaborate ritual sacrifice practiced during this period. The other three *Vedas* are, second, the *Sāma Veda* (from *sāma* which means "song"), which consists of certain *Ṛg Veda* verses arranged and organized for liturgical purposed and to be sung or chanted by the *udgatṛ* priest who, by his sweet songs, invited the Gods to attend the sacrifice; third, the *Yajur Veda* (from *yaja* which means "sacrifice"), a compilation of sacrificial formulae which were uttered by the *adhvaryu* priest who performed the manual portion of the sacrifice by preparing the cakes, straining the soma, and overseeing, in general, all the arrangings and pourings; fourth and finally, the latest text of them all, the *Atharva Veda* (probably from *atharvan*, the name for the priest who recited from this *Veda*), primarily a compilation of spells and incantations for various "magical" purposes, such as for the procurement of the attentions of a loved one, for victory in battle and success in private affairs, for averting calamities and disasters, for destroying hated rivals, and so on. A fifth priest, the *brahmin*, supervised the entire sacrifice and by silent meditation repaired any flaws or slips in the ritual. Hence the *Vedas* consist of four *Vedas*—the *Ṛg Veda*, the *Sāma Veda*, the *Yajur Veda*, and the *Atharva Veda*—and each played an important role in the *Vedic* sacrifices. We have mentioned the names of but five of the priests involved in the ritual sacrifice; seven priests were common, and for the soma sacrifice sixteen priests were employed.

The whole picture of the *Vedas*, however, is considerably more complicated than this. For to each of the four *Vedas* appendices and commentaries were later attached. Thus each of the *Vedas* has, in reality, two parts: the actual hymns themselves, called *mantras*, which are the chants of the priests; and a set of passages, called *Brāhmaṇas*, which are commentaries added later to explain and elucidate the *mantras*. In addition each of the *Brāhmaṇas* has two sets of appendices. The first is called the *Āraṇyakas*, or forest passages, which contains the rules and procedures for meditating on the *mantras* and is used by those who retire to the forest to live; the second, the *Upaniṣads*, consists of the still later philosophical portions of the *Veda* that stand as commentaries on the concluding parts of the *Araṇyakas*. So the *Āraṇyakas* and the *Upaniṣads* are appendices to the *Brāhmaṇas*, which are in turn commentaries on the four *Vedas*.

The commentaries and the appendices are further divided in such a way that portions of them relate specifically to one or another of the four *Vedas*. For example, the *Kauṣītakī Upaniṣad* and the *Aitareya Upaniṣad* are appended to the *Brāhmaṇas* of the *Ṛg Veda*. The *Taittirīya Brāhmaṇa* has the *Taittirīya Upaniṣad* appended to it, and the *Bṛhadāraṇyaka Upaniṣad* is appended to the *Śatapatha Brāhmaṇa* of the *Ṛg Veda*. Further, the *Chāndogya Upaniṣad* is a major portion of one of the *Brāhmaṇas* which is a commentary on the *Sāma Veda*, and so on for the remainder of the *Vedas*, *Brāhmaṇas*, and *Upaniṣads*.

The dates of composition of the major portions of *Vedic* literature run approximately as follows: The *Ṛg Veda mantras* probably date about 1500–800 B.C.E.; the *Brāhmaṇas* about 1000 to 600 B.C.E.; the *Āraṇyakas* about 800 to 600 B.C.E.; and the *Upaniṣads*, in the main, are usually dated 800 to 200 B.C.E., though some later *Upaniṣads* date into the Christian era itself. All four of these portions taken together, then, constitute what is technically called "the *Vedas*." But a common practice has been to refer to the *mantras* alone of the four parts of the *Veda* as "the *Vedas*" and to reserve the names *Brāhmaṇas*, *Āraṇyakas*, and *Upaniṣads* for the later additions to those *mantras*. That practice will be followed here as well. That is to say, from now on when we use the words *Vedas* or *Veda* we will be talking primarily about the *mantras* or hymns of the *Ṛg Veda*, or the *Sāma Veda*, or the *Yajur Veda*, or the *Atharva Veda*; the other three parts of this early Indian literature will be referred to as the *Brāhmaṇas*, the *Āraṇyakas*, and the *Upaniṣads*.

In the discussion that follows I want to pursue in some detail only two of these texts: first, the *Vedas*, and in particular the *Ṛg Veda*, and then the *Upaniṣads*. Thus we turn next to a philosophic examination of the *Ṛg Veda* and the *Vedic* way to human happiness.

# *D.*

# *The Ṛg Veda and Its Philosophy*

The *Ṛg Veda* is the world's oldest religious text still in common use today. It contains 1028 hymns gathered together into ten *maṇḍalas* (literally "circles"); the entire collection of these hymns and chapters is called "the *Ṛg Veda saṁhitā*." The *Ṛg Veda* together with the other three *Vedas*, the *Sāma*, the *Yajur*, and the *Atharva Vedas*, and the *Brāhmaṇas*, the *Āraṇyakas*, and certain early *Upaniṣads*, are collectively called *śruti* (from √śru, "to hear") by the Indians. *Śruti* means "sacred scripture" and, literally, "that which is heard by the *ṛṣis*," seers, wise men, or prophets, as a result of ancient traditions and timeless revelation. *Śruti*, furthermore, is juxtaposed by the Indians to the less authoritative *smṛti* (from √*smṛ*, "to remember"). The *smṛti* includes sayings, compositions, and the teachings and commentaries of the later orthodox authors, sages, and saints of Hinduism, together with the various revered law books and texts which include descriptions of minor ceremonies and sacrifices, and certain specially revered epic poems such as the *Bhagavad Gītā*. In addition, the *smṛti* contains the *Purānas*, certain ancient myths and legends, the *Sūtra* literature or instructive aphorisms, as well as the two major Indian epics, the *Rāmāyaṇa*, the collection of stories about the Indian hero Rāma, and the *Mahābhārata*, the massive group of legends and tales about the Indian family of the *Bhāratas*, from which epic comes the *Bhagavad Gītā*.

Further, among the *smṛti* are the longer verse texts called *śāstras*, chief of which are the *Artha Śāstra*, on the science of statecraft and politics, and the *dharma śāstras*, on the science of the sacred law; one such *dharma śāstra*, the Laws of Manu, we shall examine shortly (see below, pp. 85–100). The *smṛti* literature also includes such things as the *tantra* (which means "a loom" or "ritual and doctrine"). The *Tantra Śāstras* are books revealed by Lord Śiva and other divine beings for use in this particular final period in the world's history, a period called "the *kali yuga*." The *kali yuga* is the period of moral and spiritual decline—that is, the modern iron age—in which evils, suffering, and decadence are at their height. The *tantra* contains, consequently, advice and consolation in the form of psychological insights combined with certain spiritual and mental techniques and rituals designed especially for this modern *yuga* or historical period.

By and large, however, the most significant earliest texts for Hinduism are the sacred revelations of the four *Vedas*, and the most revered of the *Vedic śruti* is the *Ṛg Veda*.

The hymns of the *Ṛg Veda* can be divided into two periods which correspond roughly to parts of the ten *maṇḍalas*, or books, of this oldest of the four *Vedas*. The first period includes the earliest hymns from Book I (verses 51 to 191) and all of Book II through Book IX. They reflect the Āryan commitment to a polytheism wherein certain major deities seem to share power and honor equally. The second and more recent period includes the remaining hymns from Book I (verses 1 to 50) and all of the hymns of Book X. What we note as we move through these *Ṛg Vedic maṇḍalas* are certain changes in stress, intention, and doctrine: there is a gradual move from religious polytheism towards a modified polytheism called "henotheism"; there is a gradual development of a clearer and fuller doctrine of life after death; and, side by side with these changes, the role of the public, as opposed to the household, ritual sacrifice becomes more and more important; and with the growth of the importance of the ritual sacrifice, the power of those who conducted the sacrifice, the *brahmins*, the priests, grows as well. The history of *Vedism* is really the history of the growth of the power of the *brahmin* class. Consequently, it has been the custom among Indologists to refer to the philosophy and religion of the *Vedas* as *brāhmaṇism* or *brahminism*, the philosophy and religion of the *brāhmaṇs* or *brahmins*, in order to distinguish this early religion from later Hinduism, proper. I shall follow that practice here, as well. So what we are looking to, then, is a systematic examination of the philosophy and religion of *brahminism*. We will begin our discussion with a description of the religion of the *Ṛg Veda*, then move on from there to an examination of the metaphysics, the epistemology, and the ethics of *brahminism* as found in this great text.

## 1. THE RELIGION OF THE ṚG VEDA

The origins of man's religious beliefs are shrouded in hoary antiquity. Any discussion of those origins is fraught with problems and perils for the hearty philosophic adventurer that inevitably make any systematic discussion both problematic and perilous. Did people become "religious," whatever that means, out of fear or love? Out of shame or pride? Out of necessity or curiosity? Do people now become religious or turn to religion for similar reasons? If I asked you, Why are you religious?, or not religious?, what would you answer? It doesn't help, of course, if you answer, I'm religious because my parents were, or, I'm religious because I was brought up and raised that way. By answering in this way you are giving a causal expanation of your religiosity and not a rational account or explanation of it: you would be confusing a cause with a reason, and what we're hunting for here, as philosophers, are reasons. So we return to the question. Suppose now you are religious. Then we can ask, Why are you religious?, What reasons have you for being religious?, and, Are your reasons for being religious the same as or similar to a *Vedic brahmin's* reasons for being religious?

As a start to our discussion about the origins of religiosity we might simply ask: what does "religion" mean? Perhaps if we knew at the outset what we were searching for, and knew it with as much clear-eyed perspicacity as possible, our hunt for origins and reasons might be more effective. There is a double meaning to that word "mean," incidentally, for it can refer either to the sects or institutions that are called "religions" or to the verbal definition of the word whose meaning is being sought. So "religion" means, in the first sense, religions such as Hinduism, Buddhism, Christianity, Islam, and Judaism. This use of "means" is called its *extensional use* or the *denotation* of the term "religion." Hence, the denotation of "man" would be each and every individual man born and remaining to be born, and the extension of "man" would be the members of the class of all actual and possible alive, once alive, and yet to be alive human beings. Thus both the extension and the denotation of a term point to the individuals that the term names. But our discussion about the meaning of "religion" is not, obviously, concerned with the extension of that term; rather, it is concerned with what all those five major world religions have in common that makes us call them "religions." In other words, we are seeking the verbal definition of "religion."

This second, verbal notion of "meaning" is called the *intensional use* or *connotation* of a term. The intension or connotation consists in laying out defining characteristics such that anything which satisfies or meets those defining characteristics is the thing in question, and anything which does not satisfy those characteristics is not the thing in question. The intension of "man" would probably be "rational animal," since man is the only animal that is rational and anything which is not rational and also an animal is not a man. There are problems with such a definition, to be sure, and not the least of them is the question about the intension of "rational" and possibly even "animal," too. So it is fair to ask: are babies of men also men? But they are not rational. How about idiots, the feeble-minded, lunatics, and terribly intelligent monkeys—are they or aren't they rational animals? But here's a less problematic example of intension: the intension of "triangle" is "a plane figure bounded by three straight lines." No one would seriously quibble about that definition. In fact within all common formal systems of logic and mathematics certain terms are defined intensionally, and generally there's no quibbling about those formal definitions. The dictionary is, by and large, another source for the connotations of terms, for most dictionary definitions are simply verbal synonyms or connotations of the words being defined. However, some dictionaries are illustrated lexicons. If they give a picture instead of a verbal synonym for a term, then we might ask: are they giving the intension or are they giving the extension of a term?

A whole host of terms, on the other hand, can never finally and ultimately be defined connotatively. Suppose I ask you to define "yellow" for me. You hem and haw a bit, prowling for a definition. Finally you say: Over there, see that chair, that's yellow. I remind you that I'm looking for the intensional meaning of the color word "yellow" and not an example, not a *denotatum*, or instance, of the concept. So you turn to the dictionary. It says things such as this about "yellow": "Having the color of ripe lemons, or sunflowers," which would help you to recognize yellow if you had an example of a lemon or sunflower in front of you or knew what they were; or it says complicated things about wavelengths of light: "The color of the spectrum between green and orange, including wavelengths centering at about 5,890 angstroms," and then, in case you didn't get it the first time, it adds immediately, "the color of ripe lemons." The definition of "yellow" in terms of its light waves won't help you in spotting the color yellow in the world. The first part of the definition relies on your knowing something about green and orange; and the second part simply tells you what to expect from a pointer reading on a mass spectrometer when that instrument is presented with a yellow object.

Curiously enough, the meaning of "yellow" that we are after here can only be obtained by seeing something yellow and having someone say, "There, that thing, old boy, is yellow"; that is, yellow can only be defined *ostensively*—by pointing. Now it so happens that a whole host of words, all of them relating to so-called "sense qualities" or what Galileo and John Locke in the seventeenth century called "secondary qualities," can only be defined ostensively, by pointing to a *denotatum*, or example, of the term in the space-time world while simultaneously naming aloud the object of both the term and the pointing. Thus terms that name secondary qualities must all be defined ostensively in this same nonintensional way—terms or qualities such as rough, smooth, sweet, sour, loud, soft, acrid, pungent, green, yellow, and so on. In other words, to understand the meaning of these terms it is essential that one experience directly the quality denoted by the term.

It is obvious that "religion" is not a term like "yellow." But certainly "religious experience" may be a term like "yellow" in that both require one to have direct, personal, immediate experience of the entity named in order to understand the meaning of the term, whether that be a religious experience or a yellow object. "Religion" will be like "yellow" only if "religious experience" is a necessary part of the definition of "religion"; and this is certainly not obvious. "Religion," as ordinarily understood, refers to a social institution of some kind, created or developed by man to accomplish certain ends, to reach or realize certain goals; while "religious experience" is not an institution at all but a reference to an experience. Were we to define the adjective "religious" in place of the noun "religion," we might then resort to talk about experiences, but as things stand now that move is not necessary here.

Please keep in mind this discussion about ostensive definition, secondary qualities, and the immediacy and privateness entailed in defining certain concepts such as *yellow* and *religious experience*, for we will be coming to it again in our presentation of the *Upaniṣads* (see below, pp. 111 and 128).

To return to our question. What is the intension or connotation of "religion"? When we refer to *Vedic* or Āryan religion, what are we committing *Vedism, brahminism,* or Āryanism to? What is it that all religions have in common that can be isolated and then identified by a synonym or set of synonymous terms? Must there be a God in order to have a religion? But most Buddhists are atheists, and yet Buddhism is a religion. Must there be a change of personality or character, a conversion experience, in order to have a religion? But then psychoanalysis would be a religion. Is religion simply doing good to your fellow man and being good to yourself? But this confuses religion with morality; or does it?

For the present we might tentatively say that religion is the way to either an other-worldly or transcendent person or place or state of Being—for example, to a metaphysical person called "God," or to a metaphysical place called "heaven," or to a metaphysical state or condition called "liberation." In the *Ṛg Veda,* "religion" may be defined precisely as the way that leads to those transcendent persons and places called "the Gods" or "heaven"; but as Hinduism evolved and as *brahminism* faded into the background, the new religion became more and more abstract, until finally what distinguished that religion from other institutions in the society was its ability to lead its practitioners to unusual *states* of Being or consciousness and in particular to a condition called "liberation," or what in Sanskrit is called *mokṣa* (see below, p. 99). For the present, however, *Vedism* as a religion simply helps to put man into a relation to the Gods and heaven, whereby he may realize certain of his aspirations and goals as a consequence of those same Gods' being *for* him rather than *against* him. Whatever else it is, *Vedic* religion, unlike the later Hindu religion, is not an institution designed to produce permanent metaphysical or psychological changes of personality or character.[1] What, then, is Vedic religion?

The reconstruction and interpretation of the ancient *Vedic* religion is an activity fraught with peril for any Indologist. As Daniel Ingalls and Auguste Barthe have well said, the only persons who could enlighten us as to what *Vedism* was really all about are the *Vedic ṛṣis*, themselves, and they're all dead. But with this warning before us, we're going to plunge into an interpretation of *Vedic* religion, realizing that it's probably not going to please everyone. It is an interpretation which explains much that we do know about the *Vedas*, however, and it also explains why *brahminism* finally came to an end, and why it was superseded by the religion of the *Upaniṣads*. To set the scene for this interpretation of *Vedic* religion let me say a brief word about the practice that lay at the heart of that religion: the ritual sacrifice.

The ritual sacrifice that was part of the public, as opposed to the household and private, *Vedic* ritual was an all-important part of the life of *Vedic* man. The sacrifice homologized the universe in such a way that it was believed that the continued existence of both the world and the Gods, themselves, depended on that *Vedic* ritual.[2] The homology expressed in the sacrifice is that wherein the sacrificial place with its fires and grounds represents the universe as a whole, hence the homology ("same measure" or "to speak the same" in Greek). Thus, by a kind of imitative magic, whatever one does to or with or at the sacrifice must be done in turn or in return by the Gods to the world. And this is extremely important for two reasons: first, the desired results brought about through this discovered homology or identity between the two realms of the sacrifice and the world will come about necessarily, automatically, and independently of the will of either the Gods or man; second, it would follow from this that whoever knew the secret formula, verse, or sacred word, called *brahman*, could compel the return favors of the Gods; hence the *brahmins* became incredibly important and powerful because they alone knew *brahman*.

The Vedic sacrifice was undertaken for the purpose of renewing cosmic life. Through it *Vedic* man renewed himself and also secured the things that made life meaningful for him, things such as sons, wealth, property, cattle,

[1] But see J. Gonda, *Change and Continuity in Indian Religion* (The Hague: Mouton & Co., 1965), p. 18: "The periodical ritual acts reflect and are identical with the ever-proceeding process of renewal of all cosmic life and matter.... That is to say, if the sacrificer [the patron, not the priest] follows, in his mind, the construction of the fire-place in the ritually correct way, he undergoes a modification of his status, a renewal of his personality, a spiritual rebirth.... [T]his self-realization is the essence and deeper significance of a ritual act, whether Vedic or post-Vedic."

[2] As J. Gonda has said: "[M]an adds to the god's power, that he [the god] may have power to reciprocate and that life processes may not stagnate because of any lack of potency." *Ibid.*, pp. 214–215.

and other material goods; and through it *Vedic* man assured himself a place in the next world, the heaven of the Gods, heroes, and ancestors of the race. The sacrifice maintained and revivified the universe, and man himself, and his relation to that totality. It is no wonder that it was important, and no wonder that the power and importance of the *brahmins* grew and became sacred and secured.

The evolution which one finds in *Vedic* thought at this point, then, is the gradual change from dependence on the Gods to dependence on the *brahmins*. Since the Gods can be compelled to do the bidding of the priests who know the sacred formulas of the sacrifice, and since it is not the Gods that are wanted, anyway, but only their Power to maintain and control the cosmos, then it follows that the Gods can be dispensed with. That is to say, the Gods are only intermediaries between the Power that will yield the goods of the universe and keep the cosmos in order, and the men who want that Power. Now the priests have taken the Gods' place; they have become like the Gods, they are Gods on earth. Thus by the end of the *Vedic* period, roughly sometime in the ninth century B.C.E., *Vedism* had evolved, theoretically, into a kind of ritual atheism dominated by the power and prestige of the priests.

But a more violent change in *Vedic* religion was waiting to make its appearance. This violent change would displace the priests from the religious stage just as previously the priests had displaced the Gods. This change will come about as we leave the *Vedic* period and move into the period of the *Upaniṣads*.

What, then, was *Vedic* religion designed to do? What was it that the public sacrifice ultimately aimed at? The answer, together with the interpretation of *Vedic* religion that I shall offer, can be summed up in one word: Power. The justification for this interpretation of *Vedic* religion will be found in the analysis of the four statements of "the formula for power" that follow. That formula looks like this:

a. There are Gods with Power.
b. Man wants and needs Power.
c. There is a way to Power.
d. The *Vedas* describe that way.

Let me take each of these four statements of the formula for Power, explain and then comment briefly on each one.

### *a. There Are Gods with Power*

The problem of proving the existence of God or the Gods does not seem to have been terribly bothersome for the authors of the *Vedas*. Concern about this problem never reached, even in later Indian philosophy, the paranoiac proportions that it reached in the West, for example, during the patristic and scholastic periods of Christianity. There are probably two major reasons for wanting rational arguments to prove the existence of God, and the Indians do not appear to have been caught up with either. First, rational proofs to demonstrate God's existence are necessary when one feels one's own certainty about God's existence waning. For when the seeds of skepticism regarding God begin to sprout, one probably turns to the security of a good argument to prove that God exists. In times of dwindling personal God-concern, arguments to show that God exists would tend to increase. Second, rational proofs to demonstrate God's existence are necessary when one feels the obligation to proselytize or make converts of others to or for one's own religion. If one does one's proselytizing nonviolently and does not make converts with the sword, one is likely to turn to rational persuasion and demonstrable arguments to prove that God exists. If one goes out into the world preaching one's own brand of good news or gospel, the implication is that that gospel is superior to all other gospels. All proselytizing is built upon a conviction of theological superiority. But neither the *Vedic brahmins* nor later Hinduism seem to have been especially afflicted with either the problem of skepticism or the sin of superiority.

Arguments to show that the Gods exist occur in the *darśanas* or philosophic systems later in the history of Hindu thought. But at these early stages of Vedism in the first millennium B.C.E., the general tendency is to assume that they do exist and that, aside from a few *Ṛg Veda* passages that suggest the existence of a few skeptics, they are the sources of all power. With regard to that theological skepticism, here are some passages that, taken out of the context of the hymns, may sound quite modern and rather familiar. They concern Indra, the Āryan God of storms and battle:

> Striving for strength bring forth praise to Indra,
> a truthful hymn if he in truth exists.
> One and another say, There is no Indra.
> Who has seen him? Whom then shall we honor?[3]

And here's another, but in praise of Indra:

> Of whom, the Terrible (Indra), they ask, Where is he?
> Of him they also say, He does not exist.
> The enemies' wealth like the gamblers' stakes, he sweeps away.
> Believe in him: For, Oh men, he is Indra.[4]

While both hymns appear to offer skeptical comments about Indra, they direct attention to another more obvious point. Those who "strive for strength" and those who seek to "lessen their enemies' wealth" turn to

[3] *Ṛg Veda*, VIII. 89.3, Griffith.

[4] *Ṛg Veda* II.12.5, translated by A. A. Macdonell, *Hymns from the Rigveda* (London: Oxford University Press, 1922); hereafter "Macdonell" or "after Macdonell."

Indra in order to accomplish these ends. Indra has power, and it is this power that man is attempting to lay hold of. If in the process the *ṛṣi* mentions in his hymns that skeptics do exist, so much the better as far as his own petitions to the Gods are concerned. For in mentioning the possibility of skepticism, the worshipper emphasizes that by comparison he, himself, has been truly faithful; also, he subtly implies that if he doesn't get what he wants, he might join the skeptical ranks. In both allusions there occurs some not-so-subtle divine-arm-twisting.

The thesis that the Gods have power was probably derived from observing the effects of that power in the natural world. This is one of the most common theories about the origin of religion and religious beliefs. Man was and still is enormously impressed by the destructive as well as the constructive forces in nature. Even today, despite all our scientific and philosophic worldliness, a violent spring cloudburst can send chills of terror down the spine of the most obdurate sophisticate. We are, all of us, alternately impressed and terrified at the forces in nature, and those forces of rain, sun, growth, flood, drought, and famine represent real, terrifying power.

Indra is the God of the thunderstorm. In the popular myths of the *Ṛg Veda* it was he, Lord Indra, who slew the demon that had dammed up all the waters inside the mountains, thereby causing a massive drought. Everything was dying or dead and the world was threatened with extinction. Then Lord Indra smashed the demon and released the pent-up waters in a mighty rushing torrent—the monsoons came, spring came, and the earth bloomed:

> 7. As an axe fells the tree so he slew Vṛtra (a "barrier"),
> broke down the enclosures (dams?) and dug out the rivers.
> He split the mountains like a new made pitcher. Indra
> brought forth the cattle with all his companions.[5]

In the *Ṛg veda* there are more hymns dedicated to Indra than to any of the other *Vedic* Gods, and not simply because Indra is a divine savior-hero. For Indra is also the God of justice and punishment *par excellence*, he wields not the sword in vain against transgressors and other wicked beings:

> 8. You, Oh Indra, are the wise one and the punisher
> of guilt. Your sword lops limbs as you smite the sinner,
> Those men who injure the laws that are like friends to them,
> the laws of Varuṇa and Mitra.
>
> 9. Men who lead evil lives, who break agreements, and
> injure Varuṇa, Aryaman, and Mitra,
> Against these enemies, Oh mighty Indra, sharpen,
> as terrible death, your bull [thunderbolt] of fiery color.[6]

[5] *Rg Veda* X.89.7, Griffith.

[6] *Ibid.* X.89.6–9.

Finally, so as to leave no doubts in anyone's mind that Indra can, indeed, accomplish these things, the worshipper concludes, extolling Indra's incomparable Power:

10. Indra is sovereign lord of earth and heaven;
    Indra is lord of waters and of mountains.
    Indra is master of those who prosper and the wise;
    Indra must be invoked at work and at rest.

11. Greater than days and nights, the Giver of all is
    greater than the earth and the oceans' waters,
    Greater than the limits of earth and the wind's expanse,
    Greater than all rivers and all our lands, greater than
    all of these is Lord Indra.[7]

But Indra is not the only deity with Power. The Indian pantheon is populated, according to legend, with 33,333 Gods and Goddesses. The more prominent among these deities, however, are the following: *Agni*, the Lord of fire; *Dyaus*, the Indian counterpart of the Greek God Zeus, the Lord of the Grecian heavens and sky; and *Uṣas*, who is associated with the dawn. Here is part of a lovely and familiar hymn to her:

1. Dawn on us with prosperity, Oh Uṣas, daughter of the sky,
   Dawn with great glory, Oh Goddess, lady of the light,
   dawn thou with riches, Oh bounteous one.

5. Like a good matron Uṣas comes carefully tending
   everything.
   Rousing up all living things, she stirs all creatures
   with feet and makes the birds of air fly up.

6. She sends the busy forth, each man to his own pursuit;
   delay she knows not as she springs forth.
   Oh thou rich in opulence, after thy dawning, birds
   that have flown forth no longer rest.

7. This lovely Dawn hath yoked her steeds afar, beyond the rising
   of the sun.
   Borne on a hundred chariots she, with her auspicious
   rays, advances on her way to men.

8. To meet her glance all living creatures bend low
   before her brightness; excellent one, she makes the light . . . .

9. Shine on us with thy radiant light, Oh Uṣas, daughter
   of the sky.
   Bring to us great store of high felicity, and beam down
   now on our solemn rites.[8]

Other prominent Gods mentioned in the *Ṛg Veda* include *Viṣṇu*, the God who was both a creator and an ever-present moral judge in the creation; *Pṛthivī*,

[7] *Ibid.* X.89.10–11.

[8] *Ibid.* I.48.1, 5–9.

the Goddess of the earth; *Soma*, the Lord of the ritual sacrifice, wherein the heady and inebriating juice called *soma* was drunk by the priests; *Yama*, the Lord of the dead, departed spirits, and the underworld; *Āpas*, the Lord of the waters, oceans, streams, and lakes; *Vāyu*, the Lord of the wind; the *Maruts*, who were storm Gods; and *Sūrya*, the Lord of the sun, to whom the following beautiful hymn was directed:

> Aloft his beams now bring the God who knows all creatures
> that are born, that all may look upon the Sun.
>
> Away like thieves the stars depart, by the dark nights
> accompanied, at the all-seeing Sun's approach.
>
> His beams, his rays, have shone afar astride the many
> homes of men, flaming aloft like blazing fires.
>
> Swift-moving, visible to all, maker of light thou art,
> Oh Sun, illuming all the shining space.[9]

We can conclude that there are Gods and that they have the Power. This Power is a natural power—rain, dawn, sunlight—such that the Gods in giving or withholding it can directly affect the lives of men.

But the Power is also supernatural as well, for the *Vedic* Āryans believed in a life after death. After the body dies, a part of the self that inhabited that body rises out of this world and goes to another place. The dead go to the world of the Gods and the warrior-heroes, or to the world of the ancestors and the Fathers; all the dead do this apparently, and no distinction is made between the righteous dead and the wicked dead. But in the later *Vedas* things become a bit more complicated. A distinction is made there in which the general principle that governs who goes where and why would appear to be, "Heaven for the righteous and hell for the wicked,"[10] Thus, there is the following passage in a hymn directed to Yama, Ruler of the departed:

> Become joined with the Fathers and with Yama.
> With your good works seek rewards in highest heaven.
> To your home return, all imperfections leaving,
> And unite with another body, full of vitality.[11]

And many hymns make an outright appeal that immortal life may be granted by the Gods:

> May I attain to that, his well-loved mansion, where men
> devoted to the gods are happy . . . ,
> Happily would we go to your dwelling places where there are
> many horned and nimble oxen . . . .[12]

[9] *Ṛg Veda*, I.50.1–4, Macdonell.

[10] S. Radhakrishnan, *Indian Philosophy*, Two Volumes (London: George Allen and Unwin, 1951), Vol. I, p. 115.

[11] *Ṛg Veda* X.14.8, Macdonell.

[12] *Ṛg Veda* I.154.5, 6, Griffith.

In addition to these two heavenly possibilities—life with the Gods or life with Yama and the Fathers—there appears to be a third; it is referred to only once in the *Ṛg Veda* and is obscurely called "the house of clay." It occurs in a pitiable lament raised to Lord Varuṇa:

> 1. Let me not yet, King Varuṇa, enter into the
>    house of clay: Have mercy, spare me, Mighty Lord.
>
> 2. When, Thunderer, I move along tremulous like
>    a wind-blown skin: Have mercy, spare me, Mighty Lord.
>
> 3. Oh Bright and Powerful God, through want of
>    strength I erred and went astray: Have mercy, spare
>    me, Mighty Lord.[13]

However unclear the places of the afterlife of the *Vedic* Āryans may have been—and the texts certainly do not help in clarifying whether there are two or three or more such places—the point is that the afterlife was terribly significant for the worshipper, and that the Gods held the Power that determined the worshipper's place in that afterlife. For only the Gods could keep one from the house of clay (the grave?), and only the Gods could deliver one to heaven. Therefore, once again, the Gods have the Power, and it is the Power of not only life and death, but the Power of afterlife and afterdeath as well.

We move to the second of the four statements of the formula for Power.

### *b. Man Wants and Needs Power*

Man is thrown into a world he never made, a world which seems indifferent to his hopes and callous to his aspirations; a world where he faces a hostile environment that not only threatens to frustrate his desires but that intends, finally, to devour and destroy him as well. Man reacts to the indifference, hostility, and threats with fear and anxiety. So overwhelming and so universal is this anxiety about the world and its future states that we might conclude that anxiety is a defining characteristic of "man": man is the only living creature that is capable of fearing the future. And fear of the future (no one really fears the past or the present) is precisely what we mean by "anxiety." Bertrand Russell has spoken most poignantly to this existential and essentially universal condition of man:

> Brief and powerless is Man's life; on him and all his race the slow, sure doom falls pitiless and dark. Blind to good and evil, reckless of destruction, omnipotent matter rolls on its relentless way; for Man, condemned to-day to lose his dearest, to-morrow himself to pass through the gate of darkness, it remains only to cherish, ere yet the blow falls, the lofty thoughts that ennoble his little

[13] *Ibid.* VII.89.1–3.

day; disdaining the coward terrors of the slave of Fate, to worship at the shrine that his own hands have built; undismayed by the empire of chance, to preserve a mind free from the wanton tyranny that rules his outward life; proudly defiant of the irresistible forces that tolerate, for a moment, his knowledge and his condemnation, to sustain alone, a weary but unyielding Atlas, the world that his own ideals have fashioned despite the trampling march of unconscious power.[14]

Not only is man defined as the anxiety-possessing animal; he is also the only creature who has developed means and techniques for allaying that anxiety. Confronted with a hostile world over which he has no power, threatened by an environment that renders impotent his attempts to ameliorate threat, faced with a wholly-other nonself beyond him that he can neither control, bend, nor mold to his own purposes, man indulges his terrors and fears; he may even find his way in the world by cultivating, rationalizing, and then worshipping those very terrors and fears. In the modern world we have made a fetish of our fears for the sake of security, and we have come to deify those things which will allay and temporize our insecurity, such as military hardware, household luxuries, money, and all the other material possessions that convince and assure us that we are, really, immortal, and that we have nothing to fear after all.

In the ancient Western world, Hellenistic man found two philosophic ways of assuaging his torment and anxiety. The problem he faced was that of a self threatened by a world over which that self had no control. For after the fall in the fourth century B.C.E. of the Greek city-state, that comforting, nurturing, maternal heritage of the Hellenic period, and following the destructive Peloponnesian Wars with their disquieting aftermath of bloodshed and tyranny, the ordinary citizen of the new Hellenistic world felt isolated and estranged from the old, comfortable city-state values. He was left with nothing to believe in, bereft of anything in which to put his hopes and trust. The picture that we get of Hellenistic man is all too familiar today: a frightened man in a frighteningly big world. For example, a senior graduates from high school and is ceremoniously but precipitously thrust from that warm and friendly environment into a new and indifferent world. For four years he or she had been involved in the academic busy-ness of the high school, where the potentialities for individual freedom with respect to life within the school may have been relatively limited but where there was, nonetheless, a great deal of security. The student's home was near by; the church, the community, the friends and relatives that helped to define the limits of his freedom were similarly near at hand, providing further security. Freedom and security are curiously related in that environment and in an inversely proportional way:

[14]Bertrand Russell, "A Free Man's Worship," in *Mysticism and Logic* (Garden City, N.Y.: Doubleday Anchor Books, 1957), p. 54. Reprinted by permission of Harper & Row, Publishers, and George Allen & Unwin Ltd.

the more you have of the one, the less you have of the other. But now the senior graduates and leaves home. His or her own Hellenistic period dawns; the old customs, the religious and social habits of a lifetime, familiar faces, loving embraces, and the warmth of that old and traditional pattern are suddenly swept away. The big city or the big university—the big world—is suddenly there to take their place. The challenge of the unfamiliar and the hostility of the wholly-other produces the threat to the self. The city-state is gone, the old Gods and the traditional ways have been overthrown. One is alone, separated and isolated, and the attendant anxiety may be overwhelming.

The threat of the hostile world cannot be eliminated, but the anxiety that it causes to the self can be temporarily dulled. Our graduated high school senior, alone for the first time, finds that going home for the weekend, calling parents long distance nightly, using alcohol and drugs, indulging in distractions such as movies, TV, and books might all dull the anxiety and perhaps even remove it for long periods; but the world, the hostile unfamiliar and wholly-other, is still there to threaten and torment the self when it returns from home, or the alcohol wears off, or the movie house closes. Man wants something more permanent, he wants something that will solve, not salve, his problem. The world and the self have to be brought into a relationship that will remove the anxiety permanently, once and for all.

The Hellenistic Greeks found two philosophic ways of treating the problem of the relationship between the world and the self. Since it is the world that threatens the self, the first way involves making the world less imposing, less important, and less threatening by shrinking it, tearing it down, or becoming indifferent to it altogether. The followers of the Greek philosopher Epicurus (342–210 B.C.E.) accepted that sage's advice and adopted a simple mode of life that was as independent of the threatening world as they could make it. Hence the Epicurean way (don't identify it with the way of sensual indulgence; Epicurus was a hedonist, all right, but a most ascetic one) is for all practical purposes the way of the religious nun or monk. The Epicurean way involves the shrinking or contraction of the world with the subsequent avoidance of dependence on, and a consequent lessening of, threats from that world. The self is freed, ultimately, from the fear and anxiety that such a world previously held. The Epicureans believed, for example, that *death* was not to be feared; for death was merely the scattering and dispersal of the atoms that made up the body. There was, consequently, no threat of a life after death that could disconcert or upset a man in this life. Moreover, the Gods were not to be feared, for the Gods were simply unconcerned and independent congeries of atoms that could never hurt you or torment you. Neither could *the world* hurt you, if you simply avoided it and its entanglements, stayed in your own private world, and cultivated those simple intellectual pleasures that made life significant, enjoyable, and worthwhile. The Epicurean way is followed, for example, by the student who shrinks his college or university world to the manageable dimensions of his dormitory or his rooming house, the classroom or the library. The Epicurean way leads to the abolition of the gigantic overwhelming world in order that the self may survive.

The Hellenistic Greeks also found a second and different way of solving the problem. Since the world threatens the self, the second way would be to make the self stronger than the world by enlarging the powers of the self, or by giving all power to the self. The followers of Zeno the Stoic (who died in 264 B.C.E.) held that the cultivation of the inherent and potential powers of the self would give that self power, ultimately, over the entire world. It was believed that immanent within each man was a *logos* or an aspect of the divine, a part of the holy transcendent logos of the universe. Man could surmount his fears of death and the world by a mystical intuition of the identity between the immanent *logos* in the self and the universal *logos*, transcendent and beyond that self. The later Roman Stoics, such as Marcus Tullius Cicero (106–43 B.C.E.), Epictetus (60–120 C.E. or "Christian Era"), Plutarch (46–120 C.E.), and the Roman emperor Marcus Aurelius (121–180 C.E.), armed with the comforting elements of this basic Stoic doctrine, were all in the forefront of Roman politics and imperial activities for over 200 years. The Stoic way is followed, for example, by the student who intentionally cultivates his inner powers by intuitively tapping his own inner hidden resources, by reminding himself that he is that power or that God that transcends the campus, the university, the world. Such a believer, like his ancient Greek and Roman counterparts, does not shy away from the world but comes rather to dominate and to influence it. If the follower of the Epicurean way can be seen as the shy and quiet scholar on campus, then the follower of the Stoic way can be seen as the extroverted, self-assured, big man or woman on campus.

In conclusion, we might say that both the Epicurean and the Stoic have achieved happiness but in two entirely different ways. The Epicurean meets the problem of the relationship between the self and the world by making the world smaller and less important and less threatening. The Stoic meets the same problem by making the self more important—recognizing the power in the self and using that power to dominate and conquer the world. In discussing the *Vedas*, I hope to show that the *Vedic ṛṣis*, or wise men, adopted their own version of what we have called "the Epicurean way" to human happiness. And in our discussions of the *Upaniṣads* we shall see that the *Upaniṣadic ṛṣis* adopted their version of what we have called "the Stoic way" to human happiness.

Man is defined by his pain, his suffering, and his anxiety. He is the only living creature to known, to be conscious of, his pain, suffering, and anxiety: he is *homo agonistes*. But if there are powers that seize man, manipulate him,

96695

and turn his life into an agony, then the way out of the agony would involve controlling those manipulating powers. The goal becomes one of turning from being the object of manipulation to becoming the manipulator, the controller. Man needs the power that will enable him to escape the terrors, the uncertainties, and the untoward realities of the world. But, granted that power is needed, power to overcome all the other unconscious powers in the world that thwart, inhibit, torture, and finally kill man, one final question remains: where is that power to come from? The answer in the *Vedas*, of course, is that it comes from the Gods. The problem then becomes one of getting that power and the security and happiness that accompanies it.

### c. *There Is a Way to Power*

The Gods have the Power, man needs that Power, so the problem becomes one of finding out how to get it. The threatening world outside of man, the world that produces the anxiety and suffering, whether potentially or actually, can be overcome or conquered. The Epicureans, we have seen, decided that peace and serenity could be attained by shrinking the world and lessening its importance, thereby making the threat of the other, the world, minimal if not nonexistent. The Stoics, on the other hand, discovered that peace and serenity could be had, not by manipulating the world and man's beliefs about it, but rather by manipulating the self and man's beliefs about it. Peace and serenity for the Stoic could be attained by enlarging the self, by giving it a new significance it had not had before, thereby making the threat of the other, the world, minimal if not nonexistent.

But, curiously enough, both the Epicureans and the Stoics believed that the power to shrink the world or magnify the self lay within easy grasp of each individual Epicurean or Stoic. The power to change the world or change the self, in other words, lay within reach of each individual world-changer or self-changer. The *Vedic brahmins* were not so optimistic.

How does one get the Power? There seem to be two ways. One way would involve influencing the Power Group and appealing to or forcing them to give up their Power; a second way would be to join the Power Group somehow and seize Power as a member of the Group. The first is the *Vedic* way, the second, the *Upaniṣadic* way. The first way entails influencing, cajoling, entreating, appealing, and then finally forcing the Gods to do one's bidding. The second way entails becoming a "God" oneself and then doing as one pleases.

The *Vedic way to Power* assumed, essentially, that the Gods were anthropomorphic beings, susceptible to being influenced by human wiles and persuasion. They had the Power, but they could be entreated to share it or give it up, for a while at least. The way in which this entreating could be accomplished was through the process of the ritual sacrifice.

As time went on, the conception grew clearer that the Power was separable from the Gods; that is to say, the Gods weren't identical with their Power; rather, the Power was something they used, too, and it was not part of them or in them. This momentous discovery proved, eventually, to be the downfall of *brahminism*, as we shall see. The momentous discovery was that what one wanted was Power: not the Gods, not heaven, not food, not honor, not victory, not wealth, not even the *brahmins*, but Power. For once one had Power, then all these other things naturally fell under one's control as well. As Franklin Edgerton has said regarding the *Vedic* sacrifice:

> Before the dawn of history it had developed into a ritualistic cult, a complicated system of sacrifices, the performance of which was the class privilege of a guild of priests. . . . At first merely a means of gratification and propitiation of the gods, the sacrifice gradually became an end in itself, and finally, in the period succeeding the hymns of the Rig Veda, the gods became supernumeraries. The now all-important sacrifices no longer persuaded, but compelled them to do what the sacrificer desired; or else, at times, the sacrifice produced the desired result immediately, without any participation whatsoever on the part of the gods.[15]

The Power that is now at the beck and call of the priest who knows the compelling formula has an interesting history that should be mentioned at this point. That Power comes to be called *Brahman*, and this concept will be with us throughout our discussion of later Hinduism. Initially, and in its original use, *brahman* appears to have meant "hymn" or "evocative chant"; the word applied to both the hymns and evocative charms or magical spells of the early *Vedas*. Thus any utterance that is sacred and magical is *brahman*. But as time passed, *brahman* came to be identified not with the uttered words, hymns, chants, or spells but rather with the power evoked by those utterances; *brahman* was not identified with the Gods but rather with what the Gods had: Power. Franklin Edgerton puts the point well, again, when he says:

> The spoken word had a mysterious, supernatural power; it contained within itself the essence of the thing denoted. To "know the *name*" of anything was to control the thing. The *word* means wisdom, knowledge; and knowledge . . . was (magic) power. So *brahman*, the "holy word," soon came to mean the mystic power inherent in the holy word.[16]

And to the man who knew the holy word, the holy Power that it manifested was immediately available as well: "All human desires and aspirations were accessible to him who mastered it."[17]

[15]Franklin Edgerton, *The Bhagavad Gītā* (New York: Harper Torchbooks, 1964), p. 111.

[16]*Ibid.*, p. 116.

[17]*Ibid.*

A final stage of development of *brahman* from holy word to holy Power now emerges. *Brahman* comes to be seen as the power inherent in everything, the totality, the whole, since nothing does anything without this power. Hence the universe itself comes to be identified with *brahman*, and *brahman* becomes identified with the holy All. Now he who knows *brahman* (the holy word) can grasp *Brahman* (the holy Power) and thereby control *Brahman* (the holy All) or the totality of all that exists. And since this power over the totality, the entire universe, is in the hands of those who know the holy word and can conduct the ritual and compelling sacrifice, the prestige and importance of the priests become enormous.

We may glimpse the nature of the *Vedic* power sacrifice by examining one of the most common and most powerful of the many kinds of ritual Āryan sacrifices: the soma sacrifice. The soma plant, the focal point of the entire ritual, was gathered from the clefts of the rocks in the high mountains at night and by moonlight. It was regarded as a sacred plant; hence there may have been some ritual accompanying its gathering. From what we can understand from the *Ṛg Veda* the plant was brought to the place where the soma ritual was to be carried out, and there it was washed and cleaned. Then the stalks of the plant were crushed in a stone mortar by a wooden pestle, and the bruised and crushed remains were laid between stones and pressed. As the pressing stones or (later) wooden boards, were brought together, the juices trickled out onto a cleansing sieve, usually lamb's wool. Next the juice was strained and, finally, consumed by the priest or priests. The priestly celebrants chanted exuberant hymns to the soma to accompany both the crushing and the pressing ceremonies, hymns which invited Indra to come to the sacrifice and partake of the sacred soma juice, and which ecstatically anticipated the drinking of the juice:

> To waters with the stones they
> drive thee, tawny-hued,
> most rich in sweets,
> Oh Soma, to be Indra's drink.[18]

And again,

> Him, green, beloved, many-eyed,
> The Sisters with the
> pressing stones
> Send down to ridges of the sieve.
>
> This Sage, exalted by our praise,
> flows to the purifying cloth,
> Scattering foes as he is cleansed.[19]

[18] *Ṛg Veda* IX.30.5, Griffith.

[19] *Ibid.* IX.26.5; IX.27.1.

Once the juice was filtered and cleaned, it passed into wooden cups or vats. Tawny or brownish-red in color, it was drunk either mixed or undiluted. Dilution was usually with curds, water, or milk, but we are not told in what proportions:

> The plant is washed in waters,
> pressed by men, the milk-
> cows sweeten it with their milk.
>
> Led by the men he (Soma) takes
> the milk for raiment . . . .[20]

Then the juice is poured into cups, perhaps as many as three (*Ṛg Veda IX*.1032), and it is drunk for Indra by the priests or perhaps symbolically by Indra, himself, by being poured into the fire or perhaps onto the ground. Evidence seems to indicate that one of the priests, possibly the *hotṛ* priest, called Lord Indra or the other Gods to the sacrifice and then offered the libation.

The states of consciousness produced by drinking the soma vary from ecstatic mystical exaltation to wild, rapturous intoxication:

> 1. Drink, Indra; the juice is shed
> to make thee joyful: Let loose
> the bay steeds . . . .
>
> 2. Drink thou of this (soma), . . . . for
> power and rapture.
> The men, the pressing-stones, the
> cows, the waters have made
> this soma ready for thy
> drinking.
>
> 4. . . . let this sacrifice increase
> thy vigour.[21]

The descriptions of the states of consciousness that occurred upon drinking the soma continue:

> We have drunk soma . .. and in the wild raptures of the juice . . . have become immortal, we have attained the light and discovered the Gods.[22]

> These glorious drops that give me freedom have I drunk. Closely they knit my joints as straps secure a chariot.[23]

[20]*Ibid.* IX.62.5; IX.95.1.

[21]*Ibid.* VI.40.1, 2, 4.

[22]*Ibid.* VIII.46.14; VIII.48.3.

[23]*Ibid.* VIII.48.5.

And,

> . . . the soma brings wild delight . . . in the wild joy of soma the Gods wrought their glorious deeds.[24]

It was in these ecstatic states that the *brahmins* had their visions, sang their praise and joy of the Gods, and brought about the miraculous events for which the sacrifice was conducted: the acquisition for themselves or their patrons of wealth, cattle, sons, cities, and, finally, heaven itself.

The soma sacrifice up to this stage would seem to cut across the conclusions we drew previously regarding the grasping of *Brahman* or the holy Power simply in virtue of knowing the name. We saw previously that what the late *Vedic* sacrifice finally came down to was the acquisition of Power by ritual compulsion. The soma sacrifice seems to abrogate that previous conclusion. More importantly, it seems that one or the other, either ritual compulsion or the soma sacrifice, would have to be superflous. In other words, if ritual compulsion can bring Power on demand, then what's the use of quaffing soma? And if quaffing soma can bring Power, then what's the use of ritual compulsion?

The foregoing is a problem, of course, only if ritual compulsion and quaffing soma are distinct activities and only if they both lead to the same approximate results. But these assumptions may be wrong. I would suggest in fact that ritual compulsion and quaffing soma are really not separate activities, for the soma-quaffing ceremony is simply an adjunct to the ritual compulsion ceremony. Moreover, what is sought in the ceremony is actually a double end. The ritual compulsion part of the *Vedic* sacrifice yields the Power that was discussed earlier, while the soma-quaffing part yields states of consciousness—wild, rapturous, and mystical transports of mind. The *brahmins* who performed the ceremonies, therefore, sought *both* Power and these ecstatic, mystical states. There is no problem, therefore, for the precise reason that there was but one ritual with two aspects and two ends sought.

We now turn to the fourth statement of the formula for Power:

### *d. The Vedas Describe that Way*

We have seen that the way to Power is described in *Vedic* ritual and even in the soma sacrifice, though the notion of Power there is specifically related to ecstatic states of consciousness rather than to naked, holy Power itself. The conclusion we can draw, then, is simply to reiterate that the *Vedas* themselves, as part of the oral tradition of the *Vedic brahmins*, constitute the source, the divinely revealed *śruti*, of all descriptions of the way to *Brahman*, the way to the holy Power. The hymns, the songs, the chants, the myths, the stories, and the ecstatic descriptions of the Power of the *Vedas* constitute the

[24]*Ibid.* I.85.7, 10.

fount of all later Hinduism, and while this point has been only briefly illustrated here, it will be more amply illustrated as we discuss the metaphysics of the *Vedas*. I will assume that the fourth statement needs no further elaboration here.

### *e. Summary*

The formula for Power constitutes the key to *Vedic* religious life, and from its four statements a number of observations and conclusions about *Vedic* religion necessarily follow. I list five major characteristics of the *Vedic* religion:

#### 1) Power Oriented

The late *Vedic* religion was oriented to the gaining of Power, and this Power was obtained by the compulsory ritual of the sacrifice. Once the way to the Power had been found, the Gods could be ignored, for it is their Power that becomes all important to the *Vedic* priests and their patrons, and that Power is separable from the Gods. As a result the Gods become of secondary concern, and it would seem to follow from this that the Gods become negligible, unimportant, and, for religious-Power purposes, nonexistent. *Brahminism* then leads, oddly enough, to a kind of atheism; in other words the Power orientation of *Vedic brahminism* would lead to the obsole scence or uselessness of the Gods and from thence to ritual atheism. In fact, this curious result is precisely what we find occurring in the period that follows the *Vedas*, as developed in the texts called the *Upaniṣads*. The *Upaniṣads*, in declaring the ultimate reality to be *Brahman*, the holy Power in the universe, a theme taken over from late *brahminism*, become generally indifferent to the Gods.

#### 2) Excessively Ritualistic

The *Vedic* religion was organized around the sacrifices performed by the priest for the securing of goods such as wealth, sons, territory, heaven, and, in the end, the Power itself, which would deliver these various goods on demand. The ritual, as a result, became the focal point of the entire religion. We have talked about the extremely important soma sacrifice, but there were numerous and varied other sacrifices: the Fire-God sacrifice or the *Agnihotra*, offered in the morning and evening; the New-moon and Full-moon sacrifices; the Four-month or Seasonal sacrifices; the First-fruit or Harvest sacrifice; the Animal sacrifice, which consisted of the offering of a goat to both Agni, the God of the fire, and Soma, was conducted once or twice a year. In the Horse sacrifice a mighty king or ruler turned a horse loose to wander at will for one year; whatever realms the horse touched on would have to swear loyalty to the King. To ensure this the horse was followed by a band of stalwart warriors. At the end of the year the horse was returned to the starting place, slain, and covered with a garment under which the queen of the country crept and there united with the dead animal. Afterwards the horse was cooked and sacramentally eaten, with certain parts being offered to the Gods. A human sacrifice is mentioned twice in certain later *sūtras,* in ceremonies closely patterned after the Horse sacrifice mentioned above, though these references may entail only a symbolic and not a real murder.[25]

### 3) Priest Dominated

The Vedic religion was dominated by the *brahmins* who conducted the ceremonies. It was a closed profession in the sense that someone from another occupational level, a warrior, ruler, worker, farmer, or peasant, could not become a priest (a point to be touched on below in our discussion of *varṇa dharma,* the law of color, or the class or "caste" system of India). As a result of the tremendous importance of the ritual sacrifice, and given the facts that only the priests could conduct it and that the union of priests was closed to non-*brahmins,* the influence and power of the *brahmins* must have been enormous.

### 4) Aristocratic

The Vedic religion, it must be admitted, tended to be an aristocratic (from the Greek *aristos,* "the best") religion—a religion controlled or ruled by the best, whose partrons, on the whole, would be the very best, themselves, the wealthy and the noble. The keys to the kingdoms of heaven and earth were not held by or for *hoi polloi,* the common people, but for and by aristocrats. Consequently the masses of people—the vast majority of those who were not priests or could not have afforded the priests and a public sacrifice—would be denied the direct benefits of that public ritual. The proof for this hard-nosed and highly speculative conclusion lies in the rather scathing remarks made about the *Vedas* and the *brahmins* in the later tradition, remarks made particularly in the *Upaniṣads* and in the *Bhagavad Gītā,* as we shall see.

### 5) Pragmatic

The *Vedic* religion was eminently pragmatic or practical. The ritual and the priests who conducted it sought several instrumental or secondary ends, such as the maintenance of the cosmos, the acquisition of wealth, territory

[25]For more on these and other *Vedic* sacrifices see Arthur Berriedale Keith, *The Religion and Philosophy of the Veda and Upanishads,* Two Volumes (Harvard Oriental Series), (Cambridge, Mass.: Harvard University Press, 1925), Vol. 32, pp. 313–348.

and sons, the cultivation of ecstatic states of consciousness, the guarantee of heaven, and the control of Power. But the ultimate or primary end to which all of these instrumental ends led was, of course, the freedom from fear and anxiety that contact with a threatening world had engendered. In the practical pursuit of that ultimate end, the religion of the *Vedas* seems to have been moderately successful. For if it had not been successful at all, it probably wouldn't have endured into the twentieth century, in one form or another. And if it had been wholly successful, it probably wouldn't have been superseded by the reforming religions such as Jainism, Buddhism, and Vedānta [literally "the end (*anta*) of the *Vedas*"—that is, the *Upaniṣads*].

This completes our discussion of the religion of the *Vedas*, and in particular the *Ṛg Veda*. We turn next to the metaphysics of the *Ṛg Veda* and to an examination of a story about the creation.

## 2. THE METAPHYSICS OF THE ṚG VEDA

### *a. Why is there anything at all?*

Why did things come into being—your house, this room, this book? Why did you come into being? After all, those things, as well as you, might very well not have existed! Your house need not have been built. Your parents might have had another child, and not you! Now, if this talk makes some kind of sense, then it might make equally good sense to make the same assertions of all things or beings—that is, that they too might not have been produced or lived; and then it might make equally good final sense to assert that, quite possibly, nothing at all might have existed—neither tables, chairs, mountains, oceans, planets, stars, galaxies, nor the entire universe, the totality or whole. But if that final assertion does make some kind of sense, then our original question is a meaningful one: why is there anything at all? And, further, why is everything the way it is and not different?

People who ask such questions are generally and by nature unsatisfied with causal explanations of the sort offered by the natural scientist. The questions raised here are really metaphysical questions, questions about ontology and cosmology, rational theology and rational psychology. They are not questions about genetics and the biological laws of the human species, nor do they seek answers in the latest theories of the astronomer or the astrophysicist regarding the origin of the universe.

Why is there anything at all? Metaphysics ["beyond (*meta*) physics or beyond matter (*physis*)," as its name is taken by many to imply] is the domain we are hunting answers in right now, and metaphysics as cosmology provides extremely well-stocked areas for the kind of hunting we have in mind. Martin Heidegger, the contemporary German existential philosopher, asks in the opening lines of his *Introduction to Metaphysics:*

> Why are there things rather than nothing? That is the question. Clearly it is no ordinary question. "Why are there things, why is there anything at all, rather than nothing?"—surely this is the first of all questions . . . .

And in the *Ṛg Veda* it is similarly asked:

> No one knows whence creation has arisen; . . . whence was it born? and from whence came all this creation? . . . Who knows then when it first came into being?[26]

Why is there anything at all? Let me explain what all this means. My daughter plays a curious game with her friends in which one child gives an answer and the other children must try to guess the question to that answer. Now the evidence before us in the *Vedas* and other cosmological texts would seem to indicate that a similar game was being played there. For we have a great number of similar stories or myths in those texts that look as if they were all attempting to answer the question, Why is there anything at all? The answers are varied and yet strangely similar. They all start with a beginning of sorts, a first event, a first substance or stuff, a first act from which all later events, substances, or acts would seem to come. They say, "In the beginning God created heaven and earth," or, "In the beginning was the Word and the Word was God," or, "In the beginning was the Puruṣa, the Person," or, "In the beginning was *Brahman*," and so on. But some of these so-called beginnings are not really beginnings at all. Thus *Genesis* I.1 in the Hebrew *Old Testament* says, "In the beginning God created the heavens and the earth." But that "beginning" is no true beginning, for quite obviously God preceded the creation of the heaven and the earth, and therefore in some sense of "beginning" God existed before the beginning.

One creation story, out of quite a few in the *Vedas*, gives every appearance of beginning with a true beginning, a beginning out of a pure nothing, for obviously in talking about a "true beginning" you either begin with something like a God or a heaven or an earth, or you begin with a nothing. Here's a story that seems to begin with a nothing, and it seems to be a true beginning in the sense that there seems to be nothing, literally nothing, neither being nor nonbeing, prior to it:

1. Nonbeing then existed not nor being;
   There was no air, nor sky that is beyond it.
   What was concealed? Wherein? Under whose protection?
   And was there deep unfathomable water?

2. Death then existed not nor life immortal;
   Of neither night nor day was there any sign.[27]

[26] *Ṛg Veda* X.129.7, 6, after Macdonell.

[27] *Ibid.* X.129, 1, 2.

But then, rather mysteriously, a real something suddenly appears following that beginning. It is called the *One*:

> But the One, without breath, breathed by its own nature.
> Apart from it there was nothing.[28]

Examined from one point of view, the hymn at this stage is plainly self-contradictory: on the one hand, it seems to say that in the beginning there was nothing; it also seems to say that there was the One, a something-or-other.

I think that two conclusions can be drawn from cosmologies that deal with beginnings of this sort, and both of these conclusions relate quite directly to *Ṛg Veda* X. 129, the hymn here under discussion. First, no cosmology can speak meaningfully about true beginnings in which there is nothing; none do, as a matter of fact, but, more strongly, none can. Even the *Vedic brahmins*, apparently, recognized this in their speculations, for while this hymn begins with an apparent nothing, it is obvious from what follows that this is a strongly qualified nothing and that the One has been there all along. In a similar situation in the oldest of the *Upaniṣads*, the *Bṛhadāraṇyaka* (ca. 800 B.C.E.) there is a remarkable parallel situation regarding beginnings in which a nothing is at first postulated but then in the next moment also mysteriously qualified:

> In the beginning there was nothing at all here. This world was covered over with death, with hunger, for hunger is truly death.
> Then he made up his mind: "I wish that I had a body."[29]

Who is this obscure "he" that suddenly appears?

> So he went on chanting. From him, while he was singing, water was produced.[30]

Later hymns in the same *Upaniṣad* by-pass the need for such qualification by simply speaking about true beginnings with real beings, thus:

> In the beginning this world was Self (Ātman) alone in the form of a Person.
> Looking around, he saw nothing but himself. He said first, "I am."[31]

And again,

> Truly, in the beginning this world was Brahman.
> It knew only itself: "I am Brahman." Therefore it became the All.[32]

[28] *Ibid.* X.129.2.

[29] *Bṛadāraṇyaka Upaniṣad,* I.2.1, author's translation of all *Upaniṣads* unless otherwise noted.

[30] *Ibid.* I.2.1.

[31] *Ibid.* I.4.1.

[32] *Ibid.* I.4.10.

And, finally, the *Bṛhadāraṇyaka* says,

> In the beginning this world was first the Self, one only. He wished: "I wish that I had a wife, then I would procreate. I wish that I had wealth; then I would offer a sacrifice." So great, indeed, is desire.[33]

The first conclusion, again, is that no cosmology can meaningfully begin with a nothing and from that nothing expect to get a something, a creation. If one attempts it, one ends, as with *Ṛg Veda* X.129, in a self-contradiction. The *Bṛhadāraṇyaka Upaniṣad* attempts it, as we have seen, but finally gives up in its later creation stories and resorts to the acceptance of a something—a strange "he," or a Self, or a *Brahman.*

The second conclusion I want to draw follows from the first and its allusion to the self-contradictory nature of *Ṛg Veda* X.129; for to state that there is nothing and then to state that there is also something, the One, is patently self-contradictory. I want to argue that something is going on here with language other than a logical mistake. It is the same sort of going-on that one finds in the hymn when it says, "But the One without breath breathed by its own nature." Language is being used here in a shocking, self-contradictory way that serves to pull the listener or reader up short. The apparent contradictions are employed as flagging or warning devices to remind the reader that something special, something wholly extraordinary, is being communicated. What is this something special? I am going to argue that this same flagging throughout the later texts of Hinduism, such as the *Upaniṣads*, the *Bhagavad Gītā*, and the *Purāṇas*, stands as a warning to the listener or reader that the subject under discussion is by its nature beyond linguistic description and that a new kind of attention is being demanded of him.

We will have occasion to look further at this contradictory use of language in our later discussions, but the interesting thing for our purposes now is that it occurs here in *Ṛg Veda* X. 129:

> 3. At first there was darkness concealed in darkness. This All was undifferentiated ocean.
> All that existed then was empty and without form. By the great power of heat the One came into being.
>
> 4. In the beginning desire entered the One, the first seed and origin of spirit. Sages who searched their hearts with wisdom discovered the bond between the existent and the nonexistent.
>
> 5. Their ray of light shot across the darkness. What was above it and what below?
> Creative energy was there and fertile power. Below was energy and above was impulse.

[33] *Ibid.* I.4.17.

But the author of the hymn suddenly takes a new approach:

> 6. Who knows for certain and who can declare whence it was born and from whence came all this creation?

Can't God tell us? Doesn't sacred scripture know? No, for

> The Gods are later than this world's creation. Who knows, then, whence it first came into being?

And the author ends rather strangely on a wryly sceptical note:

> 7. No one knows whence creation has arisen, and whether the One has or has not produced it. He who sees the All from highest heaven he alone knows—and maybe even he does not know.[34]

Another and even more famous *Vedic* creation hymn deserves our attention. We are back once again with cosmological beginnings, but in place of nothings this time we begin with somethings—namely, a *puruṣa,* which means "person" or "man." This hymn, *Ṛg Veda* X.90, is called by translators "The Hymn to *Puruṣa*." In the beginning, it says, there was a gigantic man, and from the parts of the body of this man, or *puruṣa*, the All, the totality, was created. One curious thing about the hymn is the sudden and inexplicable appearance of the Gods, who do the dividing and sacrificing of the man's body. Where did they come from? Do they constitute a beginning also? Or are they in some unexplained way part of the man, too, as is everything else? The hymn illustrates, among other things, the metaphysical doctrine of pan-en-theism (all is in God, but part of God transcends the all); the origin of the *varṇa dharma* system of occupational classes or *varṇas* from the various parts of the man; and the origin of mankind as part—an intimate, spiritual part—of the totality, inextricably tied to everything else in the creation from the dust of the earth to the highest of the Gods. Here, then, is this mysterious, beautiful, and delightfully philosophic hymn of creation:

> 1. The Puruṣa has a thousand heads; a thousand eyes and a thousand feet. He pervades the earth on all sides and fills a space ten fingers wide.
>
> 2. The Puruṣa is all that has been and all that will ever be. He is the Lord of immortality which grows greater still by food from the sacrifice.
>
> 3. Such is his greatness. But even greater than all of this is the Puruṣa. All creatures are one-fourth of him, and three-fourths of him are the immortals in heaven.
>
> 4. With three-fourths the Puruṣa rose in heaven and one-fourth of him again was here on earth. Then he

[34] *Ṛg Veda* X.129.3–7, after Macdonell.

spread himself out to every side over those who eat (Gods, men, animals) and over those who do not eat (rivers, mountains, earth).

5. From him Virāj (the female creative counterpart of Puruṣa, the male creative principle) was born and form Virāj Puruṣa was born. When he was born he spread eastward and westward over the earth.

6. When the Gods spread out the sacrifice with the Puruṣa as their offering, its sacred oil was spring, summer was the fuel and the holy gift was autumn.

7. They sprinkled the Puruṣa as he lay on the sacred grass. With him all the Gods, the Sādhyas (celestial beings), and the Ṛṣis (sages) sacrificed.

8. From that great first sacrifice the dripping oil was gathered up. It made the creatures of the air, and all beasts both wild and tame.

9. From that great first sacrifice were born the hymns of the Ṛg Veda and the Sāma Veda. From it were born spells and charms and the Yajur Veda.

10. From it were born horses and all those with two rows of teeth. From it were born cattle, and from it goats and sheep.

11. When they divided Puruṣa, into how many portions did they arrange him? What was his mouth? What his arms? What his thighs and feet?

12. The brahmin was his mouth; his two arms made the rājanya (kṣatriya); his two thighs the vaiśya; and from his feet was made the śūdra.

13. The moon was born from his mind, and from his eye the sun was born. Indra and Agni were born from his mouth, and from his breath came Vāyu (wind).

14. From his navel came the middle sky and the heaven was made from his head. From his feet came earth, and from his ear the four quarters, North, East, South, and West. Thus they formed the worlds.

15. Seven sticks made the fence around the fire, three times seven the layers of wood on the fire when

the Gods bound their victim, Puruṣa, and offered sacrifice.

16. The Gods sacrificing made the sacrifice sacred. These where the first holy ordinances. These mighty ones thereby reached to highest heaven where dwelt the Sādhyas, the ancient Gods.[35]

And there the creation hymn ends. Two observations are in order regarding this remarkable cosmological catalogue. First, the Indians who composed, and others who now revere, this sacred hymn play a certain game with words and objects to which we should call attention. Briefly, it is a game that attempts to show that everything is not what it seems to be, but rather many ordinary things stand as signs for something else that is extraordinary. The Puruṣa is a man but not really a man; he is not this or that but rather the totality, the All; his head is not really a head but heaven; his feet are not really feet but the earth; and so on. The Indians love this language of metaphor and they employ it throughout their later philosophy as well as in these earliest texts. The *metaphor game*, if that is what we can call the activity that employs language this way, assumes that nothing is what it appears to be but rather that everything is something else. One tends to see in microcosm, at the sacrificial fire, for example, what exists really in macrocosm: the creation of the whole or totality from Puruṣa. The metaphor game keeps one on one's metaphysical toes, certainly, and puts one into a philosophic mood to accept sudden and thunderous shifts in language use, shifts from the literal to the symbolic, similetic, or metaphoric. Just as the use of self-contradiction in *Ṛg Veda* X.129 served to remind the reader or listener that something unusual and special was being discussed in that hymn—namely, a being beyond all possible linguistic description—so now the playing of the metaphor game further serves to engage the reader's or listener's attention at another, equally unusual, level of reality and language. This game will be played throughout the *Upaniṣads* and the *Gītā*, and we shall have occasion to note it later in this work.

The second observation has to do with the designation of the parts of Puruṣa into the four occupational classes. The four classes are referred to by the terms *varṇa*, which means "color," and *dharma*, which means "law." Thus *varṇa dharma* means "the law of color." The danger of reading too much contemporary racism into this expression certainly exists, and one must be wary of reading modern psychological theories into this ancient social standard. But having been thus warned, I am nonetheless going to lead you into a rather contemporary sociological interpretation of what might very likely have been the case with the origin of *varṇa dharma*—that is, the origin of the four classes or *varṇas* in ancient India.

[35] *Ṛg Veda* X.90.1–16, author's translation.

### *b. Varṇa Dharma: What and Why?*

*Ṛg Veda* X.90.12 says, once again, "The brahmin was his mouth; his two arms made the rājanya (kṣatriya); his two thighs the vaiśya; and from his feet was made the śūdra." The fact that the text quoted is a *śruti* text serves to ground the *varṇa* system in a sacred, traditional context, and that grounding gave a kind of absolutist legitimacy to the entire system that flowed from it, one that lives and endures in India even to this day.

There are two approaches one can take in order to seek explanations and possibly justifications about *śruti* assertions regarding *varṇa.* The first is simply to ask: why did God, the *Ṛṣis,* or Authors, or the eternal Tradition establish the *varṇa* system? This *religious approach* is generally intellectually unfruitful, however pious it might seem. The religious approach, as I am defining it here, seeks a kind of theodicy, a justification of God's purposes and activities for man or to man. Thus the religious approach seeks answers to the question: "Why did God establish the *varṇa* system?," and it accepts such answers as, "Because God thought it best," or, "Because God said that man would be happier this way," or, "Because that's the way men naturally divide up," or, "Because God did and that's all." I find all of these responses to be intellectually uninteresting, because they led nowhere beyond saying something about God's goodness and wisdom. Religious answers, of the type cited, serve a different function than answers of or from a sociological or psychological source. The religious approach to questions about *śruti* produces religious answers that serve to promote faith, increase emotional stability, or eradicate insecurity and pain; they do not provide us with insight into the empirical, sociological, or psychological grounds for establishing a *varṇa* system. For those kinds of grounds we must forsake the transcendental, religious approach for the mundane, *naturalistic approach.* To employ the naturalistic approach to *śruti* in no way implies that the religious approach is false or wrong. All it does imply is that there are multiple meanings to *śruti* and, hence, multiple approaches can safely and productively be employed.

The naturalistic approach to *varṇa dharma* asks of it: why did these people establish the *varṇa* system, or more specifically: what need was there for the employment by the Āryans of the *varṇa* system? what human need was being met by the system of class or *varṇa*? I mention four possible answers:

1. *Religion.* The *varṇa dharma* was established by God or by the eternal, the beginningless Tradition; it was heard or seen by the *ṛṣis* and told to the people. Thus the explanation and justification for *varṇa* lies in its transcendental timeless origin and its ability to satisfy some human emotional or religious need. But this is the religious answer we previously discussed and subsequently rejected as being uninteresting. We pass therefore to a second answer.

2. *Āryan Tradition.* The *varṇa dharma* was established in a tribal tradition that may predate the arrival of the Āryans into India. The Āryans sought to pattern their three upper classes of priests, warriors, and producers after the three classes of Gods: the heavenly Gods, the sky Gods, and the earth Gods. Like similar social divisions among the Pythagoreans or the Spartans, or those idealized by Plato in his *Republic*, this structure had its real origins in the prehistorical customs of the Indo-European peoples of the eastern Caspian regions of Asia. But, one might well ask, so what? This Āryan tradition account is merely a genetic history of the possible origin of the *varṇa* system, whereas we are seeking a rational explanation for *varṇa*. In giving this account of *varṇa* in terms of Āryan tradition we have solved nothing, for we have to ask the original question all over again, only now we ask it of the proto-historical Āryan tradition: What human need was being met by the system of caste, class, or *varṇa*? Since that question is not answered merely by referring to the Āryan tradition, whatever it was, we pass on to a third answer.

3. *Fear of the Harappāns.* The *varṇa dharma* was established to combat the threat posed by the Harappāns after that Indus Valley people had been conquered by the Āryans. The fear may have been that intermarriage with the racially distinct Harappāns might attenuate the felt superiority of the Āryan conquerors in customs, religion, trade, and rulership. After all, it is sometimes argued, *varṇa* means "color," and what could be more logical than that *varṇa dharma*, the law of color, was set up for the precise purpose of protecting the lighter-skinned long-nosed Āryans from contamination with the darker-skinned (*kṛṣṇa* or black) and short-nosed (*anāsa* or noseless) Harappāns? This view has been especially popular in the present century, although there is no real historical evidence to confirm it. The *Vedas*, save for one passage in *Ṛg Veda* X.90 on the origin of the four classes, are remarkably silent about *varṇa dharma.* One must be wary, however, of this counterargument that is used to reject the Fear-of-the-Harappāns argument. The counterargument, a species of what is technically called *the argument from silence* in Western philosophy, looks something like this:

1. If *varṇa dharma* had heen instituted to protect the Āryans from the Harappāns (for reasons of race, color, custom, religion, or whatever), then the *Vedas* would have said so.
2. But the *Vedas* do not say so; they are silent about the whole affair.
3. Therefore the *varṇa dharma* was not instituted to protect the Āryans from the Harappāns.

This argument is *valid*, but, because the premises may not be true, the argument may not be *sound* (a "sound argument" is one whose form is valid and whose premises are all true). There are two reasons why the argument from silence, as used above, may have false premises. First, in a text as fundamentally "theological" as the *Vedas* any other mention of *varṇa dharma* might be out of place; it is not a text on sociology, psychology, or racial fear. Second, in texts as ancient as the *Vedas* other references to *varṇa dharma* might have been lost; it is possible that the *Vedas* that we have are incomplete. For these and similar reasons, the argument from silence cannot be used to refute or even to establish the fear of the Harappāns as the origin of *varṇa dharma*.

Many of the other defenses of the Fear-of-the-Harappāns argument are derived from twentieth-century sociological and psychological knowledge of racial and cultural bias and are in themselves indefensible, unless one is willing to first defend much broader empirical generalizations such as: All men are everywhere the same, and especially *the same* with respect to the defense of customs, culture, and standards of tribal intermarriage. For our purposes it is not necessary to follow out the argument in which this generalization would stand as a major premise. It is sufficient to say that the *Vedas* are silent on this third answer, but this silence is no reason to yield to the Fear-of-the-Harappāns argument. We pass on, consequently, to a fourth answer.

4. *Practical Purpose.* The *varṇa dharma* was established in order to serve the very practical purpose of dividing up the occupations in the tribe, thereby ensuring a more efficient and workable occupational and social system. If each man, woman and child in the society knew what his productive purpose and function in the society was to be, this would yield not only a more efficient society but happier and more contented persons as well. Consider for a moment your own situation. Wouldn't you be happier if you were engaged in the kind of occupation you were fitted by your nature to do? Your *occupation* (from the Latin *occupare*, "to seize or take possession of")—the work that you do without necessarily being fitted temperamentally for it or having any special natural predilection for it—would then become a true *vocation* (from the Latin *vocare*, "to call"), the work that you have been called to do in virtue of your special nature temperament, talent, or fitness. One of the reasons people take aptitude and interest tests is to determine what kinds of tasks or jobs they would be best suited to be called to. The underlying assumption is, once again, that a person is happiest and does his best work when his job is his vocation and not his mere occupation. The Vedic Āryans in instituting the *varṇa dharma* (the argument concludes) were simply using an ancient variety of the modern aptitude and interest test. They knew that sons of *brahmins* would be happier being *brahmins*, that sons of *kṣatriyas* would be happier being *kṣatriyas*, and so on.

The *varṇa dharma* is an Indian variant of a similar occupational system theoretically introduced, as we mentioned earlier, by the Pythagoreans and Plato in the West in the sixth and fourth centuries B.C.E. It may well be that the caste, class, or occupational system found among the Greeks and Āryans was a system indigenous to the Indo-European language family established for social expediency and personal happiness (the "practical purpose" argument). Plato's system, however, unlike the Indian *varṇa* system, did not rest on inheritance. At quite an early age, around seven years, boys and girls were to begin a series of skill tests and intelligence examinations that were continued, for many of them at least, through the next fifteen or so years. These tests and examinations determined who was fitted for doing what tasks in the imaginary social utopia that Plato described so elegantly in his *Republic*. Plato believed that every man and woman was fitted by his or her nature or soul to become either a ruler (an administrator or philosopher king), or a defender of the state (a warrior or guardian), or a producer (a businessman or farmer). His scheme for his state thus carries one less category than the *varṇa dharma* (although it is believed that the original Āryan system had only three classes, as well), but the idea was precisely the same: the individual and therefore society function best when the individual is happiest; and the individual is happiest when he is doing what he is fitted by his nature and by his calling to do. The *varṇa dharma* helps a person to find his nature and then the vocation best suited to that nature. Therefore we have an extremely plausible naturalistic reply to the question with which we began this discussion what human need was being met by the system of vocational class or *varṇa dharma*?

This ends our discussion of the metaphysics and cosmology of *Ṛg Veda* X.90 and our discussion of the metaphysics of the *Ṛg Veda*.

## 3. THE EPISTEMOLOGY OF THE ṚG VEDA

The problem of writing about the theory of knowledge or the theory of truth and meaning in the *Vedas* is that the *Vedic* texts seem totally unconcerned with epistemological problems. The claim that anything is epistemological in the *Vedas* is largely the result of a philosophic reconstruction by the Indologist. But given these *caveats*, let us push ahead using a reconstruction of our own with regard to a basic and favorite epistemological question: how do I know that I know anything?

To move the reconstruction quickly, let's assume that "knowledge" can be defined as "justified true belief." This is a commonly accepted definition among philosophers, and we will stick to it throughout this book. Let's assume, further, that we are trying to discover whether a particular statement, call it *p*, can be known. But for any statement to be known, it must satisfy the definition above: that is, three necessary conditions must be fulfilled before *p* can be said to be known. Putting all this together, we have something like this: I know that *p* if and only if, first, *p* is true; second, I believe *p*; and, finally, I have evidence (a justfication) for *p*; in other words, all knowledge is justified or evidenced true belief. Furthermore, we know whether or not a belief is true only by finding, having, or being able to state the conditions under which we could produce evidence for our belief. With this definition in mind we turn to the *Vedas*, and in particular to the *Ṛg Veda*, for a brief discussion of its epistemology.

The *Vedic* Āryan was a practical man. His religion was practical; his association with his environment as a herdsman, farmer, and warrior was practical; his interests in the world, in wealth, sons, cities, and land were all practical. Hence, by extrapolation, one would suppose that his knowledge about the world around him would rest on simple, uncomplicated, straightforward sensation. In other words, the *Vedic* Āryan was what is called a "realist" in his epistemology. Moreover, he was very likely what we would today technically call a *naive realist*; he would maintain that physical objects and the world in general are exactly what they seem to be: red dawns are red; tawny soma is tawny; sweet milk is sweet; bulls are just exactly what they look like; and trees, earth, and sky are as they appear. The view is *naive* because it is uncritical, and in uncritically basing knowledge on sensation it must admit not only that things such as fires, bows, and chariots are as they appear to be, but that all things are exactly as they appear. It must admit such absurdities, therefore, as that straight spears half immersed in water not only look bent in that water but really are bent; that double images obtained by pushing one eyeball toward the other really produce doubles of everything thus seen in the world; and so on.

Or consider the diagrams intended to produce illusions. According to naive realism there could never by any illusions or hallucinations, for things in the world really are exactly as they appear to consciousness: whatever properties these physical lines in the diagrams appear to have or seem to have are precisely the properties they must have. Here, for example, is the rather familiar Miller-Lyer illusion:

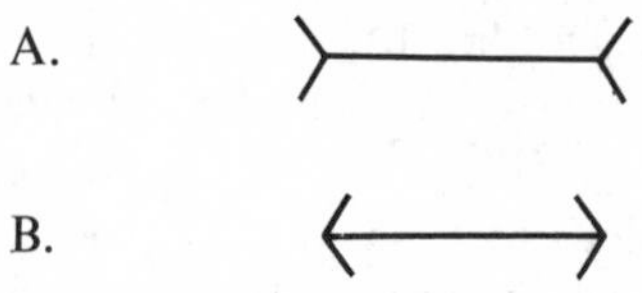


Line A *looks* larger than line B. Hence, naive realism must conclude that line A *is* larger than line B, since naive realism holds, in general, that *looks* and *is* are identical. However, a careful measurement reveals that line A is the same length as line B; hence naive realism is false if not absurd.

Not only was the *Vedic* Āryan a naive realist in his epistemology, grounding most of his knowledge claims in sensation; he must also have believed, that the *brāhmins*, the *ṛṣis* or seers, could see with eyes other than physical eyes, and could hear their *śruti* or sacred revelations with ears other than physical ears. Therefore, it must be supposed that the *Vedic* Āryan also accepted *revelation* and even *intuition* or *mystical insight* as two other legitimate ways or means of grounding true belief and turning it and the entire *śruti* tradition into knowledge.

In conclusion, we might say that the *Vedic* Āryan probably resembles very closely the common-sensical, unsophisticated, ordinary citizen of the twentieth century in his epistemological approach to the world. As with his religious views, so also with his views of the world and the *śruti*; he is first and foremost a hard-headed practical realist, a person of wordly affairs. His uncritical epistemology entails, first, a theory of sensation that grounds his true beliefs about the world, and second, a theory of revelation and intuition that grounds his true beliefs about the Gods and heaven. *Vedic* man is a familiar figure to twentieth-century man, from whom he attracts not a little sympathy, understanding, and compassion. What he knows about his world and his Gods he places into his hymns, adoringly but agonizingly expressing his attitudes and feelings to both. Here, for example, is a hymn to Prajāpati, the Lord of the universe. Consider the question the hymn asks and then consider the possible ways (such as through appeals to sensation, revelation, or intuition) of coming to know the answer to that question:

1. As the Golden Seed he arose in the beginning; when born he was the only Lord of all that existed. He supported the earth and this heaven. What God with our gifts shall we worship?

2. He who gives breath, who gives strength, who commands that all the Gods obey, whose shadow is life immortal, and the lord of death, as well. What God with our gifts shall we worship?

3. Who through his greatness has become the sole ruler over those who breathe and those who slumber; He who is lord of the two-footed and the four-footed. What God with our gifts shall we worship?

4. Whose are, through his greatness, these snowy mountains? Whose are the ocean and the great river Rasa that surrounds the world? His are the embracing arms and all the regions he embraces. What God with our gifts shall we worship?

5. By him are the heavens strong and the earth steadfast, by him the sun and the earth are supported. By him the regions between sun and earth were measured. What God with our gifts shall we worship?

6. To him the heaven and earth, upheld by his aid, look up, trembling in spirit, as over them the risen sun shines. What God with our gifts shall we worship?
7. When the great waters came containing the seed of all within and generating fire, then sprang the one life spirit of the Gods into being. What God with our gifts shall we worship?
8. Who through his greatness beheld the waters that bore the power and generated worship, he who was the one God beyond all the other Gods. What God with our gifts shall we worship?
9. May he not injure us who is earth's father, he of the just laws, heaven's creator, who has brought forth the mighty and shining waters. What God with our gifts shall we worship?
10. Oh Prajāpati, none other than you understand all these created beings and you alone. Oh Prajāpati, when we call unto you grant us our hearts' desire. Oh Prajāpati, may we become lords of wealth.[36]

And here is a lovely hymn to Rātrī, the Goddess of night, using common images all too familiar to practical, realistic contemporary man:

1. The Goddess Night has glanced about with her eyes. She is everywhere approaching and has put on all her loveliness.
2. The immortal Rātrī has filled all the wide space to its depths and heights, and her radiance drives out even the darkness,
3. She comes and drives out her sister Dawn, and then darkness, too, disappears.
4. All have drawn close to us for at Her coming all come home, as birds to their nest upon the tree.
5. The families have all gone home to rest, home the beasts and birds, home even the hawks whc lust for prey.
6. Oh Night, guard us from the she-wolf and the wolf; guard us from the thief, and be good for us to pass.
7. For darkness, shutting out all, has come near me, black and blinding. Oh Dawn, drive it away along with my debts.
8. Oh Daughter of the Sky, I have offered my hymn as a cow is offered. Oh Night, accept my sacrifice as praise to my conqueror.[37]

[36] *Ṛg Veda* X.121.1–10, after Griffith.
[37] *Ibid.* X.127.1–8.

## 4. THE ETHICS OF THE ṚG VEDA

If we assume ethics to be that discipline which deals with the systematic analysis of *right* and *wrong* in human conduct, then the *Vedas* as a whole will be an ethical disappointment for us. One will look in vain in these ancient hymns for any systematic treatment of ethics. And the *Ṛg Veda*, in particular, is no better off than the other three *Vedas* in this matter.

The picture we do get from examining the hymns is that early on, perhaps before the Āryan incursions into India, the Āryan tribes appear to have regarded one of their deities, Varuṇa, as the God whose function in the world was primarily moral. And, at a later historical stage, it would appear that Varuṇa's singular moralistic function is replaced by an abstract principle, *Ṛta*, which becomes the essential moral power in the universe, a principle that insures perfect justice and order among the inhabitants and entities of the universe. In addition to these two speculative ethical elements in the *Ṛg Veda*—besides Varuṇa and, later, *Ṛta*—there must be an element that predates them both, an element known largely by extrapolation from what we already know about any community of persons, any randomly selected tribe or clan, however modern, however primitive. I want to speak to this last point first, call it "tribal ethics," and then turn to Varuṇa and *Ṛta* in our later discussion of the ethics of the *Vedas*.

### *a. Tribal Ethics*

As I indicated, this earliest period of Indian ethics can be known only by extrapolation, whereby we infer a possibility from a series of facts. The series of facts would be what we already know from the *Vedic* hymns such as those quoted above, from anthropological studies of primitive societies, and from our own common sense about what it takes for a community of people to live, and to live harmoniously, together. What the hymns, the anthropological studies, and common sense say is that harmonious living depends on rules and customs, on morals and standards that essentially tell the members of the tribe, clan, or community what constitutes acceptable and unacceptable behavior in the community. The belief in the existence of a Varuna and the acceptance of a principle such as *Ṛta* simply serve to give a legitimacy to the rules and customs, but they (Varuṇa and *Ṛta*) are nontheless separable, logically separable, from those rules.

Thus if Varuṇa will always punish those who steal a neighbor's cattle, then the rule that says "Thou shalt not steal" is grounded in Varuṇa's dislike and disapprobation of stealing. But the belief in the existence of Varuṇa is not really essential to the community's rule against stealing. Stealing would be wrong, the community must know, even if Varuṇa had never existed, and it will be wrong long after he has ceased to exist for the simple reason that stealing, like murder, is socially and institutionally disruptive and therefore unacceptable within the community. Tribal ethics encompasses a set of rules that do not depend essentially on Gods or moral powers in the universe for their legitimacy and acceptability. What makes it ultimately necessary for all men to follow tribal ethics is not that Varuṇa will get you if you don't watch out, or that *Ṛta* or the eternal *dharma* or the law of *karma* will in the end set things right, again by seizing and punishing you: what makes it ultimately necessary and essential for all men to follow tribal ethics is that if they don't there won't be any tribe.

What is at work here is a very simple utilitarian principle resting on the most practical, common-sense rule: stealing, murder, rape, cheating, breaking contracts, and lying are socially disruptive, hence they are socially unacceptable forms of behavior; if you want the tribe to survive, then don't steal, don't murder, don't rape, don't cheat, and so on. In other words stealing, murder, and so on are socially wrong. Tribal ethics, then, must have consisted, as it still does, of a set of extremely useful moral prohibitions, and we can find numerous instances of these prohibitions tucked away in the hymns to trees, dawn, ponds, and the Gods, but especially in the hymns to Varuṇa.

### *b. Varuṇa*

The belief in the existence of Lord Varuṇa simply served, *inter alia*, to provide a reason for not engaging in unacceptable social behavior. Perhaps no tribal ethics ever existed without, or in the absence of, a Varuṇa of some sort or other that served to legitimize the rules forbidding certain types of unacceptable behavior; perhaps the wrongness of certain actions, in terms of sheer social expediency, or as utility, or as practical necessity for the very survival of the tribe, was too complicated to explain or too obvious to need explanation. But whatever the reason, the tribe must have found it expedient and morally necessary to turn Varuṇa from a pure nature deity into a moral watchdog. Originally, Varuṇa was a sky God and his name probably meant "coverer" or "enfolder." Sarvepalli Radhakrishnan says of Varuṇa:

> He covers the whole starry expanse of heaven "as with a robe, with all the creatures thereof and their dwellings" (cf. *Ṛg Veda* VIII.41). . . . Varuṇa's figure is steadily transformed and idealized till he becomes the most moral god of the Vedas. He watches over the world, punishes the evildoers and forgives the sins of those who implore his pardon. The sun is his eye, the sky is his garment and the storm is his breath (cf. *Ṛg Veda* VII.87.2). Rivers flow by his command; the sun shines, the stars and the moon are in their courses for fear of him (cf. *Ṛg Veda* I.24.10; I.25.6; I.44.14; II.28.8; III.54.18; VIII.25.2). By his law heaven and earth are held apart. He upholds the physical and the moral order.[38]

[38] *Indian Philosophy*, Vol. I, p. 77.

It is an easy move, as we shall see, from this athropomorphic protector of the world, the omniscient judge of the universe, to the later abstract concept of *Ṛta* which symbolizes the impersonal, rather than the personal, moral and nomological principle of the universe. Radhakrishnan continues and displays another side to this divine Indian Solomon not previously touched on:

> He is the supreme God, the God of gods, harsh to the guilty and gracious to the penitent. He conforms to the eternal law of the moral world which he has established. Yet in his mercy he is willing to forgive those who offend against him. "He is merciful even to him who has committed sin" (*Ṛg Veda* VII.87.7). In almost all the hymns to Varuṇa we find prayers for the forgiveness of sin.[39]

Taking our cue from Radhakrishnan's description, let's return to the *Ṛg Veda*. Here is a beautiful and touching hymn to Varuṇa that illustrates some of Radhakrishnan's observations:

1. Sing forth a hymn sublime and solemn, grateful to
   glorious Varuṇa, imperial Ruler.
   Who has, like the priest who slays the slaughtered
   offering, spread out earth as a skin in front
   of Sūrya.

2. In the treetops he has extended the air, put milk
   into cattle, and spirited speed into horses.
   Placed intellect into hearts, fire in the waters,
   Sūrya in heaven and Soma on the mountain.

3. Varuṇa lets the waters flow as from a big cask
   opening downward, through heaven to earth
   and air's mid-region,
   From it the world's Lord waters the earth as the
   shower of rain sprinkles the barley.

4. When Varuṇa wishes offerings of milk he moistens
   the sky, and the earth to its very foundations,
   And then the mountains suddenly become clothed
   with rain clouds and the mighty Maruts,
   putting forth their strength, make the mountains tremble.

5. I will declare the wonderous power of māyā of
   the mighty Varuṇa, the immortal Lord,
   Who, standing in the heavens, has measured out
   the earth using the sun as measure.

6. Indeed, none have ever compelled or hindered
   this most wise God's mighty māyā,

[39] *Ibid.*

By which, despite their torrential flood, the
sparkling waters still cannot fill the
sea wherein they pour their waters.

7. If we have sinned against the ones who love
us, or have ever wronged a brother,
friend or comrade,
The neighbor who is close to us or a stranger
who is not, then, Oh Lord Varuṇa, take
from us this wrong.

8. If, as gamblers, we cheat at play, have cheated,
done any wrong whether unknowingly, or
on purpose,
Then take away these sins like loosened bonds,
and, Oh Varuṇa, let us be your own beloved
ones.[40]

The hymn is interesting for a number of reasons, for it actually lists a number of tribal prohibitions that must have been recognized at the time as transgressions and hence as constitutive of tribal ethics—for example, the mistreatment of brothers, friends, neighbors, and even strangers, and cheating at gaming. But this tribal ethics, together with Radhakrishnan's comments earlier, introduce some ethical problems and moral questions that need critical philosophic scrutiny.

One problem is involved with this question: are the moral laws, which prohibit harming your fellow man and cheating, *right* because Varuṇa instituted them, or did Varuṇa institute them because they are right? Call this "the problem of the justification of rightness." A second problem involves Varuṇa's ability to forgive transgressions of the moral law. The question is whether or not God can erase the effects of sin and make it seem as if the wrong action had never been done. There also is the further puzzle regarding what implications such divine forgiveness has for the moral life of *Vedic* man and, perhaps, for modern man as well. Call this second problem "the problem of divine forgiveness." Let me discuss each of these ethical problems that are connected with Varuṇa and then, within the context of the second one, take up the discussion of *Ṛta*, the abstract principle of order in the universe.

### c. *The Problem of the Justification of Rightness*

The problem here is this: is the moral law right because God approves of the law and then creates it as right, or is the moral law right independently

[40] *Ṛg Veda* V.85.1–8, after Griffith.

of God's affirming it and despite any of God's approvings or affirmings towards it? The first view represents what is technically called "ethical subjectivism," the second, "ethical objectivism." The question, then, is: does the *Ṛg Veda* support ethical subjectivism or ethical objectivism?

Let me make this question clearer with some definitions. *Ethical subjectivism* holds that the rightness (or wrongness) of an action is wholly dependent on humanlike attitudes or feelings, such as feelings of approval (or disapproval). *Ethical objectivism* holds that the rightness (or wrongness) of an action is wholly independent of humanlike attitudes or feelings. Suppose I ask you if cheating is wrong and suppose you think that it is. Then I ask you why you think it's wrong. One kind of answer you might give is that cheating is wrong because it is disapproved of by the society in which we live. The ethical subjectivist would argue that it is precisely that disapproval that makes cheating wrong.

But suppose I approve of cheating and you don't; what then? Is cheating right or wrong? Or suppose our society disapproves of cheating but another society says cheating is okay; what then? Now we are involved with another technical position in ethics: "ethical relativism." *Ethical relativism* holds that given two contradictory ethical judgments, both may be right. Thus cheating is right to me and wrong to you, and these apparently contradictory judgments are both right. Notice that ethical relativism seems to be based on ethical subjectivism; the latter defines or states the origin of rightness (it lies in the feelings of the moral agent), while the former demonstrates the applicability of rightness in cases of contradictory moral judgments. All of this is rejected by the ethical absolutist, the chief philosophic opponent of the ethical relativist. *Ethical absolutism* holds that given two contradictory ethical judgments, only one can be right, even though nobody may actually know which one. Thus if I hold that cheating is right or sometimes right, and you hold that it is always wrong, ethical absolutism maintains that one of us must be incorrect.

Our problem, now, is to determine the *Vedic* stance with respect to ethical subjectivism, objectivism, relativism, and absolutism. One way of approaching the question is simply to ask; has the law been created by Varuṇa or is it separate and wholly independent of Varuṇa? The hymns seem to suggest that the law is, if not created by Varuṇa, certainly administered by him, and in some sense the laws even seem quite dependent on him for their application and efficacy. This would mean, then, that there is a certain ethical subjectivism in the *Ṛg Veda*, for the inherent rightness of the laws appears to be dependent on the humanlike approval of those laws by Varuṇa (as well as the other deities). This ethical subjectivism is further grounded in the fact that Varuṇa can forgive sins and thereby alter the effects of moral transgression. More on this below in our discussion of the problem of divine forgiveness.

Here is another hymn to Varuṇa. Note in particular the relation of the law to Varuṇa:

1. Oh God, Oh Varuṇa, when we as men violate your law day after day,
2. Then give us not as prey to death, to be destroyed by you in your wrath or in your fierce anger when displeased.
3. To gain your mercy, Varuṇa, we bind your heart with hymns, even as the charioteer binds his tethered horse.
7. Varuṇa knows the path of birds that fly through heaven, and, master of the sea, he knows all the ships thereon.
8. True to his holy law, he knows the twelve moons with all their progeny as the months with all their days. . . .
9. He knows the pathway of the wind, the spreading, high and mighty wind; he knows the Gods who dwell above.
10. Varuṇa, true to holy law, sits down among his people; he, the most wise one, sits there to govern all.
11. From there he perceives all wonderous things, both what has been, and what hereafter will be done.[41]

At this stage it is not terribly clear whether the law and Varuṇa are separate, identical, or related by some form of inclusion wherein the law is immanent in Varuṇa or vice versa. But several conclusions emerge. First, there are moral laws in the universe and they are related to Varuṇa in some way or other. Second, men are able to disobey or transgress these moral laws. Third, Varuṇa knows when transgression of the moral law occurs. Fourth, Varuṇa will punish those who transgress the moral laws. And finally, Varuṇa can be persuaded, under certain conditions, not to punish those who transgress the moral law. The fifth point is the most important point here, for it means that the consequences of disobedience (punishment, death, destruction by Varuṇa's wrath, or whatever) are not automatic—which means that Varuṇa has control over at least some aspects of the law and that it does not control him. In the end Varuṇa dominates the law; it is truly "*his* law," and he can choose to punish or not to punish offenders as he sees fit.

[41] *Ibid.*, I.25.1–3, 7–11.

But more than a few puzzles must be cleared away before any such conclusion can stand. We must first explore the forgiveness of sins and what I shall call "the Forgiveness Game."

### *d. The Problem of Divine Forgiveness*

Varuṇa's worshippers live in fear and trembling of their Lord's quick and paralyzing wrath, but their apprehension is mixed with hope and optimism, for they know that Varuṇa is equally quick to impart forgiveness. Here is that fearful concern, beautifully stated in one of the older sections of the *Ṛg Veda*:

> 3. May we be in your keeping, Oh Leader, wide-ruling
> Varuṇa, the lord of many heroes. . . . [P]ardon us,
> admit us to your friendship.
>
> 5. Loose me from sin as from a bond that holds me;
> may we strengthen the foundations of your
> order. Let not my thread be severed while
> I weave my song, nor my life-work be shattered
> before my time has ended.
>
> 7. Strike us not, Varuṇa, with those terrible weapons
> which at your bidding wound the sinner. Let
> us not pass away from the light into exile. Scatter
> those who hate us that we may live.

But something rather strange emerges in the next verse, refocusing our attention on the relationship between Varuṇa and the law. Up to this point it has seemed that Varuṇa controlled the law, administered it, and perhaps could, on occasions of forgiveness, even hold it in abeyance. But perhaps that only seemed to be the case:

> 8. Oh mighty Varuṇa, now and hereafter, even as of old,
> will we speak forth our worship. For in yourself,
> invincible God, your unchangeable statutes are
> fixed as if carved in rock.

So it would seem that the law never changes; but, oddly enough, the consequences of disobeying it may nonetheless be assuaged by forgiveness:

> 9. Remove far from me whatever sins I have committed;
> let me not suffer, Oh Lord, for the sins of
> others. Many full morns have yet to dawn
> upon us; while we live in those morns, Oh
> Varuṇa, we pray you to give us guidance.[42]

[42]*Ibid.*, II.28.3, 5, 7–9.

The liberation from sins that Varuṇa is capable of giving needs careful analysis. First, however, let us experience as deeply as possible the flavor of these hymns directed to Varuṇa, hymns imploring his aid, protection, and forgiveness:

1. Truly wise are all creatures through his greatness which kept earth and spacious heaven apart, which urged the high and mighty sky to motion with the star, our sun, of old, and which then spread the earth before him.
2. With my heart I ponder the question, How may Varuṇa and I be united? What gift of mine will he accept without anger? When may I look and find him gracious?

Then, sounding like a veritable *Vedic* Job, the worshipper continues,

3. Anxious to know my sin I question others; Oh Varuṇa, I seek the wise and I question them. And this self same answer all the sages give back to me: Surely Lord Varuṇa is angry with you.
4. Oh my Lord, what has been my chief transgression that you would thus slay the friend who hymns your praises? Oh unconquerable Lord, do but tell me and quickly, sinless will I approach you with my homage.

The worst possible moral-religious situation that could ever arise for a human being has just been described. Imagine being in a state of having offended God but not knowing what your offense was. That is surely a nightmare that Franz Kafka alone did not dream. The way out of this particular moral-religious madness for the worshipper is to ask God's forgiveness, not only for all known offenses, but for all unknown offenses as well. But the catalogue of the possibles and the actuals continues:

5. Free us from sins committed by our fathers, as well as those that we ourselves have committed. . . .
6. It was not our own will that betrayed us but seduction, thoughtlessness, Oh Varuṇa, wine, dice and anger. The old and stronger are always near at hand to lead the young and weaker astray, and even gentle sleep does not remove all evil doing.

This is a curious reference, indeed, to what can only be described as sinning in dreams. The wretched sinner continues:

7. As a slave may I render service to my bounteous
   Lord. May I, free from sin, serve the
   God inclined to anger. This gentle Lord
   gives wisdom to the ignorant and leads
   the wise man to riches.
8. Oh Lord Varuṇa, may my hymn of praise come
   close to you and lie within your heart.
   May all be well with us, in rest and in
   labor. May the Gods keep us with their
   blessings forever.[43]

Having sampled the flavor of these imploring hymns, we are now in a position to look critically at the topic that will conclude our discussion of ethics and value theory in the *Vedas*: the forgiveness of sins.

Let us begin by asking: what is presupposed by the doctrine of the forgiveness of sins? In particular, what is assumed in asserting that Varuṇa can forgive sins? Recall for a moment the five conclusions we arrived at earlier: there are moral laws; these laws can be transgressed; Varuṇa knows when the laws are transgressed; Varuṇa will punish the transgressor; but, finally, Varuṇa can be persuaded not to punish the transgressor. It is this fifth conclusion that we ordinarily refer to as the practice of forgiving sins. But we stand in need of a sharper and finer delineation of this forgiveness.

### e. *The Forgiveness Game*

A number of necessary conditions must be fulfilled in order for the forgiveness of sins to occurs. Here are six of them:

- $C_1$ A moral law exists: *Ṛta*
- $C_2$ Disobedience by the moral agent to the moral law occurs: *pāpa*
- $C_3$ The consequences of this disobedience are real and threatening to the moral agent: *karma*
- $C_4$ Repentance occurs in the moral agent: contrition
- $C_5$ The forgiver exists: Varuṇa or *Ṛta*
- $C_6$ A relation exists such that $C_5$ sees $C_4$ and excuses $C_2$ by preventing $C_3$

The mechanism of the Forgiveness Game (the schema that accepts the six necessary conditions above) is meant to apply only to the *Ṛg Veda* and the person of Varuṇa. Whether other Forgiveness Games can be played with the same set of conditions depends, of course, on further analysis and interpretation of items $C_1$ through $C_6$. I call this schema *the rules for the Forgiveness Game*, for that is exactly how this set of conditions can be seen in the *Ṛg*

[43] *Ibid.*, VII.86.1–8.

*Veda.* One need only make a simple conditional statement out of the list to see what the single rule of the game is and to see that a game is precisely what is being played; and to see that $C_1$ through $C_6$ constitute the rules or reduced rule of this game: if $C_1$ and $C_2$ and $C_3$ and $C_4$ and $C_5$, then, if $C_5$ sees $C_4$ and excuses $C_2$ by preventing $C_3$, forgiveness exists.

Let me turn next to a brief discussion of the six necessary conditions for playing the *Ṛg Veda* Forgiveness Game. The game employs some concepts that lie at the heart of later Hinduism, so it is important to ferret them out at this point, early in the history of Hinduism, and note their rather singular workings.

$C_1$ *A moral law exists: Ṛta*

In Sanskrit *Ṛta* means "fit," "right," "true," and its original meaning in the *Vedas* would seem to follow these meanings. In the *Vedas*, as we mentioned briefly above, *Ṛta* also carries the meaning of "order" or "sacred order," and it is variously translated as "eternal law" or "eternal order." Now the law and order referred to by *Ṛta* is a natural as well as a moral order. *Ṛta* is apparently not only a *descriptive law*, empirically detailing or summarizing what is true about the world, or what is the case, or what behaviors are truly exhibited by entities in the world, but it is a *prescriptive law* as well, morally ordering or imperatively commanding what ought to be true about the world, or what ought to be the case, or what behaviors ought to be exhibited by entities in the world. Thus *Ṛta*, as a descriptive as well as a prescriptive law, oddly identifies what *is* with what *ought to be.*

But *Ṛta* is also personified in the *Ṛg Veda.* Established by the Gods, *Ṛta* can be praised, flattered, and cajoled, and this kind of attention paid to *Ṛta* would appear to benefit the worshipper. Here is an example of a priest praising *Ṛta*; by doing so he hopes to raise his fee for the sacrifice (the payment from his patron, which is here a payment in cows):

8. Ṛta has varied food that gives strength; the
 thought of Ṛta removes transgressions.
 The hymns in praise of Ṛta, arousing and
 glowing, have opened the deaf ears of
 the living.

9. Firmly grounded are Ṛta's foundations: in
 its fair form there are many splendid
 beauties;
 By holy Ṛta long-lasting food is brought to
 us; by holy Ṛta the cows are brought
 to pay us for the sacrifice.

10. Fixing Ṛta, Indra now upholds it; swiftly
 moves the might of Ṛta and wins the
 rewards.

To *Ṛta* belongs the vast deep earth and
heaven, the cows of the sacrifice, to
*Ṛta* they render their milk.[44]

What interests us is the emergence of *Ṛta* as a moral law, and in particular as a principle of justice. Ordinarily "justice" simply means "to each according to his due"; everyone gets what's coming to him, evil to him to whom evil is due, and good to him to whom good is due. But *Ṛta* does not seem to have been stated in precisely these terms. The principle of *Ṛta* is hazier than this. Eventually the concept of *Ṛta* will evolve and change until, finally, in the *Upaniṣads* it will be replaced by the principle or law of *karma*, which will fully and completely guarantee that justice will always be done. The *Upaniṣads* will thus have to add to the law of *karma* the doctrine of *saṁsāra* or rebirth (transmigration or metempsychosis) to further guarantee that justice will never be mocked but always fulfilled, and if not in this life, then in the next.

At the present point, however, we can state with some assurance that $C_1$ is fulfilled, as far as the *Vedas* go, by the principle of *Ṛta*.

$C_2$ *Disobedience to the moral law occurs: pāpa*

*Pāpa* means "sin" or "transgression," and we have abundant evidence of its existence in the *Vedas*. Recall, again, the *Ṛg Veda* passage where the transgressor cries out:

Remove far from me whatever sins I have committed;
let me not suffer, Oh Lord, for the sins of
others.[45]

This is a curious passage in many ways, and one might profitably pause to ask: how is it possible for one to suffer from the sins of others? Is it possible that one could, for example, inherit sin from one's natural parents (mother and father)? Or from one's "original" parents (Adam and Eve or Manu)? While we don't wish to attribute what Gottfried Leibniz, the great polymath and theodicist of the German Enlightenment, called "metaphysical evil" or "original sin" to the *Vedic ṛṣis*, still it is worth pondering: how, indeed, can I be made to suffer from the sins you or even my ancestors have done? Recall, again, the *Ṛg Veda* plea:

Free us from sins committed by our fathers, as
well as those that we ourselves have
committed.[46]

[44]*Ibid.*, IV.23.8–10.
[45]*Ibid.*, II.28.9.
[46]*Ibid.*, VII.86.5.

But there is a very obvious answer to our question. I suffer for your sin when you violate the law and implicate me, either directly (when you go through a red light and strike my bicycle and me) or indirectly (when you raise your daughter improperly, she marries my son, and we all live miserably ever after).

Another and perhaps more interesting critical philosophical question (because it is about meanings) emerges at this juncture. How does disobedience occur? How do I go about the business of disobeying *Ṛta* or the law or *dharma*? The question might be answered: you merely do what the law says you shouldn't do, or you simply don't do what the law says you should do; thus we have "sins of omission" and "sins of commission." But it's not really that simple at all. One might well ask, for example: in order to disobey the law, do I have to *know* the law? Could I violate a law I don't even know anything about? The *Ṛg Veda* says that Indra's laws are unchangeable and fixed as if carved on a mountain. Suppose I've never been up that particular mountain. Can I still be held responsible for not knowing that the law I disobeyed was truly Indra's law? Ignorance of the law is no excuse, someone might say; but who said so, when, and why?

But to return to our original puzzle, one might also ask: in order to disobey the law, do I have to know what I did? In other words, can a person who acts unknowingly—who just does things spontaneously, without taking note of what he's doing—can such a person ever disobey the law? Suppose that I accidentally and unknowingly, carelessly and dangerously, pass with my bicycle in front of a car that is, unbeknownst to me, forced to stop suddenly while I pedal ignorantly on; after this sudden unannounced stop, a second car strikes him from behind, and someone is seriously injured in that second car as a result. Have I disobeyed a law—a law with respect to either the improper operation of a bicycle, or not injuring one's fellow human beings? Have I disobeyed a law when I am in total ignorance of what I did? Legally I am guilty, of course, of inattentive cycling, but am I morally culpable? Or further, suppose I know exactly what I did but I didn't know that it was wrong. Suppose I knowingly pass in front of the first car, then calmly watch the chain reaction of the events that leads up to the injury in the second car. I see the bruises, the blood, note the pain and agony with olympian bemused detachment, because I don't know that what I did was wrong, and then I pedal on, with rising anticipations, to another intersection. Did I disobey the law?

One of the problems that enters into this seemingly simple picture, of course, is the problem of intent or motive. The *Ṛg Veda* would seem to argue that intention or motive and conscious awareness of sin are not necessary at all to disobedience of *Ṛta* or *dharma* and the terrible guilt that follows disobedience. Thus the sinner prays that whatever sins he has committed be removed, even those, it must seem, that he is not aware of—those that he did not intend to do or of which he is ignorant:

> Whatever the offence may be that we mortals have committed against the Gods in heaven, if foolishly and stupidly we have violated your laws, Oh Lord, do not destroy us for our sins.[47]

So the question of disobedience of the law becomes far from simple when the matters of intention and knowledge are brought in. But these problems aside, $C_2$ is fulfilled in the *Vedas* by the existence of *pāpa*.

$C_3$ *The consequences of this disobedience are real and threatening to the moral agent: karma*

In the *Upaniṣadic* tradition that follows the *Vedas,* these consequences will be called *karma,* but in the *Vedas* that concept is not employed. However, in order to have the Forgiveness Game played at all, whether in the East or the West, *karma* or something very like *karma* must exist, and those *karmic* results must be untoward, frightening, and threatening.

*Karma* has a number of meanings. In Sanskrit its original sense is "action" or "work," but here the meaning is "the results or consequences of action" and, more specifically, "the unwanted, to-be-avoided-at-all-costs results or fruits of action." Thus the *karmic* results of disobedience entail suffering and pain for me in the future because *Ṛta* in the *Vedas,* or the law of *karma* in the *Upaniṣads* and *Bhagavad Gītā,* says disobeyers must be punished, the crooked made straight, the disorder turned to order. If the *karma* (as "result" or "consequence," now) of my disobedience were unreal or illusory, or if the *karma* of my disobedience were continually pleasant or just plain eternally unthreatening to me, then I would never have occasion to play the Forgiveness Game. But the consequences of disobedience are most real and most threatening. Hear again the sinner's tragic wail:

> While I weave this song, let not my thread be severed; nor before my time, let not my life-work be shattered.
>
> Varuṇa, strike us not with those dread weapons which at your bidding wound the sinner. Let us not pass from the light into exile.[48]

As we have seen previously, the consequences of disobedience could mean that one would not enter heaven, or worse yet:

> Let me not yet, King Varuṇa, enter into the house of clay: Have mercy, spare me, Mighty Lord.[49]

[47] *Ibid.*, VII.89.5.

[48] *Ibid.*, II.28.5, 7.

[49] *Ibid.*, VII.89.1.

Thus, it would seem, $C_3$ is fulfilled in the *Vedas* by what is later to be called *karma*.

$C_4$ *Repentance occurs in the moral agent: contrition*

The disobedient moral agent is sorry for what he has done and knows about, for what he has done and doesn't yet know about, and even for what he has not yet done. Repentance (from the Latin *poena* which means "punishment") is regret, sorrow, or contrition with respect to past sins. I may be said to repent when a number of seemingly necessary conditions are fulfilled; ordinarily these would include, first, the commission of some sinful act and, second, the feeling sorry about having done it. But these two apparently necessary conditions for repentance, as a little thoughtful attention must show, are not really necessary at all. For I can repent the doing of some good action or even (if the *Vedas* are correct on this) some action that I have not yet done, or that I am not yet aware that I have done. Further, merely feeling sorry about what I did, or will do, or might have done or what have you simply won't do either. "Feeling sorry" is not strong enough. I feel sorry about a lot of things I have done, but I'd probably do them over again if I had the chance (they were worth it, you see). To be truly repentant you must not only feel perfectly dreadful about what you did, but you must also wish that you had not done it; and further you must feel that if you had it to do over again you would not do it. This point is important for it entails that if you had it to do over, then you *could* choose not to do it. In other words, repentance entails free will in the commission of sin.

Suppose, for example, that you claim you're sorry you stole some book; and suppose that you really had the whole thing to do over again; but suppose something or someone compelled you to steal it the second time around as well as the first; then it must be the case that you are not really free, and repentance is not possible or even thinkable. Thus, wherever there is no free will, and wherever there is, for example, some sort of divine determinism or fatalism, then, not only can there be no contrition or repentance, but also there can be no sinning, disobedience, or sinners. In other words, without free will—without the ability and the possibility to do differently than you did or had done—there could be no possibility of true contrition or repentance: Without free will, finally, the Forgiveness Game would be impossible, precisely because condition $C_4$ could never be fulfilled.

But granted that free human or free humanlike will is necessary to repentance, and granted that the sorrow one feels at past sins entails a wish that one had the chance not to do the action again, what else is necessary to repentance? Is it merely mouthing *mea culpas* and cries of contrition? But tape recorders and parrots can be programmed or taught to utter repentancelike sounds. And was the author of this previously mentioned prayer lying or truly penitential when he cried:

> Oh bright and powerful God, through want of strength
> I erred and went astray: Have mercy, spare me,
> Mighty Lord.
>
> Thirst has seized your worshipper, though he stands
> in the midst of the water-floods: Have mercy,
> spare me, Mighty Lord![50]

So what counts must be what is truly in the heart of the penitent, his intentions, his state of inwardness. But since only Varuṇa can judge those intentions, it might be best for us to leave the necessary condition of contrition or repentance at that; for it would appear, as far as our work is concerned, that $C_4$ is fulfilled in the *Vedas* by what is called "contrition."

### $C_5$ *The forgiver exists: Varuṇa* or *Ṛta*

Common sense, of course, demands that if there is to be forgiveness, then there must be a forgiver. But the forgiver need not be a Person; it could be a mechanism as impersonal as *Ṛta* or as disembodied as the law of *karma*. The forgiver must merely take account, as we shall see in $C_6$, of the repentance or contrition of $C_4$ in order to pardon, excuse, or modify the consequences of $C_3$, and that "taking account" could be done by *Ṛta* as well as by Varuṇa of the thousand eyes. Thus instead of stating, "All moral upsettings of the universe will be set right and the upsetter punished," *Ṛta* could as easily state, "All moral upsettings of the universe will be set right and the upsetter punished, *unless* the upsetter feels remorse at what he has done." For it would be an easy step to have a repentance-forgiveness clause built into *Ṛta* such that remorse or repentance in the sinner could then mitigate, abrogate, or blunt the usual and ordinary effects of the punishment against moral upsettings. So it is possible to see the forgiver as simply part of the impersonal mechanism of either *Ṛta* or, later, the law of *karma*.

However, the more obvious interpretation of the Forgiver is as a personal God who can allay the punishment fixed by *Ṛta* in *Ṛta*'s attempts to set the moral order right after it has been violated. But the curiosity noted previously returns again at this point on one interpretation, at least, of the relation between Varuṇa and *Ṛta*. For suppose that Varuṇa exists (and this is assumed without argument throughout the *Ṛg Veda*), and suppose further that *Ṛta* is sovereign such that even if Varuṇa forgives, *Ṛta* can't alter the consequences of the punishment for the repentant sinner. If *Ṛta* is a principle

[50] *Ibid.*, VII.89.3–4.

of the moral order (without a repentance-forgiveness clause), an eternal law resetting all upsettings, and if *Ṛta* is an impersonal mechanism that is unable to take into account order or directives from the Gods, then repentance is pointless.

Let me make this clearer with an example. Suppose that there is *Ṛta*, the eternal law of justice that operates to redress all wrongs and to reset all moral upsettings. Suppose you upset the moral order. Now *Ṛta* begins to operate; the machinery is set in motion to punish you and reset the moral imbalance of the universe. But suddenly you repent, you're truly sorry for what you did. You start to play the Forgiveness Game. Varuṇa exists, he takes account of your contrition (there are problems here that we'll get to below) and says, in effect, "I forgive you." But that's not enough—not for you at least. You aren't just looking for words; a simple verbal bouquet won't do. "I forgive you," alone and by itself, is empty, a mockery to the repentant sinner who is looking for more than a benediction. The repentant sinner wants action that will cancel the effects of *Ṛta*. The roof is about to come down around his ears and he wants an architect, a carpenter, and a mason, not a well-wisher. So Varuṇa must be able to influence *Ṛta* to such an extent that the punishment for sinning now set in motion can be halted, restrained, and eliminated. But if *Ṛta* is sovereign, all-powerful, and impersonal, and if it does not have that ability to "take account" of repentance mentioned previously, then Varuṇa is impotent, forgiveness is meaningless, and no one can play the Forgiveness Game.

To conclude this discussion about the relation between the Forgiver and *Ṛta* we can say two things. First, if Varuṇa is sovereign, all-powerful, and dominant over *Ṛta*, and if that eternal principle of justice and order can be started and stopped at the will of God, then the Forgiveness Game can be played. Second, if *Ṛta* is sovereign, all-powerful, and dominant over Varuṇa, then two things may follow: one, if the impersonal mechanism by which *Ṛta* operates does not have a repentance-forgiveness clause built into it together with a way of detecting repentance and effecting forgiveness, then the Forgiveness Game cannot be played; two, if the impersonal mechanism by which *Ṛta* operates does have a repentance-forgiveness clause built into it, together with a way of detecting repentance and effecting forgiveness, then the Forgiveness Game can be played. But problems about the nature of Varuṇa are still bound to arise; we will treat these below in $C_6$.

In whatever manner the above problems resolve themselves, the *Ṛg Veda* would appear nonetheless to hold that the Forgiver—Varuṇa or possibly some deity like Varuṇa—does in fact exist, and that $C_5$ as a necessary condition for the Forgiveness Game is thereby fulfilled.

$C_6$ *A relation exists such that $C_5$ sees $C_4$ and excuses $C_2$ by preventing $C_3$*

Actually the problem of the relation between the Forgiver—Varuṇa or God—and *Ṛta* or the law of *karma*, dealt with in $C_5$, will emerge to haunt us again. The problem takes on a new dimension now, since we have to analyze the properties of the Forgiver as represented by such predicates as "sees" and "excuses" as used here in $C_6$. The Forgiver sees and takes account of more than just the usual kinds of things, for he sees into the hearts of men and there searches out man's true feelings. Here is a rather typical hymn-description of Lord Varuṇa and his powers. It might be useful to recall once again that Varuṇa's name comes from the Sanskrit root $\sqrt{var}$ which means "to cover," as if Varuṇa, somehow, covered everything and was indeed everywhere:

1. To bring Varuṇa to us, sing you a song to the all-
   wise Maruts [storm Gods],
   This Varuṇa who knows and guards well the thoughts
   of men like a herdsman with his cattle.
   Let all the others die away.

2. Varuṇa I will praise with all the songs and hymns
   my fathers sang and with all my own songs
   as well—
   Varuṇa, dwelling at the source of all the waters
   surrounded by the seven sisters, the seven
   rivers.
   Let all the others die away.

3. Varuṇa has enveloped the nights, and with his magic
   art he has brought forth the morns. He is
   visible over all.
   Those dear to Him, following His law, have prospered
   in the three dawns, morning, noon and evening.
   Let all the others die away.

4. Varuṇa, visible over all the earth, brought forth
   the four directions of the sky;
   He measured out the eastern place that is the
   starting point of his wanderings; this God
   is like a strong herdsman.
   Let all the others die away.

5. Varuṇa, Who supports the world of living things,
   Who knows the hidden names, mysteries
   of the morning sunlight beams.
   He cherishes great wisdom as heaven brings forth
   each varied form.
   Let all the others die away.

6. Varuṇa, in Whom all wisdom finds a center even
   as the nave is set within each wheel.

Come, hasten to honor Trita (heaven), the great
expanse of the triple worlds; as cattle,
come, hasten to gather in the fold just as
they are brought in to be yoked.
Let all the others die away.

7. Varuṇa wraps these regions in his robe; he contemplates the tribes of Gods and all the works
of men.
Before the home of Varuṇa all the Gods follow his
decree.
Let all the others die away.

8. Varuṇa is an Ocean far-removed, yet all the worship
given by all the realms ascends through heaven
to Him.
With his shining foot He overthrew the magical arts
of the friends of darkness and went to heaven.
Let all the others die away.

9. Varuṇa, ruler, whose bright far-seeing rays penetrated
all three earths, and pervaded the three highest
realms of heaven.
Firm is the throne of Varuṇa; over the seven rivers
he rules like a King.
Let all the others die away.

10. Varuṇa, after His decree overspread the dark nights
with a robe of light.
Varuṇa, Who measured out the ancient foundations, Who
tore apart earth from heaven and, separated thus,
set the Unborn eternal Being supporting heaven.
Let all the others die away.[51]

Varuṇa, at the very least, would seem to be omniscient. The *Ṛg Veda* hymn just quoted would seem to bear out something very close to omniscience, and, indeed, the Forgiveness Game would seem to demand something very close to omniscience. If I'm going to excuse you for something you've done, and if I'm going to excuse you on the basis of your contrition over your deed; then (if I'm going to make a good job out of my excusing you) I must be able to know when you're really contrite and when you're not. Now I could make a bad job out of it, as often happens in more mundane civil and criminal court cases. The murderer says, "Your honor, I'm sorry for what I did, I wish I'd never done it; at least give me a break; give me a light sentence." The judge, who may be inclined to leniency, because both the law and his temperament allow it, has a problem now. For he must establish the veracity of the murderer's claim to be truly repentant. So begins a pre-sentence investiga-

[51] *Ibid.*, VIII.41.1–10.

tion—a parade of witnesses, friends, family members, teachers, probation officers, and so on—all for one particular purpose: to find out if the murderer would do it again, in which case he might not be sorry; or whether he would not do it again, in which case he might be sorry.

The analogy between the Divine Forgiver and the jurisprudential forgiver, when stretched too far, shows some serious flaws, but the idea is there: if the jurisprudential forgiver could suddenly become the Ideal Observer of the murderer's heart (and really know that he was contrite) and the murderer's future (and really know that he wouldn't backslide), then the judge's problems would be solved. He would not only know the murderer's heart and future, but he would know them with certainty. But now we're talking about a kind of factually certain knowledge, and two questions then arise with respect to Varuṇa and this knowledge: does Varuṇa have to know with certainty everything about everything? (is Varuṇa *totally omniscient*?) or does Varuṇa merely have to know with certainty everything about something? (is Varuṇa *selectively omniscient*?). The case for selective omniscience—limited but nonetheless certain and errorless knowing—is merely that Varuṇa need know only the hearts and minds of his forgiveness candidates and needn't know all the other trivial events that have occurred, are occurring, and will occur in the history of the universe. Varuṇa doesn't need the total omniscience that would tell him how many spokes there were in Genghis Khan's first chariot, where every sparrow fell from every sky and at what precise moment in time on June 30, 1640 (old style), and what yeasty doughs failed to rise in what ovens throughout the world yesterday. All Varuṇa needs, the argument concludes, is selective omniscience to get about his job of knowing a limited number of hearts and minds and forgiving the truly contrite.

But several arguments urge that selective omniscience must always entail total omniscience. One of them simply points out that to know the hearts and minds of forgiveness candidates really involves knowing the hearts and minds of every human being, if not every sentient or feeling creature in the universe, since all such beings are potential forgiveness candidates. This would entail knowing the past, present, and future events of every such being, which must entail knowing all of the actual as well as the possible other events that relate to those beings. And that knowledge would have to be total. Thus, if Varuṇa is selectively omniscient (so the argument runs), then he must also be totally omniscient.

Or we might take another tack. To know with certainty that something was *not related* to a particular forgiveness candidate's contrite heart and future action would certainly entail knowing the nature of anything and everything that was not thus related and why it was not thus related. And to know all those nonrelated events and things involves knowing everything; hence, selective omniscience entails total omniscience.

Thus the conclusion is established, it would seem, that if anyone wishes to play the Forgiveness Game he is driven to holding that the Forgiver is totally omniscient, for what He knows with certainty must indeed be everything about everything.

But the person who holds that total omniscience is a property of the Forgiver is driven into what I shall call "the paradox of total omniscience." For if the Forgiver is totally omniscient, then the Forgiver knows what He, the Forgiver, is going to do in the future: either He will forgive or He will not forgive the forgiveness candidate. But now there is no need any longer to know everything. The Forgiver need only peer into the future in order to see whether He will forgive or not forgive and then do now what he sees he will do then. Total knowledge of hearts and futures is not needed to know whether forgiveness occurred at all; from which it follows that total omniscience reduces to selective omniscience. From which we can conclude that selective omniscience is true only if total omniscience is true, and there appears to be a problem for those who play the Forgiveness Game using $C_6$; thus the paradox of total omniscience.

But $C_6$ refers to a property of the Forgiver other than that of future seeings. That other property is the property to excuse or forgive. $C_6$ states that what is excused is the disobedience, $C_2$, and that the Forgiver shows this by preventing $C_3$, the real and threatening consequences of the disobedience. What we are talking about, of course, is the ability of the Forgiver to substitute other consequences for the ones the sinner would ordinarily get for his sin. We are interested primarily in the powers of the Forgiver in this matter, and in particular with His omnipotence. We can parallel our discussion of omniscience above by asking: is the Forgiver *selectively omnipotent* (does He hold power in a limited way) or is He *totally omnipotent*? It's important to keep in mind just what the power of forgiveness entails; it is not a matter of excusing the disobedience but rather of averting the untoward, hideous, and painful consequences that follow from that disobedience.

Let us look more closely at this point. First, does it make any sense to talk about forgiving the disobedience if nothing is done about the unwanted results? Suppose I kill a man and come before the Forgiver. I am truly contrite, I wish I hadn't done it, and I'll never do it again, and the Forgiver knows this. "I forgive you," He says. "I forgive you, and I sentence you to die in the electric chair." What meaning does forgiveness have in that case? Or suppose He says, "I forgive you, but you'll have to pay for your crime, and that's out of my hands." What difference does His forgiveness make then if it doesn't make a difference? It might be nice to know that God forgives me for my committing a murder, but if I don't receive anything more, for ever and ever, except a compassionate wink of the divine eye, a pat on the back by the divine hand, and a loving word from the divine lips, then who needs it? Forgiveness that can't prevent the roof from falling in is no forgiveness at all. Forgiveness that doesn't end by producing fruitful results is fruitless. Or suppose the

Forgiver decides not to forgive me for my murderous deed. Suppose, reading my heart and future, he says, "I don't forgive you, but incidentally, I release you from the results of your deed." Why, then, who cares about the kind words, the pat, the wink? To fail to forgive and then to prevent the consequences as provided by the law must surely be, at least within the confines of the Forgiveness Game, a practical contradiction. And, I would contend, to forgive and not to prevent the consequences of the disobedience from occurring would also be an example of a practical contradiction: thus, excusing entails preventing, and both excusing without then preventing as well as not excusing and then preventing are practically inconsistent activities; while both excusing and then preventing as well as not excusing and then not preventing are practically consistent activities within the Forgiveness Game.

Second, if the Forgiver excuses by preventing the consequences of the disobedience from occurring, then what is the nature of His power with respect to those consequences? In other words, how powerful must the Forgiver be in order to forgive the disobedience by preventing the consequences? Three points are crucial here. One: If *Ṛta* or the law already has a repentance-forgiveness clause built into it, then obviously there is no need for a Forgiver and no issue of how much power He has. Two: If the law has no repentance-forgiveness clause built into it, and if it specifically says that under no circumstances can one be forgiven the consequences of one's act, then once again there is no need for a Forgiver, for there is absolutely nothing a Forgiver could do. Three: If the law is either open with respect to repentance-forgiveness or positively direct on the necessity of a Forgiver, then only under those circumstances could a Forgiver's forgiving be effective. In other words, the law must provide covertly or overtly for a Forgiver, either by saying nothing contradictory about the existence of or the possibility of such a Person or by stating straightforwardly what the place of such a person is in *Ṛta*, the eternal law of justice, the law of *karma*, or whatever. Only if this third possibility is operative does the power of the Forgiver, how much and what kind, become a real and live issue.

Suppose then that *Ṛta* does provide covertly or overtly—and it must surely be the former, given what little we know about *Ṛta*—for the possibility of forgiveness of consequences by a Forgiver. The question then stands: how much power must the Forgiver have to do his job properly? Once more, I want to suggest that the Forgiver is either selectively omnipotent or totally omnipotent. If the Forgiver were selectively or limitedly omnipotent, He could do everything logically possible to aid repentant sinners, but He could not do anything that was not in some sense connected with preventing those consequences. He couldn't, we would assume, drain a river in flood, walk on water, raise the dead, turn water into wine, and so on, unless real forgiving were involved with each event in some way. If the Forgiver were totally omnipotent, on the other hand, He could do anything that was logically possible for repentant and nonrepentant sinners, anything at all. He could not, however, lift the unliftable elephant, make Wednesday come before Tuesday, or make the class of brahmins identical with the class of nonpriests, for all of these "do-ables" involve logical contradictions.

I want to argue that the Forgiver of the *Ṛg Veda* is totally omnipotent because He must be capable of moving heaven and earth to keep untoward consequences away from His repentant charges. Recall that the selectively omnipotent Forgiver can do everything logically possible for His repentant sinners. But in that case He can do *anything* (logically possible) for His penitents. But He must be totally omnipotent in order to do anything. Recall the examples that defined the limitations on the selectively omnipotent Forgiver. We said He couldn't drain a river in flood unless it involved preventing pain-filled consequences. But this does not mean He couldn't drain rivers; it is not a limitation on his powers but rather a condition under which His powers can be operative. And the same argument would apply to the other *apparent* limitations on the power of the Forgiver. The Forgiver is and must be totally omnipotent, for He is and must be capable of preventing any and all painful consequences from occurring to all His repentant sinners.

Two objections follow, however. First, it might be charged that the Forgiver, under these conditions, cannot forgive a nonrepentant sinner—and surely this is a limitation on his power? Second, don't the conditions really limit the Forgiver by placing narrow restrictions on what He *must* do, once someone has repented? That is, He *must* forgive all repentant sinners; He is not free to do otherwise. Both objections can be met, I believe, by reminding the reader that the world of *Ṛta* is a just world where eternal order, balance, and harmony hold sway. Thus, to forgive the unrepentant sinner (the first objection) and to fail to forgive the repentant sinner (the second objection) would be unjust, and both would be practically inconsistent, practically impossible, in the world of the *Ṛg Veda*.

Thus we can conclude that the Forgiver is not only totally omniscient but totally omnipotent; at least he must possess these properties within the limits set by our assumptions about *Ṛta*, the eternal order of the universe. Thus we can conclude our discussion of necessary condition $C_6$, the final condition of playing the Forgiveness Game, by stating that whenever $C_5$ sees and knows $C_4$ (repentance), He sees and knows with total omniscience; and that whenever he excuses $C_2$ (disobedience) by preventing $C_3$ (consequences), He prevents with total omnipotence.

This concludes our discussion of the Forgiveness Game and of the problem of divine forgiveness, *Ṛta*, and the ethics of the *Ṛg Veda*. We shall return to many of the issues raised here when we take up the ethics of the *Upaniṣads* and the ethics of the *Bhagavad Gītā*. We have also completed our investigation of the *Ṛg Veda*, its religion, its metaphysics, its epistemology, and its ethics. We will return to these four topics and the *Ṛg Veda* when we have finished our examination of the next set of texts in the history of early Indian thought: the *Upaniṣads*.

# E.

# *The Upaniṣads and Their Philosophy*

The *Upaniṣads* are the collection of works which form the basis for the philosophical commentaries on the *Vedas*. The dates of composition of the twenty most important *Upaniṣads* (out of the over 200 that have come down to us) span a period from about 800 to 200 B.C.E., usually referred to as "the age of the *Upaniṣads*." It is an exciting time in the history of Indian thought, for it is witness to the rise of many heterodox and heretical philosophic and religious beliefs, among them the anti- or nonsoul theory of Buddhism, the atheism of Jainism as well as of Buddhism, and the metaphysical materialism of the *Cārvākas*. It is a time of churning and rending, when the philosophic and religious life of man is turned inside out and upside down and when the foundations are laid for both later Hinduism and Buddhism—foundations that have remained intact up to the twentieth century. In the vanguard of this philosophic renaissance, a rebirth epitomized by a rebellion against the ritualistic, aristocratic, and seclusive religion of the *Vedas*, stands that set of revolutionary philosophic compositions, the *Upaniṣads*.

But to understand the revolutionary and reforming character of the *Upaniṣads* it is essential to sketch out some of the background, and some of the assumptions of these most influential Sanskrit texts. To that end we shall briefly examine the *Upaniṣads* as secret teachings, and explore the social, moral, and psychological assumptions of the age. We can then turn more profitably and systematically to the religion, the metaphysics, the epistemology, and the ethics of the *Upaniṣads*.

## 1. THE SECRET TEACHINGS

The *Upaniṣads* have been called "the secret teachings of the *Vedas*," and for three good reasons. First, *upaniṣad* is a compound word formed from three simple ones: *upa* ("near"), *ni* ("down"), and *sad* ("to sit"). The initial *s* of *sad* changes to the *ṣ* of *ṣad* in virtue of a grammatical rule of Sanskrit which says that if the dental sibilant, *s*, is preceded by a vowel such as *i*, then the dental sibilant must be altered to the lingual sibilant, *ṣ*. And this is precisely what happens. *Upa-ni-sad* becomes *upaniṣad*, which means "to sit down near or close to." The important part of the compound, however, is *upa*, which means "near" or "close to." For why sit down "close to"—and close to whom? Tradition says that the *śiṣya*, the pupil or, really, the disciple, is to sit close to his *guru*, the teacher or, really, the master, in order that what is imparted to the *śiṣya* by the *guru* may be heard by no one else. And why should it be heard by no one else? The obvious answer is that the teachings were secret; they were meant only for those who were allowed to sit down near (cf. *Bṛhadāraṇyaka Upaniṣad* III.2.13). Hence for etymological reasons alone the *Upaniṣads* can justifiably be referred to as "secret teachings."

Second, the relationship between the *guru* and the *śiṣya* bespeaks a very special relationship, and not merely that between an ordinary teacher and an ordinary pupil. What made the relationship extraordinary was that the *guru* chose the *śiṣya* and the *śiṣya* chose the *guru*. Tradition would seem to indicate that the *śiṣya* was chosen only after he had proved that he was capable and had the right to sit down near (see below, p. 101 for example, and *Chāndogya Upaniṣad* IV.4.1–5). What was to be taught was for the qualified pupil only. One of the qualifications would be a moral one (always being truthful, perhaps); another would be occupational (always being a *brahmin*, at least in one's heart, perhaps). Hence, for reasons relating to the qualification of the *śiṣya*, the *Upaniṣads* can justifiably be referred to as secret teachings.

Third, the character of many of the passages in the *Upaniṣads* meant that they could be understood or ought to be understood only by a qualified *śiṣya* in the presence of the *guru*. I am saying two things here really. One is that the *Upaniṣads* have meanings which lie beyond the literal, ordinary, common-sense meanings of bills of lading, novels, and daily conversation. Only in a private, face-to-face, quiet meeting could these meanings be explained and understood (cf. *Chāndogya Upaniṣad* VIII.7–12). It follows that both teaching and learning at this level are simply sit-down-near affairs. The second thing is that the *Upaniṣads*, according to the tradition, have great magical and mystical power and they ought to be heard and understood, therefore, only by those who will use that power well. And the possibility of the misuse of that power made the explanation of the compositions a sit-down-near affair, once again. Hence the *Upaniṣads* can only and ought only to be taught and understood as secret teachings.

We have mentioned three good reasons to refer to the *Upaniṣads* as the "secret teachings" of the *Vedas*. We should be warned, however, not to read too much of the magical, the occult, and the mysterious East into this epithet. I am using "secret teachings" in a purely descriptive way, and the meaning of that description is to be found in the three good reasons mentioned previously.

## 2. BACKGROUND TO THE UPANIṢADS: THE LAWS OF MANU

As part of the background to the *Upaniṣads* we should note a number of social and religious practices that were already formed or were being formed in the Indian society. Most of them are rather neatly catalogued in a work which probably comes from the late *Upaniṣadic* period (about 300 B.C.E.): *The Mānava Dharmaśāstra.* The author of these "treatises on the law by Manu," or simply the *Laws of Manu*, was a mythical figure, first mentioned in the *Vedas* as a holy seer and as Father Manu, child of the Sun. But whether the *Laws of Manu* have a mythical or an historical author, they do present, and in some detail, the political, social, moral, and religious rules under which the Indians of that period, as well as the early *Upaniṣadic* period, lived and moved and had their earthly being. There are four areas of the *Laws of Manu* that I want to touch on in backgrounding the *Upaniṣads:* the *varṇas*, already mentioned in our discussion of the *Vedas;* the *āśramas*, or stages of life; the *Arthas*, or aims or goals of life; and finally the ethics of the *Laws of Manu.*

### *a. The Four Varṇas*

The four *varṇas* are familiar to us from our discussion of the *Vedas* and in particular *Ṛg Veda* X.90 (see above, pp. 51–53). They encompass the four occupational classes that originated from the parts of the *puruṣa*, the gigantic primordial man whose body is divided at the original and first sacrifice of the Gods. By the time of the *Upaniṣads* these four occupational classes were fully accepted by the Indians as inheritable classes. That is to say, with the introduction of the concepts of *saṁsāra* or rebirth, and the law of *karma* or moral justice, the *varṇa* that one belonged to was no accident, no chance affair, but rather it was dependent on one's previous life, and especially the moral quality and religious character of that life. The four inheritable occupational *varṇas* were:

1) *brahmin*, the priest-teacher *varṇa*,
2) *kṣatriya*, the warrior-ruler *varṇa*,
3) *vaiśya*, the tradesman-farmer *varṇa*,
4) *śūdra*, the servant-laborer *varṇa*.

There is some evidence at this stage for the presence of outcaste or noncaste classes, and there are even a few references to members of degraded castes such as the *caṇḍāla* and the *paulkasa*. A *caṇḍāla* was the child of a *śūdra* father and a *brahmin* mother, and a *paulkasa* was the child of a *śūdra* father and a *kṣatriya* mother. But marrying beneath one's station or having offspring beneath one's station, as above, was not the only way of defining the outcaste or noncaste. For it was in terms of one's vocation that *varṇa* could be detected, and outcastes always had the dirtiest jobs:

> Though some caṇḍālas had other means of livelihood, in theory their main task was the carrying and cremation of corpses, and they also served as executioners of criminals. According to the lawbooks the caṇḍāla should be dressed in the garments of the corpses he cremated .... No man of higher class might have any but the most distant relations with a caṇḍāla, on pain of losing his religious purity and falling to the caṇḍāla's level .... [L]ike lepers in medieval Europe, they were forced [by the fourth century C.E.] to strike a wooden clapper on entering a town, to warn the Āryans of their polluting approach.[1]

But why had the *caṇḍālas* come to such an occupation? Or, why had their parents mismated? The answer is found, of course, in *saṁsāra* and the law of *karma* (see below, pp. 102–4).

### b. *The Four Āśramas*

The four *āśramas* or stages of life may have been established to provide the young Hindu, from birth to death, with proper signs, directions, and rites of passage by which to guide and conduct his life. Ideally, it has been argued, the average Hindu lived to the ripe old age of 100 years. The *āśramas* were divided, therefore, into four equal 25-year periods. But this is merely an ideal approximation and not a rule. One progressed or moved, however, from one stage or level to the next as the various aims and goals (*arthas*) of the several stages were satisfied. The four *āśramas* were:

#### 1) Brahmacarya, the Student Stage

According to the *Laws of Manu*, the student must find a teacher and then live as a student of sacred knowledge under the *guru's* direction:

> The [student] who has been initiated must be instructed in the performance of the religious vows, and gradually learn the Veda, observing the prescribed rules.
>
> Every day, having bathed and been purified, he must offer water to the gods, sages and manes, worship the gods, and place fuel on the sacred fire.

[1] A. L. Basham, *The Wonder That Was India* (London: Sidgwick & Jackson, Ltd., 1954), p. 145. Reprinted by permission of the publisher.

> Let him abstain from honey, meat, perfumes, garlands of flowers, condiments for flavoring foods, women . . . .
> Let him abstain from perfuming his body, applying coloring to his eyes, the use of shoes and umbrella, from sensual desire, anger, covetousness, dancing, singing and playing music.
> From gambling, idle disputes, backbiting, and lying, from looking at and touching women, and from hurting others.
> Let him always sleep alone . . . .[2]

It was, obviously, no easy thing to be a student of sacred knowledge.

### 2) Gṛhastha, the Householder Stage

According to the *Laws of Manu*, the householder stage is the most excellent (the most important) stage of all because it supports and maintains the persons of the other three stages through its property, riches, and gifts. In this stage one acquires a wife, property, sons, and wealth:

> Having bathed, with the permission of his teacher . . . a twice born man [*brahmin*, *kṣatriya*, or *vaiśya*] shall marry a wife of equal caste who is endowed with auspicious bodily marks.[3]

And here are some examples of the laws for the *brahmin* at this stage:

> Having dwelt with a teacher in the first quarter of life, a *brahmin* shall live during the second quarter in his house, after he has wedded a wife.
> A *brahmin* must seek a means of subsistence which either causes no or as little pain to others as possible, and live by that except in times of distress.
> For the purpose of gaining bare subsistence, let him accumulate property by following those irreproachable occupations which are prescribed for his caste but without fatiguing his body.
> Let him never, for the sake of subsistence, follow the ways of the world; let him live the pure, straightforward, honest life of a *brahmin*.[4]

The life of the householder for the other *kṣatriya* and *vaiśya varṇas*, as well, is a life devoted to *dharma*, the laws of God and man.

### 3) Vānaprastha, the Forest-Hermit Stage

When a twice-born householder sees his wrinkled skin, his hair gone white, and sees his grandchildren, then it is time to move on to the stage of the forest-dwelling hermit. The closest parallel in the West is retirement at 65 from a job or profession, except that retirement in the *vānaprastha* stage

[2] *Laws of Manu*, II.173, 176–180, G. Bühler, trans., *Sacred Books of the East*, Vol. XXV (Oxford: Clarendon Press, 1886).

[3] *Ibid.*, III.4.

[4] *Ibid.*, IV.1–3, 11.

is for religious purposes. Here, for example, is what the *brahmin* must do:

> Abondoning all food raised by cultivation, and abandoning all his belongings, he may depart into the forest, either committing his wife to his sons, or accompanied by her.
>
> Taking with him the sacred fire and the implements required for domestic sacrifices, he may go forth from the village into the forest and reside there, duly controlling his senses.
>
> Making no effort [to procure] things that give pleasure, chaste, sleeping on the bare ground, not caring for any shelter, dwelling at the root of trees.
>
> These and other observances must a *brahmin* who dwells in the forest diligently practice; and in order to attain complete [union with] the Self, [he must study] the various sacred texts contained in the *Upaniṣads* . . . .
>
> Or let him walk, fully determined and going straight on, in a north-easterly direction, subsisting on water and air, until his body sinks to rest.[5]

**4) Sannyāsa, the Ascetic Wanderer Stage**

When the forest hermit arrives at the stage in his life when he can abandon all attachments to worldly objects, then it is time to move on to the final *āśrama*, the life of the wandering ascetic. The word *ascetic* is particularly apt here, and one should not read into it the picture of the emaciated yogi sitting on a bed of nails. *Ascetic* comes from the Greek *asketikos*, which means "exercised" or "athletic," for it was the name given to the kind of training an athlete went through before he entered the Olympic games. Consequently, *askētikos* really means "mental and physical discipline," which is precisely the way that *ascetic* should be read. The fourth stage is that of the wanderer who has mentally and physically attuned his mind and body to be receptive to spiritual enlightenment:

> . . . after abandoning all attachment to worldly objects . . . . He who after passing from order to order, after offering sacrifices and subduing his senses, becomes, tired with alms and offerings of food, this ascetic gains bliss after death.
>
> Having studied the Vedas in accordance with the rule [*brahmacarya āśrama*], having begat sons according to the sacred law [*gṛhastha*], and having offered sacrifices according to his ability [*vānaprastha*], he may direct his mind to final liberation.
>
> Departing from his house fully provided with the means of purification, let him wander about absolutely silent, and caring nothing for enjoyments that may be offered [to him].
>
> Let him always wander alone, without any companion in order to attain [final liberation], fully understanding that the solitary man, who neither forsakes nor is forsaken, gains his end.
>
> He shall neither possess a fire, nor a dwelling; he may go to a village for his food, indifferent to everything, firm of purpose, meditating and concentrating his mind on *Brahman*.

[5] *Ibid.*, VI.3–4, 26, 29, 31.

> Let him not desire to die, let him not desire to live . . . . Delighting in what refers to the Self, sitting [in the *yoga* posture], independent, abstaining from sensual enjoyments . . . .
>
> By deep meditation let him recognize the subtle nature of the supreme Self, and its presence in all organisms . . . .
>
> By not injuring any creatures, by detaching the senses [from objects of enjoyment], by the rites prescribed in the *Veda*, and by rigorously practicing austerities, [men] gain that state even in this world.
>
> When by the disposition [of his heart] he becomes unattached to all objects, he obtains eternal happiness both in this world and after death.[6]

The key to this fourth and final *āśrama* lies in a rare attitude of mind, an attitude of desirelessness and unattachment. This attitude, we shall see, defines the condition of *mokṣa* in the *Upaniṣads*, and it will be the goal of later Hindu religion and philosophy. Here it is the essence of the fourth *āśrama*, the *sannyāsa āśrama*, and it perfectly defines the *sannyāsi* who has attained *jīvanmukti*: freedom or liberation while still living.

But there is, nonetheless, a proper place and appropriate time for attachments and desires within the Indian framework. A tradition has evolved that associates these appropriately timed and properly placed goals within the Indian philosophic scheme. These goals are called *arthas*, and four of them form part of the background to the *Upaniṣads*.

## c. *The Four Arthas*

The four *arthas* or *ends* or *goals* of life tend to be associated with one or another of the four *āśramas* or stages of life. Let us look briefly at each of these *arthas* and then attempt to see them in the perspective of the *āśramas*.

### 1) Artha, the Goal of Wealth

The word *artha* has many meanings in addition to "goal," and here it means "wealth" and "material wealth" in particular. It is quite legitimate at a certain stage of one's life to pursue material ends, to take a wife, land, house, children, "the whole catastrophe," as Zorba the Greek says. It is proper and correct for the twice-born (the members of the first three *varṇas*, who are called *dvija* or *twice-born*) in the *gṛhastha āśrama* to aim for property, money, cattle, sons, cars, yachts, and so on, provided it is not in itself distracting and fanatically carried out nor gained by immoral means. Thus the goal (*artha*) of wealth (*artha*) is quite appropriate to the *gṛhastha*.

Finally, there are traditional texts that will teach you and train you in all aspects of this undertaking. One, for example, will counsel you on the art of politics, kingship, leadership, and diplomacy. Here is an example of the hard art of political survival as advised to a King by Kautilya, the Machiavel-

[6] *Ibid.*, VI.33–34, 36, 41–43, 45, 65, 75, 80.

lian author of the *Arthaśāstra* (321–296 B.C.E.):

> Assisted by a tried council of his officers, the King shall proceed to create spies: spies under the guise of a fraudulent disciple, a recluse, a householder, a merchant, an ascetic practicing austerities, a classmate or a colleague, a firebrand, a poisoner, and a mendicant woman.
>
> Having set up spies over his prime ministers, the King shall proceed to watch both citizens and country people. Societal spies formed as opposing factions shall carry on disputations in places of pilgrimage, in assemblies, houses, corporations, and amid congregations of people.
>
> Spies lying in wait or living as inmates in the same house may make use of weapons on occasions of royal sports or musical and other entertainments. Spies under the disguise of nightwalkers or of firekeepers may set fire to the house of the wicked . . . .
>
> If a King is energetic, his subjects will be equally energetic. If he is reckless, they will not only be reckless likewise, but also eat into his works. Besides, a reckless King will easily fall into the hands of his enemies. Hence the King shall be ever wakeful.
>
> In the happiness of his subjects lies his happiness; in their welfare his welfare; whatever pleases himself he shall not consider as good, but whatever pleases his subjects he shall consider as good. Hence the King shall be ever active and discharge his duties; the root of wealth is activity, and of evil, inactivity. In the absence of activity acquisitions present and to come will perish; by activity he can achieve both his desired ends and abundance of wealth.[7]

**2) Kāma, the Goal of Love**

The word *kāma* means "sensual" or "sexual love." It is what the Greeks called *eros*, and it is not to be confused with either *Platonic love* or with the Christian *agapē*. It constitutes a legitimate pursuit for Indians at the *gṛhastha āśrama*, for without it there would be no procreation. But erotic love at the hands of the Indians has become a refined art that relates human beings in one of the most delightful pastimes known to the species. Sex was not looked upon as sordid or vulgar, but it was, at one stage in one's development, an extremely important and beautiful art, to be embraced and enjoyed for its own human sake and not for some "higher" romantic or religious end. The peculiarly Western puritanical attitudes towards sex and the human body in general do not enter India until the coming of the missionaries, either Muslim or Christian. Regarding *kāma*, A. L. Basham has observed:

> Sexuality was not looked on as a mere vent for the animal passions of the male, but as a refined mutual relationship for the satisfaction of both parties. The sophisticated townsman for whom the *Kāmasūtra* [see the selection below] was written was advised to consider the satisfaction of his mistress as well as his own, for she was as passionate as himself, and it was even said by some that her pleasure in sex was greater than his.

[7] *Kautilya's Arthaśāstra*, R. Shamasastry, trans. (Mysore: Wesleyan Mission Press, 2d ed., 1923), I.11, 13; XIV.1; I.19.

The significance of sex for the classical Indian is expressed in Sanskrit descriptions of some sixteen different forms of kissing and numerous sexual positions, achieved and graphically described through man's inventive genius. Basham continues:

> There was much tenderness in lovemaking, though it often culminated in very violent embraces; it was a favorite poetic convention to describe lovers of both sexes, whether married or single, as displaying the tokens of their passion to their confidential friends, in the form of the marks of nails and teeth.[8]

Here is a brief example that serves to set the mood of the *Kāmasūtra*. See if you think the advice from this great work on the art of lovemaking is sound:

> For the first three days after their marriage husband and wife should sleep on the floor and abstain from intercourse . . . . For the next seven days they should bathe to the sound of music, adorn themselves, dine together, and pay their respects to their relatives and to the other people who attended their wedding . . . . On the evening of the tenth day the husband should speak gently to his wife . . . to give her confidence . . . . Vātsyāyana [the sage who authored *Kāmasūtra*] recommends that a man should at first refrain from intercourse until he has won over his bride and gained her confidence, for women, being gentle by nature, prefer to be won over gently. If a woman is forced to submit to rough handling from a man whom she scarcely knows [arranged marriages were the rule] she may come to hate sexual intercourse, and even to hate the whole male sex . . . or she may grow to detest her husband in particular, and will turn then to another man.[9]

### 3) Dharma, the Goal of Duty

The word *dharma* has several meanings, all bound up in the rather vague English word "duty." *Dharma* means "law," "rightness," "righteousness," and "practice." As "righteousness," *dharma* means "the duty one ought to show to both the laws of God and the laws of man." When one is behaving properly, religiously and morally, then one is being *righteous;* one is following one's *dharma*. But since the duties that one has to God and man depend a great deal on the *varṇa* one belongs to, the inheritable occupation and nature that one has, then *dharma* and duty both refer to the vocation one has, the profession to which one has been called. One is called to one's station and its duties—that is, one's *varṇa*, with all the attendant attachments, responsibilities, and possibilities inherent in that *varṇa*—in virtue of the character or quality of one's own past life or lives. Thus one is rewarded or punished for past lives according to the law of *karma* by choosing for oneself in that past life a morally appropriate *varṇa* and vocation in this life. And notice this: in

[8] Basham, *op. cit.*, p. 171.

[9] *The Kāmasūtra*, K. R. Iyengar, trans. (Lahore, 1921), III.2, quoted in Basham, *op. cit.*, p. 172.

a curious and interesting sense one really calls oneself to that vocation, for what one is *now* is wholly and totally by one's own previous choosing. And that vocation is one's *dharma.* So *dharma* simply means "the duty (*dharma*) one has in virtue of one's vocation (*dharma*) to follow and obey the laws (*dharma*) of God and man." It's a complicated and tangled concept, to be sure.

But what are the laws of God and man that one is duty-bound to follow and obey? The central work on *dharma* in Indian Sanskrit literature, as we have seen, is the *Laws of Manu*, mentioned briefly above. These *Laws* deal with every subject under the sun, setting out in clear and concise language the duties of men and women, the *varṇas*, the twice-born in the *āśramas*, and so on. One of the more striking and timely aspects of the *Laws* is the attitude of its author towards woman, an attitude not unlike that expressed in other traditions regarding women.

*a*) *Woman*

In the five major world religions—Judaism, Christianity, Islam, Hinduism, and Buddhism—it is notable that all seem to share one common attitude towards women: an attitude of paranoiac suspicion and fear, mixed with not a small amount of violent persecution. These five religions are, as a little reflection will show, male-dominated. Their founders were males; their chief priests, bishops, and popes are males; their holy prophets, evangelists, and seers are males; their Gods, divinities, holy judges, angels and archangels, are more frequently male or masculine (a grammatical gender rather than a designation of sexual classification) than female or feminine. Thus, in Judaism it is Eve (the word means "woman" in Hebrew) who is created second while man, Adam, is created first; and it is Eve who is created out of Adam's body, not warranting a fresh, new creation of her own; it is Eve who falls into temptation first and sins first, lured to a Fall, no doubt, out of her own inherent feminine weakness by a wily masculine serpent who probably knew he couldn't talk the ever-faithful Adam into biting into that first fruit; and it is Eve who then, full of sin and a certain serpentine wiliness of her own, imitates her slithering mentor and brings about the Fall, like her Greek tragic counterpart, Pandora, of Adam and with him all of mankind. For her reckless frailty, God curses her and woman in general, behaving every inch the male He apparently seems to be, with a command that rings down through the generations straight into the twentieth century:

> To the woman He said, "I will greatly multiply your pain in childbearing; in pain you shall bring forth children, yet your desire shall be for your husband, and he shall rule over you."[10]

[10] *Genesis* 3: 16.

But if God played favorites in the *Old Testament*, it would appear that He played the same game in the *New Testament*. The attitude towards women begun earlier is carried over into that later work. Here is St. Peter, the disciple of Jesus, in a letter in 60 C.E. on the submission, weakness, and necessary subjection of women:

> Likewise you wives, be submissive to your husbands, so that some . . . may be won without a word by the behavior of their wives, when they see your reverent and chaste behavior. Let not yours be the outward adorning with braiding of hair, decoration of gold, and wearing of robes . . . .

And then the cruelest cut of all, as St. Peter describes woman as "the weaker sex"—the one and only sex that is weak:

> Likewise you husbands, live considerately with your wives, bestowing honor on the woman as the weaker sex . . . .[11]

Woman is not the beloved partner of man; rather, as "the weaker sex," she walks either behind him or in front of him but never beside him.

St. Paul shares the Petrine attitude towards women when he commands, sometime in 55 C.E., first, the veiling of women and, second, the silencing of women:

> I want you to understand that the head of every man is Christ, the head of a woman is her husband, and the head of Christ is God. Any man who prays or prophesies with his head covered, dishonors his head, but any woman who prays or prophesies with her head unveiled dishonors her head—it is the same as if her head were shaven. For if a woman will not veil herself, then she should cut off her hair; but if it is disgraceful for a woman to be shorn or shaven, let her wear a veil. For a man ought not to cover his head, since he is the image and glory of God; but woman is the glory of man. For man was not made from woman, but woman from man. Neither was man created for woman, but woman for man.[12]

Paul hearkens back to *Genesis* to justify the silencing of woman:

> As in all the churches of the saints, the women should keep silence in the churches. For they are not permitted to speak, but should be subordinate, as even the law says. If there is anything they desire to know, let them ask their husbands at home. For it is shameful for a woman to speak in church.[13]

The Judeo-Christian tradition regards women as second-class citizens to say the least, and other contrary passages in the *Bible* that stress the equality of

[11] I *Peter* 3: 1–3, 7.

[12] I *Corinthians* 11: 3–9.

[13] I *Corinthians* 14: 33–35.

man and woman in the sight of God cannot ameliorate the inequality that is stated here—an inequality that appears to have been justified by divine sanctions.

One might well ask: why has this attitude towards women been put in this way? What is the origin of the fear and the anxiety thus displayed? What were the founders of these religions—Moses, Paul, and Peter—trying to say through these prohibitions and justifications that they couldn't come right out and say bravely, manfully, straightaway? We will return to this below, but the reader is invited to pause and marvel.

Buddhism is not allowed to escape unscathed from the generally pervasive and weird *contretemps* between the sexes. Because of Gautama Buddha's initial prohibitions against women becoming nuns in the Buddhist religious order or receiving enlightenment within that order, there are a number of curious stories of women who, in early Buddhism, are miraculously changed into men by the Buddha in order to receive enlightenment; rather than becoming "honorary men" they really change into males.[14] Further, Buddha warns his disciples that if women become nuns or are admitted into an order of nuns, then Buddhism, which would have endured for 1000 years, will last only 500 years.[15] Thus there is the story about the first woman to be admitted to the order, and of Gautama's dire prediction about the results of her being allowed to enter. There was a woman, Mahā-Pajāpatī, the aunt of Gautama, who had nursed and raised the future Buddha and Savior of mankind when his own mother, Māyā, had died shortly after his birth. This old aunt-mother came to the Buddha to plead with him to be allowed under the rules and discipline of the order to leave the household life, the *gṛhastha āśrama*, and move on to the houseless life as a nun. Gautama had refused to allow her to do so. When, shortly thereafter, he traveled to the town of Vesāli, the old aunt followed him. She persuaded a disciple of Buddha's, whose name was Ānanda, to plead her case to the Buddha. But, again, Gautama refused to allow this precedent of letting women enter as homeless equals to the monks. Finally, after Ānanda pleaded on a second occasion, Buddha relented and allowed women to enter the order and be ordained, provided that they obeyed eight stringent rules. Here are two of these new rules introduced to remind women what they are, and to help them keep their place:

> A priestess of even a hundred years' standing shall salute, rise to meet, entreat humbly, and perform all respectful offices for a priest, even if he be but that day ordained.

[14]Cf. Edward J. Thomas, *The History of Buddhist Thought* (London: Routledge & Kegan Paul, Ltd., 1971), pp. 183, 193.

[15]Cf. *Vinaya* II.253; *Anguttara-nikāya* IV.274.

> From this day on the priestesses shall not be allowed to reprove the priests officially, but the priests shall be allowed to reprove the priestesses officially.[16]

There follows Gautama's dark prediction about the future of the order, now that women have managed to wheedle their way in, together with three of his reasons for being suspicious of women. I mention here Gautama's forebodings and two of his reasons:

> If, Ānanda, women had not retired from household life to the houseless one, under the Doctrine and Discipline announced by The Tathāgata [Buddha], religion, Ānanda, would long endure; a thousand years would the Good Doctrine abide. But [now] Ānanda . . . not long, Ānanda, will religion endure; but five hundred years, Ānanda, will the Good Doctrine abide.

Buddha gives one of his reasons for his fears: women are physically and emotionally weak:

> Just as, Ānanda, those families which consist of many women and few men are easily overcome by burglars, in exactly the same way, Ānanda, when women retire from household life to the houseless one, under a doctrine and discipline, that religion does not long endure.

Then Gautama Buddha compares women to a disease among sturdy plants:

> Just as, Ānanda, when the disease called rust falls upon a flourishing field of sugar-cane, that field of sugar-cane does not long endure . . . .[17]

Just as the Christians may have picked up their attitudes about women from their predecessors, so also, of course, the Buddha's attitude towards women was either something in the wind, or something borrowed from the Indians who preceded him. We turn to the best expression of that Indian attitude, and it lies in the *Laws of Manu* and their expressions about women. There had been, of course, a rather long and honorable history of women disciples, *sannyāsīs* and teachers, from the *Upaniṣads*, so it may well be that the women being talked about initially in the *Laws* are simply your good and ordinary, run-of-the-mill, decent women, if there be such creatures. For the *Laws* say many things that make them sound pro-feminist and really rather modestly liberal when compared to the passages previously mentioned. Here are some of those modestly liberal sentiments:

> Where women are honored, there the gods are pleased; but where they are not honored, no sacred rite yields any rewards.

[16]*Culla-Vagga* X.1: 3–4, in Henry Clarke Warren, *Buddhism in Translation* (New York: Atheneum, 1963), pp. 444, 445.

[17]*Ibid.*, p. 447.

> Where the female relations live in grief, the family soon completely perishes; but that family where they are not unhappy always prospers.[18]

And this sentiment even continues with some mention of the reason for being good to, but wary of, woman:

> The house on which female relations, not being duly honored, pronounce a curse, perishes completely, as if destroyed by magic.
>
> Hence men who seek [their own] welfare, should always honor women on holidays and festivals with [gifts of] ornaments, clothes, and [dainty] food.[19]

But, suddenly, the same familiar misogynous fears and suspicions come creeping out:

> Day and night women must be kept in dependence by the males [of] their [families], and, if they attach themselves to sensual enjoyments, they must be kept under one's control.
>
> Her father protects [her] in childhood, her husband protects [her] in youth, and her sons protect [her] in old age: a woman is never fit for independence.[20]

And why isn't she fit for independence? What fears, jealousies, envies, and dank forebodings haunted Manu and his brethren? Is woman like a fungus rust in Hindu society? Why? Is she so uncontrollably and voluptuously sensual that men fear for their own celibacy if they are *brahmacarya*, or fear for their wive's infidelity and their own cuckoldry if they are not? Modern psychologists seem to hold that the male is the creature who is most easily sexually aroused and that the female is not. To many modern psychologists it is the male who should be crowned with the epithet "uncontrollably sensual" and not the female. Is it the case that these males have projected onto the female their own easily aroused and guilty sensual feelings, and having thus guiltily projected they set about the business of restraining, not themselves, but her? Thus the male projects his own feelings onto the female by some sort of sick empathizing, and then blames the female for having those feelings. Other explanations stand in the wings awaiting their moment on the stage, undoubtedly; but the projection-empathy explanation, perhaps backed by contemporary psychological insights, seems to offer a well-grounded answer to the question: why all this fear, anxiety, and suspicion about the female? The answer on the projection-empathy theory is simply that what a man fears most in himself he projects as real feelings onto others where he believes he can control, cure, or suppress those ill-wanted feelings.

[18] *Laws of Manu*, III.56–57, Bühler.

[19] *Ibid.*, III.58–59.

[20] *Ibid.*, IX, 2–3.

Manu then continues in language that seems to .rumble out of *Genesis*:

> Him to whom her father may give her, or her brother with her father's permission, she shall obey as long as he lives, and when he is dead, she must not insult his memory.[21]

Or out of the *New Testament:*

> Though [he be] destitute of virtue, or seeking [his] pleasure [elsewhere] or devoid of good qualities, [yet] a husband must be constantly worshipped as a god by a faithful wife.
>
> . . . if a wife obeys her husband, she will for that [reason alone] be exalted in heaven.[22]

And while a husband may marry again after the death of his wife, the widowed wife is forbidden to do so, and more:

> A faithful wife who desires to dwell with her husband after his death, must never do anything that might displease him who took her hand, whether he be alive or dead.
>
> At her pleasure let her emaciate her body by [living on] pure flowers, roots, and fruit [so that she will not be attractive to other men, apparently]; but she must never even mention the name of another man after her husband has died.[23]

Thus the Indians and others on the status of women in the world.

*b*) *Ethics*

The *Laws of Manu* take up other matters in relation to *dharma* than those already mentioned. In particular we should notice their discussion of ethics and the sources of ethical rules. The *Laws* provide the solution to a rather nasty puzzle in ethics, one associated with what is called "deontological ethics." The deontologist holds that certain acts are always and forever morally right and that one knows them to be right immediately (without looking at the consequences of the action, for example) and with certainty (doubts about the rightness of this select class of special acts never arise). Because things that are known immediately and certainly are said to be known by intuition, deontologists by and large are classified as "moral intuitionists." Most deontologists from Immanuel Kant (1724–1804) to H. A. Prichard (1871–1947) and W. D. Ross (1877–1940) would accept the dictum that certain acts such as promise keeping, nonkilling, and truth telling are always

[21] *Ibid.*, V.151.

[22] *Ibid.*, V.154–155.

[23] *Ibid.*, 156–157.

right. But the deontologist is beset with puzzles about the rightness of these acts together with the deontological theory in general; among these is the deontological puzzle. Suppose that you accept the dictum that promise keeping and truth telling are always right. But suppose a situation arises where if you tell the truth, you will also have to kill someone. For example, suppose you are a doctor and a deontologist. A patient comes to you for a physical examination, and before the examination he makes you promise that you will tell him what you discover about his physical condition, and suppose you agree to do this. Upon examining the patient you discover that he has an extremely serious cardiac condition. In your opinion the least emotional shock could kill him, and giving him this news would mean an undoubtable wipe-out. What do you do? If you lie, you may save his life. If you tell the truth, you will probably kill him. Suppose, as we did, that both telling the truth and saving his life are morally right in your deontological mind, and yet if you do one, you violate the other. What do you do? Call this "the deontological puzzle."

Deontologists in the West have traditionally turned to two ways out of the deontological puzzle. The first involves an appeal to some kind of extra-rational principle such as intuition. In a moral dilemma one simply intuits on the spot which of two right actions is best under the circumstances. A second way out involves having a list of action preferences. In a moral dilemma one simply consults one's list, notes that, for example, saving life always takes preference over telling the truth, and so one lies to one's patient and saves his life.

But the *Laws of Manu* furnish us with what amounts to a third way out, which is simply an amalgamation of the foregoing two ways out. It involves setting up a list (the second way out), not of action preferences now, but rather of four ordered criteria for deciding and adjudicating conflicts; and it also involves justifying the ordering of these four criteria by intuition (the first way out). The *Laws* give the order of the criteria for determining rightness as follows:

> These are the four intuitively grounded [*prādu*] and precise [*sākṣa*] criteria [*lakṣaṇa*] of *dharma*: first, the *Vedas* [that is, all *śruti*]; second, the remembered traditions [*smṛti*]; third, the customs and habits of good men [*sadācāra*]; and fourth, one's own predilections [*priyātman*, pleasure or conscience].[24]

Thus, if the deontological puzzle arises, one checks to see, first of all, what the *Vedas* say. If the *Vedas* (*śruti*) command you always to tell the truth, but the remembered traditions (*smṛti*) command you never to kill, then with respect to the previous dilemma with your cardiac patient, and because the *Vedas* take moral precedence over the *smṛti*, you must simply do what the

[24]*Laws of Manu*, II.12, author's translation.

*Vedas* command you to do, even though the *smṛti*, or the good men of the society, or your own conscience, tell you differently.

But while the four criteria may be able to adjudicate a deontological puzzle of the sort mentioned, the puzzle remains in cases where, for example, the *Vedas* simultaneously command both truth telling and nonkilling. In such cases, where one cannot do both simultaneously as with the cardiac patient, one could then proceed in the reverse order by looking first to the remembered traditions or *smṛti* of the society. What does the *smṛti* say that one should do in such instances? Should even the *smṛti* prove to be useless in this regard, either because it is identical with the *śruti* (*Vedas*) in advising that both truth telling and nonkilling are always right, or because it advises nothing at all in either regard, then one might move to the third criterion of moral rightness, the advice from the morally good men of the tribe. One talks to one's minister, parents, Dear Abby, and so on. Again, if this third route also fails, because they all tell you to do both (failing to appreciate your deontological puzzle), or they advise nothing at all, or their advice is conflicting, then you have no choice but to move on to the fourth and final arbiter of all moral disputes and all deontological puzzles: your own conscience—your own inner feelings about what is best. Presumably, if you are a deontologist, you will await some sort of intuition to seize you in making your moral choice, but it is not certain that this is what the *Laws of Manu* are advising. In fact, it is not at all certain whether the *Laws of Manu* are deontological texts, or teleological texts (texts that determine moral rightness in virtue of the nature of the consequences of an act). I use them here simply to illustrate a point in ethical theory: by the method of serially ordering these four criteria one might be able to resolve certain deontological puzzles, and perhaps other similar conflict situations involving moral choices.

We turn now to the fourth and final *artha*: freedom or religious salvation.

#### 4) Mokṣa, the Goal of Liberation

The word *mokṣa* has several meanings in the *Upaniṣadic* period. It comes from the Sanskrit root $\sqrt{muc}$, which means "to release," "to free," "let fly" or "shoot." For the *Upaniṣads*, what is released is the self, and what the self is liberated or released from is desire. But a disturbing puzzle develops in treating *mokṣa* as just another *artha*. The other three *arthas—artha, kāma,* and *dharma*—are, as we have seen, proper and legitimate goals or ends for the twice-born to pursue in the various *āśramas* that make up one's ordinary life. But *mokṣa* is a strange sort of "goal," extraordinarily unlike the others; for *mokṣa* can be reached only when all desire and attachments have been given up, including, oddly enough, the desire for *mokṣa*, itself. This situation has produced what has come to be called "the paradox of *mokṣa*": if I desire *mokṣa*, I'll never get it; but if I don't desire *mokṣa*, I'll never get it either. It's as if one were trying to desire to get rid of desires, or trying to give up trying; the whole enterprise is doomed and ruined as soon as one realizes that the goal involves negating the means to the goal. A curious puzzle, indeed, is this paradox of *mokṣa*.

The way out of the paradox of *mokṣa* involves not treating *mokṣa* as an *artha* at all. Rather, *mokṣa* must be seen as a by-product, an epiphenomenon, something like happiness or pleasure, that comes from doing something else well. *Mokṣa* is not a goal at all. But then what is *mokṣa* or liberation? The response to this question is answered well and at length in the *Upaniṣads*, which are the texts about *mokṣa* in Hinduism. Consequently, without further backgrounding we turn finally to the *Upaniṣads* and to the four areas of religion, metaphysics, epistemology, and ethics found within these powerful and influential compositions.

## 3. THE RELIGION OF THE UPANIṢADS

The essential thrust of the religion of the *Upaniṣads* contrasts starkly with the religion of the *Vedas*. This thrust in the *Upaniṣads* is directed towards producing permanent states of human inwardness and subjectivity. The reformation of Hinduism begins with the *Upaniṣads*' denial, in effect, of the exclusive efficacy of the outwardly directed sacrifices, rites, and activities of the priests. The overwhelming thrust is away from works and sacrifices and towards states of the self and subjectivity—towards the Stoic way discussed earlier (see p. 39). From the *Upaniṣads* onward religion receives quite a different focus. As a tentative approach to this new *Upaniṣadic* religion we might attempt a definition somewhat as follows: "religion" is the way, *yoga*, or discipline by which one attains *metanoia*, self-transcendence, or metaphysical self-transformation (see p. 29). The details of this metaphysical self-transformation through the yogas will become apparent as we progress in our discussions of both the *Upaniṣads* and the *Bhagavad Gītā*.

### *a. The Reformation of Vedism*

One of the most striking examples of this new religion that removed *Āryan Vedism* or *brahminism* from the forefront of the Indian scene lies in a story from the *Upaniṣads*, which discusses the criteria for determining who can and who cannot be a *śiṣya* and lead the *brahmacarya* life. It is the story of a young boy, the son of a *śūdra* mother and an unknown father, who wants to take up the life of a student of sacred knowledge:

1. Once upon a time Satyakāma Jābāla addressed his mother Jabālā: "Madam! I desire to live the life of a student of sacred knowledge. Of what family am I?"

2. Then she said to him: "I do not know this, my son, of what family you are. In my youth, when I went about a great deal serving as a maid, I got you. So I do not know of what family you are. However, I am Jabālā by name; you are Satyakāma by name. So you may speak of yourself as Satyakāma Jābāla."

3. Then he went to Hāridrumata Gautama, and said: "I will live the life of a student of sacred knowledge. I will become a pupil of yours, sir."

4. To him Hāridrumata then said: "Of what family, are you, young man?" Then Satyakāma replied: "I do not know this, sir, of what family I am. I asked my mother and she answered me: 'In my youth, when I went about a great deal serving as a maid, I got you. So I do not know this, of what family you are. However, I am Jabālā by name; you are Satyakāma by name.' So I am Satyakāma Jābāla, sir."

5. To him Hāridrumata then said: "Only a brahmin would be able to explain thus. Bring the fuel, young man. I will receive you as a pupil. You have not deviated from the truth."[25]

What does it take to qualify as a *brahmacārin*? It takes, among other things, a certain inner subjective state: the willingness never to deviate from the truth. The criterion for *brahminhood* is no longer just who your parents were but rather the willingness never to deviate from the truth. If one follows the reasoning here and follows it consistently, one is led to the obvious conclusion that being a *brahmacārin*, being a *brahmin*, are states or conditions open to anyone who possesses a certain attitude. A *śūdra*, even a *caṇḍāla*, might become a *brahmin* and follow the path of *brahmacarya*. We have come upon a religious reformation, a philosophic revolution, indeed.

Reform was surely in the Indian winds during the period from about

[25]*Chāndogya Upaniṣad* IV.4.1–5. All the translations from the *Upaniṣads* are the author's unless otherwise indicated.

800 to 400 B.C.E. There is a general religious retreat from the aristocratic, priest-dominated, heaven-goaled, sacrifice-centered *karma-kaṇḍa* (way of sacrificial works) of the *Vedas* towards a more open, liberal, liberation-goaled, knowledge-centered *jñāna-kaṇḍa* (way of intuitive knowledge). A statement attributed to Gautama Buddha (563–483 B.C.E.) in its aphoristic directness and verbal simplicity catches the spirit of the times: "I preach but one thing," Gautama said, "suffering and the release from suffering."

Gautama Buddha was incorrect when he said he preached "but one thing." As a matter of fact he preached two quite distinct things. First, he proclaimed that all life, all sentient, animal existence, was shot through and through with suffering and pain; and second, he proclaimed that there was a possibility of release from that suffering and pain. Both of these things are necessary conditions for "religion," as we defined it earlier, and for any religious life. Call the first "the awareness of pain," and call the second "the awareness of the way out of pain." More to the point, let us call the first condition "the awareness of *saṁsāra*" and the second condition "the awareness of yoga." These two concepts are introduced for the first time in the religion of the *Upaniṣads*.

### b. *Saṁsāra*

*Saṁsāra* is a compound Sanskrit word derived from the root $\sqrt{sṛ}$ which means "to flow," and the prefix *sam* which means "together"; hence it has the original sense of "a flowing with or together." It has come to mean simply "rebirth" and is variously translated as "transmigration," "reincarnation," or "metempsychosis"; it is closely parallel to the Greek Orphic and Pythagorean doctrines of *palingenesis* which literally means "to be born again." In the later Indian literature, *saṁsāra* has taken on the added meanings of "the round of birth and death" and "the phenomenal world," where its primary intention is that of suffering, pain, and misery. The awareness of the misery and suffering entailed by *saṁsāra*, the worldly round of birth and death, constitutes the first and necessary condition for the existence of religion and for the religious life.

In the *Bṛhadāraṇyaka Upaniṣad*, the most ancient *Upaniṣad* we have, a curious question prefaces a discussion of rebirth, and it is repeated before a similar discussion in the *Chāndogya Upaniṣad*. In both *Upaniṣads* a young *śiṣya*, Śvetaketu, goes to a *kṣatriya* (and not a *brahmin*!) teacher, Jaibali, who asks him:

> "Do you know how people here, on dying, separate in different directions?"
> "No," he said.
> "Do you know how they return again to this world?"
> "No," he said.

> "Do you know why that other world is not filled up with the many who go there, again and again?"
> "No," he said.[26]

Why doesn't that other world fill up, indeed? Could this have been a problem for *Vedic gurus*? The question is not explicitly answered in the *Bṛhadāraṇyaka*. Instead, the above questioning is followed by an ancient description of journies after the bodies' death that take those souls "who know and those who truly worship faith" to the *Brahma*-worlds from which they never return. But those souls "who merely practice charity, austerity, and sacrifice" are born again on the earth; and those who do not know these two ways are reborn as insects and biting animals: the other world, presumably, never fills up because of the fact of rebirth. The *Bṛhadāraṇyaka* looks, then, to three ends of the soul's going: the *Brahma*-world, the returners as men, and the returners as lower animals.

The *Chāndogya Upaniṣad*, the next oldest of the *Upaniṣads* we have, gives a more explicit answer and at the same time provides a reason or rationale for rebirth. Thus, Jaibali again asks the youth Śvetaketu:

> "Do you know why that other world is not filled up?"
> "No, sir."[27]

And much later in the text, after a discussion of rebirth, we have Jaibali concluding:

> "Thus for this reason it is that the other world is not filled up."[28]

In between that question and this conclusion there is an expanded account of Śvetaketu's previous dialogue with Jaibali. And here the *Chāndogya* parallels but differs noticeably from the earlier account in the *Bṛhadāraṇyaka*. First, there is a virtual repetition of the description of the deaths of ascetics whose selves go to the Gods. Then follows the account of the deaths of sacrificers whose selves go to the Fathers and are then reborn on earth as plants, trees, and beans, thus preventing, it would appear, a population explosion in heaven. But after this the *Chāndogya* provides a rationale for the mechanism of rebirth by speaking of conduct, both good and bad, as the nomological or lawlike criterion of how, when, and where rebirth shall occur; for to complete the rebirth picture we must have criteria regarding who goes where and when. This nomological criterion that determines who goes where and when will eventually be called "the law of *karma*." Here is a description of the law of

[26] *Bṛhadāraṇyaka Upaniṣad* VI.2.2.
[27] *Chāndogya Upaniṣad* V.3.3.
[28] *Ibid.*, V.10.8.

*karma* from the *Chāndogya* in one of the most famous passages in Indian philosophic literature:

> Those whose conduct here has been good, they will enter a good womb in the next life, the womb of a *brahmin*, a *kṣatriya*, or a *vaiśya*. But those whose conduct here has been evil, they will enter an evil womb, the womb of a dog or a pig or a *caṇḍāla*.[29]

But, in truth, while the puzzle regarding overcrowding in heaven may have been solved temporarily, overcrowding in other places on earth is still a ponderable problem. For, in theory, there is nothing to prevent millions of selves from becoming models of good *brahminic* behavior and in their next births suddenly overcrowding the wombs of virtuous matrons in some of the few most righteous families in Boston or Bombay. The prospect is ecologically staggering. But whether overcrowding in heaven or in this world or not, and whether a pleasant birth or an evil birth, the outlook that *saṁsāra* offers entails eventual pain and suffering for all. The law of *karma* metes out fair rewards and fair punishments for conduct rendered until the weary, dreary round of *saṁsāra* is ended. Hence we must discuss next the way to the ending of that pain and suffering brought on by *saṁsāra*—the way called *yoga*.

### c. *Yoga*

Religions must not only point to the source or cause of human unhappiness by labeling that source "original sin," "desire," "attachment," "lust," "ignorance," or *saṁsāra* but they must also provide a way out of that human pain and suffering; and these ways out of suffering, pain, and unhappiness, these ways to heaven, a better birth in the next life, *mokṣa*, *nirvāṇa*, or *satori*, we can simply denominate *yogas*. In general, the *yogas* may be as diverse as faith and works in Christianity, or the grace of God, or the more traditional *yogas* of Hinduism and Buddhism.

By a curious etymological happenstance *yoga* and "religion" mean approximately the same thing. "Religion" comes from the Latin *religio*, which means "to bind" or "to bind back." The meaning intended is one of disciplining or training, as one might bind or yoke oxen to a cart, or harness the self to engage in some strenuous mental, body or spiritual activity. *Yoga* also means a disciplining, a binding or harnessing, for spiritual, mental, or physical ends similar to those of religion: to escape the pain, the suffering and the unhappiness that is constantly attendant upon the human condition. Therefore, because of this etymological analysis together with the more formal explanation of *yoga* in Indian religion that follows, I want to argue

[29] *Ibid.*, V.10.7.

that *yoga* and religion as ways out of human misery have precisely the same meaning.

The word *yoga* comes from the Sanskrit root $\sqrt{yuj}$ which means "to harness," "yoke," "make ready," "set to work," "apply," "unite," or "be joined";[30] it is often used interchangeably with the Sanskrit word *mārga* which means "path" or "road." Hence *yoga* is also the path or road that leads out of human unhappiness, misery, suffering, and *saṁsāra*.

**1) Jñāna Yoga**

The principal *yoga* enjoined generally by the *Upaniṣads* is called *jñāna yoga*, the way or discipline of knowledge. While a complete explanation of this *yoga* and its object must await our development of the metaphysics and the epistemology of the *Upaniṣads*, we can nonetheless sketch out some of the details of *jñāna yoga* as it is developed in the *Upaniṣads*. What is it that one comes to know? According to the *Upaniṣads*, the transcendent spiritual Power in the universe, called *Brahman*, is immanent in the world within each individual where it is referred to as *Ātman*. What one comes to know is that this *Ātman* within and the *Brahman* beyond are really identical. But this *jñāna* or knowledge is not to be confused with a quite different knowledge: discursive, everyday, factual knowledge about a statement's being true or false. Instead, *jñāna* appears to be an immediate, intuitive, nonconceptual grasping of a *truth*. This supracognitive nature of *jñāna* places it beyond discussion, really, and one can only hint heavily at what is probably involved. We will return to this topic at greater length shortly, but suffice it to say, now, that this way to human happiness—the way that discovers the reality of *Ātman* and the Power of the Self—will constitute "the *Upaniṣadic* way to human happiness."

**2) Dhyāna Yoga**

But there is another *yoga* similarly enjoined in the *Upaniṣads* that we can refer to as *dhyāna yoga* or the way of meditation. This second path leading away from misery, suffering, and pain towards ultimate human happiness and felicity involves the control of the senses together with a disciplined, practical restraint on all natural human lustings, emotions, and appetites. The technique of *dhyāna yoga* involves controlled attention to the breath; from a reading of the appropriate passage in the early *Upaniṣads* we can detect the beginnings of meditational doctrines that then evolved from

[30]Through the Indo-European language family the Sanskrit word *yoga* is cognate with or etymologically related to the Latin words *jungo* and *jugum*, which mean "yoke," "harness," or "join," to the German word *jochen*, "to join," and, of course, to the English words "yoke" and "join."

them straight down to the popular yoga meditational theories and practices of the twentieth century.[31]

The earliest *Upaniṣads* place great stress on both the importance of the breath and the need for its control. Breath (*prāṇa*) may have been recognized quite early as the great animator of human beings, for it must have been as obvious to *Upaniṣadic* Indians as it is to us that without breath you're dead! But breath not only meant life and movement and the beginning and end of life itself, but it came to be identified in some metaphysical way with everything that exists: "When I said, 'I seek refuge in breath', breath means everything that has come into being, everything that exists here."[32] So if one could control breath, one could control the totality of being, since breath is identified with that totality. And this is precisely what the *Upaniṣads* set out to do; *dhyāna*, or meditation, becomes the way to the control of breath and thereby the control of all that exists—the control of the mechanisms that lead out of and away from *saṁsāra*. Meditation—*dhyāna* yoga—allows one to penetrate to the reality that is *Ātman* that lies hidden deep within the self:

> Just as the potential fire lies hidden in the wood, it is not seen, but it may be brought forth and seized again and again by means of the fire stick [the drill that Boy Scouts and woodsmen use to start fires] penetrating into that wood, so also does the *Ātman* have to be seized in the body by the use of the mantram "Om."

The yoga or way of doing this is then described:

> By making your body the wood and the mantram "Om" the fire drill, by practicing the art of meditation in this way, you will come to see the bright and fiery God hidden deep in your self.[33]

Thus meditational yoga constitutes the second way described in the *Upaniṣads* for the attainment of release from *saṁsāra*, from the pains and sufferings of rebirth. We shall have occasion to return to both of these yogas, *jñāna* and *dhyāna*, later in this book (see pp. 165–69). Both ways lead to the solution of the problem of a self confronting a hostile, threatening world (see pp. 36–40). Both ways attempt to solve that problem by enlarging the significance and importance of the self. And both ways constitute, therefore, the *Upaniṣadic* way to human happiness.

This concludes our brief discussion of the religion of the *Upaniṣads* as glimpsed through the concepts of *saṁsāra* and *yoga*. We turn next to the

[31] See A. L. Herman, *The Theory and Practice of Indian Yoga* (North Hollywood: Center for Cassette Studies, Inc., 1973).

[32] *Chāndogya Upaniṣad* III.15.4.

[33] *Śvetāśvatara Upaniṣad* I.13–14.

metaphysics of the *Upaniṣads* and a rather lengthy commentary on the nature of the ultimately real as seen in these most important compositions of early Indian thought.

## 4. THE METAPHYSICS OF THE *UPANIṢADS*

Writing about the nature of the ultimately real in the *Upaniṣads*, at least in one sense, reduces to a relatively simple task. Inquiring into the metaphysical status of the Gods, man, and the world, we discover that all three can be very neatly put aside; for, according to the *Upaniṣads*, none of them qualifies for the title "ultimately real." Rather, the *Upaniṣads* generally (with minor exceptions) seem to assert that *Brahman* alone is real, because *Brahman* alone, unlike the Gods, man, and the world, is eternal, uncreated, and unchanging. This *advaita* (literally "nondual") or monistic metaphysical interpretation of the *Upaniṣads* is augmented and strengthened by the introduction of three basic concepts that will have continuing significance for the development of Indian thought: *parā* and *aparā Brahman*, *māyā*, and *Ātman*.

### *a. parā and aparā Brahman*

The *Upaniṣads* make a distinction between two aspects of *Brahman*, which they denominate variously as the formed (*mūrta*) and the formless, or the lower (*aparā*) and the higher (*parā*), or the perishable and the imperishable, or the qualified and the unqualified, or the unreal and the real. The great *advaita* philosopher, Śaṁkara (788–820 C.E.), referred to these two aspects of *Brahman* as *saguṇa Brahman* (literally "*Brahman* with properties"), the formed, lower, qualified and unreal *Brahman*, and *nirguṇa Brahman* (literally "*Brahman* without properties"), the formless, higher, unqualified and real *Brahman*. It's a handy terminology and we shall adopt it in what follows. This distinction between *saguṇa Brahman* and *nirguṇa Brahman* probably goes back to the *Bṛhadāraṇyaka Upaniṣad*. In this oldest of the *Upaniṣads* (again, early eighth century B.C.E.) it is said of *Brahman*:

> Truly, there are two aspects of *Brahman*, the formed and the formless, the mortal and the immortal, the unmoving and the moving, the existent and that which is beyond existence.[34]

Further, the formless, immortal, and unmoving *Brahman* is said to be "not this," "not that" (*neti, neti*)—beyond ordinary description and beyond

[34] *Bṛhadāraṇyaka Upaniṣad* II.3.1.

ordinary predication; and yet *nirguṇa Brahman* is also said to be the Truth of truth and the Real of the real, and the very essence of the breath that stands within all creatures. This interpretation of the dual nature of *Brahman* is continued in the *Muṇḍaka Upaniṣad*, a text from the early Buddhist period (probably late sixth century B.C.E.), in which two kinds of knowledge are set forth:

> There are two kinds of knowledge as the knowers of *Brahman* are said to declare: a higher [*parā*] and a lower [*aparā*].
>
> Of these, the lower is the *Ṛg-Veda*, the *Yajur-Veda*, the *Sāma-Veda*, the *Atharva-Veda* . . . . Now, the higher is that by which the Imperishable is apprehended.
>
> That which is invisible, ungraspable, without family, without class (*a-varṇa*), without sight or hearing is It, without hand or foot, eternal, all-pervading, everywhere present, exceedingly subtle: That is the Imperishable, which the wise see as the womb of all being.
>
> As a spider secretes and then draws back [its web], as herbs grow from the earth, as the hairs of the head and body grow from a living person, so from the Imperishable arises the entire universe.[35]

And the two-*Brahman* theme continues at *Muṇḍaka Upaniṣad* II.2.8–9, *Praśna Upaniṣad* V.2–5, and in the *Maitrī Upaniṣad* where we find:

> There are, truly, two forms of *Brahman*: the formed and the formless. Now that which is formed is the unreal; that which is the formless is the real, it is *Brahman*, it is light.[36]

To describe formed or *saguṇa Brahman* as "unreal" brings us next to the cause of this unreality, and the second of our major metaphysical concepts: *māyā*.

### *b. māyā*

The means by which *nirguṇa*, or higher, *Brahman* is enabled to manifest Itself as *saguṇa*, or lower, *Brahman*, is called *māyā* (the word is cognate with the English words "measure" and "magic"). *Māyā* means many things, and looked at from one point of view it is simply a neat answer to the pressing cosmological question: how did there come to be anything at all?

The *Upaniṣads* answer this all-important cosmological question about origins by indicating simply that the power or *māyā* of God made all this. While all creation comes forth from the Unmanifest and Imperishable, it is

[35] *Muṇḍaka Upaniṣad* I.1.4–7.

[36] *Maitrī Upaniṣad* VI.3.

the Great Lord or Īśvara who does the actual creating, and does it with this *māyā*:

> Know that nature (*prakṛti*) is *māyā* and that the user of *māyā* is great Īśvara. And the whole world is filled with beings that are part of him.[37]

*Māyā* here takes on a double meaning, actually, for it is the product of that power of creativity as well as the power itself. The *Bṛhadāraṇyaka Upaniṣad* speaks about *māyā* as the magic power by which Indra both conceals and reveals himself. *Māyā*, again, comes to have a kind of double sense, the sense of product and process, revealing and concealing, displaying and hiding. But its fundamental sense remains that of power or creative energy, and it is ultimately the power that higher *Brahman* must wield in order to manifest lower *Brahman*. Thus the reason that there is anything at all is that higher *Brahman* with Its *māyā* and through the instrumentality of the Great Lord brought this all into being.

But several questions are bound to occur at this moment to the curiosity-ridden reader. If all that exists is divided into higher and lower *Brahman*, and if Īśvara or the Great Lord Creator is part of lower *Brahman* (as product or creation), then where did that Īśvara come from? And if Īśvara is a product or manifestation of higher *Brahman*, then higher *Brahman* is not the unmanifest and formless after all. But if *māyā* is brought in at this point once again to save the transcendental purity of higher *Brahman* from metaphysical contamination with lower *Brahman* by being inserted between the two, then a similar question can be raised with respect to the relation between higher *Brahman* and *māyā* (as the power to bring Īśvara into existence).

This latter question can be put into the form of a rather nasty puzzle, "the dilemma of *māyā*," which raises serious questions about the metaphysical nature of *māyā* itself. Here is that dilemma: either *māyā* is real or it is not. If it is real, then higher *Brahman* is not the only reality in the universe, as the *Upaniṣads* want to maintain. So *māyā* cannot be real. But, if *māyā* is not real, then as a power to produce lower *Brahman* and the world it would be impotent. So, the dilemma of *māyā* concludes, *māyā* itself must either threaten the monistic metaphysics of the *Upaniṣads* or it must be impotent and powerless; and neither of these conclusions is wanted by the *Vedāntins* (the philosophers devoted to defending the *Upaniṣads*).

We shall return to this entire matter in our discussion of *Vedānta darśana* or the philosophical system of the *Upaniṣads* (see pp. 191–92). For the moment, it is enough to say that *māyā* is the creative power, the magical art, by virtue of which *nirguṇa Brahman* manifests the creation and at the same time conceals or hides Itself from the beings in that creation.

[37] *Śvetāśvatara Upaniṣad* IV.10.

### c. *Ātman*

The third metaphysical concept we shall briefly examine here is *Ātman*, the supreme Self or Spirit. As the selections below from the *Upaniṣads* indicate, *Ātman* can be interpreted as closely parallel to the Christian notion of Spirit or Light or Christ as in St. Paul's phrase in *Galatians* 2: 20: "[I]t is not I who live but Christ that liveth in me," and as in the moving claim in *John* 1: 9 about "the Light that lighteth every man that cometh into the world." For the *Ātman*, like the Christ and the Light, is impersonal God, Godhead, or the holy Power in the universe, and it lies deeply concealed within all beings. Throughout the *Upaniṣads* the *Ātman* is curiously identified with life, breath, God, and *Brahman*; in fact, *Ātman* is seen as the totality of all that is; consequently, if it is everything, then it is anything. It is also like the Greek and Christian *logos* or Word, as when the author of the Fourth Gospel says, once again (*John* 1: 1): "In the beginning was the Word, and the Word was with God, and the Word was God." Simply replace *Word* with *Ātman* and *God* with *Brahman* and you would have a *Upaniṣadic* statement about *Ātman*. Following *John* further (1: 2–5), we have another passage to which the seers who constructed the *Upaniṣads* would also probably assent:

> [The *Logos*] was in the beginning with God; all things were made through him, and without him was not anything made that was made. In him was life, and the life was the light of men. The light shines in the darkness, and the darkness has not overcome it.

Thus *Ātman* is a familiar concept to the West when it is seen in its mystical setting as the Christ, *Logos*, Light or Spirit.

Looked at philosophically, the concept of *Ātman* leads us into several extremely tough metaphysical problems that become part of the heritage of the *Upaniṣads*. I want to examine three of these problems about *Ātman* and offer some rather tentative solutions to them. In order to do so, suppose we try to discover what this revolutionary concept of *Ātman* was all about and what the seers of the early *Upaniṣads* probably meant by it.

#### 1) Six Parables about *Ātman*

The *Upaniṣad* in which *Ātman* receives its most extensive and most intriguing treatment is the *Chāndogya Upaniṣad*, the second oldest of the 200 or more *Upaniṣads* that have come down to us. The *Chāndogya* was probably composed sometime in the eighth century B.C.E. Though it contains much that faces back to the traditions of the *Brāhmaṇas* and the *Vedas*, it also contains a great deal that is radical, modern, and revolutionary. Among the new and the radical is this concept of the *Ātman* or the Self. What makes it so radical a notion is first and foremost the very unusual belief that

*Ātman* cannot really be talked about, described, or discursively conceived. Its indescribability or ineffability, however, is not a function of its being a secret; rather, there is something in the very nature of *Ātman* that puts it beyond language, beyond description, and beyond mental conception in the ordinary sense. *Ātman* is not one of your common run-of-the-mill objects of knowledge. The closest that language and teachers and *gurus* can come to describing or telling students about *Ātman* is to resort to myths, symbols, metaphors and similes, stories and parables, that point to the reality represented by the word *Ātman*. In the use of these myths and symbols, however, there is always the danger that the auditor will mistakenly assume that the myth or symbol is the reality. An old Chinese Taoist warning, "Do not mistake the pointing finger for the moon," serves to remind the *śiṣya* that the myth or symbol used by the *guru* points beyond itself to that reality which words cannot describe and where language is poverty stricken.

In the same way that sense qualities (see pp. 28–29 and recall our attempt to define "yellow") must be described or defined indirectly, and by ostension or pointing, so also concepts such as *Ātman* must be similarly treated. In the *Upaniṣads*, myths and symbols become the pointing devices with which to push the *śiṣya*, who would try to understand *Ātman*, in the right direction so that he may come to see and perhaps directly experience their nonverbal, ineffable significance. Ineffable *Ātman* becomes the ineffable "yellow" of the *Chāndogya Upaniṣad*; and the pointing finger that is used to redirect the *śiṣya's* attention to *Ātman*'s indefinable and unutterable significance is the parable. Now the best way to demonstrate the use of this linguistic parabolic device is simply to see it at work: to let the *Chāndogya*, with its numerous parables about *Ātman*, speak for itself.

If there were such a thing as a logic of parables or myths, perhaps one of the first rules (and that's one of the things we mean by "logic") of such a system would be that in order for a parable to be "effective" it would have to be transparent to the reader or auditor, such that he would be able to see through the parable to the inexpressible object that the parable magnifies. The logic of parables would probably have to include a decision procedure for determining what "effective" means, and it would have to specify the conditions under which success (or lack of success) was to be found with specifiable kinds of parables. Thus some "myths" might be just patently opaque; you couldn't see through them to any higher reality, for they just wouldn't magnify or wouldn't point to anything; such "myths" would then become merely amusing stories or entertainments. Other myths might be partially transparent by pointing, for example, to a moral or a lesson; an ethical or social point would be made by and through the story but that's all; such "myths" are generally stories or, more importantly, part of *nīti-śāstra*, the Indian science of correct moral and political conduct. But our logic of myths would specify the effective or successful conditions of myths, separating the truly metaphysically transparent story from the amusing story, the fairy tale, and the story that merely teaches proper moral conduct. Such a distinction between moral stories, fairy tales, and myths does in fact seem to exist, and this distinction underlines the function of mythology: to point beyond the simply amusing and the merely moral. Heinrich Zimmer, the great German Indologist, comments on this distinction and this function when he says:

> The Greek critical philosophers before Socrates, the pre-Socratic thinkers and the Sophists, practically destroyed their own native mythological tradition. Their new approach to the solution of the enigmas of the universe and of man's nature and destiny conformed to the logic of the rising natural sciences —mathematics, physics, and astronomy. Under their powerful influence the older mythological symbols degenerated into mere elegant and amusing themes for novels, little better than society gossip about the complicated love-affairs and quarrels of the celestial upper class.[38]

Our logic of myths would have to specify the differences, then, between such older legitimate symbols and the more recent but now degenerated symbols as part of the linguistic elements of such a logic. Unfortunately, no such logic of myths exists; we are thrown back, consequently, on our intuitions and our own direct and native common sense to tell us when the myth is either transparent to a higher purpose and meaning or merely opaque to secular amusement and morality. But we shall let the parables of the *Chāndogya Upaniṣad*, our myths on this occasion, reveal to us through their own linguistic transparency the higher metaphysical reality pointed to by that ineffable concept *Ātman*.

In the sixth chapter of the *Chāndogya Upaniṣad* a twelve-year-old *śiṣya* named Śvetaketu is sent off by his father, Uddālaka, to get an education in the science of sacred knowledge. The boy returns from his educational experience some twelve years later at the age of twenty-four. When he meets his father, he is all puffed up, proud, and conceited with the *Vedic* learning that he has received. The irate father then exposes the boy's ignorance and puts the youth to shame; but, because the boy wants to learn, the father subsequently endeavors to teach the youth himself. What he teaches his son is, in effect, the non-*Vedic* doctrine about that which cannot be taught, wherein "that which has not been heard now becomes heard; what has not been thought now becomes thought; and that which has not been understood now becomes understood." In other words, the subject of the teaching will be a species of the ineffable, and the particular species they settle on is, of course, *Ātman*. Each of the simple instructional stories that follow ends with the

[38]Heinrich Zimmer, *The Philosophies of India*, ed. by Joseph Campbell, Bollingen Series XXVI (New York: Pantheon Books, 1951), pp. 25–26. Reprinted by permission of Princeton University Press.

classic mystical refrain, "*Tat tvam asi,* Śvetaketu" ("That art thou, Śvetaketu"), uttered by Uddālaka as he attempts to force Śvetaketu to see, by way of the parable, what *Ātman* is in relation to himself.

So what is *Ātman*? Read on and see. Use the parables as a microscope or a telescope; look through them and not at them; see what they are aimed at and pointing to. The first one is the parable of the rivers:

> "All these rivers flow my son, the eastern towards the east, the western toward the west. But they really flow from the ocean and then back to the ocean once again. Flowing, they become the ocean itself, and becoming ocean they do not say, "I am this river" or "I am that river." In the same way, my son, even though all creatures here have come forth from Being, they know not that they have come forth from Being. Whatever a creature may be here, whether tiger or lion or wolf or boar or worm or fly or gnat or mosquito, they become that Being again and again. For that Being is the finest essence of all this world and in that Being every creature has its Self. That is reality. That is *Ātman. Tat tvam asi,* Śvetaketu."[39]

Here is the parable of the tree:

> "My son, if someone were to cut at the root of this great tree it would bleed, but it would continue to live. And if someone were to cut at the middle of this tree, it would bleed but it would continue to live. Finally, if someone were to cut at its top, it would bleed but it would continue to live. Pervaded by the immanent Ātman the tree stands firm in all cases, joyfully drinking in the life-giving moisture. But if that life leaves one branch then that branch dies. If that life leaves another branch then it dies as well. If it leaves a third then it too dies. If that life leaves the whole tree then the whole tree dies. In the same manner, my son, understand this: when the life has left this body then this body will die in just the same way; but that life does not die. For that life is the finest essence of all this world and in that life every creature has its Self. That is reality. That is *Ātman. Tat tvam asi,* Śvetaketu."[40]

Śvetaketu asks his father for further understanding, and Uddālaka tells him the parable of the fig seed:

> "Bring me a fig from over there."
> "Here it is, father."
> "Divide it."
> "There, it is divided, father."
> "Now, what do you see?"
> "These minute seeds, father."
> "Divide one of them."
> "There, it is divided, father."
> "Now what do you see?"
> "Nothing at all, father."

[39] *Chāndogya Upaniṣad* VI.10.1–3.

[40] *Ibid.*, VI.11.1–3.

> Then the father said to him, "My son, that finest essence of the seed that you do not see, from that comes forth this great Nyagrodha tree. Believe me, my son, that which you do not see is yet the finest essence of all this world, and in that invisible essence every creature has its Self. That is reality. That is *Ātman. Tat tvam asi*, Śvetaketu."[41]

The teaching continues, and Uddālaka brings out next the parable of the salt water:

> "My son, place this salt in this water and in the morning come to me once again. Śvetaketu did so. In the morning his father said to him, "That salt that you placed in the water last night, please bring it to me." Śvetaketu looked for it but could not find it, for it was totally dissolved. Then his father said to him, "Please take a sip from this end. How does it taste?" "Salty," Śvetaketu replied. "Please take a sip from the middle. How does it taste?" "Salty," he again replied. "Take a sip from that end. How does it taste?" "Salty, as well," he said. Then his father told him to taste a mouthful and then sit with him. Śvetaketu said to him then, "It is everywhere the same." The father replied, "Yes, my son, you do not perceive that Being here but it is truly here nonetheless. For that invisible essence is the finest essence of all this world, and in that invisible essence every creature has its Self. That is reality. That is *Ātman. Tat tvam asi*, Śvetaketu."[42]

Penultimately, we came to the parable of the blindfolded man. The aim here is to show the significance of the *guru* in the *śiṣya's* seeking or understanding *Ātman*, for *Ātman* is now seen as the final and real home or goal of all creatures as they wander in the world blinded by ignorance and desire. Thus while the salt could still be tasted or sensed, as above, in the following parable the village that one has been led from blindfolded is not sensed, is not known, and is not apprehended even while the search for it is going on. Here, then, is the dramatic parable of the blindfolded man:

> "My son, follow this parallel: Just as a man might be led away from the village of the Gandhāras with his eyes blindfolded and then be abandoned in a place uninhabited by human beings; and just as there he might turn to the east, to the north, to the south, and to the west, wandering willy-nilly unable to get his bearings for home because his eyes are blinded and he had been led there with his eyes blinded; just as, then, someone removes that blindfold and tells him, "The village of the Gandhāras is that way. So go that way"; and being sensible and clever the man would go as he was directed, following village by village and inquiring at each, he would soon reach his home. So in the same way in this world, a man who has a guru will learn from him, this same truth: "As long as I remain here I will not be released. But then I will arrive at my home." For that invisible home for which we all search is the final home for every creature in this world. And it is the Self of every creature. That is reality. That is *Ātman. Tat tvam asi*, Śvetaketu."[43]

[41] *Ibid.*, VI.12.1–3.

[42] *Ibid.*, VI.13.1–3.

[43] *Ibid.*, VI.14.1–3.

Ultimately, now we have the parable of the heated axe:

> "My son, they lead up a man with his hands bound and they shout, He has stolen! He has committed a robbery! Heat up the axe for him!" For if he is truly the criminal, he will show his falseness, himself, by his own action. His protests of his innocence are false, and covering himself with lies and untruth he seizes the heated axe. But he is burned by it, so then he is killed. But if he is not the criminal, then he will show his truth by his own action. His protests of his innocence are true, and covering himself with truth, he seizes the heated axe. But he is not burned by it, so then he is released. Just as he is not burned because the truth enveloped and protected him, so this whole world has that truth as its Self. That is reality. That is *Ātman*. *Tat tvam asi*, Śvetaketu."
>
> Then Śvetaketu understood what Uddālaka had taught, truly he understood.[44]

What all this serves to point to could be summed up, inadequately to be sure, by saying that *Ātman* is both real and everywhere present. But rather that try to reduce the parables to a set of statements, let's stay with the spirit with which the parables were originally introduced and see them as pointing to the ineffable.

We are left with the final task of demonstrating the existence of three brief puzzles that come out of this discussion of *Ātman*. I want to turn to those puzzles next and make use of the parables above in elucidating them.

### 2) Three Problems about Ātman

*Ātman* is a curious philosophical concept, indeed. Parables, symbols, and transparencies aside, it's a metaphysical notion that has a lot of curious tasks to perform. For it is everywhere and yet also nowhere; it is everywhere and yet also here; and we must wonder how "nowhere" and "here" can have any meaning at all when what is referred to is, indeed, everywhere; it is the finest essence of being and still it is also life and the living sap of creatures, yet "finest essence" is to be taken quite literally while "life" is to be taken quite figuratively; and one wonders what the criteria are by which one draws the line between the literal and the figurative. The word *Ātman* performs multiple tasks and it serves them all simultaneously: *Ātman* is nonsensible, yet it is a "Self" in some sense of that word, yet ungraspable by any recognizably cognitive means. It is used to refer to the many rivers, lifes, essences, and tastes, yet it is always one only; it is the goal or home of all, yet it is all; or, to put the latter notion differently, *Ātman* is the goal of all selves or beings, yet it is the Self of those selves or beings at the same time; *Ātman* has the task of being the real, the true, the all-pervading Self. It is a busy and puzzling entity, and it deserves not a little respect and attention.

[44] *Ibid.*, VI.16.1–3.

In what follows I want to mention three problems that grow out of the welter of tasks, jobs, and uses to which "*Ātman*" has been put. These descriptions of *Ātman* at work come from the parables mentioned previously; hence, these problems relate directly to the *Upaniṣads* and to the metaphysical treatment there accorded *Ātman.* I will name the problem, discuss it briefly, and then offer a tentative solution. Our later discussion of the epistemology of the *Upaniṣads* will clear up several of the vagaries now connected with *Ātman*, especially our discussion of the knowledge of *Brahman* and several problems to be raised at that time (see pp. 127–30). But it is important to raise these several problems about *Ātman* here, so that the reader can see that the *Upaniṣads* are not without their own metaphysical hassles and can perhaps be given a clearer perspective with regard to his or her own philosophical misgivings which might have begun to appear by now regarding *Ātman.* As the reader will see, the problems that we are going to mention relate directly both to the claim that *Ātman* alone is real and to the general position of metaphysical monism rife in the *Upaniṣads.*

What I propose to do is to divide the Sanskrit expression *Tat tvam asi* into its three constituent parts and then examine a central problem connected with each. The principal reason for focusing on *Tat tvam asi* is that it easily summarizes what all six of our parables were attempting to say; and the authors of the *Chāndogya Upaniṣad* must have felt that *Tat tvam asi* did indeed epitomize the ineffable object of the parables, else they would not have repeated this particular *mahāvakya* ("great saying" or "aphorism") as often as they did. Thus, analysis will show why *Tat tvam asi* deserved the attention that it got in the *Chāndogya Upaniṣad*, and it will show what must be accepted in order to retain it.

The most expeditious way of handling the analysis of this very pithy expression is, again, to suggest a problem connected with each of the three parts of the expression, state the problem, and then attempt to answer it.

### *a*) *The Problem of Tat*

"*Tat*" is an accusative (objective-case), singular, neuter pronoun (from "*tad*" and "*ta*" in Sanskrit) which means "that" or "it"; it is usually transliterated from the Sanskrit in the context *Tat tvam asi* with an upper-case, honorific initial "T" in order to convey that something worthy of being honored is intended. Unfortunately, Sanskrit has no upper-case letters, so we can't tell by mere orthography (by a study of the shape of the letters in the original Sanskrit) what the authors of the *Chāndogya* intended for *Tat*. But a contextual examination of the six parables of the *Chāndogya Upaniṣad* makes it abundantly clear that "*Tat*" means *Brahman.* We are told by the parables that *Tat* is: That from which all beings come forth (10), and That in which all separate creatures eventually become united (10); That which is like the life in every creature (11), and That which, when it departs, all creatures die (11), but That which itself never dies (11); That which is invisible (12), but That which has power to produce and create (12); That which is never perceived (13) but That which is everywhere (13), and That which is always the same (13); That which is the final home and goal (14), and That which can be searched for, traveled to, and reached by everyone (14), and That which can be pointed to by a true *guru* for the spiritual benefit of a serious *śiṣya* (14).

This catalogue of characteristics continues, for, while the descriptions above relate to the separate characteristics of the severally different parables, each parable repeats descriptions of *Tat* that are common to all of them. Thus we are told that *Tat* is *Ātman* (or *ātman*, since we cannot distinguish the two in Sanskrit), that it is real, and, of course, that it is *tvam*—that it is in some sense Śvetaketu. But it is also (though this is not common to all of the parables) Being, Truth, the Self or self of the universe, and, finally, the whole or the totality of the universe. If one were to put all of these separate and common characteristics together, only one concept could do justice to being the entity pointed to by them and by *Tat*; that entity, of course, is *Brahman* (see pp. 107–8).

But if *Tat* denotes *Brahman*, and if all the properties or characteristics of *Tat* described above and in the parables are in fact the properties or characteristics of *Brahman*, then a problem begins to take shape that we ought to mention and worry about. For if *Tat* is, indeed, reality and being and truth, and if *Tat* is, indeed, the self of the universe and the self of all creatures, and if *Tat* has power, never dies, is imperceptible, is everywhere, unchanging, and the goal of all our endeavors, and if *Tat* and *Brahman* are, indeed, identical, then *Brahman* possesses all the properties possessed by *Tat*. But then we must know which *Brahman* this is of which we are speaking. Is it higher (*parā*) or lower (*aparā*) *Brahman*? The *Chāndogya Upaniṣad* (ca. 750 B.C.E.), in attributing all these characteristics to *Tat* or *Bṛahman*, seems to have thrown out that precise metaphysical distinction between *parā* and *aparā Brahman* that was busy finding root in the earlier *Bṛahadāraṇyaka Upaniṣad* (ca. 800 B.C.E.) and in the later *Muṇḍaka Upaniṣad* (ca. 500 B.C.E.). So what is going on here? Is *Tat* higher or lower *Brahman*? *Nirguṇa* or *saguṇa Brahman*?

There are four possible answers to "the problem of *Tat*," as we shall call this puzzle as to whether *Tat* is higher or lower *Brahman* (if it is indeed *Brahman* at all). First, *Tat* could be lower *Brahman* alone. But this answer is rejectable on the simple grounds that lower *Brahman*, even in the early *Bṛahadāraṇyaka*, is regarded as the formed, the mortal, and the perishable, and these properties certainly do not define the *Tat* of the *Chāndogya* parables. So *Tat* is not lower *Brahman*. Second, *Tat* could be both lower and higher Brahman together—and if *Tat* is the whole, and the universe, and everything, then isn't this plausible? But this answer is rejectable on two grounds. First, *Tat* is said to be the Self of the universe or the finest essence of the world, and not the universe *per se* or the world or the whole, itself. Second, since we've already rejected one of the conjuncts (lower *Brahman*) of this conjunction (lower *Brahman* and higher *Brahman*), it would be self-contradictory to accept this second "solution" here. For both of these reasons, then, *Tat* is not both lower and higher *Brahman* together. Third, *Tat* could be neither higher nor lower *Brahman* but some other being or entity or nothingness. But this is rejectable on the historical grounds that at this stage of metaphysical development in the *Upaniṣads*, there is no such being or nonbeing other than *Brahman*. So *Tat* is not neither higher nor lower *Brahman*, if you'll excuse the grammatical barbarism. Fourth, and finally, *Tat* could be higher *Brahman*, and perhaps you rather fancied it all along anyway. Higher *Brahman* wins both by default (none of the other three logical possibilities proved viable) and by textual evidence. For, just as in the earlier *Bṛhadāraṇyaka*, higher *Brahman* is said to be formless, the source of all being, imperishable, immortal, stationary, and the real of the real, so in the later parables of the *Chāndogya*, as we have seen, *Tat* takes on these same elegant and superb qualities of higher *Brahman*. Thus the problem of *Tat*, the problem about its nature and essence, is solved by identifying it wholly and solely with higher *Brahman*. But we are not out of the critical philosophical woods with *Tat*, yet.

*b) The Problem of Tvam*

"*Tvam*" is a nominative (subjective-case), singular, personal pronoun which means "you"; in the context of *Tat tvam asi* it is sometimes translated "thou" in order to indicate, as with the 'T' in *Tat*, that something honorifically special is intended. The problem of *tvam* is simply to establish what and who the "you" or "thou" is that is being referred to here. Recall that, in teaching Śvetaketu the parables about *Ātman*, Uddālaka, at the same time and by implication, introduced a dichotomy between the real and the unreal. In fact the entire dialogue between them rests upon this covert but fundamental dualism. For if *Tat* alone is real, then by implication everything else must be either *Brahman* or nothing. That is to say, everything in the universe must be either *Brahman* and real or non-*Brahman* and nothing. Therefore, theoretically, one could take the objects, entities, or happenings that make up the whole or the totality, enumerate them one by one, and classify them as *Brahman* (higher *Brahman*) or non-*Brahman* (or lower *Brahman*). We know the properties of each in a way, already, for we know the properties of *Tat* from the parables of the *Chāndogya*. And so we know that any event or thing which lacks those properties will be non-*Tat* or non-*Brahman* or lower *Brahman*; and any event or thing which has those properties mentioned in the *Chāndogya* parables will be *Tat* or *Brahman* or higher *Brahman*. Thus we have a kind of decision procedure for determining which things are *Brahman* or real and which are not. We could, if we wanted, write the individual names of everything in the universe on separate three-by-five cards, set up two boxes, one marked "*Tat*" and the other marked "non-*Tat*," and proceed to put all the cards into one box or another. So here's "water," and it goes into the non-*Tat* box; and here's "eternal being," and it goes into the *Tat* box. Here are "fire" and "squirrels," and they go into the non-*Tat* box along with "the second battle of the Somme" and "God Bless America"; here are "essence of the world" and "Truth," and they go into the *Tat* box along with "unchanging Being" and "immortal." So far so good. But then we get hard cards such as "God," "*māyā* itself" (see pp. 108–9) and the toughest cards of all: "you," "self," "me," and "I."

The problem of *tvam*, then, is this: which box, the *Tat* or non-*Tat* box, do we put *tvam* (you, self, me, I) into? That is, what is the nature of the self? Is it *Brahman* or non-*Brahman*, higher *Brahman* or lower *Brahman*? Śvetaketu is ignorant of this knowledge; the *Vedas* could not teach him about the true nature of the self because that's not what the *Vedas* teach. Śvetaketu's ignorance is excusable. So what Uddālaka teaches him, of course, is the *Tat*, and, as we have seen, the manner of teaching is by persuasive parables and not rational arguments. What he must know about the self, his self, cannot be gotten discursively and by argument; it can be gotten only by sudden and immediate intuition. And that is one of the reasons for employing parables. We will return to the knowing of this *Tat* nature of the self (see pp. 127–30), but for now our task is simply to establish the metaphysical nature of *tvam*.

If *tvam*, or you, is *Tat*, then a problem develops that we will take up below in examining the problem of *asi*, for it turns out that there are not two things here, *tvam* and *Tat*, but really only one thing: *Tat*. The "you" that is real here is not an individual personality complete with your memories, your consciousness, your desires, your ambitions, your wants, and your needs, all standing separate from my memories, my consciousness, my desires, and so on. These items, and the three-by-five cards that mentioned them, have long before been dropped into the non-*Tat* box. The "you" that remains, if any "you" remains at all, must be the "you", therefore, that is *Tat*. Now for the *Chāndogya* and the other major *Upaniṣads* that take up this theme, the *tvam* that is *Tat* is *Ātman*; that is, *tvam* is Self with a capital "S" to distinguish it from the personal self that is identified with your desires and your personality. The word "*Ātman*" means "Self," and it carries in most of its uses in the *Upaniṣads* the force of *Tat* or *Brahman*. Thus the problem of *tvam* is removed or solved by simply saying that *tvam* is *Ātman*, and that is the only real "you" that there is.

This solution is underscored by the general *Upaniṣadic* denial of a personal life after death—a denial that any sort of real personal you survives for eternity side by metaphysical side with another real *Tat*. In the *Bṛhadāraṇyaka Upaniṣad* when a disciple asks her *guru*, the great sage of the *Upaniṣads*, Yājñavalkya, if there is personal survival of the self after death, a survival of Mary and John, of Mani and Sushila, he both frightens and bewilders her by claiming that there is none. And the reason that there is none, and the reason that you are not real save in the special sense that you are *Ātman*, is that such a survival would entail a metaphysical duality and thereby contradict that unique monistic metaphysical assumption on which the *Upaniṣads* seem to be constructed. Here, at any rate, is a portion of what the great Yājñavalkya says to his disciple and wife, Maitreyī:

> After death there is no consciousness or knowledge . . . . For where there is duality there, indeed, one sees another, smells another, hears another, speaks to another, thinks of another, understands another. But where everything is really and truly only Ātman, then how could one smell, see, hear, speak to, think about, or understand another? Impossible! Where all is one, by what means could one understand that other by which everything is understood, or come to understand himself, even, the understander.[45]

In such a monistic universe there is no place for *tvam* that is not at-one with or identical with *Tat*. You are, consequently, *Tat*; you are identical with the real, the unchanging, the truth, and the all-being one. And you are not Mary or John, Mani or Sushila. Thus the problem of *tvam* is answered out of the tradition and the assumptions of the *advaita* metaphysics that is presupposed in these early *Upaniṣads*. The nature of this identity and a puzzle it raises will be dealt with in the third and final problem connected with *Ātman* and the metaphysics of the *Upaniṣads*. The nature of both *Tat* and *tvam* will be made clearer, it is hoped, as a consequence of our discussion of this remaining problem.

c) *The Problem of Asi*

"*Asi*" is a verb taken from the Sanskrit root $\sqrt{as}$ "to be"; it is in the second-person singular indicative mood, hence it combines with "you" to mean "you are." This verb can be ambiguous, however, and it will be important to recognize which one of the several meanings of "are" or "is" is intended by the *asi* of *Tat tvam asi*, "you are That."

Philosophers have traditionally identified three senses of the verb "is," and it will help us in our analysis to make these three meanings clear. First, there is the *is* of predication; second, the *is* of existence; and finally, the *is* of identity. Let me very briefly explain these three senses of *is* and then focus attention on the third, the *is* of identity, by mentioning a problem connected with interpreting the *is* of *Tat tvam asi* as that of identity.

The *is* of predication is easily illustrated in statements such as "The chariot is red," "The world is *māyā*," and "God is good." Here, predicates such as "red," "*māyā*," and "good" stand in relation to subjects such as "chariot," "world," and "God," and these predicates attribute certain properties such as redness, *māyā*-ness, and goodness to those subjects. It is

[45] *Bṛhadāraṇyaka Upaniṣad* II.4.12, 14.

important to keep in mind, then, what the subject is, what the predicate is, and what the property is that is being assigned to that subject by that predicate through the copula or verb *is*. Sanskrit, like English, has a basic grammar composed of subject (the nominative case, as we saw above with *Tat*), predicate (the accusative case, as we saw above with *tvam*) and copula (the present indicative verb *asi*), so parallels between the two grammars can be easily pointed to. It should be clear, therefore, from the context in which *Tat tvam asi* occurs that *asi* is not the *is* of predication. *Tat* is not a property of you in the sense that redness is a property of the chariot or *māyā*-ness is a property of the world. Since we know that *Tat* refers to *Brahman*, then to argue that *Brahman* is one of your properties is to miss the point that the parables were trying to make. Still, it is interesting to speculate what kind of sense could be made from a statement that attributed *Brahman*-ness to you.

The *is* of existence can be simply illustrated in statements such as "Mani is" or "The color blue is" or "God is." This use of the copula bothers many contemporary Western philosophers, for it seems to leave the statements that employ it dangling and looking for an object: "God is what?" one is tempted to ask. But that uneasiness results simply from treating the *is* of existence as if it were the *is* of predication. The *is* of existence merely calls attention to the beingness of or the reality of or the space-time occupancy of their subjects. In the statements above the sensible and perfectly meaningful claims being made or the propositions being asserted are: that Mani lives, that blue is manifested, and that God lives, has being, or is real. But while some philosophers might feel uneasy and become loathsomely contentious over such a usage as we find with the *is* of existence, the one thing they and we can all agree on is that the verb in *Tat tvam asi* is not the *is* of existence. The verb asserts neither being nor nonbeing, neither existence nor nonexistence, of either the subject or the predicate in saying *Tat tvam asi*—as anyone can see by a casual inspection of the assertion. So we move on to the third and final meaning of *is*.

The *is* of identity is easily illustrated in statements such as "She is Sushila," "All brothers are male siblings," and "God is God." The subject term and the predicate term are meant to be logically interchangeable without loss of meaning or truth to the proposition; in fact, this is precisely what the *is* of identity asserts: that there really aren't two things, one named by the subject term and another named by the predicate term, but that they each name or point to one and the same thing, entity, or process. Thus "she" names "Sushila" and "Sushila" names "she," and both point to some one person, real or imaginary. "Brothers" names "all male siblings," and "male siblings" names "all brothers," since what we have here is a definition where the connotation and the denotation of both terms are the same (see p. 27). Finally, the self-identity expressed by the last statement, "God is God," simply shows another use to which the *is* of identity has been put: to call attention to the fact that every individual thing is always taken to be the same with itself. That is, everything is reflexively self-identical. It should be clear from the context of the parables of the *Chāndogya Upaniṣad*, once again, that *asi* is, indeed, the *is* of identity, and that what is being claimed is quite simply that *Tat* and *tvam*, That and You, higher *Brahman* and *Ātman*, are identical. In other words, *Tat tvam asi* is saying that you are *Brahman* and *Brahman* is you in the same way that "she" and "Sushila" are identical.

But what way is that? The identity must be both an identity of properties (hence the *is* of predication is actually applicable here) and an identity of objects (the same object is being pointed to by both the subject and predicate term). That is to say, what we have here is connotative (intensional or property) identity as well as denotative (extensional or individuals-pointed-to) identity: there is only one being but it is called by two names, hence the properties of one must be the properties of the other. Thus *Ātman* is *Brahman*, and *Brahman* is *Ātman*, both connotatively and denotatively, if these two notions make any sense now.

But if we are dealing with higher *Brahman*, then the claim is that there are no properties at all, hence no predicates are applicable to *Brahman*. And if *Brahman* is identical with *Ātman*, then *Ātman* is propertyless and predicateless, as well. But then a problem looms: for if there are no predicates by virtue of which *Brahman* and *Ātman* can be identified, then in what sense can they be called "identical"? Perhaps the defenders of the *is* of identity for *Tat tvam asi* wish to fall back from connotative or property identity (and they must, if there are no properties) to denotative identity. They may say *Brahman* and *Ātman* are identical, not *vis-à-vis* their properties, but rather in that each concept points to the same ultimate reality. Of course that reality can be described only in parabolic language, and that was the whole point of our examining the descriptions of *Tat* and *tvam* previously. We shall return to this discussion later in our treatment of the epistemology of the *Upaniṣads* (see pp. 124–30).

Where do we stand now with respect to the problem of *asi*? Precisely what is being identified? If there are properties, then there is no problem of identity, but there is a problem, a contradition, with the alleged propertyless nature of higher *Brahman*. If there are no properties, then there is no problem about higher *Brahman*, but there is a problem about identity and what's being identified. On the other hand, if we are speaking denotatively and *Tat* and *tvam* as objects are, indeed, propertyless, then, while the above problems don't arise, several serious questions do. Why do the parables assign properties to *Tat*, calling it "real" and "true" and so on? Thus if *Tat* and now *tvam* point beyond themselves to higher propertyless *Brahman*, then why does the *Chāndogya* take so much time in talking about the property-nature of *Tat*? Further, is *Tat* and *tvam* point beyond themselves, then what function does the *is* of identity serve anyway? Does *Tat tvam asi* in the end simply mean that what *Tat* points to is the same thing that *tvam* points to? If so, in what sense? Finally, doesn't this purely denotative interpretation of *Tat* and *tvam* render nugatory a rather traditional interpretation of *Ātman* as immanent *Brahman* and of *Brahman* as transcendent *Ātman*, where "immanent" and "transcendent" clearly refer to metaphysical properties? The issues these questions raise have been stumbling blocks to the understanding of these metaphysical matters about identity for many centuries. However, we shall not dwell here on these issues, for a far more serious problem awaits us—one that emerged for the first time in the *Upaniṣads* and continued to plague Indian philosophers up through the twentieth century. Let us call this problem "the dilemma of monism."

The philosophical monism lurking in *Tat tvam asi* poses a problem for common sense, for logic, for epistemology, and for metaphysics. Monism is essentially reductionist doctrine, for it says that all plurality is really a unity, that all apparent multiplicity is ultimately one, and that all that seems separate is actually together and single. Thus, for logic all distinct instantiations are really one; for epistemology all multiple knowings and truths are really one; for metaphysics all separate beings are really one—and all these must be really one or else they are unreal. Common sense reels under the onslaught of philosophical monism, and the person also reels who faces either being the One, himself, or being nothing, himself. Being the One or *Brahman*, of course, is precisely the message that *Tat tvam asi* hopes to convey to the self in order that the self might escape being unreal and being nothing. But ego clings to itself, to its memories, hopes, fears, and consciousness, to its selfness; faced with the Oneness that is *Brahman* and with the loss of personality, ego may find the alternative of *Tat tvam asi* a bleak one, indeed. This bleak alternative is plaintively expressed in the dilemma of monism:

1. If *Brahman* is real, then I am not real.
2. If I am real, then *Brahman* is not real.
3. Either *Brahman* is real or I am real, but not both (the monistic assumption).
4. Therefore, either I am not real or *Brahman* is not real.

The dilemma of monism concludes, then, that one of us, metaphysically, has got to go: either *Brahman* goes or I go. The *Upaniṣads* say that I must go, for only *Brahman* is real. Or, perhaps to soften the blow of the dilemma of monism, the *Upaniṣads* say that we can "both" stay provided that I can see myself as *Ātman*. But then there is no "both" at all, for the *is* of identity has driven home the point that *Ātman* and *Brahman* are one; and the self that I would save is driven out once again from the arena of reality. The dilemma of monism will be challenged by later *Vedānta* philosophers, several of whom will want to make personal selves and the world into *Brahman*, as well.

This concludes our analysis of *Tat tvam asi* and our presentation of the metaphysics of the *Upaniṣads*. We shall return to the issues, questions, and problems raised here in our development of the epistemology of the *Upaniṣads*. Because realizing the identity of *Brahman* and *Ātman* is tantamount to achieving *mokṣa*, and since *mokṣa* is the proper and universal end for all beings, it will be important for us to grasp just what is entailed by *mokṣa* and by the kind of knowledge that leads to *mokṣa*. This knowledge is called *jñāna*, and *jñāna* yoga, we have seen, is the way of knowledge that is introduced for the first time in the *Upaniṣads*. This doctrine of *jñāna yoga* will occupy our attentions in the epistemology of the *Upaniṣads* that follows.

## 5. THE EPISTEMOLOGY OF THE *UPANIṢADS*

The *Upaniṣads* undoubtedly describe two routes to *mokṣa*, as mentioned in our discussion of yoga (see pp. 104–7): *jñāna* yoga, or the way of knowledge, which we will again discuss here, and *dhyāna* yoga, or the way of meditation, which we will not be discussing here. The *Upaniṣads* are the *locus classicus* for *jñāna* yoga, for in no other set of texts is this way to *mokṣa* described with such force and persistence. It will be well, therefore, to try to discover what kind of knowledge *jñāna* is and what it is not.

### *a. Statements and Propositions*

Earlier in this volume we defined "knowledge" as "justified true belief." Let me extend that definition now by distinguishing between two technical concepts: "propositions" and "statements"; I'll conclude by arguing that it is only propositions that can be known. A proposition is not a sentence; rather, it is technically defined as the meaning of an indicative sentence or statement. A statement is a sentence that asserts or tells us something or other. A statement, therefore, must be a sentence (a well-formed, grammatically correct utterance) and it must state, assert, or indicate that something or other is the case. Now the proposition is what is known, and what is known about a proposition is that it must be either true or false. The proposition is conveniently expressed by an utterance beginning with the word "that" followed by the statement. The statement, "All elephants are large," expresses the proposition "that all elephants are large."

Our interest from this point on will be in the meanings and propositions of statements and not in the statements themselves. Here are several examples of purported statements and their propositions:

| *Statement* | *Proposition* |
|---|---|
| S1 All *brahmins* speak Sanskrit. | P1 that all *brahmins* speak Sanskrit |
| S2 All tall *brahmins* are *brahmins*. | P2 that all tall *brahmin*. are *brahmins* |
| S3 I exist now. | P3 that I exist now |
| S4 All cobras drink $\sqrt{-1}$. | P4 ? |
| S5 The *Upaniṣads* are Thursday. | P5 ? |

Each putative statement S expresses a proposition P such that S1 expresses P1, S2 expresses P2, and S3 expresses P3. Now if a statement expresses a proposition—that is, if any well-formed English sentence in the indicative mood has a meaning or is meaningful—then we can say that the proposition expressed by the statement is going to be either true or false. And in this technical vocabulary all "meaningful" sentences are sentences that express *bona fide* propositions; acquiring knowledge is simply the process of finding out whether the proposition thus expressed is true or false.

### b. Knowledge as Justified True Belief

But the test of meaningfulness of a sentence is tied directly to the evidence for turning all purported true beliefs into knowledge. Unless there is justification for true beliefs, there can be no knowledge, but merely unsupported belief. For example, take S1, All *brahmins* speak Sanskrit. What does it mean? It purports to mean P1, that all *brahmins* speak Sanskrit. Does it not have a meaning, then, and isn't S1 therefore meaningful and isn't S1 therefore true or false? But how do we know if S1 is really meaningful? Couldn't S1 be mistaken for a putative statement such as, say, S4, All cobras drink $\sqrt{-1}$, or S5, The *Upaniṣads* are Thursday? Both S4 and S5 seem to express propositions (you can make up a P4 and a P5 without any difficulties at all), and it looks, therefore, as if both S4 and S5 are likely condidates for being statements and being ultimately either true or false. But what evidence would count for your belief that the *Upaniṣads* are Thursday when the *Upaniṣads* just aren't the sorts of things to which one can attribute days of the week? Or what would show that "All cobras drink $\sqrt{-1}$" was either true or false?

The answer is that neither S4 nor S5 can be shown to be either true or false. For reflect on how you would go about gathering evidence either for or against them. Recall the three criteria for knowledge and for being able to say that you know something or other. Thus to say, "I know that all cobras drink $\sqrt{-1}$," implies, first of all, that I believe that all cobras drink $\sqrt{-1}$, second, that it is true that all cobras drink $\sqrt{-1}$, and third, that I have evidence for my belief that in fact makes it true. But neither S4 nor S5 can qualify as statements or objects of knowledge, for it is not logically possible to find evidence for them or to justify them—since square roots aren't the kinds of things anyone drinks and Thursdays aren't the kinds of things that a collection of texts can be. Since they are not capable of being justified, now or ever, and since they are then neither true nor false, and since therefore they don't express propositions, then we can say that both S4 and S5 are technically *meaningless*.

But what about S1, S2, and S3? Are they meaningful or meaningless? Can evidence be found to justify a belief in the truth or falsity of these statements? They all seem to express the propositions attributed to them, for no doubt it is logically possible (in the sense that there is no logical contradiction entailed) to find evidence that would show whether they were either true or false; hence they are meaningful. Suppose S1 is believed to be true; now that makes it a very likely candidate for knowledge, but only a candidate, for it must pass the hurdle of justification. The evidence sought here is sensory evidence, because the claim is empirical. We simply poll all the *brahmins* we can lay our hands on and find out if they speak Sanskrit. When we come upon one, which is very likely, who cannot speak Sanskrit, then S1 is proved false. Note this: S1 is *meaningful* but *false*. Furthermore, we also know that the statement, "Some *brahmins* speak Sanskrit," call it S1′, is true; and we also know that "Some *brahmins* do not speak do not speak Sanskrit," call it S1″, is true; and we know these statements for they are both true beliefs justified, in this case, on empirical grounds, i.e. by sensory evidence.

S2, which does not make an empirical claim, is justified on nonsensory grounds. For you wouldn't run around the empirical or sensory world to see if all tall *brahmins* were indeed *brahmins*; nor would you try to see if all tall *brahmins* were tall. Rather, we discover statements such as S2 to be true by merely analyzing the meanings of the terms. It would be self-contradictory to deny statements such as S2, for denials of such logically true statements are always self-contradictory. We can say quite simply that S2 is known to be true merely in virtue of the *meanings of the words* involved.

We can adopt at this time several useful technical terms. Let's say that S2 is an *analytic judgment* (a logically certain judgment whose denial is self-contradictory) and that it is justified *a priori* (not by sensation or through sensory observation of the world). And let's say that S1 is a *synthetic judgment* (a judgment that is not logically certain, but only probable, for its denial is not self-contradictory but only interesting) and that S1 is justified *a posteriori* (by sensation or through sensory observation of the world). We could even generalize at this point and say that all synthetic judgments are only probably true (with a high degree of probability, in most cases, to be sure), that their denials are not self-contradictory, and that they are all justified, or proved true or false through sensory observation of the world. Further, all analytic judgments are logically certain—true by definition or known to be true simply by analyzing the meanings of the words involved in the statement or by deriving them from the axioms, definitions, and rules of inference within a formal system; also, their denials are self-contradictory. It is rather a truism in many philosophic circles that all synthetic judgments are known *a posteriori*, and all analytic judgments are known *a priori*, and that, just as there are no analytic *a posteriori* judgments, so, also, there are no synthetic *a priori* judgments. Try to think of some examples, if you can. But then we come to the curiosity of S3 and certain *Upaniṣadic* attitudes regarding the claims of *jñāna* yoga.

S3, "I exist now," could be justified *a priori* by definition or by inference from other judgments or statements, or it could be justified *a posteriori* by sensation through identifying the self with the body. But most philosophers who go around asserting strange things such as "I exist" and "I am" prefer to say that S3-like statements are justified neither by sensation nor by inference but rather by something called *intuition*. By boldly evoking this magic name they hope to gain the best of both worlds. They yearn for the *certainty* that lurks in all analytic *a priori* statements, but they also seek the new, the factual, and the informative that lurk in all synthetic *a posteriori* statements and that is wholly lacking in the trivial tautologies of the analytic statements (after all, who finds anything exciting, new, and factual about "All *brahmins* are *brahmins*" or "All short *śūdras* are short"?). And so the intuitionist claims that S3, "I exist now," is both certain and informative, and that he knows this without doubt, without sensation, and without inference from any other statements. Further, the denial of S3 is not self-contradictory in any logical sense, so S3 must be a synthetic statement. But the denial of S3 is weird, to say the least (try saying, "I do not exist" or "I am not" aloud to yourself). So S3, the intuitionist claims, is synthetic. But, he adds, S3 is not known or justified *a posteriori* by sensation; therefore, it must be justified *a priori* and by intuition. Hence, S3 is a synthetic *a priori* judgment, both certain (synthetically, not logically) and informative. The claims of *jñāna yoga* can be seen in precisely this same sense.

Take the following statements and the claim that they are meaningful because they are justifiable, by intuition in this case, and not by sensation or inference, and that, therefore, when known, they are known immediately and with certainty to be true.

S6 I am *Ātman*.
S7 *Ātman* and *Brahman* are identical,
S8 I am *Brahman*.

*Jñāna yoga* is the way in which S6, S7, and S8 are known to be true: *jñāna* is the justification for believing that S6, S7, and S8 are true. S6 simply says, in effect, that my true Nature, my real Self, is *Ātman*. The *Upaniṣads* indicate that knowing this leads to *mokṣa*. Further, one discovers the truth of S6 by having the experience oneself. One simply penetrates deeply into the self and discovers through this penetration that there, deep within, is the true Self, the *Ātman*. In discovering this true nature of oneself one can then say, "I am *Ātman*" or "*Ātman* alone is real." In a way, the experience cannot be described or verbally transmitted to others; one must have the experience for oneself. In this sense, experiencing *Ātman* or the Self is like the experience of the secondary qualities known through sensation (see pp. 28–29). Thus I experience secondary qualities such as red, sweet, rough, loud, and acrid, but I cannot really verbally describe these qualities directly to anyone else—for example, to anyone who might inquire what the sensation of red is like. The only way to reveal to you what the experience of red is like is to present you with a red object. All the telling in the world, all the metaphors and similes I could think of or conjure up, wouldn't give you that experience of red. So it is with all secondary or sensory qualities: you can know them only by directly experiencing them yourself. And so it is with *Ātman*: to know *Ātman* is to have the direct, immediate experience of *Ātman*, Itself. Words can't describe, words can't replace, words can't catch up that experience. And the *Upaniṣads* point to the path that leads to that experience, and that path is called *jñāna* yoga.

S7, apparently, is the statement that stands at the heart of the mystic *mokṣa* experience. It is what one discovers about the nature of the Self or *Ātman* in realizing that S6 is true. For what one sees is that the *Ātman* is the transcendent *Brahman* immanent in oneself. Or to put the whole *jñāna* discovery into the form of a curious conundrum: *Ātman* is immanent *Brahman*, and *Brahman* is transcendent *Ātman*. And the intuitionist claims that the truth of S7, hence the evidence or justification for S7, is found through *jñāna*—through intuition.

S8 not only follows by inference from the conjunction of S6 and S7 but it is also grounded or justified by *jñāna*. One immediately, clearly, and indubitably sees that one's true nature is pure Godhead, pure holy Power, pure *Brahman*, and this is known neither by sensation nor by inference, but by intuition. Hence, we can conclude from our previous discussion that S6, S7, and S8 are synthetic *a priori* judgments—judgments which are factual (about the real world) but also necessary, certain, and indubitable.

In summary, then, it would seem that the *Upaniṣads* could, indeed, make room for all three kinds of knowledge: logically certain knowledge; synthetically possible, empirical knowledge; and synthetically necessary intuitive knowledge. Various puzzles and problems are connected with all three, however, and we will be at some pains to point these out as we proceed through several of the *darśanas* or speculative philosophical systems that occur later in this text. For the moment it might be well to take these three kinds of knowledge—rational or logical knowledge, everyday empirical knowledge, and mystical, intuitive knowledge—and sketch the several difficulties that each meets and will meet in later Indian thought. For, as it seems to turn out, neither logical, nor empirical, nor intuitive knowledge, whether claimed in the eighth century B.C.E. or the twentieth century C.E., can escape all the epistemological traps, snares, and pits that have been laid, whether intentionally or not, by critical philosophers and their reputable camp followers.

### 1) Problems with Logical Knowledge

To count as examples of logically justified true beliefs, statements about those beliefs must be either (1) logically derived from a premise set that is itself composed of justified true propositions or (2) logically true simply in virtue of their form alone—that is, in virtue of the meanings and the grammatical and syntactical juxtapositions of the concepts in the statements. For example: All spitting cobras are cobras; $2 + 2 = 4$; All *brahmins* are members of the first *varṇa*; and so on. But all such statements are trivially true and empty of factual content. Hence, while logical certainty may be a highly sought-after quality, it would always seem to be accompanied by a stark uninterestingness. Logically justified knowledge that depends on the grammatical and syntactical associations of concepts in a statement purchases its certainty at the price of interestingness and novelty, too high a price to pay merely to be able to cry, "This is certain!"

But logically justified true statements might also be derived from a premise set, so attention shifts now from the derived conclusion to the premises from which it was derived. But these premises must be either trivially true and analytic, in which case the criticism above holds once more, or else derived from another premise set, in which case everything said here will hold of that previous premise set as well; or else they are either empirical statements or intuitively justified statements, themselves. If they are either of the latter, we can move on to a discussion of those two types of statements. The critic's point, again, for statements that are logically justified true beliefs is simply that they are either trivially true, devoid of factual content, and blatantly uninteresting, or else derived from other statements which possess those same logical and psychological properties.

### 2) Problems with Empirical Knowledge

To count as examples of empirically justified true beliefs, statements about those beliefs must be grounded in sensory experience, either direct (I saw it with my own eyes) or indirect (I saw what the laboratory instruments said, or I heard it from an expert). But the problems with sensory justification of knowledge are enormous, and not the least of these is the task of trying to be certain about what one claims to see, what the instrument claims to register, or what the expert says he saw. The fact that I could misperceive and be having illusions, hallucinations, or the like, or that I could report wrongly by a slip-of-the-tongue what I thought I saw, introduces an element of uncertainty into the whole empirical process that renders synthetic judgments of this *genre* unhappily probable at best (see pp. 58–59). The point about empirically justified true beliefs, the critics say, is that they are never certain, and at their hopeful best they are merely probable.

#### 3) Problems with Intuitive Knowledge

To count as examples of intuitively justified true beliefs, statements must be grounded in intuition—an often sudden and immediate feeling of certainty. But the problems with intuition as a justification of true beliefs are enormous. In trying to combine certainty with novelty and factualness—in claiming factual certainty for its synthetic *a priori* judgments—intuitionism neatly avoids all the criticisms and problems in items 1 and 2 above, but it opens itself up to a whole new range of attacks.

For example, what happens when two contradictory intuitions clash? How do we adjudicate your intuition that God exists together with mine that He does not? Since intuition seems to rest on a feeling, a strong feeling to be sure, that is private and subjective, how do we ascertain whether that feeling is a genuine intuitive feeling and not just another strong feeling? If the intuitionist says, as he apparently must, that we should check the empirical world to see whether the intuition is correct or not, to see whether God exists, the Self exists, *Ātman* is *Brahman*, and so on, then he has really given up his own case: intuition is seen as a way or a means of believing, but not a justification or final ground of knowledge. Thus the point, again, for statements about intuitively justified true beliefs, the critics say, is that their very subjectivity and privateness makes them suspect as true grounds of knowledge, and this kind of criticism makes us search elsewhere in order to justify intuition, if we must, as well as to provide ourselves with alternatives to this putative ground of knowledge.

This ends our discussion of the epistemology of the *Upaniṣads*. We turn next to the fourth and final philosophic subdivision of the *Upaniṣads*—ethics—for a presentation of one of the most important concepts to come from these texts and the whole of the Indian tradition: the law of *karma*.

## 6. THE ETHICS OF THE *UPANIṢADS*

The *Upaniṣads*, since they are, among other things, guides to life, abound in moral pronouncements of the usual and expected sort. They assume, generally, the *dharma* system of the *Laws of Manu*, they accept the moral law of the *Vedas*, and they expect right behavior for the sake of happiness in this world and the next. There is really only one new moral dimension present in the *Upaniṣads* that is not found in the *Vedas*, and that is the law of *karma*.

### *a. The Law of Karma*

*Karma* or the law of *karma* is an essential element to the *Upaniṣadic* concept of rebirth. We have seen references to it in our discussion of *saṁsāra* above, but I want now to speak about it more explicitly. The doctrine is as old as the *Bṛhadāraṇyaka Upaniṣad*, where the principle of karma is regarded as a great secret not to be spoken of in public. In that *Upaniṣad*, the law is covertly assumed:

> This is what happens to the man who desires.
> To whatever his mind is attached, the
> self becomes that in the next life.
> Achieving that end, it returns again
> to this world.[46]

In the *Chāndogya Upaniṣad* the same theme appears once again, wherein those of good conduct go on to a good womb, and those of evil conduct are also rewarded, appropriately and justly (see p. 104). The doctrine of *karma* then becomes a device for linking up conducts and consequences in this life and in the next. Finally, by the time of a later *Upaniṣad*, the *Śvetāśvatara* (ca. fifth century B.C.E.), the doctrine of *karma* is stated in the way that it is most popularly known to this day:

> According to its actions, the embodied
> self chooses repeatedly various forms
> in various conditions in the next life.
>
> According to its own qualities and acts,
> the embodied self chooses the kinds
> of forms, large and small, that it
> will take on.[47]

Thus each self gets not only what it deserves, but also what it wants.

Two comments before we continue. First, we will have to ask what kind of law this law of *karma* is, so that we can be precise with respect to the doctrine of rebirth; second, since there is no God according to the above account who is responsible for the meting out of punishment and discipline

[46] *Bṛhadāraṇyaka Upaniṣad* IV.4.6.
[47] *Śvetāśvatara Upanisad.*, V.11–12.

under this law, the law of *karma* works automatically. We must inquire how this is possible. Franklin Edgerton says of this automatic law:

> It is man's relation to propriety or morality, *dharma*, which alone determines. For more than two thousand years, it appears that almost all Hindus have regarded transmigration, determined by "Karma," as an axiomatic fact. "By good deed one becomes what is good; by evil deed, evil."[48]

The reason for regarding transmigration as determined by *karma* as an "axiomatic fact," of course, is that both rebirth and *karma* are asserted by the *Upaniṣads*, hence orthodoxy compels assent on this matter.

### *b. Right and Wrong under the Law of Karma*

What's going on with this law of *karma*? The doctrine seems to be saying something like this: for some kinds of behavior *b* there will be a result *r*, such that if *b* is good or bad then *r* will be good or bad. But this needs further explanation. Suppose that we have three kinds of behavior: good (*bg*), bad (*bb*), and indifferent (*bi*). Then there will be three types of results to these three behaviors: *rg*, *rb*, and *ri*. If the law of *karma* works, it would be impossible to have *rb* or *ri* associated with or follow from *bg*, and the same could be said for the other behaviors and results. Further, if the law of *karma* is just, and that seems to be what the *Upaniṣads* imply, then each person must get exactly what is coming to him, his due, no more and no less.

Could there be any overcompensation or undercompensation? Suppose that I angrily shout at a librarian who is bothering me, and shortly afterward a truck roars into the library loaded with concrete culverts and squashes me so that I die horribly. Haven't I been overpaid—such a harsh result (being squashed) for such a trivial behavior (shouting at a librarian)? There are two ways to account for such apparently extraordinary evils. First, perhaps a mistake was made, for there are chance events, fortuitous and unaccountable clashings of bodies. Second, one must distinguish short-term justice from long-term justice; thus the squashing may have been a just payment for a long line of unpaid-for and nasty acts done previously by me. Let's briefly consider each of these alternative explanations.

First, to say that I was squashed when I ought only to have been bruised is to admit overcompensation and to admit, consequently, that an injustice was done. But an apologist might respond that the injustice will be made up by a better birth, a *karma reward*, as he might call it, in my next life. It's the law's way of apologizing for accidents and correcting overcompensation. So justice is done. But I don't think this will work. The law of *karma*, according

[48]Franklin Edgerton, *The Beginnings of Indian Philosophy* (Cambridge, Mass.: Harvard University Press, 1965), p. 30.

to the consensus of the *Upaniṣads*, operates with respect to my behavior, joining that behavior to certain results, good to good and bad to bad. And while I must be reborn, there is no legitimate *Upaniṣadic* ground whatsoever for assuming that I must be rewarded later for being accidentally squashed by a truck now. The *karma* theory, as the *Upaniṣads* state it, cannot compensate me for chance wicked acts done to me now by giving me future better births. So it seems that if such a mistake was made, then there is no justice under the law of *karma*.

However, the law of *karma* can justify such accidental acts by explaining the squashing in terms of my being in the library because of my past *karmic* acts. Hence my gravitating to ground-floor locations where cement trucks might suddenly show up was brought about by my past lives. Hence the law of *karma* can explain and perhaps even justify my being squashed in the library, though it cannot, as a result of that alone, give me a better birth next time around.

Second, suppose that it was no "accident." Suppose I was being "paid off" for years and even lives of past bad behavior. We are, of course, put in the position of asking, "Why wasn't I paid off before now?" The law of *karma* is not like those natural laws (inertia, gravity, chemical and physiological statements summarizing relations between events) that "pay off" immediately; rather, it operates with respect to a whole host of past deeds, in this life and conceivably in others, too. Justice will be served in the long run; if short-run injustices are noted, one must remember that they are *short run*. The truck squashing me was *rb*, not to the librarian incident but to a whole host of other *bb*'s that suddenly and unforeseeably surfaced—like bubbles clinging to the side of a glass that grow and grow, and then suddenly burst to the top.

The problem, of course, is that we can explain bubbles in water through hydrodynamical laws, and predict rather accurately what amount of gas in the bubble will cause it to surface, when, and with what results. No such prediction seems possible with the law of *karma*, nor should we seek any. We will return to the lawlike nature of *karma* shortly.

While every *bg* and *bb* behavior will eventually produce an *rg* and *rb* response, and do it without remainder (do it justly in the long run), there are certain kinds of behavior, *bi*, that are *karma*-indifferent. Common sense—with a little help from ethical theory—tells us that many things that we do do not have moral (*karmic*) effects: autonomic responses such as blinking the eyes, yawning, and sneezing, and actions wherein no "moral" activity is involved at all, such as walking on the sidewalk, stretching the arms, talking to people, and so on. A whole host of *prima facie* activities are *karma* neutral, as we know from the experienced neutral results of these acts in the past. But this reliance on experience can be easily challenged now under the reign of the law of *karma*. If we are *a fortiori* to believe that *rg* or *rb* can result from *bg* or *bb* performed in a past we-know-not-when, then a cloak of mystery, uncertainty, and unpredictability is thrown over the entire moral venture. For if one can't explain the *rg* and *rb* happening now in terms of known, identifiable, and isolatable *bg* and *bb* in the immediate past, then how can one be sure that the act one is performing now, which might *seem* to be *bi*, is not really *bb* or *bg*? Perhaps one guide might be a list of prohibited or enjoined acts from the *śrūti* or *smṛti*. But what about proposed actions that are not even mentioned there—such as drinking Coca-Cola or buying foreign cloth? Surely one knows whether they are right or wrong only by noting their immediate effects. And the law of *karma*, with its unpredictable and unforeseeable habit of suddenly surfacing and paying off, would obviate such experimental tests for right and wrong.

My point is this: one of the best guides we have for acceptable and unacceptable behavior is the fact of the immediate results, pleasurable or painful results, connected somehow to that behavior. The law of *karma*, as this interpretation would have it, with its possible delayed results and odd overcompensations for past deeds, throws this entire right-pleasure, wrong-pain correlation out of theoretical alignment. I can't trust the present consequences I get from present actions as a guide for future moral behavior because, pow!, I may suddenly get paid back for what I thought was a right action by a runaway truckload of concrete culverts.

Finally, under this interpretation, of course, there may be no *bi*'s at all: If experienced past consequences can no longer guarantee a sharp separation between present *bg* and *bb*, then neither can consequences guarantee which acts are *bi*—if, indeed, any are. Today's sneeze, yesterday's stretch, tomorrow's laugh, may lead to a sudden meeting with a concrete truck, thereby causing my observant friends to avoid sneezing, stretching, and laughing, at least in the library.

However, though living under the umbrella of the law of *karma* may prove to be morally unsettling, isn't it nice to know everyone is going to get, or has gotten, what's coming to him or her sometime, somewhere? Perhaps this feeling for justice will outweigh the insecurity in action that the law produces. But to believe that one may be every moment of every day gathering *karma* with every snort, blink, and scratch is somewhat exhausting. And the latter surely follows from the fact that we can no longer be certain, because of delayed *rb*'s and *rg*'s, which behaviors are really right, which are really wrong, and which are really neutral.

### c. *The Law in the Law of Karma*

The law of *karma* is a curious-blend of both descriptive and metaphysical elements. On the one hand it states predictively that if you do so-and-so (and we've seen now that this might mean anything and everything that you do), you can expect (you know not when) certain moral results. It says that whenever *bg* or *bb*, then—absolutely, not merely probably—*rg* or *rb*. There is no question of statistics or empirical test runs to establish this relationship; it is an *a priori* metaphysical law, with an empirical content and empirical consequences.

*Karma* shows the same sort of relationship to the cosmos as Ockham's law of parsimony. William of Ockham (1300–1349) had said, or so many philosophers believe, that one ought not to multiply entities beyond necessity. Ockham's law can be interpreted prescriptively, *for best results keep things simple*, or descriptively, *Nature herself is simple*, that is, this law reflects nature's own simplicity. In a similar way, the law of *karma* is descriptive of the world, and yet with prescriptive force it commends itself to the disciple. The law of *karma* is universally operative: *watch out lest ye fall into sin.*

As with most full-blooded empirical laws one can *explain* past events and *predict* future events given the law of *karma.* Why did the concrete truck crush me? Well (explanation), sometime in the past you exhibited $bb_1$, $bb_2$, . . . , $bb_n$, and there is a law that says: whenever $bb_1$, $bb_2$, . . . , $bb_n$ occurs, then $rb_1$, $rb_2$, . . . , $rb_n$ must occur. We have seen $rb_1$, the concrete truck crushing you, so there must have been a *bb* sometime in your past life or lives. What will happen if I shout at a librarian? Well (prediction), sometime in the future you can expect *rb.* Why? Because: whenever $bb_1$, $bb_2$, . . . , $bb_n$, . . . ; and so on.

But a most disturbing thing about the law of *karma* as a descriptive or (as Franklin Edgerton calls it) a natural law is that it is not itself grounded or justified empirically. We cannot be sure that we have seen real cases of *bb* followed by real cases of *rb* for reasons of the moral uncertainty pointed out previously. The law of *karma* is not meant to be empirically lawlike in the sense that it comes from repeated observations of past empirical associations of *bb*'s and *rb*'s. It is not empirically justified, and consequently it cannot be compared to a natural law at all. To this extent, the law of *karma* is like the principle of causation: every event must have a cause. Karl Potter has summarized this similarity very well. Of the "law of causation" he observes:

> Thus the "Law of Causation" is not a law at all, but a principle. As such it serves an extremely important function: it formulates a basic presupposition of scientific inquiry . . .;

and of the "law of karma":

> If the "Law of Karma" is to be thought of as parallel in function to the "Law of Causation," it, too, must be viewed as a principle, a principle which formulates a certain program for moral inquiry.[49]

[49]Karl H. Potter, "The Naturalistic Principle of Karma," *Philosophy: East and West* Volume XIV, Number 1, April 1964, p. 40.

Both the causal principle and the *karma* principle then have exhortative functions: the former urges us to keep looking for explanations of physical phenomena; the latter urges us to seek explanations for moral occurrences—it "commits us to seeking a deterministic order beneath the quantum order or whatever other incompletely determined order science may arrive at through further investigation."[50] More particularly, the *karma* principle urges us to seek out the cause of habituation or bondage in our own lives and to seek release from such binding habituation. The upshot for our purposes is simply that *karma* as a principle is assumed for heurisitic or practical reasons, and that these reasons justify its acceptance.

The point that *karma* must be an assumption or presupposition and that it cannot, as a consequence, be proved by any of the valid means of knowledge has been pointed out by Eliot Deutsch in his book *Advaita Vedānta, A Philosophical Reconstruction.* Deutsch refers to the law of *karma* as a "convenient fiction," for it enables the Indian to solve a number of rather baffling problems that would otherwise be insoluble. Among the four or so problems it solves, according to Deutsch, is the general problem of evil:

> The last problem for which *karma* offers a solution is the one most frequently pointed to: the problem of inequality and evil, of why there are such great differences among men in spiritual and mental capacity or why men occupy such different places within the socio-economic order.[51]

To such puzzles the law of *karma* has an answer:

> The spiritual and intellectual differences between *jīvas* are the result of their conduct. The place in society that they occupy at any one time is the result of their past action.[52]

And because the law of *karma* itself cannot be established through any of the *pramāṇas* or valid means or ways of knowing, we can call it a fiction, but a convenient or useful one. Whether one dubs it a fiction, a principle, a heuristic device, or an assumption, the point is that it is not capable of proof in the ordinary sense but it is accepted nonetheless as an essential element in rebirth theories.

This concludes our discussion of the ethics of the *Upaniṣads* and with it our general presentation of the philosophy of the *Upaniṣads.* Before turning to the philosophy of the *Bhagavad Gītā*, I would like to compare the philosophy of the *Vedas* with that of the *Upaniṣads.* We shall address the four fields of philosophy together with one additional category that relates the philoso-

[50] *Ibid.*, pp. 43–44.

[51] Eliot Deutsch, *Advaita Vedānta, A Philosophical Reconstruction* (Honolulu: East-West Center Press, 1967), p. 78.

[52] *Ibid.*

phy of the *Vedas* and the *Upaniṣads*: Man. The reason for introducing this latter category will be apparent as we launch ourselves into the *Bhagavad Gītā* and its philosophy.

## 7. THE *VEDAS* AND THE *UPANIṢADS*: A COMPARISON

### *a. Metaphysics*

The *Upaniṣads* in comparison to the *Vedas* make tremendous philosophic changes in all five of the categories touched on below. These changes are expected, of course, and for the simple reason that the *Upaniṣads* set out to do a different sort of job on the world, man, and the Gods than the *Vedas* did. The *Upaniṣads* are reflective, thoughtful, and, in their own way, critical texts, and what they are reflective, thoughtful, and critical about, among other things, are the *Vedas*. And in critically thinking about the naive metaphysics of the *Vedas*, they evolve a theory of reality that shows a sophistication and perspicacity unparalled in the ancient world. By calling the metaphysics of the *Vedas* "naive" I intend nothing disrespectful, for the *ṛṣis* of the *Vedas* are no more naive than the ordinary, unreflective, common man of the twentieth century. What is probably real to the latter are rocks, plants, animals, and man, together with his relatives and friends in heaven, as well as God, who superintends the whole affair from on high. If questioned, this modern, average man, like his *Vedic* counterpart, would undoubtedly admit that this serial ordering of these real entities is significant in the sense that plants are more valuable and real than most rocks, that animals are more valuable and real than most plants, and that God is more valuable and real than all the rest. Hence, there is an ontology of levels specially ordered by the values of those respective levels. *Vedic* man differs not at all in his metaphysics (I would venture to guess) from the common man of every time and clime.

But *Upaniṣadic* man turns himself very quickly out of this circle of naive *Vedic* metaphysics. The concept of *Brahman*, as well as the concepts of higher and lower *Brahman*, evolves out of the *Vedas* and the *Brāhmaṇas*, along with the curious notion of *māyā* that attempts to make the distinction between these levels of *Brahman* possible. In our discussion of the *Bhagavad Gītā* we will return to this *Upaniṣadic* metaphysics, for the *Gītā* will accept as presuppositions all of the metaphysical machinery of the *Upaniṣads*.

### *b. Epistemology*

The epistemological position of the *Vedas* is based on the metaphysical realism described above. It assumes in a rather ordinary, common-sense way that what one sees, hears, tastes, smells, and touches is pretty much what's really out there in the world: at least we have no good grounds for assuming that the naive metaphysics does not lead to a naive epistemology. The metaphysical pluralism of the *Vedas*—the metaphysical view that holds that there are many real, enduring, constant, and abiding things in the world, such as rocks, trees, elephants, *brahmins* and Gods—leads naturally to naive realism in epistemology: what we come to know about the world is exactly the way the world really is. The *Upaniṣads*, however, with their doctrine of the ultimate reality of *Brahman* and *Ātman*, and their doctrine of *māyā*, call into sharp question this "real world" of trees, rocks and man, this entire world of *saguṇa Brahman*: knowing the unreal, the illusory, is not really knowing at all. The value of what is known becomes a function of the reality of the object of knowledge; the metaphysics colors (or distorts) the epistemology, imbuing it with value (or disvalue). And what is worth knowing is only that which is most real. Since *Ātman* is most real, it becomes the only entity worth knowing or the only entity that can be really known—all else being imbued with *māyā*. And the locus of *Ātman*, the *Upaniṣads* are at some pains to point out, is the Self, where the religious-mystical-epistemological motto becomes *Tat tvam asi*. Hence attention, both metaphysical and epistemological, is drawn towards the Self: metaphysics and epistemology threaten to reduce to psychology.

### c. *Ethics*

The ethics of the *Vedas* must also be seen as relatively uncomplicated and simple. There is justice in the universe, but it operates under the aegis of *Ṛta* like any other compensatory law; justice in the universe is like a physical law that explains why everything stays in its place or, if removed from its place, returns there. Thus *Ṛta* can explain equally well why the spear you threw fell back eventually to the earth, and why the contract you broke led eventually to your punishment: that's the way the physical and moral universe is—a cosmos, not a chaos, as ordered under *Ṛta*. The law of *karma* in the *Upaniṣads*, compared to the system of *Ṛta* in the *Vedas*, is simply a more complicated way of taking and keeping moral notes on the universe. The point is that the universe is just: everyone gets what's coming to him, either in this life or, with *saṁsāra*, in the next or the next or the next, however long it takes to right the imbalance.

Finally, *varṇa dharma* is a law in the *Vedas* calling, one must suspect, for some kind of obedience. However, it would seem that *varṇa dharma*, as well as the system of the *arthas* and the *āśramas*, is late *Vedic*. In fact it is not until the time of the *Laws of Manu* that all three receive any sort of explicit philosophic and historical treatment.

We can conclude that the relatively simple ethical philosophy of the *Vedas* is eventually replaced in the *Upaniṣads* by the highly complex machinery of social, personal, and religious values represented by such concepts as the *arthas*, the *āśramas*, *saṁsāra*, and law of *karma*.

### *d. Religion*

With the introduction of the yogas and the sort of do-it-yourself or save-yourself religious reforms of the *Upaniṣads*, the power of the priests and the practices and beliefs associated with the *Vedic* ritual are considerably augmented. We have, for purposes of contrast, exaggerated the break between these two religious traditions but not, I believe, overstated them. Thus *Upaniṣadic mokṣa* as the goal of the new religion replaces the *Vedic* pleasng-the-Gods and the *Vedic* aim of obtaining-the-heavenly-worlds. In fact, given the power that speculative philosophy developed late in the *Vedic* period, the Gods are replaced by the notion of *Brahman*. This holy Power of the universe can now be obtained by *jñāna yoga*, self-discipline, and individual effort, rather than by priestly sacrifice and *Vedic* ritual. Morality is removed from the religious sphere since it can no longer bring one to a *permanent* place in heaven as the *Vedas* had previously taught, for both good acts and evil ones become equally binding; as a consequence, the *Upaniṣadic* philosophy on this matter of the bondage of actions introduces serious complications into Hinduism. For if all acts bind one, then the good as well as the wicked acts continue to hold one to *saṁsāra*. If that is so, then it would appear that *mokṣa* is possible only if one gives up all acts and acting. Hence, in the *Upaniṣads*, there is either the danger of suicide or the problem of inaction and quietism. The latter has always been a problem for Hinduism, and, as pointed out by theologians such as Albert Schweitzer, "world and life negation" or quietism has had a long and disturbing history in Hinduism.[53] This problem will be solved, however, in the *Bhagavad Gītā* by the doctrine of *karma yoga*, which shows one how to act in the world without having one's acts produce bondage and rebirth (see pp. 158–62).

Finally, the *Upaniṣads* replace, in principle, the polytheism or theism of the *Vedas* with the metaphysical doctrine of *Brahman*. And with the introduction of higher *Brahman* or *nirguṇa* or *parā Brahman* as the ultimately real Being in the universe, Hinduism turns to ritual or religious atheism. It is saved from the full consequences of this atheism, however, by the introduc-

[53]See Albert Schweitzer's classic attack against Hinduism in his famous *Indian Thought and Its Development* (1936) (Boston: Beacon Press, 1962), Chap. 2; and then see a classic defense of Hinduism against Schweitzer's attack in S. Radhakrishnan's, *Eastern Religions and Western Thought* (1939), 2d ed. (Fair Lawn, N.J.: Oxford University Press, 1969), Chap. 3.

tion of lower *Brahman* or *saguṇa* or *aparā Brahman*. Both concepts of *Brahman* will play a heavy role in the philosophy of the *Bhagavad Gītā*, as will the doctrine of the Forgiver, somewhat like Varuṇa in the *Vedas*, when the Forgiver is seen as a divine Savior, Lord Kṛṣṇa.

### e. Man

The changes in the concept of man and his nature between the time of the *Vedas* and the period of the *Upaniṣads* is most striking. We have already seen that for all practical purposes man in the *Vedas* is a relatively simple metaphysical being. The philosophy which discusses him focuses on some kind of simple dualism, such that when the body dies something survives that goes on to the heavens. This *Vedic* dualism is replaced in the *Upaniṣads* by a metaphysical monism. But even here something still survives the death of man, and this something is, among other entities, the ultimately real Self of man.

The stratified social and occupational *varṇa* system of the *Vedas* is rent but not sundered by the *Upaniṣadic* doctrine that every person, apparently including women, low *varṇa*, and non*varṇa*, is capable of the life of the student of sacred knowledge. As we saw in the story of Satyakāma Jābāla, behaving like a *brahmin* is more important than being born a *brahmin* (see pp. 100–101). This stress on behavior and behavioral attitudes rather than on birth and parentage as a determiner of who shall be capable of salvation or highest happiness constitutes a radical reform of early *Vedic* Hinduism; it will be reflected later in the *Gītā*, where the possibility of "highest happiness" is open, universally, to everyone. Thus man's dependency on priests and sacrifice as reflected in the *Vedas* tends to drop away, and what emerges in its place is a stress on the importance of the guru and the guru's reflections as handed down in the *Upaniṣads*.

Finally, the simple picture that we get of the self in the *Vedas*, where that self is merely a mobile soul that moves from earth to heaven at the death of the body, is totally superseded in the *Upaniṣads*. The self of the *Upaniṣads* is, on the one hand, a complex, sheathed being, consisting of various layers and states of consciousness which are all capable of the activities of an ego or *jīva*; on the other hand, this self in the *Upaniṣads* becomes a Self, an *Ātman*, the metaphysically ultimate center of man's consciousness. This complicated *Upaniṣadic* self and Self will be carried over into the *Gītā*, where they will become the focal point of salvation. And around these two selves will revolve the four yogas, also to be discussed in the *Gītā*.

As a result of this philosophical comparison between the *Vedas* and the *Upaniṣads* three striking points emerge. First, there is a general move from relative philosophic simplicity and common-sensicalness in the *Vedas* to philosophic complexity and esotericism in the *Upaniṣads*. Second, this move is carried along by a revolution in religious and philosophic thought sometime between 1000 and 800 B.C.E. in which philosophic esotericism gains the ascendancy. Third, in subsequent centuries there is a move away from the religious way of dealing with the world, man, and the Gods towards a metaphysical way of seeing these three entities. Thus by the fifth century B.C.E. two quite distinct views of the world, man, and the Gods emerge within early Indian thought. We shall refer to these two views as "the religious view" and "the metaphysical view" and note the role they play in the *Bhagavad Gītā*.

This completes our philosophical comparison between the *Vedas* and the *Upaniṣads*. We turn now to the *Bhagavad Gītā* and its philosophy.

# *F.*

# *The Bhagavad Gītā and Its Philosophy*

## 1. BACKGROUND TO THE *BHAGAVAD GĪTĀ*

The *Bhagavad Gītā* [literally "the song (*gītā*) of the Lord or God (*bhagavan*)"] forms part of India's greatest, and the world's longest, epic poem, *Mahābhārata*, and it has been accurately described as "the *New Testament* of Hinduism." A number of parallels between the *Gītā* and the *New Testament* make this description apt and instructive.

First, and most obvious, both the *Gītā* and *New Testament* are chronological continuations of previous cultural and religious traditions; the *Gītā* continues a tradition whose roots stretch into the historical *Upaniṣads* and *Vedas*, and the *New Testament* continues a tradition whose roots can be found in the *Pentateuch* and other books of the Hebrew *Old Testament*. In other words, neither the *Gītā* nor the *New Testament* sprang fully grown and complete from any sort of literary immaculate conception. Further, since the dates for the *Gītā* lie some 200 to 400 years earlier than those of the earliest books of the *New Testament*, it might be more accurate to say that the *New Testament* is the *Bhagavad Gītā* of Judaism.

Second, the *Gītā* and the *New Testament* not only claim to be continuations of the previous traditions, but each also claims an authenticity, an Authorship, of its own that tends to transcend if not to contradict those previous traditions. They are not merely repetitions of old doctrines, but in many places they challenge the old doctrines. When Jesus, speaking with this new-found authority, states (*Matthew* 5: 38–39): "You have heard that it was said, 'An eye for an eye and a tooth for a tooth.' But I say unto you, Do not resist one who is evil,' he is, in effect, doing more than drawing an obvious theological conclusion from the Law of Moses. He is setting himself up as a new prophet who is able to speak with authority, as he does throughout the

Sermon on the Mount (*Matthew* 5): "You have heard that it was said to the ment of old . . . but I say unto you . . . ." Jesus' other claims, as we shall see next, serve to underscore the point that the *New Testament*, far from being merely Judaism from another point of view, actually represents a revolution of the Judaic religion; and as a revolution it must needs turn over or convert the old for the sake of that new. The *Gītā* is in precisely the same position. It speaks derogatorily and deprecatingly of the previous *Vedic* tradition in just enough places to warn the listener or reader that something new is about to occur. For example, early in the *Gītā* we have this classic passage, almost as if the author had been trying to say, "You have heard that it was said by the *Vedas* . . . but I say unto you here and now . . . .":

> When you escape from this tangle of delusion then you shall ascend to the level of total indifference as to what should be heard and what has been heard in the *Vedas*.
>
> The *Vedas* are as much use to an enlightened brahmin as is a tank of water in a place flooded on all sides by water.[1]

The *Gītā* represents a bold, innovative religious stroke in Hindusim, continuing, but at the same time altering, the previous tradition. Both the *New Testament* and the *Gītā* emerge as radical, revolutionary departures from the staid, conservative traditions from which they sprang. But they took place nonetheless within well-defined limits; not all of the old pieces were swept from the board.

Third, and finally, a number of new and quite specific claims made by the authors of both the *New Testament* and the *Gītā* provide a turning point for the older Judaic and *Vedic* traditions. This turning proved to be too sharp for Judaism, and as a consequence a new religion, Christianity, was born. But early Hinduism simply found space for its own new maverick child and added the new text, the new revolution, to itself. The specific claims made by those two new texts bear, moreover, a startling resemblance to one other. Both the *New Testament* and the *Gītā* set forth and defend a doctrine of a Savior or *Avatār*. They both make the claim, moreover, that this Savior is God. Further, both claim that one of the ways to salvation or happiness for human beings is to be found through dedication or devotion or love to or for this God. And finally, both texts make the claim that the way to salvation (through devotion to this God) is open to all persons and not just to the high-born or the well-born. Let us consider these specific within the context of the *Bhagavad Gītā*.

The *Gītā* claims to be the faithful record of a conversation that took place between an incarnation of God, Kṛṣṇa, and a man, Arjuna, sometime

[1] *Bhagavad Gītā* II.52, 46. See also VI.1, 46; VIII.28; IX.20, 21; XI.48, 53. All translations are the author's.

in India's immemorial, mythical past. The setting of the recorded conversation is on or near a chariot on a darkened, tense battlefield, in the midst of two fierce armies, just before the joining of a horrendous battle between them. The chairot contains Arjuna, a *kṣatriya* warrior of the Paṇḍava family, and his driver and cousin, Kṛṣṇa. As their chariot rests precariously between the two enormous armies, Arjuna looks across at the opposing force and recognizes among its ranks his friends, relatives, and teachers, men that he knows and loves; for the battle is part of a civil war:

> "And Arjuna looked and saw standing before him fathers and grandfathers, teachers, the brothers of his mother, cousins, sons and grandsons, friends . . . .[2]

Arjuna is moved to pity at those he sees, not knowing where his duty lies; suddenly his bow slips from his hands, he trembles at what he was about to do, and, despondently, he refuses to fight: "Arjuna, in the midst of the battle, sat down on the floor of his chariot, cast aside his bow and arrows, his heart overcome with grief."[3]

At this moment in the story Arjuna's charioteer and cousin, Kṛṣṇa, steps forward and begins the dialogue that continues for about 653 more verses. In the course of this dialogue Kṛṣṇa gradually reveals his true nature to Arjuna; for he is the preserver of the universe and the Savior of mankind. Throughout their long conversation, Kṛṣṇa attempts to get Arjuna to realize his true *dharma* or duty and to follow it, whatever the results, whatever his personal feelings. The message that Kṛṣṇa preaches is not merely a message for Arjuna, however, any more than Christ's message was merely for his twelve disciples. Rather, Kṛṣṇa's sermon or song is for all those who have ears and can hear; it is, as he says, an eternal message for all mankind, for all times and for all places. This universal character of the *Gītā* is probably what makes this delightful Sanskrit text so enormously popular. And to this extent, finally, the *New Testament* and the *Bhagavad Gītā* make an identical claim for the hearts and attention of all men, everywhere, to all those who are "weary and heavy laden." Let's see what the doctrine and the promise of this *New Testament* of Hinduism is like by turning first to the religion of the *Gītā*.

## 2. THE RELIGION OF THE *BHAGAVAD GĪTĀ*

In our discussion of the religion of the *Vedas* (see above, pp. 36–40) we talked about the ways to human happiness in terms of two possible relationship between the self and the world. The first of these two ways, the Epicurean and *Vedic* way, entailed shrinking or minimizing the importance of this world in relation to the self; with the consequent loss of this world-threat to

[2] *Ibid.*, I.26.

[3] *Ibid.*, I.47.

the self, a measure of security and happiness could be achieved. The second way, the Stoic and *Upaniṣadic* way, lay not in shrinking the world but rather in enlarging the self by making it overwhelmingly important in the face of a threatening and anxiety-producing world. If, as in the *Upaniṣads*, one could see the self as *Ātman* (see above, pp. 105–6)—as the holy Power of the universe, Itself—then the threat of the world could be removed entirely. Both of these ways to happiness, the *Vedic* way and the *Upaniṣadic* way, are still present in the *Bhagavad Gītā*, insofar as the *Gītā* stands as a speculative philosophic extension of *Vedic* and of *Upaniṣadic* doctrine. But in that extension, the *Gītā* develops a new way to human happiness of its own, which interestingly combines both of the previous ways. Part of this new way is found in the wholly unique relationship that Lord Kṛṣṇa bears to Arjuna, that God bears to man.

### *a.* *The Savior Game*

The Savior Game of the *Bhagavad Gītā* is an interesting inversion of the Forgiveness Game of the *Ṛg Veda* (see above, pp. 69–82). Where the Forgiveness Game discussed the necessary conditions for being forgiven one's sins (from man's point of view), the Savior Game discusses the necessary conditions for being a Savior (from the Savior's point of view). It is a game in that specifiable rules govern the play or activity of being a Savior, and being a Savior to a specifiable end. In the Forgiveness Game the end was reached when forgiveness occurred; in the Savior Game the end is reached when the Savior accomplishes his or her or its end, whatever that may be.

Recall once more the plot of the *Bhagavad Gītā*. Lord Viṣṇu is incarnated in the world as Kṛṣṇa, Arjuna's cousin and charioteer. Arjuna won't fight his friends and relations, so Kṛṣṇa's task is to convince him that he must do his duty, take up his arms and defend the clan. But for purposes of the Savior Game our attention must be fixed on the character of the divine charioteer, Lord Kṛṣṇa. Where did Kṛṣṇa come from? What are his origins? What purpose or service does he serve in the world?—what does he save and from what?—and, more importantly for the Savior Game, what conditions must exist in order for a Savior to be functional or operative in the world? Some of these questions the *Gītā* answers outright; others can be answered only by inference from what we already know of "Saviors" in other world religions.

Of his origins and function Kṛṣṇa, himself, says:

> You and I have passed through many births, Arjuna; I know all of them but you do not.
>
> Though unborn, for the *Ātman* is eternal, though Lord of all beings, yet using my own nature, I come into existence using my own *māyā*.

For whenever there is a decaying of *dharma*, and a rising
up of *adharma*, then I send Myself forth.

I come into existence time after time to protect the good,
to destroy the wicked, and to reestablish the holy *dharma*.[4]

Thus it is that Kṛṣṇa is the incarnation of the unborn, eternal *Ātman* and Lord of all beings. Further there is a condition under which this Lord leaves the place where he was and comes into the world. And, finally, having come into the world, having preached or taught the message to reestablish righteousness or *dharma*, the Lord leaves the message behind and retires from the world. His message, of course, constitutes the ways or yogas by which men can save themselves once the Savior is gone; and Kṛṣṇa is a true and real Savior, as he tells Arjuna:

But those who lay all of their actions on Me, intent on
Me, worshipping and meditating on Me with yoga,

For these, when their minds are fixed on Me, Oh Pārtha,
I am their Savior from the ocean of
deathly existence.[5]

But putting these several questions aside temporarily, for they will be answered directly in what follows, we can go about the business of setting up the conditions under which the Savior Game could be played or engaged in. In other words, as with the Forgiveness Game previously, what we want to establish now are the set of necessary and sufficient conditions for a being—any being, for that matter, even you and I—to be called "Savior." A number of necessary conditions must be fulfilled in order for a Savior to exist. We shall consider five such conditions:

$C_1$ A Lord or God exists; Viṣṇu

$C_2$ In some time and place trouble occurs: *adharma*

$C_3$ The Lord recognizes the trouble and responds to it by descending or crossing over into that time and place as (for instance) a man: *Avatār*

$C_4$ The *Avatār* teaches the way or ways out of the trouble: yogas

$C_5$ The Lord then returns to the place from which he came but leaves behind his message about the ways: *Bhagavad Gītā*

The mechanism of the Savior Game is meant to apply to the *Bhagavad Gītā*, but the same Game could be said to exist wherever these five necessary conditions are fulfilled. For example, in *Vedic brahminism* Lord Varuṇa seems a very likely precursor or predecessor of Lord Kṛṣṇa and, with one

[4]*Ibid.*, IV.5–8.

[5]*Ibid.*, XII.6–7.

notable exception to the conditions listed above, he could be a likely candidate for Savior and for playing the Savior Game. The exception is that Lord Varuṇa does not seem to have been an *Avatār* or Descender into the world in the sense to be explained below. There is another sense in which, given the philosophical assumptions the *Gītā* makes, all of us are Saviors, for all of us can meet precisely the five conditions described above. Let us look more closely at these conditions.

### $C_1$ A Lord or God exists: Viṣṇu

Viṣṇu has traditionally been regarded as the second Person of the Hindu trinity. His function is to preserve and maintain the world, just as Brahmā's function is to create and bring the world into existence, and Śiva's, the third Person of the trinity, is to dissolve and end the creation. As Preserver and Maintainer, Viṣṇu emerges as Protector and Redeemer in the Indian tradition, and that is why we find him here, in the *Gītā*, a likely candidate for Savior.

But what makes Viṣṇu God? As Kṛṣṇa, he answers the question in one of the passages quoted above: "Though unborn, for the *Ātman* is eternal, though Lord of all beings . . ."; that is, he is essentially *Ātman*, the Self, *Brahman*, the holy Power in the universe, a concept here carried over from the *Upaniṣads*. Viṣṇu is *Ātman* with all the essential characteristics of *Ātman*—an uncreated, wholly real, eternal, and pure being; it is that and that alone that makes him Lord and God. But, as we have already seen in the *Upaniṣads*, all men have *Ātman*, all possess that aspect of *Brahman* within them, and the *Gītā* simply accepts and continues this metaphysical assumption about the ultimate nature of man. In doing so, the *Gītā* makes it possible for all men to become Saviors in the very simple sense that all men are capable of satisfying this first necessary condition of the Savior Game.

### $C_2$ In some time and place trouble occurs: *adharma*

We are concerned here not so much with when and where the trouble occurs but rather with its nature as *adharma*. To begin with, the Indians believed, and the *Gītā* seems to have accepted this belief, that the chronology of the world can be divided into four quite distinct periods or ages. These periods, named after the four possible numbers one can get in casting an oddly shaped oblong Indian gaming die, are called *yugas* in Sanskrit. The first throw of the die yielded the side with four dots, and the golden age or *kṛta yuga* was born. Then, after 1,728,000 years, the next *yuga* began, the *treta yuga*, represented by the die with three dots. After 1,296,000 years the *treta yuga* ended and the *dvapara yuga* began, corresponding to the side of the die with two dots. After 864,000 years of the *dvapara yuga* the final age began, the period corresponding to the side of the die with one dot, the unluckiest throw of the whole game. That age is the *kali yuga*, the age that we are in now and that will last for 432,000 years. The *kali yuga* is the age of iron, the age of misery, trouble, pain, and suffering, and it is the age that encompasses the time described in the *Bhagavad Gītā*: *kali yuga* is the time of *adharma*.

The word *dharma* means many things in Sanskrit, as we saw in our discussion of the *Laws of Manu* and the four *arthas* (see pp. 91–92). It means "law," "rightness," "righteousness," "duty," "practice," and "vocation." It's a grand, busy word, and it has many jobs to do in Sanskrit—too many, in fact. Why didn't people hire a new word to help it out when they saw it would have to be so busy, putting in overtime, as it were, in so many different places? Working so hard, such words have the semantical equivalent of a nervous breakdown, and they cease to have any precise meaning. Becoming ambiguous (the name for this nervous verbal disease), they have to appear in public ever after dressed up in quotation marks. Other nervous words that suffer from the same semantic collapse spring to mind: "Freedom" and "free," "democracy," "God," "salvation," "communist" and "capitalist," "logical" and "valid," "truth" and "true," "happiness," "love." These are just a few examples of overworked, broken down, nearly meaningless, ambiguous, busy, busy words. Why do we work such words so hard? It's worth pondering.

Now, if *dharma* has all those meanings, we may expect *adharma* to have a lot, too. But oddly enough this doesn't seem to be the case. I want to take *adharma* to mean quite simply "unrighteousness." Here, "unrighteousness" will mean what happens when the laws of man and God, or the traditional laws of society, whatever they may be, are violated or transgressed. But they are not transgressed merely because the world consists of vicious, ruthless, and brutal violators and transgressors. For if man were that wicked, he would be beyond redemption, and the whole Savior Game would be impossible. Rather, *adharma* occurs because men have forgotten the *dharma*, the true law, and the function of the Savior is simply to remind men what the *dharma* was and to show them how to recover it. The Savior, then, is rather like a Socratic teacher who reminds his pupils, according to Plato, what the shock of birth has caused them to forget. Thus at the very end of the *Gītā* the grateful Arjuna says to his Lord and teacher: "My ignorance has been destroyed. I have been reminded of my duty through your grace. I now stand firm with all my doubts removed."[6]

Unlike the Socratic teacher, the Savior is God, and he speaks with an Authority beyond that of either the rational philosopher or the Socratic teacher. Interestingly enough, the method Kṛṣṇa uses to teach Arjuna is a version of the Socratic dialectic—the method of question and answer that

[6] *Ibid.*, XVIII.73.

Socrates used to elicit recollection from his associates. The aim of both dialectics would appear to be the same: to recall righteousness, truth, duty, and *dharma* to the mind of the troubled, doubting, and bewildered associate, *śiṣya*, or disciple.

> $C_3$ The Lord recognizes the trouble and responds to it by descending or crossing over into that time and place as (for instance) a man: *Avatār*

The *Avatār* is technically "one who crosses over," and what the Savior does is to move from heaven to earth by crossing over the metaphysical boundary that separates the two. It is important to realize, of course, that one may speak cogently of these matters at all sorts of levels of meaning. One can take heaven, like earth, as a place in space and time, and then interpret the "crossing over" quite literally. I see nothing disturbing in such an interpretation; many people take their Gods, heavens, and hells in precisely this straightforward way. The mistake lies in assuming that the literal is the only meaningful interpretation of religious symbols and mythology. At another level of interpretation one can take heaven, unlike earth, as a metaphysical level of reality or being that transcends space and time. At this point, then, one leaves the literal or religious interpretation of the Savior as well and moves on to a metaphysical interpretation. Or one can take heaven, the Savior, and *adharma* as states or conditions of consciousness or the self. When one "crosses over" on this interpretation or at this level of meaning, one moves from one state or condition of the self or inner being to another, just as one can move from deep sleep, to dreaming sleep, to wakefulness, or from a state of ignorance to knowledge, or from hallucination or illusion to seeing or understanding truly and clearly. We can then say—rather meaningfully, too—that one has crossed over from a lower to a higher state of knowledge or understanding, or of being or reality. All growth, all progress, is by stages such as this.

It would seem that the Lord must have two abilities in order to become *Avatār* or Descender. In other words, if Viṣṇu exists ($C_1$) and if *adharma* exists ($C_2$) then to turn Viṣṇu into an *Avatār*, to make him Kṛṣṇa, two other conditions must exists. First, the Lord must recognize the *adharma*; that is, he must know the time of unrighteousness is at hand, and so he must have certain powers of omniscience (recall our earlier discussion regarding Varuṇa and the paradox of total omniscience, p. 80). Second, the Lord must respond to what he does recognize; he must have the power to do something about what he recognizes (see above, pp. 80–82). This response, in turn, is manifold and complicated, for three questions or puzzles emerge.

First of all, does the Lord necessarily have to respond as an *Avatār* to *adharma*: is it automatic or cosmically necessary? Or does the Lord freely choose to descend and set the *dharma* right again? Is *Ṛta* or some other cosmic principle of order operative over and above even Viṣṇu, such that he cannot choose but to descend as *Avatār*? Or is the Lord moved by compassion and love for man and creation, moved by the suffering he sees, to descend and thereby make the crooked straight? The *Gītā* seems to take the stand that God freely chooses to descend in order to make the world safe for *dharma*, and this stand seems to be implied in Kṛṣṇa's statements to Arjuna: "[U]sing my own nature, I come into existence through my own *māyā*," and "For whenever there is . . . *adharma*, then I send Myself forth into the world."

But if the descent is freely chosen, a second puzzle emerges with respect to it. If the Lord freely chooses to come to earth to set things right because he feels compassion for man, then isn't the Lord's compassion singularly odd? For, on the one hand, the *adharma* surely stands as a just and equitable punishment for transgressions committed by man; turning things around, as Kṛṣṇa intends to do, is surely to fly in the face of just punishment and therefore justice, itself: Kṛṣṇa's coming forth is unjust. On the other hand, if Viṣṇu is driven into being the *Avatār* out of love, compassion and sorrow at man's dreadful suffering, then Viṣṇu in possessing these humanlike qualities of desire and attachment is as imperfect as the men he is trying so desperately to save. This latter point, call it "the paradox of the *Avatār*," simply holds that it seems impossible for a being who possesses desires and attachments, and is therefore imperfect, to attempt to lead other imperfect beings to perfection. We will have more to say about the paradox of the *Avatār* when we complete $C_4$ below.

A third puzzle that emerges with respect to the Lord's response to the *adharma* he recognizes is simply this: After the Lord freely chooses to be moved by his love for man—and, if he is nothing else, Lord Kṛṣṇa is surely a God of love—then he must make a body or vehicle for himself for his descent. The body must not be too low or too humble in the continuum of things (who would listen to the sermons of a cricket?) nor too grand and overwhelming (who would listen very long to a disembodied blinding light?). So a physical body is made and Viṣṇu comes to earth as Kṛṣṇa, a man. The descent into material existence constitutes, from the metaphysical point of view, a de-evolution, a reversal of the stages of progress on the metaphysical continuum. It is, consequently, a metaphysical imperfection, since it constitutes, it would appear, a falling back from a higher level into a metaphysically lower level of reality. Thus the paradox of the *Avatār* would seem to have a new dimension. If the Lord must make a body for himself in order to play the *Avatār*, doesn't the existence of such a vehicle as well as the descent for the Lord constitute an imperfection?

$C_4$ The *Avatār* teaches the way or ways out of the trouble: *yogas*

The Savior can save in at least two ways. On the one hand he could come, gather up any and all possible savees, and leave with them. Call this "indiscriminate salvation." On the other hand, the Savior could come, set conditions for salvation, gather up those who satisfy the conditions, and leave. Call this "discriminate salvation." With both indiscriminate and discriminate salvation one simply plays the Forgiveness Game either without or with conditions, respectively. But the Forgiveness Game for Viṣṇu, as well as for Varuṇa before him, placed specific conditions on salvation; hence we find discriminate salvation being espoused in the *Gītā*. Those specific conditions in the *Gītā* are the yogas, or the ways to salvation, of which four are enunciated and discussed (see pp. 158–69).

Return for a moment to our story. Lord Kṛṣṇa attempts to persuade Arjuna that he must do his duty and fight in the just war that confronts him. Arjuna responds that the so-called "just war" is really an unjust war, because the family he is bound by duty to defend is the same family he is bound by duty to fight; and fighting, as a way out of this peculiar dilemma, will earn him, by the law of *karma*, nothing but evil. Kṛṣṇa understands Arjuna's dilemma, and it would seem that there is no easy way out. If he fights, he's doomed because he'll be fighting his family. If he doesn't fight, he's doomed because he will have failed to do his duty as a *kṣatriya*. But he must either fight or not fight; there is no third way. Therefore he is doomed. That is Arjuna's dilemma, and he's apparently stuck with it. Arjuna says: "Far better would it be for me if, unarmed and unresisting, the enemy, Dhṛtarāṣṭra's sons, with their weapons in their hands, would slay me in the battle."[7] But, as have seen, this is not "far better" at all, as the dilemma above indicates and as Kṛṣṇa is quick to respond.

Kṛṣṇa points this out with a second dilemma, which we might simply call "the dilemma of action," and he elaborates it at some length. The dilemma of action presuppose three things. First it presupposes the law of *karma*, and the belief that all actions have results that are either good or bad, right or wrong. Second, it presupposes that all men must act, and that none can cease from acting. Third, it presupposes that the final or ultimate goal for all beings is to escape *saṁsāra*, the round of birth and death, in which all creation has become entangled. The dilemma of action is simply the universalization of Arjuna's dilemma previously mentioned, and, being universalized, it applies to all men, everywhere and for all time. In effect it says something like this: If one does good acts, this produces good results. If one does evil acts, this produces bad results. Good acts and bad acts will produce these good or bad results either in this life or a later one. Therefore, the ultimate effect of all acts, good or had, is bondage to future good or bad results—future necessary rewards or punishments. Therefore, no matter what one

[7]*Ibid.*, I.46.

does, one is in bondage. Putting it more simply: If you do good acts, you're doomed to be reborn to reap the rewards. If you do wicked acts, you're doomed to be reborn to reap the punishments. You must do either good acts or wicked acts; there is no third possibility (yet). Therefore, you are doomed to be reborn.

But there is a way out of the dilemma of action and hence a way out of Arjuna's dilemma as well. It involves a third possibility regarding acts—a way or manner or attitude of doing or acting that fails to produce the seemingly "inevitable" *karmic* consequences. The name for this third possibility is "*karma* yoga."

*Karma* yoga is introduced early in the *Gītā* simply because, given the nature of the self of the hero of the *Gītā*, it is that yoga most fitted for that hero's individual nature or *svabhava*. That is to say, *karma* yoga is the yoga for *kṣatriya* types of persons, and Arjuna is that type of person. Before describing *karma* yoga and the other three yogas discussed in the *Gītā*, we ought to look into three concepts introduced in the *Upaniṣads* but organized and related in an interesting new way in the *Bhagavad Gītā*. The three concepts are *guṇa*, *varṇa*, and yoga, and they and their interrelationships make for some fascinating feasts of reason. So let us adjourn temporarily (until p. 175) our discussion of $C_4$ and the yogas in order to look at three extremely important concepts.

### *a*) *The Three Guṇas*

Two late *Upaniṣads*, the *Śvetāśvatara* and the *Maitrī*, first introduced the doctrine of the *guṇas* into the *śruti* literature, probably shortly after 500 B.C.E. The doctrine of the *guṇas* may well have appeared slightly earlier in the doctrines of the philosophical system called *Sāṁkhya*, but dates at this stage are moot and the historical origins of the *guṇas* are probably not worth arguing about anyway. Whatever the origins, whether *Upaniṣadic* or *Sāṁkhya* this much is beyond debate: the doctrine of the *guṇas* has had a profound affect on practically all Indian thought (Buddhism being one notable exception) down to the present day.

One can see the thrust of the doctrine if one sees the *guṇas* as the three basic and essential properties, qualities, or characteristics that all things or processes must have in order to exist. In the *Maitrī Upaniṣad* the three *guṇas* are named and described: *Sattva guṇa* is the quality of purity, goodness, and rightness; the other two *guṇas*, *tamas* and *rajas*, are catalogued as well:

> The nature of the *tamas guṇa* is delusion, fear, depression, sleepiness, tiredness, forgetfulness, old age, sorrow, hunger, thirst, . . . anger, heterodoxy, ignorance, . . . stupidity . . . .
>
> The nature of the *rajas guṇa* is inner lusting, attachment, feelings, jealousy, outer lusting, maliciousness, hatred, . . .

> envy, insatiability, . . . distraction, ambitiousness, . . . hatred of the unpleasant and lusting for the pleasant . . . [8]

The *Gītā* follows this tradition of the *Upaniṣads* and *Sāṁkhya*, wholeheartedly accepting the doctrine of the *guṇas*. That doctrine can be summarized by three basic principles:

1. Every object in the universe is a compound of the *guṇas* which forms that object's *guṇa* nature.
2. The characteristics or qualities exhibited by an object are determined by the object's *guṇa* nature.
3. The *guṇa* nature of an object is determined solely by the quantity of *guṇa* present in the object, such that whatever *guṇas* are masked or dominated by another *guṇa* do not show their properties, and those that do dominate do show their properties.

Some examples should help to exhibit these three principles. Suppose we accept the belief that the three *guṇas* manifest certain opposing, contradictory characteristics: *sattva* is the *guṇa* or quality of lightness, illumination, truth, and knowledge; *rajas* is the *guṇa* of energy, passion, activity, and movement; and *tamas* is the *guṇa* of lethargy, laziness, inertia, and stupidity. Now, since everything that exists is simply a combination of these three *guṇas*, it should be possible to catalogue every object in the universe as predominating in one or another of these three qualities. The *guṇa* which predominates or dominates the other two *guṇas* reflects, then, the actual *guṇa* nature of the object, and the *guṇas* it masks are merely the potential *guṇa* natures of the object. Thus the book you're holding now predominates in *tamas guṇa*; it is just lying there, heavily, inertly, while you hold it, and whatever other *guṇas* the book contains (the ones being temporarily or permanently masked by *tamas*) are for the moment unnoticed and inactive. But hurl the book across the room, and suddenly it exhibits its *rajas guṇa*: it is in motion, in splendid activity as it speeds swiftly and surely to the wall. At the wall it suddenly reactivates its potential *tamas* nature and crash! bang! plop! it turns into its immobile, heavy old self again as it falls sluggishly to the floor. Take next the reading light by your chair. It exhibits *tamas* nature when off, but turned on its exhibits both *rajas* nature, as the light waves rush and charge energetically around the room, and *sattva* nature, as those light waves flashingly illuminate the darkness and make the room glow with their brilliance.

But physical objects are not the only entities that exhibit their *guṇa* natures: people do, too. Here the *Bhagavad Gītā* steers its speculative course into controversial seas, but in doing so it exhibits a philosophic acumen and

[8] *Maitrī Upaniṣad* III.5.

an insightful brilliance exemplified by few other comparable works. For the *Gītā* argues that all human beings can be divided or separated into three ideal classes of persons, and that what separates one class from another is that the people in those classes exhibit three quite separate *guṇa* natures or personalities. Let us work slowly into this subject by comparing a relatively modern psychological triadic classification with the triadic philosophy of the *guṇas.*

### *b*) *Somatotypes and Personality Types*

It makes a kind of intuitive sense to divide people into types, groups, or classes. It's handy for all kinds of reasons to classify people as Democrats, Republicans, and Independents; as conservatives, liberals, and middle-of-the-roaders; as Christians, Hindus, and Buddhists; as communists, capitalists, and socialists; as cool-tempered, hot-headed, and lazy-minded; and so on. But classifying people by ideology, temperament, and personality is a risky business. People don't generally wear their philosophy of life, their ideologies, or their personal beliefs on their sleeves for all to see and admire. You have to work hard to fit people into ideological, philosophic, or religious groupings, such as those above, even though the classes and the classifying might seem intuitively sensible and obvious.

Many classifications, however, are easily made. For example, we can very neatly classify people as blonde, brunette, and redhead; as tall, short, and medium; as white, black, and brown; as hairy, bald, and balding; as skinny, fat, and medium build, and so on. Fitting people into these categories is, most of the time, relatively easy. One simply peers, trusts one's senses, appeals to an empirical standard or rule, and, most of the time, quickly makes the classification. The classification of people according to how they look we can call "somatotyping"; while the classification of people according to political and religious beliefs and temperament we can call "personality typing." Somatotyping (from *soma*, the Greek word for body) is really a complicated and careful empirical classification of people according to their bodily differences and similarities. It is complicated because many kinds of measurements are necessary; still, it is far more accurate than classifying people according to their personalities. Suppose, however, that the personality one had, the kind of person one was psychologically, was related to the kind of body one had, such that if one knew one's somatotype one could immediately know one's personality type? This was precisely what the physician and psychologist William H. Sheldon proposed in his pioneer study of the relation of somatotypes to personality types. Sheldon's ingenious work and his intriguing hypothesis will provide us with an interesting approach to the study of the three *guṇas* and their relation to the *varṇas* and the *yogas.*[9]

[9]See William H. Sheldon, *The Varieties of Human Physique* (1940), *The Varieties of Temperament* (1942), and *The Varieties of Delinquent Youth* (1949). Reprinted by Hatmes Publishing Co., New York, 1970, 1969, and 1970, respectively.

Sheldon created the now-famous terminology of "ectomorphy," "mesomorphy," and "endomorphy" to describe what he hypothesized as the three ideal body types. I say "ideal," for Sheldon was working with possibles rather than with actuals—with ideal limits rather than with real or existing limits. By "ectomorph" Sheldon meant the body type most clearly represented by the tall, thin, fragile person; by "mesomorph," the muscular, athletic, heavy-boned person; by "endomorph," the soft-fleshed, rounded, fat person. Sheldon rated somatotypes on a scale from 7 to 1, with 7 standing for the most extreme exhibition of the trait and 1 for the lowest possible. A person's somatotype was ranked, then, according to three possible traits with each trait coded by a number, and each number ranging from 1 to 7. Thus every person was somatotyped by a set of three numbers, with each set of three standing for or measuring an individual's endomorphy (the left-hand number), mesomorphy (the middle number), and ectomorphy (the right-hand number). Thus a fat, fat person would be ranked ideally as 7/1/1; a muscled, athletic person would be ranked ideally as 1/7/1; and a thin, thin person would be ranked ideally as 1/1/7. Sheldon also adopted three geometrical figures to stand for endomorphy, mesomorphy and ectomorphy: and they are the circle, ○, the inverted triangle, ▽, and the vertical line, |, respectively.

Some historical examples have been suggested that would exhibit the kind of mixing of endo-, meso- and ectomorphy that are typical of actual citizens of the planet, since the ideal types mentioned above rarely occur. Thus Henry Kissinger would be about 6/4/3, Muhammad Ali perhaps 2/7/3, and Abraham Lincoln roughly 1/5/6.

In an extremely interesting article[10] Juan B. Cortes and Florence M. Gatti make use of a so-called "Self-Description Test" that allows one to discover one's own somatotype by answering six key questions about one's temperament. They argue (and the results are not, of course, unchallengeable) that on the basis of a simple test involving some eighteen predicates one can describe oneself temperamentally as well as somatically. If this kind of mental test were accurate, one could discover one's somatotype by knowing one's psychological character; or one could work in the other direction and predict what responses someone would give on such a Self-Description Test simply in virtue of knowing whether one was a 7/1/1, a 1/7/1, a 1/1/7, or some less ideal combination thereof. The results would be revealing for a student of oneself—and, of course, we are all continually trying to find out more about ourselves. More importantly for our purposes as students of Indian thought, it would be rewarding to take Sheldon's hypothesis about the one-to-one or constant relationship between somatotype and personality type and relate it to the doctrine of the *guṇas*. For if we could express endo-, meso-, and ectomorphy in terms of the *guṇas*, then we would have a simple

[10]"Physique and Propensity—for Achievement, Sex, Politics, Aggression, Religion, Crime, Esthetics, Economics, Sociality," *Psychology Today*, October 1970.

test for measuring the *guṇa* nature of each and every one of us. The next section will suggest that such a relation between *guṇa* nature and somatotypes is possible, and we shall see that taking this suggestion as a working hypothesis can lead to some fascinating results for students of the *Bhagavad Gītā.*[11]

### c) *Guṇatypes, Varṇas, and Yogas*

Now let us join up the personality types and somatotypes above with the *guṇas* of the previous section. First, let us see why the *guṇas* are so terribly important to the theory of salvation in the *Gītā*, and then we shall explore how and why somatotyping can fit into this picture in a helpful and meaningful way.

#### 1) Guṇas and Varṇas

From our previous discussion we know that the *Gītā* assumes everything is composed of combinations of the *guṇas* and that from these *guṇa* combinations all the qualities, characteristics, and modes of the world can be explained. Thus human personality must also be explainable in terms of the soul's or self's *guṇa* nature. Supposedly, therefore, one could explain the groupings of similar souls or selves under the rubric of the *varṇa dharma* system simply in virtue of the fact that all *brahmins* have the same general *guṇa* nature, all *kṣatriyas* have the same general *guṇa* nature, and similarly for all *vaiśyas* and *śūdras*. All this is precisely what the *Gītā* claims, as Lord Kṛṣṇa explains to Arjuna:

> There is no being on earth nor among the Gods in heaven that is free from the three *guṇas* . . . .
> Among all *brahmins, kṣatriyas, vaiśyas*, and *śūdras* . . . their karmas have all been allotted according to the *guṇas* born in their own natures.[12]

There follows a catalogue of the *guṇa* characteristics of the *brahmin* and *kṣatriya*, and a brief description of the proper activities for the *vaiśya* and *śūdra*. First, the *brahmin*'s *guṇa* nature:

> Serenity, self-control, ascetic discipline, purity, patience, and uprightness, true knowledge, practical knowledge, and religious faith, these are the natural dispositions of the *brahmin*.

[11]Before we begin the next section and our continuing discussion of $C_4$ and the yogas, please take The Personality Description Test in Appendix I, p. 280, a variation of the Self-Description Test mentioned above. Follow the directions, complete the test, and then look at The Key to the Personality Description Test in order to find out what your own somatotype formula might be. When you've found your three-digit somatotype, ask yourself whether you think the formula is correct.

[12]*Bhagavad Gītā* XVIII.40–41; see also IV.13.

Seond, the *kṣatriya*'s *guṇa* nature:

> Heroism, vigor, firmness, skill, not fleeing from battle, generosity, and lordly nature, these are the natural dispositions of a *kṣatriya*.

Finally, the *vaiśya* and *śūdra*:

> Agriculture, tending cattle, and trade are the natural dispositions of a *vaiśya*. And service is the natural disposition of a *śūdra*.[13]

It may seem a bit strange to speak of activities such as cattle tending as natural dispositions in the same context as such other *bona fide* qualities as serenity and heroism. For cattle tending and even agriculture in and of themselves do not seem to be qualities of human souls at all. But the implication may be that occupations such as agriculture, cattle tending, trade, and service are all expressions of self-qualities—that is, of one's *guṇa* nature. If one is a *vaiśya*, then one has a *guṇa* nature that finds satisfaction in the pastoral and trade occupations. If one is a *śūdra*, then one has a *guṇa* nature that finds fulfillment and happiness in service. This explanation of the juxtaposition of quality-talk with occupation-talk seems to be supported by the next *śloka*, which says: "Man reaches perfection by being devoted, each one, to his own special innate disposition."[14] The argument used in these passages is, then, simply this:

1. If one follows one's *guṇa* nature, then one will achieve happiness.
2. The *varṇa* one belongs to is the best indicator of what one's *guṇa* nature is.
3. Therefore, if one follows the *dharma* or vocation of one's *varṇa*, then one will achieve happiness.

Now it was an easy matter for the Indian of the epic period or the *Gītā* period to know what his *guṇa* nature was: he simply looked for its outward sign in the *varṇa* to which he belonged. Hence, if he was a *brahmin*, then *sattva guṇa* predominated in his self; if he was a *kṣatriya*, then *rajas guṇa* predominated in his self; and if he was a *vaiśya* or a *śūdra* (for the two have a similar *guṇa* nature), then *tamas guṇa* predominated in his self. The best confirmation for this hypothesis is to be found in the establishment of the three special yogas for each of these three *guṇa* natures. If men differ by nature, one from the other, it would be senseless to suggest that the *way* to ultimate happiness is to be identical for all three. Part of the rich insight of the *Gītā* lies in this singular recognition and acceptance of separate *guṇa* natures, separate and different personalities consonant with distinct and

[13] *Ibid.*, XVIII.42–44.

[14] *Ibid.*, XVIII.45.

nonoverlapping *dharmas* or vocations. It was a relatively easy move to the conclusion that there must be a distinct and separate yoga or way to human happiness, or to *mokṣa*, for each of these three distinct *guṇa* natures.

### 2) Guṇas and Yogas

The *Gītā* accepts wholesale the beliefs and concepts that were part of the *Upaniṣadic* tradition. But it adds to that tradition in an interesting and exciting manner. One of the putative aims of the philosophy of the *Gītā* is simply to enlarge, extend, and universalize the tradition inherited from the *Upaniṣads* in the same way that the *Upaniṣads* tended to enlarge, extend, and universalize the tradition it inherited from the *brahminism* of the *Vedic* period.

Thus *mokṣa* or liberation is still the goal for man in the *Gītā* as it was in the *Upaniṣads*; and *saṁsāra* still looms darkly as the alternative to *mokṣa* for the unsuccessful yogi searching for liberation; and the law of *karma* still stolidly stands as the mechanism underlying the principle of *saṁsāra*. But while the *Gītā* recognizes the techniques of the yogas as the ways to liberation and happiness, it extends the number of yogas to four by introducing two relatively new yogas into Hinduism (see pp. 105–6 for the discussion of *jñāna* yoga and *dhyāna* yoga in the *Upaniṣads*). Important reasons for the introduction of these two new yogas relate directly to, first, the new religiously enfranchised *śūdras*, previously neglected in the *Upaniṣads*, and second, the increase in the power of the *kṣatriyas*. In other words, the *Upaniṣads*, despite their revolutionary flavor and intent, remained essentially *brahmin* compositions. The *jñāna* yoga of the *Upaniṣads* was essentially a yoga for *brahmins*; and the other classes or *varṇas*, as well as the other noncaste or outcaste classes (see pp. 85–6) seemed to have been especially excluded from the official *Vedic-Upaniṣadic* religion. If these other classes had not existed, there probably would have been no need for reform. Buddhism and Jainism, to mention two religions of the pre-*Gītā* period, are prime examples of reformation religions; without these, there probably would have been no need for the *Bhagavad Gītā*. In fact, the *Bhagavad Gītā* might be seen as Hinduism's counterreformation to Buddhism and Jainism.

The two new yogas which the *Gītā* brings into Hinduism are *karma* yoga, or the way of spontaneous action, and *bhakti* yoga, or the way of devotion to a personal God. Let's have a look at them now.

### Karma Yoga

*Karma* yoga is designed for the active man, a man like Arjuna, a man of the *kṣatriya varṇa*. Recall "Arjuna's dilemma": Arjuna must act, but if he does, then the act will produce either bad consequences or good consequences, and both are binding. Thus action with consequences leads to bondage, which leads to *saṁsāra*, which leads to more bondage . . . the round of birth and death goes on and on without surcease. But yoga promises to break the cycle of rebirth; and *karma* yoga in particular does it by introducing a new technique of action. *Karma* yoga has been called "the way of actionless action"; it offers the man of action, the man with *rajas guṇa* nature, a way of acting in the world that does not lead to bondage. Lord Kṛṣṇa explains to Arjuna:

> Let your concern be with the act alone and never with its consequences. Do not let the consequences of the act be your concern, and do not be attached to inaction.
>
> Firmly fixed in *karma* yoga, perform your acts, renouncing attachments, indifferent to success and failure. This indifference is called *karma* yoga.
>
> Those endowed with unattachment to the consequence of action leave behind in this world both good and evil. Therefore unite yourself to [*karma*] yoga.
>
> The wise, united to unattachment, renounce the fruits which action produces, and freed thereby from the bondage of rebirth, they go to that place free from suffering.[15]

The *karma* yoga doctrine espoused by Kṛṣṇa for Arjuna is double edged, for it offers practical as well as religious advice. In discussing $C_4$, the fourth condition of the Savior Game, we ought not to overlook that aspect of *karma* yoga that stands as simple practical advice—advice that can produce immediate results right here, right now. All "religious advice" from a Savior is surely meant to have long-term results, preferably in the next life or the next metaphysical realm. But *karma* yoga can produce results here and now, and in this practical sense it has a certain similarity to *dhyāna* yoga; both are more obviously practical when compared to the other two yogas, *bhakti* and *jñāna.*

The practical advice contained in the *karma* yoga doctrine is simply this: don't worry. Worry can devour you and defeat you, for worry, anxiety, and fear are future-directed, consequence-oriented concerns, and those concerns about the future can gnaw at you, disrupt and ruin any chance you might have at a good performance in actions now. Suppose you are going to take an examination, bake a cake, or ride a bicycle. Suppose you're worried about failing or falling. Now that worry about the consequences of the present action can redound back on the action and ruin it. In other words, worry, concern, anxiety, and fear can make you fail the examination, ruin the cake, and tumble from the bicycle. So the practical advice of the *Gītā* is: learn the technique of *karma* yoga, let go of the results of your action, don't be concerned with consequences, and put all your talents and energies to work

[15] *Ibid.*, II.47–48, 50–51.

on the act itself; learn to give up the fruits of actions, be unattached from the future ends of action, the world, and the desires for things; give up thirstings and lustings and wantings. That is the kind of good practical advice that leads to true humility, true poverty, and true happiness. Recall the *karma* yoga advice of Jesus of Nazareth (4 B.C.E.–28 C.E.) to his disciples in the Sermon on the Mount:

> And he said unto his disciples: therefore I tell you, do not be anxious about your life, what you shall eat, nor about your body, what you shall put on. For life is more than food, and the body more than clothing.

And then, speaking feelingly and with all the authority of a good *karma* yogi, Jesus asks his disciples to regard and imitate the birds of the air and the flowers and grasses of the field:

> Consider the ravens: they neither sow nor do they reap, they have neither storehouse nor barn, and yet God feeds them. Of how much more value are you than the birds! And which of you by being anxious can add one cubit to his span of life?

The advice is practical, psychologically useful, down-to-earth, homely counsel on how to live well, without fear and distraction. Jesus continues:

> If then you are not able to do as small a thing as that [add a cubit by worry: one is reminded of Shakespeare: "Cowards die many times before their deaths; the valiant never taste of death but once"], why are you anxious about the rest? Consider the lilies, how they grow; they neither toil nor do they spin; yet I tell you, even Solomon in all his glory was not arrayed like one of these. But if God so clothes the grass which is alive in the field today and tomorrow is thrown into the oven, how much more will he clothe you, O men of little faith!

Jesus then reminds his disciples to be concerned only about what really matters, "the Kingdom of the Father"; then all the consequences ("these things") shall be added as well:

> And do not seek what you are to eat and what you are to drink, nor be of anxious mind. For all the nations of the world seek these things; and your Father knows that you need them. Instead, seek his Kingdom, and these things shall be yours as well.[16]

Jesus concludes his message with the famous words, "Fear not, little flock. . . ."

The Christian tradition contains further instances of this practical advice of *karma* yoga, advice undoubtedly intended as a propaedeutic, a

[16]*Luke* XII: 22–31.

necessary precondition, to the religious advice which is also a part of *karma* yoga: the anxious man in this world cannot be the religious man for the next world. Standing high in this Christian *karma* yoga tradition is the work of Meister Johannes Eckhart (1260–1327), the great German mystic and theologian. In one remarkable sermon, Eckhart analyzes the concept of "poverty" as used in the Beatitudes in Jesus' Sermon on the Mount. In particular, Eckhart's analysis is concerned with the beatitude "Blessed are the poor . . ." and the meaning of "poverty" in that context. Eckhart begins by distinguishing between outward and interior poverty:

> There are two kinds of poverty. One is outward poverty, and this is good and much to be commended in him who makes a voluntary practice of it for the sake of our Lord Jesus Christ whose wont it was on earth.

A nice point in social criticism, surely, for the wretched suffering poor of the world are for the most part the involuntary poor and not the poor, in any sense of word, of which Eckhart or Jesus speaks. He continues:

> About this [outward] poverty I shall say no more. But there is another poverty, an interior poverty. Whereto refers this saying of our Lord, "Blessed are the poor in spirit or poor of spirit." And I would urge you now to be this same if ye would understand my argument. . . .

Eckhart moves now to define and explicate the notion of "interior poverty and the truly poor man." He says:

> A poor man is one who wills nothing, knows nothing, has nothing. It is on these three heads that I propose to speak.

The analysis begins with Eckhart's picture of the Christian *karma* yogi:

> In the first place, a poor man wills nothing. Some folk mistake the sense of this; those, for example, who win personal repute by penances and outward disciplines (and are highly esteemed, God a' mercy, though knowing so little of God's truth!). To all outward appearance these are holy, but they are fools within and ignorant of the divine reality. These people define a poor man to be one who wills nothing. Explaining this to mean that he never follows his own will at all, but is bent on carrying out the will of God.

Eckhart may have something like "the Lord's prayer" in mind, here, with its affirmation, "Thy will be done," meaning "Let God's will be done." But Eckhart wants to go beyond even this in defining "the poor man." First, he pays an offhand compliment to the mistaken folk:

> In this they are not bad; their intention is good, and we commend them for it: God keep them in his mercy.

However, he takes them farther to task:

> But I trow that these are not poor men nor are they the least like them. They are much admired by those who know no better, but I say they are fools with no understanding of God's truth. Peradventure heaven is theirs by good intention, but of the poverty in question they have no idea.

Then Eckhart presents his own case for understanding the poor man, the Christian *karma* yogi, and in doing so he says something truly extraordinary:

> Supposing someone asked me, what then is a poor man who wills nothing? I should answer this. As long as it can be said of a man that it is in his will, that it is his will, to do the will of God, that man has not the poverty that I am speaking of because he has a will, to satisfy the will of God, which is not as it should be.

This could only be spoken by a mystic who has transcended religion itself. The more orthodox, of course, will see this as nothing but heresy, as apparently the Church did; a year after his death in 1327 Eckhart was condemned and his writings publicly burned.

> If he is genuinely poor a man is as free from his created will as he was when he was not [before he was born]. I tell you by the eternal truth, as long as ye possess the will to do the will of God and have the least desire for eternity and God [or any other desire for any other fruit or result of action, for that matter], ye are not really poor: the poor man wills nothing, knows nothing, wants nothing.[17]

Thus we have *karma* yoga and the *karma* yogi as the truly poor man described within the Christian tradition.

### Bhakti Yoga

Something extremely important is, in general, missing from the religion of the *Vedas* and *Upaniṣads*. It is so essential an element, many Indologists have argued, that without it the *Vedas* and the *Upaniṣads* are simply philosophical texts at most or primitive superstitions at the very least. What is missing, and what turns the philosophy of Hinduism into the religion of Hinduism, is better illustrated than talked about. Notice for yourself how the following verses differ from all the hymns or texts taken thus far from the Indian tradition, and I think you'll see what has been absent from the religion of the *Vedas* and the *Upaniṣads*. It is a moving and emotional cry from man to God spoken in the *Bhagavad Gītā*:

[17]Franz Pfeiffer, *Meister Eckhart*, trans. C. De B. Evans, two volumes (London: John M. Watkins, 1947), Vol. I, pp. 217–218. Reprinted by permission of the publisher.

> You are the Father of the worlds, of all that moves and does not move. You are the object of its worship and its greatest teacher. There is none equal to You, so how can there be one greater than You, even in the three worlds? Oh One of Unrivalled Might!
>
> Therefore, Revered Lord, bowing down and prostrating my body before You, grant me your grace. As a father to his son, as a friend to his friend, as a lover to his beloved, show mercy to me, Oh God.
>
> I have seen That which none has seen before. My heart rejoices but also quakes with fear. Oh God, show me once again Your form, be merciful, Lord of Gods, Resting Place of the Universe.[18]

What has been missing, of course, is the passionate, emotional, and affective-feeling side of the religious life: *bhakti* or devotion to a personal God. The *Bhagavad Gītā* begins a long tradition of Hindu devotionalism, and the plea quoted above comes from that tradition where we see the *bhakta*, the religious devotee, calling out to his beloved Lord Kṛṣṇa.

In the *Gītā* Lord Kṛṣṇa very plainly tells Arjuna that one of the ways he may attain to the highest happiness is by utterly and completely dedicating himself to the person of Lord Kṛṣṇa:

> Arjuna, you must see that my devotees never perish. For those who take refuge in Me, even though they are born from a womb of sin, even though they are women, *vaiśyas*, or even *śūdras*, they go to the highest goal.

It is important to remember, of course, that the yoga of devotion is designed primarily for the members of these two *varṇas*, the *vaiśya* and the *śūdra*, fitted as they are by their very *guṇa* nature for *bhakti* yoga. But men and women from other *varṇas* may follow the path of *bhakti* yoga as well, it would seem:

> How much easier then for holy brahmins and devout royal seers. This is a fleeting and sorrowful world; while you are in it, lovingly dedicate yourself to Me.
>
> Fix your mind on Me; be dedicated to me; sacrifice to Me; lay yourself devotedly before Me; discipline yourself and with Me as your Supreme goal, to me you will truly come.[19]

Arjuna is not told how he should turn himself into a *bhakta*, a devotee, a slave of the Lord, but enough hints are given by Lord Kṛṣṇa to make us realize that *bhakti* yoga entails the total surrender of the devotee to God:

> By bhakti he comes to know Me, what My measure is and Who I am in truth. Then having known Me truly he enters into Me immediately.

[18] *Bhagavad Gītā*, XI.43–45.

[19] *Ibid.*, IX.31–34.

> Mentally surrender all actions to Me, intent on Me alone, resorting to the yoga of the mind, have your thoughts now set only on Me.
>
> Focusing all your thoughts on Me, you will overcome all difficulties by My grace. . . .[20]

The *bhakta* takes refuge in God, where comfort and tender divine care renew his strength for life in the sorrowing world. Lord Kṛṣṇa continues:

> The Lord lives in the hearts of all beings, Arjuna. By his *māyā* he causes all beings to turn about as if they were dangling on a string.
>
> Flee to him for shelter with your entire being. By His grace you shall attain the highest peace and the eternal goal.[21]

For in virtue of the devotee's loving Lord Kṛṣṇa, the Lord returns that love to his *bhakta*:

> Listen once more to My supreme message, the highest secret of all. You are truly My beloved and so I will tell you what is best for you.
>
> Merge your mind with Me, be my *bhakta*, sacrifice to Me, prostrate yourself before Me, and you shall come to Me. I promise this to you truly for you are always dear to Me.
>
> Abandoning all duties [*dharma*], come to Me alone for refuge. Be not sorrowed for I shall give you liberation from all sins.[22]

A question might naturally occur to the reader at this point, since it was raised earlier in our discussion of the Forgiveness Game (see pp. 81–82): Can I, by my devotion and dedication to Lord Kṛṣṇa, force him to give me liberation from all sins? In other words, is Lord Kṛṣṇa free or not free to dispense liberation from sins? For it would seem that he is compelled, if he is just, to save the devotee who is truly devoted; but as a just Savior, he would seem to be ensnared, entrapped, or bound into playing the Savior Game. A dilemma can be constructed from this puzzle; call it "the Savior dilemma": If I am devout and can as a result compel the Savior to forgive me, then the Savior is not free. On the other hand, if I am devout and this does not compel the Savior to forgive me, then the Savior is capricious. Either my devotion compels the Savior's forgiveness or it does not. Therefore, either the Savior is not free or the Savior is capricious. The reader is left to mull over this Savior dilemma.

We can conclude this discussion of the second of the new yogas, *bhakti* yoga, introduced in the *Gītā*, by stating once again that it is designed primarily for the *varṇas* with *tamas guṇa* nature; *bhakti* yoga is the yoga for

[20] *Ibid.*, XVIII.55, 57–58.

[21] *Ibid.*, XVIII.61–62.

[22] *Ibid.*, XVIII.64–66.

the *vaiśya* and *śūdra varṇas*. Both the *vaiśya* and the *śūdra varṇas* coalesce, therefore, as far as *tamas guṇa* is concerned. The self or soul of the *vaiśya-śūdra* possesses a preponderance of the *guṇa* of *tamas*, just as previously the self or soul of the *kṣatriya* possessed a preponderance of the *guṇa* of *rajas*. And just as the yoga of action was appropriate to the *kṣatriya varṇa*, so also, now, the yoga of devotion is appropriate to the *vaiśya-śūdra varṇa*.

The other two principal yogas of Hinduism, *jñāna* yoga and *dhyāna* yoga, are also included in the *Gītā*, and we shall note below the place that the *Gītā* gives to these two yogas as well.

### Jñāna Yoga

As in the *Upaniṣads*, *jñāna* yoga is the way of knowledge to *Brahman*, *mokṣa*, and the highest happiness (see above, pp. 105 and 124f.). One comes to know that the *Brahman* immanent in oneself, called *Ātman* or Self, is identical with the *Brahman* or holy Power that transcends the universe. In other words, in knowing that immanent *Brahman* (*Ātman*) is ultimately and actually trancendent *Ātman* (*Brahman*), one attains to the Highest. By apprehending the true nature of the Self as *Brahman*, one attains *mokṣa*, release, or liberation from *saṁsāra*. This closely parallels the Stoic way to happiness. The *Gītā* thus follows the *Upaniṣads* in accepting this yoga. Once again, Lord Kṛṣṇa says to Arjuna:

> Only through the destruction of ignorance by *jñāna* of the *Ātman*, only by that will true knowledge (*jñāna*) shine forth like the sun, revealing the Highest.
>
> Thinking on That, merging the Self with That, making That the sole aim and object of their devotion, they reach a state from which there is no returning, their sins destroyed by true knowledge.[23]

One further query might be raised here. Why, in what is primarily a text on *karma* yoga for *kṣatriyas* or persons with *rajas guṇa* nature, is there a disquisition on *jñāna* yoga, since *jñāna* yoga obviously suits the temperaments of those persons with *sattva guṇa* nature? We shall return to this question later.

We have seen that the *Gītā* holds that the three yogas—*karma*, *bhakti*, and *jñāna*—are *varṇa*-specific; that is, each of these ways to eternal happiness, *mokṣa*, *nirvāṇa*, or the highest (the *Gītā* is ambiguous on the nature of the final goal) is meant to be used by persons with differing self-natures or *guna*-natures: by *karma* yogis with *rajas guṇa* nature, by *bhakti* yogis with *tamas guṇa* nature, and by *jñāna* yogis with *sattva guṇa* nature. The great universal, and I stress *universal*, message of the *Gītā* is that there is no one way, no one path, to heaven, God, the ultimate, the absolute, or liberation; on the con-

[23] *Ibid.*, V.16–17.

trary, the ways or yogas are suited to the many possible varieties of human temperaments. One of the closest Western parallels is the controversy between Roman Catholics and Protestants over "faith" and "works" as ways to God. The Roman Catholics seem to stress work—sacrifice, ritual, and moral activity—as the chief ways to God, Heaven, or Christ; the Protestants in turn stress faith in Christ as the chief way. This is an old controversy that goes back to the history of the early Church in Jerusalem. After the execution of Jesus, the Jerusalem center of the movement he had founded and led was temporarily thrown into panic. The disciples seem to have fled for their lives, gone underground, or behaved generally in a cowardly way—recall St. Peter's earlier three-time denial of his Lord—in the face of local as well as Roman persecution. After a time Jesus' brother, James, attempted to bring the group together, but squabbles broke out among the older disciples; a new upstartish convert to the movement, a former persecutor of the Christians named Paul of Tarsus, assumed leadership of some of the dissidents. Peter and Paul could not agree on a number of points relating to what one had to do or be in order to become a Christian. Peter insisted that only Jews could be Christians, while Paul strenuously denied this. Peter insisted that male converts to Christianity had to be circumcised; Paul strenuously denied this. And Peter insisted that the way to the Kingdom of Heaven was through the way of works—works of mercy and love, and works involving the rites and sacrificial rituals of Judaism—but Paul strenuously denied this, saying that faith in Jesus Christ and Christ crucified was enough for salvation. The rift between these two giants of the early Church was apparently healed, but the seeds were already sown for later heresies and schisms, the Reformation and Counter-Reformation, and the dozens of major and minor religious wars between the followers of the early theologies of St. Peter on the one hand and St. Paul on the other.

Now who is right? Which is the true way, the best way, the superior way—the "Roman Catholic way" of works or the "Protestant way" of faith? A neat resolution, of course, is the one we find espoused in the *Gītā*. One simply looks to one's own *guṇa* nature, finds out which *guṇa* stands in preponderance there, and then picks out the appropriate yoga or way from there. We will return to this matter in our discussion of *Gītā darśana* (pp. 194–223).

By stressing multiple ways to God, by showing that the adoption of any particular way depends on personality or *guṇa* nature, and that there is consequently no *one true way*, no absolute, final, and only way to God, one avoids all talk about orthodox and heterodox religions, one avoids talk about superior ways and superior religions, one avoids religious wars, bloodshed, hatred, and discrimination based on religious origins. Perhaps relations between India and Pakistan, Israel and the Arab world, and Protestant and Catholic Ireland would all be different today if this broad and open religious relativism had been accepted and adopted.

In answer to our previous question—why does *jñāna* yoga (and *bhakti* yoga as well) suddenly surface here in the *Gītā*, alongside the *karma* yoga which Arjuna must follow?—we can simply say this: the message in the *Gītā* is truly and spectacularly "universal." It is meant for all possible types of persons, and Arjuna represents only one type. Since all beings possess all kinds of *guṇa* natures, it is quite possible, furthermore, that the yogas, which after all are *guṇa*-nature-specific, were meant to be practiced in some sort of combination. Thus, while pure *kṣatriyas* would practice only *karma* yoga, what of those *kṣatriyas* whose *guṇa* natures contained high proportions of both *rajas* and *tamas guṇa*, or of both *rajas guṇa* and *sattva guṇa*? Might they not practice some sort of integrated yoga, consisting of some combination of *karma* yoga and *bhakti* yoga, or some combination of *karma* yoga and *jñāna* yoga? And might it not be the same with the other *varṇas*, and with other men and women in those *varṇas* as well as with those outside of them? If this did in fact happen, we would have not merely three yogas for the four *varṇas*, but some eight different possible combinations of yogas for the eight logically possible types of *guṇa* natures. I leave the reader to work out the arithmetic of such a set, merely noting two things: there is nothing in the *Gītā* to warrant all these possible combinings, but there is nothing specifically against them either.

### Dhyāna Yoga

*Dhyāna* yoga must seem, at first glance, a curious kind of extra yoga that isn't needed to get the yoga doctrine off and running. But in fact it serves as a necessary preliminary, as I shall argue, to the proper practice of the other three yogas (see above, pp. 105–6). *Dhyāna* yoga, or the yoga of meditation, is the one that is most popular in the West today, largely through the efforts of such organizations as the Krishna Consciousness Movement of Swami Bhaktivedanta, the Self-Realization Fellowship of Swami Yogananda, and the Transcendental Meditation movement of Maharishi Mahesh Yogi. But the *Gītā*, like all of the traditional texts of Hinduism, is remarkably close-mouthed on precisely what one must do in order to practice *dhyāna* yoga [or "*rāja* yoga," as it is popularly called, an easy method of religious meditation fit for kings (*rājas*) to practice]. Here, in the following passages, is practically all that the *Gītā* really says about the art of *dhyāna* yoga. First, the breathing:

> Closing out all external objects, focusing the eyes between the eyebrows, making equal the inhalation and exhalation of the breath through the nostrils,
>
> The yogi who meditates with his senses, mind and reason controlled, who is intent on *mokṣa* and who has cast out desire, fear, and anger, he is already released.[24]

[24] *Ibid.*, V.27–28.

Then comes a description of the place and position of meditation:

> The yogi should practice ceaselessly to discipline his mind, seated in a quiet place, alone, controlled within and without, free from desires and possessions.
>
> In a clean place, let him sit on a comfortable seat that he has put there, neither too high nor too low, that has been covered with sacred grass, a skin, and a cloth.
>
> Sitting there let him make his mind concentrated on a single object, with his thoughts and senses controlled, practicing yoga for the purification of the self.
>
> Let him sit, holding the body, head, and neck straight and steady, raising his eyes up to the base of the nose, not letting them wander about.
>
> Let him sit, his self serene and without worry, firm in his vow of chastity, his mind under control, his thoughts on Me alone, intent on Me alone.
>
> The yogi with his mind thus under control, attains to peace and ultimately to that supreme *nirvāṇa* which rests in Me.[25]

The passages seem to say a great deal, and in truth they tell us much about what one can expect from the practice of meditation. But they really say very little or even nothing about that practice itself: the secret of meditation remains intact.

Curiously enough, *dhyāna* yoga can be seen as an interesting Indian version of the Epicurean way to happiness, for they both depend, however briefly, on leaving the busy, noisy, rushabout, tumble-upon world. That is to say, *dhyāna* yoga—temporarily at least, and then for longer and longer periods as the practice becomes internalized and automatic—shrinks the outside world and makes it less important by reminding the yogi, first, that there is another internal world that is more important and that warrants his attention, and, second, that the external world is less meaningful, less important, and in the long run, perhaps, less real than the internal world of the Self.

The *Bhagavad Gītā* does not try to blend or combine the yogas in any way. Instead, we find passages such as the following, which would appear to imply not only a clear separation between the several yogas, but also an ordering in terms of superiority of one to the other. Remember that Lord Kṛṣṇa is speaking to Arjuna:

> Perform actions for My sake alone, and you shall attain perfection.
>
> But if you are unable even to do this, then take refuge in My yoga: renounce the fruit of action with the self under control.
>
> For *jñāna* is better than practice; but better than *jñāna* is *dhyāna*; and better than *dhyāna* is the renunciation of the fruits of action, for with renunciation there comes immediate peace.[26]

[25] *Ibid.*, VI.10–15.

[26] *Ibid.*, XII.10–12.

From what we've seen earlier in the *Gītā*, and from the fact that Kṛṣṇa is advising a *kṣatriya* here, this ordering of the yogas is only natural. For underlying this relativity of the yogas is a corresponding *guṇa relativism*, as we have already observed; certain *guṇas* predominate in certain *varṇas*, necessitating specific yogas to control and to minister to the activity of those *guṇas* and *guṇa* natures. Thus the last *śloka* is saying, in effect (and here I paraphrase unscrupulously):

> For *jñāna* yoga is better for you, Arjuna, than practice (constant effort), but better than *jñāna* for you is *dhyāna*; and better for you than all these other yogas is *karma* yoga, which is the way best suited to your *guṇa* nature.

But all the yogas are equally efficacious in reaching "perfection," whether heaven or *mokṣa*, as the *Gītā* is at some pains to point out. Again Kṛṣṇa says:

> By *dhyāna* some perceive *Ātman* in the self by the *Ātman*. Others by the yoga of knowledge, and others by *karma* yoga see *Ātman*.[27]

Thus, as we have argued previously, *dhyāna* yoga really has three functions. First, it is a psychological exercise for calming the mind; second, it is a necessary condition for practicing the other three *yogas*; and third, *dhyāna* yoga is a *bona fide* way to perfection, in and of itself. We shall have more to say about this entire business shortly.

One final question remains to be answered in our discussion of $C_4$ and the place of the yogas in the *Bhagavad Gītā*. If we grant that the yogas are specific to certain *guṇa*types or *guṇa* natures, and if we grant that one can discover one's *guṇa* nature and thereby the appropriate yoga for oneself by simply looking to the *varṇa* in which one was born, then what is a modern classless *varṇa*less person to do who has no such happy empirical indicator of his or her *guṇa* nature? That long question comes down simply to this: granted the importance of finding out who I am, so I can seize upon the yoga that is right for me, how is this to be done? We attempt an answer with a concluding section on the *guṇa*types and the somatotypes.

### *d*) *Guṇatypes and Somatotypes*

Examine once again the problem that faces us in the *Gītā* with respect to the yogas. The goal of human existence is still liberation or perfection. The way to that goal is yoga, and we have seen that there are four such yogas. Three of them, furthermore, are each appropriate to one particular *guṇa* nature. The fourth yoga, *dhyāna*, is appropriate as a possible necessary preliminary to each of the other yogas, as well as being a *bona fide* way to liberation in and of itself. The *guṇa* nature one has is the result of one's previous life; one inherits one's *guṇa* nature from that previous life; and one's

[27] *Ibid.*, XIII.24.

*guṇa* nature, finally, determines which *varṇa* one will be in. Now we can proceed back up through these statements, from *varṇa* to liberation, in the following summary way: If one knows one's *varṇa*, then one's *guṇa* nature is similarly known. If one's *guna* nature is known, then one's appropriate yoga is also known. If one's appropriate yoga is known, then one can follow that appropriate yoga. If one follows that appropriate yoga, then one will eventually reach liberation. We can conclude from all of this: if one knows one's *varṇa*, then one will eventually reach liberation.

Now, as we've indicated, the Indians with their caste-class-occupation-*varṇa* society have or had little trouble discovering their *varṇas* and thereby satisfying the first condition of the above sorites (a chain of syllogistic arguments). But other societies and other cultures in other times and places have not been so fortunate. Where class and caste are known, of course, or where soul-nature is knowable, there is no problem in discovering yogas or ways to the goal or goals of life. But knowing one's *varṇa* by the empirical method established by the Indians is surely, if all the other assumptions about the selves within that *varṇa dharma* system are correct, one of the most foolproof and obvious ways of discovering the nature of the self. I would like to mention another Indo-European self-discovery technique that roughly parallels the Indian scheme. This other technique is still used today, with some modifications, for classifying selves, hence it might give to us and other *varṇa*less, casteless drifters and seekers of the world, some insight into how we too might discover who we are, what our own *guṇa*-nature is like, that we might take up our appropriate yogas and travel the road to liberation and happiness—provided, of course, that we could accept all of the other assumptions of the religion of the *Gītā*. I want to use this second empirical technique, first introduced explicitly by Plato of Athens (427–347 B.C.E.), as an introduction to a third empirical technique for discovering who you are and what your soul nature is really like. This third empirical technique is, of course, the method of the somatotypes which we'll get to shortly.

### 1) Plato's Way Out

Plato, in his masterpiece called *Republic* (see above, pp. 56–57), sets out to establish a utopia [which can mean either "best place" (*eu-topos*) or "no place" (*ou-topos*)]. He does this by banishing all adults from his society and then raising the children in accordance with certain programs of study. At various stages in this program there will be physical and mental examinations to determine whether or not the child or adolescent or young adult, man or woman, will go on to the next level or drop out. The drop-outs take up the vocation or activity best suited to their natures or souls at that particular level. If they go on, they have a chance to learn, study, work, and live at more advanced levels, where further examinations (not necessarily written or oral) are expected and given. The citizens are being tested and categorized by their teachers in a fashion not unlike that carried out in contemporary social and educational environments.

Plato believed that his society would work for the benefit of all, if the following four assumptions could be accepted:

1. Each person has a distinct soul nature.

This is the assumption that the *Bhagavad Gītā* has made, of course. Plato believed that people were naturally divided by the following three basic soul natures. The first was the rational soul; the intellectual and the thoughtful and the naturally contemplative person had this soul nature. The second was the spirited soul; the pugnacious and naturally active person had this soul nature. If you think these classifications sound familiar, they ought to, for the *guṇa* natures of the *Gītā* and the soul nature of the *Republic* directly parallel each other. The third was the appetitive soul; the money-loving and gain-loving soul, and the naturally material-object-loving person had this soul nature. Plato assumed, furthermore, that each soul contained within itself parts of all three of these natures. In each soul, however, either its rational or its spirited or its appetitive part predominated, and that part determined the entire soul nature of each individual. The parallel to the *guṇa*-nature doctrine of the *Gītā* is striking, right down to and including Plato's belief in transmigration: that one's present soul nature is a consequence of one's previous lives and is directly inherited from those previous lives.

A second assumption that Plato seemed to accept is the following:

2. Whenever a person is living according to his soul nature, then he is happy.

If a man with a preponderance of the quality of reason in his soul is living and working at a vocation for which he is fitted by that soul quality, then he will be happy. At this point Plato joins three specific vocations to the three soul natures. Corresponding to the soul that is predominantly rational is the vocational class of the philosopher-kings, those fitted by their natures to rule, teach, and carry on the business of government. Corresponding to the soul that is predominantly spirited and active is the vocational class of the guardians and defenders, those fitted by their natures to protect and defend the people and the state. Finally, corresponding to the soul that is predominantly appetitive is the vocational class of the artisans, merchants, farmers, and peasants. Thus the vocational and social classes of the state are a direct result of the nature of the multiple selves or souls making up that state.

Socrates, the chief speaker in Plato's *Republic*, summarizes these findings to his friend Glaucon, pointing out that justice in the state as well as harmony and happiness in the soul come, in the end, to the same thing: each person and thereby each class doing what it is best fitted by its own nature to do.

> And so, after much tossing, we have reached land, and are fairly agreed that the same principles which exist in the State exist also in the individual, and that they are three in number.
> Exactly [Glaucon says].
> Must we not then infer that the individual is wise in the same way, and in virtue of the same quality which makes the State wise?
> Certainly.
> Also that the same quality which constitutes courage in the State constitutes courage in the individual, and that both the State and the individual bear the same relation to all the other virtues.[28]

And Glaucon agrees. The other virtues that Socrates has in mind, which parallel the virtue of courage for the defender or soldier with a spirited soul, are wisdom for the soul of the philosopher-king and temperance or self-control for the artisan-merchant. Socrates had previously argued that each of the three soul natures, the rational, spirited, and appetitive, had a specific end or goal that it pursued or ought to pursue, if it would be happy. The rational soul should seek and love wisdom; the spirited soul should seek and love honor; and the appetitive soul should seek and love gain; and these three ends become specific or particular for each type of soul. Socrates continues, with his friend Glaucon agreeing all the way:

> And the individual will be acknowledged by us to be just in the same way in which the State is just.
> That follows of course [Glaucon, again].
> We cannot but remember that the justice of the State consisted in each of the three classes doing the work of its own class?
> We are not very likely to have forgotten, he said.
> We must recollect that the individual in whom the several qualities of his nature do their own work will be just, and will do his own work?
> Yes, he said, we must remember that too.
> And ought not the rational principle, which is wise, and has the care of the whole soul, to rule, and the passionate or spirited principle to be the subject and ally?
> Certainly.[29]

Socrates refers to the kind of education that was used in identifying the classes of souls and thereby the classes of men. In particular, music and gymnastic, along with other devices and methods, serve to select out the various classes. This brings us to the third presupposition of Plato's *Republic*:

3. A person's specific soul nature can be empirically discovered.

[28]*Republic* 441c, d, in *The Dialogues of Plato*, B. Jowett, trans., two volumes (New York: Random House, 1937), Vol. I, p. 705.

[29]*Ibid.*, 441d, e.

Here is where the educational-selection process goes on, of course.

We continue, now, with Socrates' description of the parallel between the just or happy soul and the just or happy State:

> And, as we were saying, the united influence of music and gymnastic will bring them into accord, nerving and sustaining the reason with noble words and lessons, and moderating and soothing and civilizing the wildness of passion by harmony and rhythm.
>
> Quite true, he said.
>
> And these two [the rational and the spirited parts of the soul], thus nurtured and educated, and having learned truly to know their own functions, will rule over the appetitive which in each of us is the largest part of the soul and by nature most insatiable of gain; over this they will keep guard . . . lest the appetitive soul, no longer confined to her own sphere, should attempt to enslave and rule those who are not natural-born subjects, and overturn the whole life of man.[30]

Plato's educational plan was patterned somewhat as follows. Up through the age of 15 all citizens were to be taught reading, writing, music, the arts, and gymnastic. From 15 to 17 or 18 years of age mathematics, the key to Plato's "higher education," was introduced. By the age of 15 the few who were unsuited by nature to the higher education would begin to drop out. These were the artisans and farmers. By the age of 17 still more would have fallen by the educational wayside, unsuited by nature for the roles of warrior or ruler-teacher-philosopher-king. From 18 to 20 years of age, a strenuous course in military and physical training selected out the warrior-guardians. From 20 to 30, fewer still advanced on through the disciplines of the higher mathematics, still the key to knowledge for Plato. From 30 to 35, fewer still were ready for the advanced work in dialectic and pure reasoning that Plato had readied to train the intellect together with the theoretical study of advanced principles in morality. Finally, while those philosophers who fell by the wayside up to this point were fitted for lower levels of teaching, political, moral, social, and philosophic work, a very select few struggled on. From 35 to 50 years of age, these select few received practical in-service training in the business of running the State. At the age of 50 or thereabout these few became the aristocrats who reached the vision of the ultimate, mystical idea of the Good. Thereafter they devoted themselves to study and scholarship as philosophers, and ruled and directed the State as kings: these happy few became the philosopher-kings of Plato's great vision:

> Until philosophers are kings, or the kings and princes of this world have the spirit and power of philosophy, and political greatness and wisdom meet in one, and those commoner natures who pursue either to the exclusion of the other are compelled to stand aside, cities will never have rest from their evils—no, nor the human race, as I believe. . . .[31]

[30] *Ibid.*, 441e–442a, b., pp. 705–706.

[31] *Ibid.*, 473d., p. 737.

We move on, finally, to the last of the assumptions of Plato's utopia:

4. Therefore to be happy a person must discover and live according to his specific soul nature.

Here Plato's argument really ends: to be happy, to live well, let reason rule your soul, and find out what vocation your soul nature best fits you for. All men can be happy—the philosopher-king when he is wise; the guardian-defender when he is courageous; the artisan-farmer when he is temperate. And, Plato argues, only when reason rules the soul and guides the other two parts, the spirited and the appetitive, only when this kind of balance is maintained, is the soul (or the state) happy (or just). Hence the importance of finding out who you are—what your soul nature is—so that your vocation can be adjusted to your soul nature. For man is only happy when doing what he is fitted by nature to do.

Plato's doctrine of the soul and his early contribution to the theory of natural law have served us here simply as a parallel to the doctrine of *guṇa*-natures in the *Gītā*. I introduced such a parallel for two reasons: first, to show that the *guṇa*-nature doctrine is not as terribly silly as it might appear at first blush; for here is a rather serious and well-known Western philosopher who is saying something very similar; second, to provide an easily understandable empirical transition into a rather modern technique for determining the nature of one's self or soul in order that we, too, may search for happiness (if we're Platonists) or liberation (if we're Indians). But Plato's empirical test of the nature of the soul, or the *Gītā's* empirical test of the nature of the self, the first by examinations, the second by *varṇa*, are no longer available as tests or criteria to most contemporary soul-seekers or self-seekers. However, another test, which parallels both the Platonic and the *Gītā* way to self-discovery, is available, and I wish to return finally to that test by offering a discussion of somatotyping as a useful and likely candidate to replace the now lost Platonic and *Gītā* techniques.

### 2) Somatotyping as a Way Out

The proposal I have in mind is extremely simple. I merely wish to suggest, quite hypothetically, that there is a strong correlation between one's somatotype and one's *guṇa*-nature. After the manner of Plato's tests, we also have a test for determining self nature and vocational choice (see above, pp. 154ff., and Appendix I, p. 280). Further, after the manner of the *Gītā*, we have a fairly good description of the three *guṇa*-natures (see above, pp. 156ff.). We have now only to bring these two matters together, from Plato and the *Gītā*, to solve the problem of knowing our own *guṇa*-natures, and knowing them empirically. What we have to do is to show that a correlation exists between the three somatotypes (endo-, meso-, and ectomorphy), and a set of personality predicates and a set of *guṇa* predicates (see Appendix II, "The Table of Predicates," p. 283); then we argue that if the personality type is known (and it is known hypothetically, if you took The Personality Description Test in Appendix I), then the *guṇa*-nature and the yoga appropriate to it can also be known (by virtue of the sheer similarity between the two sets of personality predicates and *guṇa* predicates in Appendix II); we conclude that by knowing somatotype alone, one can determine the yoga appropriate to oneself.

Let us put this as crudely and simply as we can: As a result of knowing how you are built physically—endomorph, mesomorph, or ectomorph—you can tell how you are built mentally. And knowing how you are built mentally, you can tell how you are built in terms of the *guṇas*, whether with a preponderance of *tamas*, of *rajas*, or of *sattva guṇa*. And knowing how you are built in terms of the *guṇas*, you can tell what your appropriate yoga is: *bhakti*, *karma*, or *jñāna* yoga. Therefore, as a result of knowing how you are built physically, you can tell what your appropriate yoga is. Those interested in this empirical test are invited to turn to Appendix II, "The Table of Predicates," and analyze the results of the test taken in Appendix I, "The Personality Description Test."

3) CONCLUSION

This completes our discussion of the yogas and with them $C_4$, the fourth of the necessary conditions for playing the Savior Game. Let the reader recall what we are attempting here in our discussion of the religion of the *Bhagavad Gītā*. We have noted four of the five necessary conditions that must be present if one is going to have a Savior, whether in the *Gītā* or elsewhere:

$C_1$ A Lord or God exists. In the *Gītā* this is, of course, Viṣṇu, who incarnates as Arjuna's charioteer-cousin, Kṛṣṇa.

$C_2$ In some time and place trouble occurs. The *dharma* wavers and grows dim. Human suffering and pain increase as *adharma* grows.

$C_3$ The Lord recognizes the trouble and responds to it by descending into that time and place as, for instance, a man. Thus the *Avatār* or Savior is born, in this case Lord Kṛṣṇa.

$C_4$ The Savior teaches the way or ways out of the trouble. Thus the yogas are enunciated and the religion is born. I remind the reader that this is the section we have just finished.

We now conclude the discussion of the religion of the *Gītā*, which lies essentially in the Savior Game and its five necessary conditions, by mentioning the fifth and final necessary condition for that Game:

$C_5$ The Lord then returns to the place from which he came, but leaves behind his message about the way: *Bhagavad Gītā*.

If the religion is to outlast his birth, then a record of his teachings must survive. If the teachings did not survive in the *śruti* or, as with the *Gītā*, the *smṛti*, then the record of the Savior's ways out of the trouble would be lost and the Savior Game could not be played. A Savior, in other words, who speaks, teaches, or preaches to an audience that does not orally or scripturally pass the message along either to themselves or others, is no Savior at all: a Savior to be a Savior must be a remembered Savior. Furthermore, the Savior must leave the world and return to his previous Godlike form in the place from which he came, or he would be a permanent God-in-residence and not a Savior. A Savior who hung around generation after generation would merely be a divine freak and not a *bona fide* Savior.

Lord Kṛṣṇa concludes his message by counseling Arjuna regarding the disposition and use of the message he leaves behind:

> What I have given to you should not be spoken by you to one who is without a disciplined mind and body, nor to one without devotion, nor to one who is disobedient or who speaks against Me.
>
> But whoever shall teach this supreme secret to My *bhaktas*, having shown the highest *bhakti* to Me, shall without a doubt come to Me.
>
> There is none among men who does dearer service to Me than such a one, nor shall there be any dearer to Me in the whole world.
>
> And he who studies this sacred dialogue of ours, by him I shall be worshipped through the sacrifice of true knowledge, this I say truly.
>
> And the man who merely hears it, full of faith and without scoffing, will be liberated and attain to the fair worlds of those of virtuous deeds.[32]

And thus ends the message that Lord Kṛṣṇa has for the world.

The conditions necessary for the Savior Game are now complete. The Savior Game emerges as the central theme of the religion of the *Bhagavad Gītā*. It has its roots in the *Vedas* in the figure of Varuṇa, the divine Forgiver, and it extends its trunk, branches, and leaves out of the *Vedas* to influence the two major religious schools of Hinduism: the *Vaiṣṇavite*, which includes the devotees of Lord Viṣṇu; and the *Śaivite*, which includes the devotees of Lord Śiva. These *bhakti*-emotional-religious elements had probably lain buried in the non-*Vedic* rites of the indigenous peoples of the Indian subcontinent and had remained officially outside the intellectualized and formalized religion of the *Vedas* and the *Upaniṣads*. But they surface in the *Gītā* and become, from this time forward, a recognized and essential part of the religion of Hinduism.

This completes our discussion of the religion of the *Gītā*. We turn next to its metaphysics and epistemology.

[32] *Bhagavad Gītā*, XVIII.67–71.

## 3. THE METAPHYSICS AND THE EPISTEMOLOGY OF THE *BHAGAVAD GĪTĀ*

In the *Bhagavad Gītā*, two metaphysical and epistemological systems compete for the hearts and minds of the sensitive philosopher. These two systems (later called "*darśanas*") are inconsistent with one another and yet they are merged in the *Gītā*, where a strong philosophical attempt is made to get them to live peaceably and harmoniously together. Whether they can be happily harmonized depends completely on the interpretation one gives to the *Gītā*, a venture that we shall attempt shortly. The two systems are the *darśana* called "*Sāṁkya*" and the *darśana* called "*Vedānta*." Let us explore each of these extremely important philosophical systems and see how they are woven together in the *Gītā* and what comes from that weaving.

### *a. The Sāṁkhya Darśana*

The word *darśana* is from the Sanskrit root $\sqrt{}$*dṛś* which means "to see"; hence *darśana* has come to mean "a view" or "position" in philosophy—"a philosophic point of view." *Sāṁkhya darśana* traces its roots back to its founder, Kapila, who may have lived sometime in the seventh century B.C.E. The basic tenets of the system are found scattered in the *Śvetāśvatara Upaniṣad*, other later *Upaniṣads*, and the *Bhagavad Gītā*. These scattered elements are finally systematized in a rather formal way in the fourth century C.E. by the best known of the early *Sāṁkya* philosophers, Īśvarakṛṣṇa. The text he has left us is the famous *Sāṁkhyakārikā* ("treatise on *Sāṁkya*").

The *Sāṁkhyakārikā* opens with the momentous words, "From the torment of pain there arises a desire to know how to stop all pain." The *Sāṁkhya darśana*, like all the other traditional Indian *darśanas*, is primarily a practical, therapeutic undertaking: both the *āstika* and the *nāstika darśanas*[33] have been established for only one purpose—to put an end to human suffering and pain. To this extent Indian speculative philosophy stands in stark contrast to most Western philosophy, which, far from having the eradication of misery as a goal, generally has no aim or goal beyond sheer intellectual or aesthetic delight or the exercise of the reason for reason's sake alone. Yet this charge that Western philosophy is goalless or aimless is not quite fair. For Plato had pointed out quite early in the career of Western (or Greek or

[33]This is a conventional distinction in Indian philosophy. The orthodox or Hindu or *āstika darśanas* accept the authority of the *Vedas* and the *Upaniṣads* as the foundation for their views of the self, the Gods, and the world. These *āstika darśanas* include the following: *Sāṁkhya*, *Yoga*, *Nyāya*, *Vaiśeṣika*, *Mīmāṁsā*, and *Vedānta*. The heterodox or *nāstika darśanas* reject the ultimate authority of the *Vedas* and the *Upaniṣads*. These *nāstika darśanas* include Cārvāka-materialism, Buddhism, and Jainism. Even *Cārvāka* seemed to be founded to show man the way to worldly happiness.

European) thought that man is happiest and at his psychological and emotional best when he is exercising his reason; and since that rational condition is man's happiest state, and since philosophy involves the exercise of that reason, one could well conclude that speculative philosophy does produce happiness, and that it does provide for the release from torment and pain. Thus it would seem that, on this Platonic interpretation, Western and Indian speculative philosophy must be pursuing a similar goal: the cessation of pain and suffering.

This similarity between Western and Indian speculative philosophy may be extended even further to a discussion of the attitudes of mind through which the goals of each are reached. For the mental attitudes by which the Hindu *darśanas* achieved their goals are remarkably similar to those that Greek speculative philosophies used. Thus neither *mokṣa* (or heaven) nor happiness (or pleasure) is achieved by going out and straightway desiring the former and searching for the latter. Rather, these states or conditions of *mokṣa* and happiness are the epiphenomenal results or by-products of doing something else well. For example, no one gets up in the morning and honestly says, "Well, today I'm going out and search for happiness." In fact, intentionally searching for happiness is a sure way of never finding it. And the same thing can be said about *mokṣa* (recall "the paradox of *mokṣa*," pp. 99–100). In other words, the Hindu and the Western speculative philosopher reach the two conditions by precisely similar means: by forgetting about the goal and doing something else well (such as practicing yoga or exercising the mind).

Finally, one basic difference between Western and Indian speculative philosophy ought to be mentioned. For the Indian, the condition that ultimately comes about as a result of doing yoga well is a final and permanent state: *mokṣa*; while for the Westerner the condition that comes about as the by-product of philosophic activity may be merely a temporary and impermanent state: happiness. In other words, once Indian *mokṣa* is reached, one need not search for it again; while once Western happiness is reached, it must be sought for again and again. So while *mokṣa* and happiness, or liberation from pain and the achievement of happiness, may be similar with respect to the attitude necessary to reach those goals, they are quite different with respect to the quality or nature of the goal itself.

If the *Sāṁkhya darśana* seeks to lead suffering mankind to release and happiness, then how is this to be done? To answer this question, let us turn to the cause of the suffering described in the *Sāṁkhya* philosophy and briefly examine the nature of the metaphysics that underlies this cause.

The *Sāṁkhya* system of philosophy consists of an ultimate metaphysical dualism, which holds that there are two kinds of basically real stuffs in the universe: *puruṣa* (spirit) and *prakṛti* (matter). Regarding *puruṣa* the *Sāṁkhya-kārikā* says:

> XIX. . . . the spirit is observer only, and possesses isolation and neutrality; it is the seer and is wholly inactive.[34]

*Prakṛti*, on the other hand, is referred to as "primal nature" or "nature" or "matter"; from *prakṛti* the entire creation or universe, the world of producers and the produced, evolves:

> III. *Prakṛti* is not produced [has not evolved]; but the seven substances [rational will (*mahat* or *buddhi*), individuation, and the five subtle elements described below], are both producers [giving rise to other things out of themselves] and produced; the sixteen others [five sense organs, five action organs, mind, and five gross elements] are thereby produced. But *puruṣa* is neither a producer nor produced.

By a curious process *puruṣa* "entices" *prakṛti* into activity by "dancing before it," with the result that *prakṛti* is induced to go from an unmanifest state of pure potentiality into manifestation, pure activity or evolution; as a result the worlds are brought forth.

Furthermore, the *Kārikā* speaks of a plurality of spirits or *puruṣas*, all obviously identical in some sense, which are capable, somehow, of being deceived by the produced or evolved entities, and in such a way that they, these *puruṣas*, come to mistakenly identify themselves with the manifested creation of *prakṛti*. This deception is bondage:

> XX. And from this deception [the indentification of the spirit with the evolved *prakṛti*] two things happen: insensible and unintelligent body [*prakṛti*] appears as if it were sensible and intelligent; similarly, from the activity that really belongs to the attributes [the *guṇas* of the evolved entities], the *puruṣa*, which is neutral, appears as if it were active.

In his commentary written on these passages from the *Kārikā*, the *Sāṁkhya* philosopher, Vācaspati Miśra (about 975 C.E.), says of this bondage:

> The spirit, while in union with the "enjoyable" Nature, believes the three kinds of pain [internal, external, and divine sources of pain], the constituents of Nature, to be his own; and from this [self-imposed bond] he seeks liberation, isolation . . . .

Vācaspati then describes the route to liberation:

> . . . this isolation [liberation] is dependent upon due discrimination between the spirit and the three attributes [the *guṇas* of *prakṛti*]; this discrimination is not possible without the Nature . . . thus it is that for his own liberation the spirit needs Nature.[35]

[34] *Sāṁkhykārikā*, author's translation.

[35] The translation is by Ganganatha Jha, *The Tattva-kaumudī* (Vacaspati Miśra's Commentary) (Poona, 1934) in S. Radhakrishnan and Charles A. Moore, eds., *A Source Book in Indian Philosophy* (Princeton: Princeton University Press, 1957), p. 433.

Thus, curiously enough, bondage is due to the spirit's being entranced with nature, and yet it is only through this source of its entrapment that release can be found. From this initial union of *puruṣa* and *prakṛti*, the two metaphysically ultimate stuffs of the universe, comes the evolution or manifestation of the rest of the entities and the resultant bondage of all beings.

I want to turn to a few of these evolved entities because they will help to explain further the notion of the ego, that counterself or counter-Spirit that we mentioned earlier, and it will help us to focus on the mechanism of transmigration in *Sāṁkhya*:

> XXII. From *prakṛti* issues rational will, from this issues *ahaṁkāra* [ego principle]; from this ego proceeds the set of sixteen; from five of this set of sixteen proceed the five gross elements.

In other words, the totality of all that is real and is not *puruṣa* now evolves from the actuated *prakṛti*. The evolution looks something like this: from *prakṛti* comes *mahat* or rational will; from *mahat* comes *ahaṁkāra*, the ego or self-consciousness; from *ahaṁkāra* comes the set of sixteen entities [see items in Table III marked (S)], and from five of these sixteen come the five gross elements (ether, air, fire, water, and earth); the set of sixteen entities is made up of the *manas* or mind [which receives sense impressions and which, together with both the *mahat* and *ahaṁkāra*, compose the three internal organs marked (I)] plus the five subtle elements (which produce the five gross entities mentioned above), plus the five senses, plus the five organs of action. All of these sixteen elements, in turn, are evolved from *ahaṁkāra* by way of the three *guṇa* natures that compose the *ahaṁkāra*; these sixteen entities as well as the five gross entities are categorized according to the *sattva*, and *tamas guṇas* of the *ahaṁkāra*.

The *Sāṁkhya* system of cosmic evolution is important to all later Indian cosmological theories, especially to the *Gītā*, so it is worth the trouble it takes to get it straight. Accordingly, the reader is invited to refer to Table III and the four comments that follow:

*Comments*

1. S's designate the set of sixteen (items 5 to 15).
2. T's designate the entities that transmigrate from one body to another, and this transmigrating "subtle body" consists of eight entities (items 3 to 5 and 16 to 20).
3. I's designate the three internal organs (items 3 to 5).
4. The driving force behind the development of the creation from *ahaṁkāra* is *rajas guṇa*. (Items 5 to 15 have *sattva guṇa* nature and items 16 to 25 have *tamas guṇa* nature.)

TABLE III. SĀMKHYA COSMOLOGY

1. *Puruṣa* disturbs 2. *Prakṛti* into activity and evolution begins:

3. *Mahat* or *Buddhi* (T, I)

4. *Ahaṁkāra* (T, I)

5. *Manas* (S, T, I)

*Five Senses:* (S)
6. eye
7. ear
8. nose
9. tongue
10. skin

*Five Organs of Action:* (S)
11. speech
12. arms
13. reproductive organs
14. heads
15. feet

*Five Subtle Elements:* (S, T)
16. sound
17. touch
18. color
19. taste
20. odor

*Five Gross Elements:*
21. ether
22. air
23. fire
24. water
25. earth

Two things are to be noted here: first, the *ahaṁkāra*, and second, the five subtle elements which produce the five gross elements. The *ahaṁkāra* is the principle by which the ego or self is individuated. Notice that this ego or self is not *puruṣa* or spirit. Further, the subtle elements form one of the sets of entities which make up the transmigrating or subtle body:

> XL. The subtle body was the first body formed from *prakṛti;* it can enter into anything, it is permanent and is composed of *mahat*, *ahaṁkāra*, *manas*, and the subtle elements, and it is what migrates, devoid of experiences, but nonetheless invested with dispositions.

Thus the subtle body is composed of rational will, ego, mind, and the five subtle elements. Vācaspati, commenting on this *kārikā*, informs us that the subtle body was the first body to evolve from *prakṛti* and that for each *puruṣa* or spirit there is one subtle body, showing again that spirit and subtle body are taken to be different entities; further, this subtle body is so constituted that it could enter into a piece of stone; and finally, it continues to exist from first evolution to the final dissolution, thus displaying its permanence. Vācaspati continues:

> "It migrates" [means] the subtle body goes on deserting and occupying one six-sheathed physical body after the other.[36]

And why does it thus migrate? Because it is devoid of experience and can only have experience when it is connected with a body. And why does it want experience? Because it is connected with the will, and the will has certain dispositions and desires for experience that drive it; and these dispositions—virtue, vice, wisdom, ignorance, passion, dispassion, power, and weakness—invest the subtle body and thereby drive it on as well.

The *puruṣa,* standing in entranced witness to this awesome, fantastic cosmic evolution, like a child glued to a TV set, attaches itself somehow to all this hurly-burly activity and, as a result, its bondage begins. And liberation might be said to begin when the subtle body, the vehicle of the transmigrating self, first experiences pain, for at that same moment *puruṣa* which, in its deluded state now identifies itself with that same subtle body also experiences pain:

> LV. So in this world the *puruṣa* experiences the pain arising from old age and death, a pain due to the *puruṣa's* delusion that it is really the subtle body; thus pain is of the nature of this subtle body.

Pain, in a sense, turns the *puruṣa* around. For just as the evolution of *prakṛti* has been for the sake of liberating the multiply deluded spirits, so now the pain that is experienced by each spirit through the subtle body is also a pain for the sake of liberating each individual deluded spirit:

> LVI. The evolution of *prakṛti,* from *buddhi* right down to specific beings, is for the sake of the deliverance of each and every individual *puruṣa.* Thus *prakṛti* evolved not for its own sake, really, but for that of the others.

Nature or *prakṛti* thus appears as a kind of selfless but unwitting Savior, evolving and bringing pain in order that the deluded *puruṣas* might be saved:

> LVI. Just as the unknowing milk flows in order to nourish the calf, so does *prakṛti*'s flow cause the liberation of *puruṣa.*

Kapila, the author of these *Kārikās,* continues with a description of this liberation using two rather curious similes:

> LVIII. The evolving *prakṛti* works for the liberation of the *puruṣa* in the same way that people make their desires cease by satisfying them.

[36]*Ibid.,* p. 438.

> LIX. In the same way as a dancer, having shown herself to the audience, ceases dancing, so also does *prakṛti*, having displayed herself to *puruṣa*, cease her activity.

And he concludes:

> LX. Thus does generous *prakṛti*, endowed with the three *guṇas*, bring about the good of the *guṇa*less *puruṣa*, but without any reward for herself in return.

Kapila then states a principle that will have the most far-reaching effects throughout later Indian thought but that, in itself, must seem rather paradoxical at first glance:

> LXII. It is certain, consequently, that no *puruṣa* is really bound, nor is it liberated, nor does it transmigrate. But, rather, it is really *prakṛti*, with its vast and many forms of being, which is bound, liberated, and transmigrant.

The point is that in its ignorance, in its state of delusion, the *puruṣa* believes it is bound, liberated, and transmigrant. But its bondage is as illusory and unreal as its liberation. Commentators who have misunderstood this passage tend to forget that bondage in *Sāṁkhya* is delusion and cannot be, therefore, in any sense of the word, real or actual. To make this point more clearly, let us distinguish between two kinds of bondage that can obtain between spirit and body, or between *puruṣa* and *prakṛti*, or better yet, for our purposes here, between *puruṣa* and subtle body. Let us call the first kind of bondage "the entombment theory of bondage" and the second "the enchantment theory of bondage." We shall examine each in turn, exploring their relevance to the *Gītā*.

**1) The Entombment Theory of Bondage**

The most outstanding supporters of this theory of bondage are found in classical Greece among the Pythagoreans, Plato, and the neo-Platonists, as well as among many early, and even modern, Christians. And, as a misinterpretation of *Sāṁkhya*, I suspect the entombment theory can be found in the *Bhagavad Gītā* as well. But for an excellent exposition of entombment let's look at the philosophy of Plato.

In the dialogue, *Phaedrus*, Plato through Socrates speaks of the relation between the soul and the body, likening the latter to a prison in which the soul has become "bound fast as an oyster in its shell" (250c). In another dialogue, *Cratylus*, Socrates uses a similar analogy but broadens the image and attributes what we are calling "the entombment theory" to the ancient Orphics:

> For some say that the body is the grave of the soul which may be thought to be buried in our present life. . . . Probably the Orphic poets were the inventors

of the name, and they were under the impression that the soul is suffering the punishment of sin, and that the body is an enclosure or prison in which the soul is incarcerated, kept safe, as the name *soma* implies. . . .[37]

Finally, in the *Phaedo*, the *locus classicus* for Plato's discussion of the nature of the soul, the entombment theory receives its most eloquent formulation. Socrates, who is about to be executed by the Athenian state, is discoursing on the liberation and immortality of the soul. He turns to the role that philosophy plays in this liberation and draws for us the following sketch of the soul's imprisonment in the body:

Every seeker after wisdom knows that up to the time when philosophy takes it over his soul is a helpless prisoner, chained hand and foot in the body, compelled to view reality not directly but only through its prison bars, and wallowing in utter ignorance.

And philosophy can see that the imprisonment is ingeniously effected by the prisoner's own active desire, which makes him first accessory to his own confinement. Well, philosophy takes over the soul in this condition and by gentle persuasion tries to set it free.[38]

The entombment theory would seem to necessitate, then, three things: a soul, a body, and a prisoner-relationship between them. Thus this theory calls for one real imprisoning body for each real imprisoned soul, and multiple imprisoning bodies with their multiple imprisoned souls, giving us an metaphysical pluralism of a most radical sort.

A parallel to this Platonic metaphysical pluralism can be found in the Indian tradition as well, and one need only take certain passages from the *śruti* at their literal face value to see the pluralism working in this fashion. In the *Kaṭha Upaniṣad*, for example, *Ātman* is described as a Rider in a chariot: if we take the metaphysically pluralistic point of view, the passage can be read as follows:

You must know that *Ātman* rides in the chariot of the body,
The *buddhi* [intelligent will], you must realize, is the
chariot driver, and *manas* [mind] is the reins.

The senses, they say, are like the horses, and physical
objects are the things that these senses, these
horses, range over.[39]

But the question arises, Is the Self a prisoner in the chariot? Is the Self there

[37] *Cratylus*, 400c, in Jowett, trans., *The Dialogues of Plato*, Vol. I, p. 190.

[38] *Phaedo* 82e–83a, trans. Hugh Tredennick, in Edith Hamilton and Huntington Cairns, eds., *The Collected Dialogues of Plato* (London: Penguin Books Ltd., 1959), p. 135. Copyright © Hugh Tredennick, 1954, 1959.

[39] *Kaṭha Upaniṣad* I.3.3–4.

by choice or by compulsion? Does It travel willingly or not? Perhaps the best answer to these questions is found by asking another question: would the cosmos be better off if the Self were not in the body?—a question to which the *Upaniṣads* and the *Gītā* would seem to answer in the affirmative; and to this extent, and to this extent only, the real Self is a "prisoner" in a real body.

This ends our discussion of the entombment theory of bondage. Strictly speaking, it has only one precise parallel in Indian thought, and that is in the philosophy of Jainism. For, by and large, all Indian *darśanas* draw their analogy of bondage from the theory that we discuss next.

**2) The Enchantment Theory of Bondage**

In this second of the theories of bondage, the self is deluded into believing it is something that it is not. In the Indian philosophic tradition this position is classically represented in two *āstika darśanas*: the *Sāṁkhya* and the *Vaiśeṣkia.* Here, for example, is a description of the self from the latter system that displays the enchantment theory of bondage rather well. It is a commentary by one Śrīdhara from his *Nyāyakandalī* (991 C.E.) on a fifth-century work by the *Vaiśeṣika* philosopher Praśastapāda. Here is what Śrīdhara says about the nature of the self and its bondage; its similarity to *Sāṁkhya* must seem all too obvious:

> In reality the Self is neither the doer nor the enjoyer; it is wholly indifferent. And it is only when it becomes connected with such limitations as those of the body and the sense organs that it comes to have such notions, as "I" and "mine," of its being the doer and the enjoyer; and such notions cannot but be regarded as false; as they represent things as what in reality they are not. From these notions of "I" and "mine" follow an affection for the pleasant, and aversion to the unpleasant thing. . . .

There follows hard upon this affection and aversion a chain of causal events that leads directly and eventually to *saṁsāra*:

> . . . these affections and aversions give rise to activity and cessation from activity; thence follow *dharma* and *adharma*; and this lands the self into the cycle of birth and rebirth. . . .[40]

This *Vaiśeṣika* account of the deluded self's relations to the world is rooted, as we mentioned, in the earlier *Sāṁkhya* tradition. In that earlier tradition the enchantment theory of bondage is described in a most graphic way—as, for example, in the *Sāṁkhyakārikā*, where it is pointed out that the bondage of the self or *puruṣa* is illusory: the *puruṣa* was never in bondage at all; the prison was really an illusion of its own making, and, as a consequence,

[40]The translation is by Ganganatha Jha (Allahabad, 1916) in Radhakrishnan and Moore, eds., *A Source Book in Indian Philosophy*, p. 417.

the way to liberation consists simply in knowing this truth about the delusion:

> LXIII. *Prakṛti* by herself binds herself by seven forms [virtue, passiveness, power, vice, ignorance, passion, and weakness]; she causes deliverance for the benefit of *puruṣa* by a single form [knowledge].
>
> LXIV. From the study of the truth knowledge is finally reached which is complete, pure, and certain and which says, "I do not exist, nothing is mine, there is no ego."

And knowing this the deluded self, the *puruṣa*, becomes liberated. It turns away from erroneous knowledge and in that act becomes freed from enchantment and delusion:

> LXV. In this way *puruṣa*, now quiet and at ease, sees *prakṛti*, which then ceases its activities because it has been seen by the *puruṣa*:
>
> LXVI. The *puruṣa* thinks, "She has been seen by me," and *puruṣa* thus loses all interest. The *prakṛti* thinks, "I have been seen," and *prakṛti* ceases all activity.
>
> LXVII. As a result of this attainment of perfect knowledge, virtue and the other causes of bondage cease to be real causes at all; but the *puruṣa* continues to be associated with the body just as a potter's wheel continues to whirl by the sheer momentum of a previous impulse.

Thus the liberated self continues in association with the body even though the delusion has dispersed. The influence of many of the *Sāṁkhya* doctrines, from the enchantment theory itself to the nonreality of ego—an *anātman* doctrine of sorts—to the analogy of the potter's wheel and the actions of the *jīvanmukta* (one who is liberated while still living), are strong and persistent influences on both later Indian Buddhism and the metaphysics of the *Bhagavad Gītā*. Thus it is that Indian Buddhists will cry, echoing *Sāṁkhya*, there is no bondage, no way to liberation, and no liberation.

But it is in the *Bhagavad Gītā* itself that the enchantment theory receives the most direct philosophic treatment. For the *Gītā* claims that all activity is the result of the *guṇas* (*prakṛti*) acting on the *guṇas*, and that the Self (*Ātman*) is not active at all; hence how can the Self ever be truly bound by actions? But—and this is the point—the Self can be as deluded about the *guṇas* in the *Gītā* as the *puruṣa* was deluded by *prakṛti* in *Sāṁkhya*. The *Gītā* says:

> All actions are everywhere produced by the *guṇas* of *prakṛti*. He whose Self is deluded by the ego imagines, "I am the doer."
>
> But he who knows the truth about the separation between the *guṇas* and action, that man knows that all actions are merely *guṇas* acting on other *guṇas*. And knowing this, he is not bound by his actions.[41]

[41] *Bhagavad Gītā*, III.27–28.

But if the *Gītā* follows *Sāṁkhya* on the enchantment theory of bondage, it will find itself adopting or being committed to several embarrassing and *apparently* inconsistent doctrines. We shall look at five such doctrines. First, *Sāṁkhya* argues—contrary to *advaita* or monistic *Vedānta*, as we shall note below—that there is a plurality of selves:

> XVIII. From the separate allotments of birth, death, and the bodily organs, from the fact of many different actions all going on at the same time, and from the different proportions of the three *guṇas* in many different bodies engaging in action, from all this it certainly follows that there is a plurality of *puruṣas*.

And yet, as we shall see, the *Gītā*, also wants to hold the *advaita Vedānta* theory that *Brahman* alone is real, that *Ātman* is identical with *Brahman*, and that its own metaphysics is monistic rather than pluralistic. A second inconsistency that emerges hinges on the ability of *puruṣa* or *Ātman* to become deluded. The *Sāṁkhya*, as we've seen, holds that *puruṣa* can possess this imperfection, but the *Gītā* cannot consistently maintain this if, once again, it wishes to identify the Self with *Brahman*; indeed, the *Gītā* agrees with *Sāṁkhya* that *Ātman* does not act, but it also appears to argue that no properties, including being deluded, can belong to or be attributed to *Ātman*. The question then naturally arises: can the enchantment theory apply consistently to the *Gītā*? Here is the *Gītā* speaking about the nature of *Ātman*. Lord Kṛṣṇa says to Arjuna:

> The imperishable holy Self, though seated in the body, being beginningless and *nirguṇa*, It neither acts nor is It acted upon.
>
> Just as the omnipresent spatial ether contains bodies but is not affected by those bodies because of its minuteness, so also the Self though present in every body is not affected by the body.[42]

And thus it would follow that if the Self is beyond being affected, it surely cannot be "deluded" or "enchanted," and yet the *Gītā* plainly seems to hold to the enchantment theory. So, who's enchanted?

A third puzzle involving inconsistency develops as a consequence of attributing the enchantment theory of bondage to the *Gītā*, and it follows hard upon the second difficulty mentioned above. If the Self is deluded and if the cause of Its bondage is ignorance, and if the Self is nonetheless *nirguṇa* and unaffected by the body, then how can It be released, if It is released; and how can It reach the knowledge, if It does reach the knowledge, that releases It from the bondage of enchantment and delusion? It can neither become anything (liberated) nor cease to be anything (enchanted), for that would be inconsistent with the *ślokas* quoted above.

At this point one might defend the *Gītā* somewhat as follows: "You have missed the point. The enchantment is not real, just as the bondage is not real, therefore the Self does not move from bondage to enlightenment. It was

[42]*Ibid.*, XIII.31–32.

never in a condition of ignorance (*avidyā*) to begin with for the simple reason that it possesses no properties at all (it is *nirguṇa*); hence it can never become or change or alter—there is nothing to become, change, or alter." If this were the response to our criticisms of inconsistency, then it would seem that the enchantment theory is inapplicable once again as an explanation of the nature of the bondage one finds in the *Gītā*. But the *Gītā seems* to speak inconsistently to this point also. This constitutes a fourth puzzle with which we must then wrestle. See what Lord Kṛṣṇa says about the Self or *Ātman* being a friend to the self in this passage and then try to make it consistent with the *nirguṇa* doctrine touted in the reply above:

> Let a man raise his self by his *Ātman*, and let him not lower himself. For only the *Ātman* is the friend of the self, and only the *Ātman* can be the enemy of the self.
>
> The *Ātman* is a friend to him who has conquered the self by that *Ātman*, but for him who has not conquered the self, that *Ātman* will be hostile to him, like an enemy.[43]

A fifth and final difficulty, which raises a further problem of consistency with respect to the message of the *Gītā* and the enchantment theory of bondage, is this: if the enchantment theory is the theory of bondage espoused or assumed in the *Gītā*, then, as *Sāṁkhya* has stated, one escapes this delusion by abolishing the ignorance or *avidyā* of the delusion by way of true knowledge; but if one escapes delusion and is liberated from enchantment by true knowledge, then the only yoga that would be useful for that purpose is *jñāna* yoga; but if *jñāna* yoga is the only yoga appropriate to the enchantment theory of bondage, then this renders the other three yogas mentioned in the *Gītā* nugatory or useless. In other words, if the enchantment theory stands, then the yoga of this theory must make the other three yogas unnecessary. But this would be inconsistent with the fact that the *Gītā* does promulgate, preach, espouse, and recommend *dhyāna* yoga, *bhakti* yoga, and *karma* yoga. But to what end?

Given these five puzzles, then, it would seem that the enchantment theory of bondage must be regarded as a problematic assumption in the *Gītā* with respect to the Self and its relation to the body. But the alternative, the entombment theory of bondage, is surely even more problematic, simply because it would tend to make the body real. There may be other alternatives, however, than either entombment or enchantment, or there may be other alternative theories of bondage that are refinements of one or another of the two theories already mentioned. These are possibilities that should be kept in mind as we look to the second philosophical system that directly influenced the *Gītā*—*Vedānta*—and in particular the monistic variety, *advaita Vedānta*.

[43] *Ibid.*, VI.5–6.

### *b. The Vedānta Darśana*

The second *darśana* that has been found comfortably ensconced in the *Gītā* is *Vedānta. Vedānta* itself, you'll recall, means "the end (*anta*) of the *Vedas*," hence "the end or concluding portions of the *Vedas*." Since those concluding portions are the *Upaniṣads*, it follows that *Vedānta darśana* means "the philosophy of the *Upaniṣads*."

In order to explain clearly the *Vedāntic* or *Upaniṣadic* metaphysical elements that appear to find their way into the *Gītā*, I want to briefly review five basic metaphysical assumptions of the *Upaniṣadic* philosophy and indicate the ways in which the *Gītā* adopts or modifies or struggles with these five assumptions. Then we shall conclude the entire discussion of the metaphysics and epistemology of the *Bhagavad Gītā* by attempting to reconstruct from both the *Sāṁkhya darśana* and the *Vedānta darśana*, as well as from the *Gītā* itself, an interpretation of the *Gītā* that I shall call *Gītā darśana*. But for the moment let us get on with the five assumptions of *Vedānta darśana* and the *Gītā*'s reaction to them:

#### 1) The Five Metaphysical Assumptions of *Vedānta Darśana*

The *Gītā* seems to adopt or to accept in whole or in part the following five assumptions about the ultimate nature of reality, God or the Gods, man, and the world. I say "seems," for the *Gītā* at many places appears to modify or contradict these assumptions, all five of which can be traced back to the *Upaniṣads*:

1. *Brahman* alone is ultimately real

The *Gītā* seems to accept this assumption in part, and the part it does accept becomes the cornerstone of its metaphysics: *Brahman* is ultimately real. As in the *Upaniṣads*, *Brahman* seems to be beyond both existence and nonexistence in the sense that no predicates apply to It or encompass It; and yet, oddly enough, *Brahman* is everywhere; It is everywhere but nowhere—all-pervasive generally but in no place particularly. The contradictory language of the *Upaniṣadic* mystical realist simply emphasizes that the ineffable is, in fact, being talked about. Thus Lord Kṛṣṇa says:

> I will tell you about that which is the object of true knowledge, and knowing which eternal life is gained. It is the beginningless holy *Brahman* which is said to be neither existing nor not-existing.[44]

But the question as to whether *Brahman alone* is the sole reality must be left open, for diverse interpreters of both the *Upaniṣads* and the *Gītā* have taken

[44] *Ibid.*, XIII.12.

varying stands on this issue. On part of this first assumption, the *Gītā* is quite clear:

> It is outside all beings and inside all beings. It is unmoving yet moving. Too subtle to be known, It is far away, yet always near at hand [see assumption 2, below].
>
> It is undivided and whole in beings [see assumption 5, below], yet It seems to be divided. It is known to be the Preserver of all beings, yet It destroys them and creates them anew.
>
> It is the light of all lights and said to be beyond all darkness. It is true knowledge, the object of true knowledge, that which is to be reached by true knowledge. It is seated in the heart of all beings.[45]

Several of the apparent contradictions in these *ślokas* will be ameliorated when we take up assumption 2 below. For *Brahman* in the *Upaniṣads* is not merely a transcendent superreality; rather, *Brahman* is also related to existence by pervading it and engulfing it; and the *Gītā* seems to agree.

2. There are two forms of *Brahman*, a higher and a lower

The *Gītā* accepts this *Upaniṣadic* assumption, and much of the aesthetic beauty of the *Gītā* is spent in hymning the praises of lower *Brahman* made manifest in the world. Lord Kṛṣṇa again speaks to his disciple, the warrior Arjuna:

> Among thousands of men scarcely one strives for perfection, and among those who strive scarcely one of them knows Me in My true nature.
>
> Earth, water, fire, air, ether, mind [*manas*], and also reason [*buddhi*] and the ego [*ahaṁkāra*], such is the eightfold division of My nature.
>
> But this is my lower nature. Now learn My other and higher nature, the *jīva*-being, the Life by which this entire world is preserved.
>
> This Life is the womb of all beings. I am the origin of this world and its dissolution as well.
>
> There is nothing whatsoever that is higher than I. All that exists is strung on Me, like lines of beads on a string.[46]

Thus higher *Brahman* maintains the world, underlies and metaphysically causes and supports it. And yet it is important to keep in mind that lower *Brahman*, the manifested *Brahman*, is not higher *Brahman*, the unmanifested; they are logically as well as metaphysically separable:

> Those men devoid of reason think of Me, the Unmanifested and beyond existence, as having come into manifestation and into existence, never knowing that My real nature is changeless and supreme.[47]

[45] *Ibid.*, XIII.15–17.

[46] *Ibid.*, VII.3–7.

[47] *Ibid.*, VII.24.

But an interesting problem emerges at this point that we can solve only by moving on to the third metaphysical assumption of the *Upaniṣads*. The problem is this: How did the manifest, the lower nature of *Brahman*, the creation, even come into existence from the unmanifest higher nature of *Brahman*? This is a teasing puzzle for the cosmologist, for it entails questions that we faced previously: Why is there anything at all? Why you? Why me? Why the world? Why everything and anything? At such a cosmological moment the *Sāṁkhya darśana* resorted to a myth that related how *puruṣa* danced in front of *prakṛti*; and as a consequence of this dancing *prakṛti* became interested and excited enough to be enticed out of its torporous state of *guṇa*-equilibrium (see p. 179). The *Upaniṣads*, as well, have resorted to mythological talk about desire entering into the potential state of Being, and from this desire for another the One creates a second, and then the whole process is off and running (see pp. 49–50). But the *Upaniṣads* that accepted the notion of a higher, propertyless, desireless *Brahman* couldn't attribute desire to that *Brahman* and remain consistent. Thus another principle was needed to explain how it was that given the first assumption above—that *Brahman* is ultimately real—we can then move on to the second assumption, in which we are suddenly faced with a manifested *Brahman*, a world, a creation. How is such a metaphysical move possible? How can there be anything at all besides unmanifested, higher *Brahman*? Here the *Upaniṣads* replied, "By *māyā*," and the *Gītā* seems to agree:

3. *Māyā* is the power of higher *Brahman* by which lower *Brahman* is manifested.

The *Gītā* accepts this assumption from the *Upaniṣads* in order to account for this world and for man's bondage in this world; for, among its many tasks, *māyā* is the source of *avidyā*, ignorance, bondage, and *saṁsāra*. Thus in agreement with the *Upaniṣads* Lord Kṛṣṇa says:

> And veiled by my yoga-*māyā*, I am not revealed at all. This deluded world does not know that I am never born and that I never perish.
>
> This divine *māyā* of Mine, made of the *guṇas*, is difficult to penetrate. But those who take refuge in Me alone, they penetrate this illusion.
>
> The evil doers, the deluded, the vile men, they do not seek refuge in Me, for their knowledge is torn away by *māyā* and they have become like demons.[48]

The divine *māyā* of the higher *Brahman*, we must suppose, produces lower *Brahman*; and, at the same moment, higher *Brahman* conceals Itself from the beings in lower *Brahman*. *Māyā* has the same task in the *Gītā* that it had in the *Upaniṣads*; and it produces precisely the same problem, the dilemma of *māyā* (see p. 109). This dilemma can be stated in the form of a most challenging

[48] *Ibid.*, VII.25.14–15.

puzzle—one that springs up in any cosmological metaphysics that attempts to demonstrate how the imperfect, the immanent, and the manifest can result from or be caused by the wholly perfect, the wholly transcendent, and the wholly unmanifest. The dilemma of *māyā*, once again, is merely this: If *māyā* is real, then *Brahman* is not the only reality, and the first assumption that we began this section with is violated. But if *māyā* is unreal, then it could not be effective or efficacious in producing the manifest, though imperfect, world, and the second assumption as well as the third would both be violated. But *māyā* must be either real or unreal. Therefore (the dilemma of *māyā* concludes), either *Brahman* is not the only reality or there is no manifest, created world. In either case the metaphysics of the *Upaniṣads* and perhaps that of the *Gītā* as well, would be in deep philosophic trouble; thus the dilemma of *māyā*: if *māyā* is real, the monism of the *Upaniṣads* is destroyed; if *māyā* is unreal, the possibility of the world is destroyed. We will attempt a solution to the dilemma shortly (p. 220).

But however the dilemma of *māyā* may be stated and solved, *māyā* itself is employed somehow or other by higher *Brahman* to produce the manifested world. And with that manifestation there occurs, as we have stated, *avidyā*, bondage, and *saṁsāra* as well as, curiously enough, *mokṣa*; for without bondage there would be no liberation; hence *māyā* is the cause of liberation in the peculiar sense that without it liberation would be impossible. The *mokṣa* of the *Gītā*, and especially the mechanism of liberation, constitutes part of the metaphysics of the *Gītā*, and liberation and its mechanism are both entailed by another assumption which the *Gītā* seems to share with the *Upaniṣads*.

4. Bondage is the result of *avidyā*; hence, *mokṣa* will be a function of *jñāna*.

The *Gītā* agrees in part with this assumption from the *Upaniṣads*, as we have already seen in our discussion of the religion of the *Gītā*. Repetition here serves to underscore the fact that for the *Gītā* bondage, as well as *avidyā*, *mokṣa* and *jñāna* yoga are realities of a sort and hence deserve a place in the metaphysical catalogue of the *Gītā*. They raise some problems, however, not unlike that raised in the dilemma of *māyā*. For if we have four concepts, as we do, that purport to talk about or extensionally point to realities—real bondage (but recall the enchantment theory of bondage discussed in the *Sāṁkhya darśana*, above, and consider how "real" such bondage actually was), real *avidyā*, real *mokṣa*, and real *jñāna yoga*—then we may well have four similar paradoxes with these "reals" as well: the paradox of bondage, the paradox of *avidyā*, the paradox of *mokṣa*, and the paradox of *jñāna* yoga. These puzzles, which are puzzles for the reader to ponder, are raised here because they do arise in considering the *Vedānta* metaphysics of the *Gītā*.

Furthermore, all these puzzles lurk beneath the surface of the fifth and final assumption of the *Upaniṣads*, which the *Gītā* seems to share:

5. Higher *Brahman* is immanent in man as *Ātman*, and *Brahman* is identical with *Ātman*.

The *Gītā* accepts this assumption from the *Upaniṣads*, for it is the key to explaining the nature of *avidyā*, bondage, *mokṣa*, and *jñāna* yoga. Thus it is by way of the *jñāna* of *Ātman* that release occurs, that *avidyā* is dispelled, and that bondage is annulled. And it is the same *Ātman* that dwells in all beings:

> Only through the destruction of ignorance by the *jñāna* of the *Ātman*, only by that will true knowledge shine forth like the sun, revealing the Highest.
>
> Thinking on that Highest, merging the *Ātman* with That, making That the sole aim and object of their devotion, they reach a state from which there is no returning, their sins destroyed by true knowledge.
>
> This Ātman in the body of everyone can never be slain.[49]

We are led, finally, to the conclusion that the *Ātman* and That, the indestructible, transcendent *Brahman*, are identical. We reach this conclusion in virtue of the descriptions that stress the eternality, indestructibleness, and purity of both *Ātman* and the One or *Brahman*:

> He who sees that *prakṛti* alone performs all actions and that the *Ātman* is not the doer—he truly sees.
>
> When he sees that all the diverse existence of contingent beings is rooted in the One and that all that exists radiates out from that One, then he becomes *Brahman*.
>
> The imperishable holy *Ātman*, though seated in the body, being beginningless and *nirguṇa*, It neither acts nor is It acted upon.[50]

But while it is possible to show some general agreement between the metaphysics of the *Gītā* and the *Vedānta darśana*, just as we showed the same general agreement between the *Gītā* and *Sāṁkhya darśana*, several problems remain. Not the least is the fact that three mutually inconsistent philosophical schools of *Vedānta darśana* have sprung to the fore in the later history of Indian thought, each laying claim to the *Gītā* as the source for its own particular and distinct metaphysical interpretation of *Vedānta*. All three of these *Vedānta* schools seem to be in loose general agreement regarding the five metaphysical assumptions mentioned above, but each interprets concepts within the five differently or else extends the interpretation in ways that the other two would not.

[49] *Ibid.*, V.16–17, II.30.

[50] *Ibid.*, XIII.29–31.

Thus the picture one gets in looking at the *Gītā* from the vantage point of a later period is that the *Gītā* seems to mean many different things to many different people, not only to the three mutually inconsistent schools of *Vedānta*—the *advaita* or monistic school of Śaṁkara (788–820), the qualified nondualistic school of Rāmānuja (eleventh century), and the *dvaita* or dualistic school of Madhva (1197–1276)—but also to the followers of *Sāṁkhya darśana* and to the dozen or so other prominent later followers of *Vedānta darśana* as well. Moreover, when one realizes that each of these various philosophers, schools, and systems has turned to the *Gītā* for its justification, then one must realize how overwhelming the entire philosophical prospect of the *Gītā* truly is. I say "overwhelming," for either the *Gītā* is terribly (or marvelously) inconsistent, or else it is simply the philosophic victim of many inordinately hungry systematizers, each seeking to stake out his own peculiar interpretative claim. In the next section we shall examine the reasons that allow for this multiplicity of interpretations.

### 2) Conclusion

The section that follows will conclude this discussion of the metaphysics of the *Gītā* by suggesting that the *Gītā* is quite capable of generating its own consistent and independent philosophy. The *Bhagavad Gītā* is neither *Sāṁkhya darśana* nor *Vedānta darśana*, but something quite distinct and unique, which I shall simply denominate *Gītā darśana*. This third metaphysical *darśana* is, among other things, a curious syncretism of *Sāṁkhya* and *Vedānta* elements. I shall defend the contention that there is such a third *darśana* by restating the five *Vedānta darśana* metaphysical assumptions that, we argued, the *Gītā* seemed to support, and then give what I take to be the *Gītā*'s own position on these assumptions. We must keep the two previous *darśanas* clearly in view, however, in attempting to formulate *Gītā darśana*.

## c. *The Gītā Darśana*

How can so many philosophers find so many mutually inconsistent metaphysical and religious philosophies in the *Gītā*? If Śaṁkara is right, for example, it would seem that Rāmānuja and Madhva are surely wrong. And if contemporary metaphysical pluralists such as Aurobindo Ghose are right about the *Gītā*, then it would seem that contemporary metaphysical monists such as Sarvepalli Radhakrishnan are wrong. The problem of interpreting a sacred work, highly revered by a religious tradition, where one slip can lead to schism, sects, heterodoxy, or heresy is a tale familiar enough to Jews, Buddhists, Christians, and Muslims; hence there's no reason, one might conclude, why the Hindus should escape the same perplexing problem. It appears, however, that the Indians are in a peculiarly unique position to answer this fundamental philosophic question about the *Bhagavad Gītā*.

There are four possible answers to the fundamental question; that is, there are four ways that one could go about dealing with the problem of the existence of at least two mutually inconsistent interpretations of the metaphysics and epistemology of the *Gītā.* Let me briefly indicate what the four are like and then seize upon the fourth as the most plausible as well as the one that will enable us to deal most happily with a rather large number of other *Gītā*-related (philosophical) puzzles, problems, and paradoxes. Call these four answers "the contradictory interpretation," "the subjective interpretation," "the one-view interpretation," and "the two-views interpretation." In what follows, I shall state each of the first three interpretations, explain each briefly and offer a critique of each that necessitates its rejection as an answer to that fundamental question. Finally, I shall state, explain, and defend the fourth interpretation, the two-views interpretation, and from it erect the doctrine that I shall call *Gītā darśana.*

### 1) The Contradictory Interpretation

This interpretation assumes that the *Gītā* is bravely and unblushingly inconsistent. Both *advaita* and *dvaita* metaphysics abound in the *Bhagavad Gītā*; they are logically incompatible; and there's an end to it. The contradictory interpretation may also assume either that the author of the *Gītā* was a philosophic chapati-head who didn't know what he was doing, or that the author was some evil *brahmin* who knew very well what he was about and enjoyed every minute of it. But whatever the intentions of the author, the point is that the contradictions stand and there's nothing the fair interpreter of the *Gītā* can do but recognize this fact and gently point out the evidence.

I find the contradictory interpretation unsatisfactory for several very important reasons. First, adopting it forces us to give up seeking any other more philosophically plausible interpretation. Rather than writing the *Gītā* off as foolishly self-contradictory, suppose we explore the three other possible interpretations first. What must surely appear at this early stage as a superficial and unfair interpretation might in the end win us around, but it's too easy and simplistic right now. Second, if we accept that the *Gītā* is merely self-contradictory, then, as every student of logic well knows, from such an inconsistent set of premises any conclusion whatsoever could be validly drawn. If the *Gītā* is composed of a logically inconsistent set of premises then we could validly infer from it any harebrained absurdities whatsoever; that Kṛṣṇa is a *śudra*, that Arjuna is a girl, that only the *advaitins* are right about the *Gītā*, that Gerald Ford is king of the Kauravas, and so on. Third, aside from the fact that it is premature, or that it could lead to absurd but valid conclusions, the contradictory interpretation goes against a rather long and common-sensical tradition that has not, at least not yet, recognized this interpretation as applicable. Therefore the contradictory interpretation is not applicable. To a Westerner this must seem like a cheap shot, indeed, but it is built out of an appeal to the so-called "argument from silence" as well as to historical traditions; it would be stated more formally like this:

1) If the *Gītā* were self-contradictory, then someone, somewhere, within the philosophic tradition that comes from the *Gītā* would have said so.
2) But no one in the philosophic tradition of the *Gītā* has said that the *Gītā* is self-contradictory.
3) Therefore, the *Gītā* is not self-contradictory.

This use of the argument from silence would disturb Westerners for two reasons. First, there is a general philosophic suspicion about the argument from silence—a suspicion arising from a knowledge of its limited usefulness and scope in handling problems of historical interpretation; second, and more importantly, few Westerners sympathize with any appeal to "tradition" to support any argument whatsoever. For most Westerners the past and its traditions are generally antithetical to all the grand assumptions we hold about cultural progress and human scientific, social, and economic evolution. These same assumptions spill over into the area of intellectual history where the historian easily recalls that since the past and its traditions have proved false in the areas of science, society, and economics, they can prove themselves just as false in the related areas of intellectual history as well. Traditions have proved to be bastions of conservatism and barriers to progress; and this holds, the second reason concludes, for Western cultural traditions as well as for Indian philosophic traditions. So much, perhaps, for the argument from silence as viewed by a contemporary Westerner. But I ask the reader's indulgence at this point, and I ask him to see the third objection to the first interpretation not as standing isolated and by itself but rather as supportive of the two previous objections. Seen in this way, the third objection (that if the *Gītā* really were self-contradictory the tradition would have said so, but it doesn't, so it isn't) serves to strengthen the other two objections. Perhaps, then, all three of these objections will urge us to look elsewhere for an interpretation of the *apparent* self-contradictoriness of the *Gītā* before taking such a radical way out as the contradictory interpretation promises to be.

### 2) The Subjective Interpretation

This interpretation assumes that it is not the *Gītā* that is inconsistent; rather, the inconsistency lies with the subjects that come to the *Gītā*, that hear it, read it, ponder it, and then make it appear that way. Thus the need that you have in approaching the *Gītā* makes you read and see the *Gītā* from your point of view. This need is not necessarily culturally specific; Indians won't all see it in one way and Europeans and Americans in another. For Śaṁkara, Rāmānuja, and Madhva were all about as culturally identical as any three *Vedāntins* could be and yet, despite that identity, they found many basic metaphysical and religious issues worth quibbling about, and in the same text to boot. Hence, the subjective interpretation allows the *Gītā* to become all things to all people. In such a case a sort of relativism enters into the entire situation, and the result is a grand absurdity: the *Gītā* becomes anything that anyone cares to read into or out of it. Hence, if one believed he had found a *Cārvāka* materialism, or a hedonism, or a nihilism, or a national socialism or a Republicanism in the *Gītā*, then the subjective interpreter would have to say, "If you believe it's there, then it must be there."

Therefore, the subjective interpretation could lead to both relativism and solipsism that would make the *Gītā*, in the end, about as relevant to Indian thought as the names of the people in your dream last night. To escape such absurdities we must seek objective standards to establish what shall count and what shall not count as an acceptable or satisfactory interpretation. Hunting for objective standards, incidentally, is the usual way out of the morass of philosophic subjectivism, solipsism, and relativism. But in hunting for standards we are thrown back once again on the object of all our interpretations: the *Gītā*. The hunt for standards leads us away from the subject, with his needs and wants, back to the object, the *Gītā*. And those standards become the focal point of the third interpretation.

### 3) The One-View Interpretation

This interpretation assumes that only one view is promulgated in the *Gītā* and all other views are wrong. It assumes that this view can be discovered and made known; and practically every interpreter of the *Gītā*, from Śaṁkara, Rāmānuja, and Madhva to Tilak, Gandhi, Bhaktivedanta, and Maharishi Mahesh yogi, has assumed that he has done precisely that. Thus these interpreters assume that the *Gītā* is consistent, that its message is not all things to all people, and that a single and knowable theme underlies all its eighteen chapters.

The one-view interpretation simply reaffirms the problem in the original question: how can so many people find so many mutually contradictory metaphysical and religious doctrines in the *Gītā*? The one-view interpretation, in arguing that the mutually contradictory doctrines are more apparent than real, and that only one view is correct, doesn't tell us which view is the right one, nor even that the correct view has been found. All it affirms is that such a view is there. The one-view interpreter may simply feel that such an important work as the *Gītā*, considering the tradition that created or evolved it, is incapable of a logical mistake. In similar contexts these one-viewers might say "God wouldn't be illogical" or "God is never wrong." While one-view Indians can't fall back on precisely such statements with respect to the *Gītā*, one suspects that they have silently made their appeal on grounds something like that, perhaps replacing "God" with "tradition."

I find the one-view interpretation unsatisfactory because it really doesn't interpret or explain anything. True, it keeps everyone looking; undoubtedly it is the single most captivating force in *Gītā* scholarship to this day. But while it may explain why there are so incredibly many mutually inconsistent interpretations of the *Gītā*, and while, perhaps, it is an interesting logical alternative to the first interpretation (that the *Gītā* is massively inconsistent), it does not resolve the problem of those massive apparent inconsistencies. Which brings us to the fourth and final interpretation of the fundamental question about the *Gītā*: the two-views interpretation.

**4) The Two-Views Interpretation**

This interpretation assumes that the *Gītā* is not a single philosophic work at all, but, rather, an amalgamation of philosophic works. The *Gītā* consists of several messages, and it speaks, therefore, with several voices to many different people. Thus the several yogas promulgated by the *Gītā* are *varṇa*-specific; they are directed toward individual *varṇas* in the sense that *jñāna* yoga is meant for *brahmins*, *karma* yoga is meant for *kṣatriyas*, and *bhakti* yoga is meant for *vaiśyas* and *śūdras*. The *Gītā*, if we may now generalize on this example, could thereby appeal to Hindus and non-Hindus alike, as well as to *Vedāntins* of whatever ilk, color, variety, or breed. The two-views interpretation hopes to explain our fundamental philosophic question, "How can so many people find so many apparently contradictory metaphysical and religious philosophies in the *Gītā*?", by declaring that these philosophies are really right there in the *Gītā*. But they are not in the least contradictory with one another, for they don't pretend to form a logically unified set of doctrines. And just as no one would cry "Inconsistent rubbish!" at seeing the *Old* and the *New Testaments* brought together within the same book so, *pari passu*, one ought not to cry "Inconsistent rubbish!" at seeing the *Gītā* similarly brought together.

What I shall try to show is that these several works, messages, and doctrines are really dependent on two fundamental views which the *Gītā* rests upon and promulgates. I shall call these two views "the metaphysical view" and "the religious view." Seen as points of view—*darśanas*—they are, as a matter of fact, quite consistent: As consistent as the four *āśramas* or the four *varṇas*. Trouble develops when one stands upon one view and uses it as the norm or paradigm to criticize the other. This is precisely what happens with the *advaitins*, who say that only *Brahman* is real and the *dvaitins* (pluralists) are wrong; and with the *dvaitins* who say that God, Selves, and the world are all real and the *advaitins* are wrong.

But the two-views interpretation cannot be completely understood, nor can we avoid the traps mentioned previously, unless we keep certain objective standards or criteria clearly in mind. Our task, then, is to set forth the two-views interpretation as *Gītā darśana* consistent with certain objective standards. So, first, we shall discuss these objective standards. Next we shall explore the two views and their place in *Gītā darśana*. Then we will be in a position to consider several problems and paradoxes that occur in the *Gītā* and which we have touched on in earlier discussions of the *Vedas* and the *Upaniṣads*. Our *Gītā darśana* will prove to be useless, indeed, if it cannot satisfy these objective standards and solve the various problems and puzzles that occur in the *Gītā*. The solution of those problems, puzzles, and paradoxes by the two-views interpretation will complete our presentation of the *Gītā darśana* and our discussion of the metaphysics and epistemology of the *Bhagavad Gītā*.

### a) THE THREE STANDARDS OF INTERPRETATION

Any satisfactory interpretation of the *Gītā* must be able to meet three commonly accepted philosophic standards: those of common sense, consistency, and completeness. Let us consider each one separately.

#### 1. *Common Sense (a Subjective Standard)*

Any satisfactory interpretation of the *Gītā* must be capable of being stated in nontechnical, ordinary language. Where technical terms are employed, they must be definable in that simple and ordinary language. Further, the interpretation itself must meet standards on naturalness and believability. Thus, if someone were to argue that *Ātman* is composed of pink cheese or that manifest *Brahman* is a quiet custard, even though the language is clear insofar as the words are understandable, the propositions expressed would stretch the standards of justifiable credulity, if not technical meaningfulness (see pp. 125–26).

I call this standard "subjective" in the sense that it rests on the educated and enlightened feelings of the philosopher. It serves to remind us that we must trust and follow our intuitions, our hunches, and our feelings and formulate them plainly and concisely as a first step in dealing not only with interpretations of the *Gītā*, but also with the various puzzles and paradoxes that may be entailed by those interpretations. The subjective standard does not exist in a vacuum, however, but takes counsel and guidance from the two remaining standards.

#### 2. *Consistency (a Formal Standard)*

Any satisfactory interpretation of the *Gītā* must be stated in such a way that there are no internal logical inconsistencies in the interpretation nor can any be entailed by it. To say that *Brahman* alone is real and then to state that selves are also real would violate the standard of consistency. Or to say that the self is personal and that it is identical with *nirguṇa Brahman*, or that God loves the world and all of its creatures but is indifferent to human suffering, would also, *prima facie*, violate our formal and logical standard of consistency.

3. *Completeness* (*a Practical Standard*)

Any satisfactory interpretation of the *Gītā* must be capable of solving all the problems, puzzles, or paradoxes that can be raised relative to the *Gītā*. Any interpretation that solved only some but not all would be satisfactory. If the two-views interpretation resolved the dilemma of *māyā* but failed to solve the problem of evil or the problem of free will, then the interpretation would not be complete and it would be, to that extent, unsatisfactory.

Thus in setting our attention on the two-views interpretation of the *Gītā* we must keep in mind these three standards of common sense, consistency, and completeness. The two-views interpretation will be satisfactory only if it is able to satisfy all three of these criteria.

### b) THE TWO-VIEWS INTERPRETATION: *GĪTĀ DARŚANA*

Let us begin by sketching the two-views interpretation as a dualism in the *Gītā*, a dualism that forms the metaphysical foundation of *Gītā darśana*; then move to the list of the five assumptions of *Vedānta darśana* (see pp. 189–94) in order to see how *Gītā darśana* would stand with respect to them: and, finally, conclude with *Gītā darśana's* treatment of several problems and paradoxes that arise in the interpretation of the *Gītā*.

1. *The Dualism of the Gītā*

Return once again to the dramatic plot of the *Gītā*—the civil war and Arjuna's dilemma: the family he is sworn by his *dharma* to protect is the same family that he must now fight. At this point Kṛṣṇa attempts to persuade Arjuna to do his soldierly duty. In the end, and after seventeen chapters, he succeeds, but only after frightening Arjuna within an inch of his *kṣatrian* life by revealing to him the horrible and demonic side of His (Lord Kṛṣṇa's) divine nature.

In the second chapter of the *Gītā*, the art of persuasion with words, philosophy, and metaphysics begins. Kṛṣṇa adopts two persuasive tactics in countering Arjuna's final pronouncement, "I will not fight." The first is stated in what I shall refer to as a "religious argument," the second in what I shall refer to as a "metaphysical argument." Arjuna is quite able, as is the reader generally, to follow the religious arguments as they occur throughout the second chapter, but the metaphysical arguments that Kṛṣṇa offers seem to exasperate Arjuna, compelling him, finally, to cry out in despair:

> You only confuse my understanding with your perplexing words. So tell me clearly what is the one way by which I may attain *śreyas* [the highest]?[51]

The remainder of the *Gītā* is spent with Kṛṣṇa attempting to answer this question and thereby solve what we have called "Arjuna's dilemma." As the *Gītā* unravels, Kṛṣṇa moves comfortably back and forth between religious arguments and metaphysical arguments; invariably, however, he seems to lose Arjuna whenever he resorts to the latter. Finally, Kṛṣṇa gives up trying to clarify his metaphysical discourse to a questioning and bewildered Arjuna. The dialogue style that appeared early in the *Gītā* is abandoned, and Kṛṣṇa continues and then concludes the *Gītā* by simply preaching to Arjuna.

The philosophic tone and tactical style of the *Gītā* are really set, then, in the second chapter, where examples of both religious and metaphysical arguments abound. Recall, again, the problem that Kṛṣṇa faces: he must solve Arjuna's dilemma and he must get him to fight in this just war. Think for a moment about the man that Kṛṣṇa is attempting to persuade. Arjuna is a warrior—a down-to-earth meat, water, and bread man. Judging from his responses to Kṛṣṇa's religious arguments—arguments that don't bewilder or confuse him—and judging from what Arjuna, himself, has said in the first chapter of the *Gītā*, he is a man who believes in the Gods, heaven, and hell, in doing the right thing and avoiding the wrong, in obeying the laws of his *varṇa* and clan, and so forth. He is totally untutored in the metaphysical niceties of *Sāṁkhya*, *Vedānta*, and the other *darśanas*. After all, if he weren't so unsophisticated, so unwashed, so plain, normal, and ordinary, he wouldn't be facing the dilemma he now faces. Arjuna is a straight and simple good man, not a student of the *Vedas* or the *Upaniṣads*. If he hadn't been this type of man, then the *Gītā* would very probably have turned into a metaphysical debate on the nature of the Unmanifest, or *Ātman*, or something on that level. But he wasn't, so it didn't. To repeat the point, the philosophic tone is two-sided; first, the tone bespeaks religious arguments that are ordinary, down-to-earth, and plain; then it grows sophisticated, losing Arjuna, but soaring to frigid metaphysical heights.

Kṛṣṇa begins his attack on Arjuna's dilemma by giving Arjuna three metaphysical arguments that all center around the imperishability of *Ātman*. To understand the arguments, let alone to accept them and fight, demands a sophistication that Arjuna is quite unprepared to exercise. Kṛṣṇa begins the first of these arguments:

> You are mourning for those that are not to be mourned, and you speak wise words in vain. The truly wise mourn for neither the living nor the dead.

[51] *Ibid.*, III.2.

It is precisely at this point, I suspect, that Kṛṣṇa as he continues leaves Arjuna behind:

> For there never was a time when I or you or these kings did not exist. And never shall we case to exist hereafter.[52]

Kṛṣṇa then goes on to talk about the immortal Dweller in the body—the *Ātman*. At this juncture in the first argument (it is an argument for it concludes implicitly, "Therefore, fight, Arjuna!") Kṛṣṇa is plainly talking not religion but metaphysics; the subject is not God, duty, and the right, but the Dweller, the *Ātman*, the Self that never dies. Arjuna may well be left to believe that the point is still a simple religious point; no *jīva* dies, all selves are immortal, they cannot be killed, so why not fight? But this latter interpretation, which would lead Arjuna along the *dvaita* or pluralistic path and into the philosophic arms of, say, Madhva, is precisely what Kṛṣṇa does not mean, as the next *śloka* concerning the embodied Dweller seems to plainly tell us:

> Just as the Dweller in this body has passed through childhood to youth to old age, in just the same way shall that One pass on eventually to another body. The wise man is not deceived in this matter.[53]

Thus the ordinary interpretation that Arjuna's self will live forever is juxtaposed to this extraordinary interpretation concerning the mysterious embodied Dweller. I am suggesting that the former is the religious interpretation, and it is very likely the one that Arjuna himself could see and understand; but the latter regarding the Dweller is the metaphysical interpretation, and, I am suggesting, it is the one that baffles Arjuna, for it is at a level that he cannot see and understand.

The second argument relates to the impermanence of the world; it is sophisticated in the same sense that the previous argument was, and once again it leaves poor Arjuna in perplexity:

> Contacts with the material world yield cold and heat, pleasure and pain. These come and go and are impermanent and unreal. Endure them, Arjuna.
>
> The man who is indifferent to these things, to whom pain and pleasure are the same, that wise man is fit for immortality.[54]

Again, the argument takes the following form: if you see the world for what it truly is—a conglomerate of appearances and the impermanent, composed of the changing, fleeting, evanescent opposites—then you must also see that

[52] *Ibid.*, II.11–12.

[53] *Ibid.*, II.13.

[54] *Ibid.*, II.14–15.

as you rise above these opposites and this appearance your own actions cannot destroy, hurt, or harm the truly real Self: therefore, fight, Arjuna!

The third metaphysical argument plays back upon the content of the two previous arguments. It contends that since the *Ātman* or Self alone is real and can never be slain, and since fighting and slaying these men would be slaying shadows and mere appearances, then it would matter not at all if Arjuna did fight and slay: therefore, fight, Arjuna!

> Know this, that which lies immanent within all this world, that reality can never cease to be. No one can bring about the destruction of that imperishable reality.
>
> These material bodies of the eternal, indestructible, and immeasurable embodied Self within are themselves unreal.[55] Therefore, fight, Arjuna![56]

It is quite clear that Kṛṣṇa is unable to reach Arjuna at this metaphysical level, once again, and this failure is underscored by the fact that Kṛṣṇa finally resorts to an argument at the religious level. He begins by appealing to something in Arjuna that ordinary men and all noble warriors are most attached to: heaven and honor. It is as if he had finally given up trying to explain the metaphysics to Arjuna (not really, for the remainder of the *Gītā* is simply a long metaphysical treatise, with Arjuna forming at times a bewildered audience of one). Kṛṣṇa resorts instead to batting a religious argument against Arjuna's vanity and his lust for heaven and honor:

> The chance to fight is an open door to heaven for you—fortunate indeed are those warriors who get such a chance.
>
> But now, if you will not fight in this war, if you will not perform your duty and instead abandon that duty and your honor, then you will surely fall into evil (*pāpa*).
>
> Men will tell again and again of your eternal dishonor; and for one now held in high regard, such disgrace is worse than death.
>
> If you die fighting, you shall win heaven; and if you live and conquer, you shall win the earth. Therefore, fight, Arjuna.[57]

Two comments may be in order regarding what I am here calling a religious argument. First, it doesn't really solve Arjuna's dilemma at all, for it doesn't speak to the nasty problem concerning the sin that is incurred by killing members of one's family; second, if this religious argument were truly persuasive in its results and if Kṛṣṇa believed it was truly persuasive, then why didn't he stop there and let the *Gītā* become the shortest religious work in history? But Kṛṣṇa doesn't stop there; he recognizes that the argument is not

[55]The Sanskrit says *antavanta*—"having an end," hence "unreal."

[56]*Bhagavad Gītā*, II.17–18.

[57]*Ibid.*, II.32–34, 37.

successfully persuasive and that it doesn't solve Arjuna's dilemma. And this is why he spends the remainder of the chapter discussing *karma* yoga—the way of acting such that no sin befalls the actor.

But Kṛṣṇa has another message to proclaim to those who have ears to hear, and that other message is the one with which the first three arguments—those baffling, metaphysical arguments—are concerned. By the time that we have concluded the second chapter, we realize that the *Gītā* can speak out of two sides of its philosophical mouth. On the one hand it speaks an ordinary religious message about Gods, sin, death, life, heaven, doing one's duty, and doing the honorable thing in order to get to heaven; it talks about hopes and fears, aims and goals, that soldiers and ordinary people understand all too well. But, on the other hand, it speaks an extraordinary metaphysical message about the Self, the embodied Dweller within, the real and the unreal, the unchanging, the indestructible and the imperishable; it talks about ideas and entities that only *Avatārs* and metaphysicians understand, and sometimes not too well. The *Gītā* is a dualism of ways and goals, of realities and languages, and this dualism emerges here in the second chapter.

The remainder of the *Gītā* simply plays upon and draws out the implications of this initial religious and metaphysical dualism. One should not view these two levels of argumentation, together with their assumptions about what is real or important, from some higher metalevel, and then judge one as somehow more real or less real, or more true or less true than the other. Instead of talking about the religious and metaphysical views as "true or false,""real or unreal," let us speak of them relationally as "appropriate to" or "inappropriate to" a particular level of understanding or a particular person at a particular level of understanding. Thus the religious view is appropriate to Arjuna's level of understanding, and the metaphysical view is appropriate to Kṛṣṇa's level of understanding. To condemn Arjuna's level as false or to condemn Arjuna for speaking falsely about or from within the religious view would be to miss the whole point concerning the two-views interpretation of the *Gītā*; and speaking in terms of appropriateness and inappropriateness reinforces this point (but see below, pp. 216–17).

Let's turn now to an examination of the five assumptions of *Vedānta darśana* and see how the religious and metaphysical dualism that is the foundation of *Gītā darśana* would speak to those assumptions. The nature of the dualism as well as *Gītā darśana*, itself, will be clearer once we have taken up these assumptions. I would remind the reader of the three standards of interpretive adequacy set out previously (pp. 199–200). *Gītā darśana* hopes to meet those standards.

### 2. *Five Upaniṣadic Assumptions and Gītā Darśana*

Let us proceed by simply going through the five *Upaniṣadic* metaphsical assumptions discussed previously (pp. 189–93). We noted that the *Gītā* seems to adopt all five of these assumptions—"seems" because the *Gītā* at many places appears to modify or contradict these assumptions, all five of which can be traced back to the *Upaniṣads*. But now, having looked at several mutually inconsistent interpretations that claim the *Gītā* as their own, and having outlined the religious-metaphysical dualism that is found in the *Gītā*, we are perhaps in a better position to return to these five assumptions and sketch out a full-blown *Gītā darśana*. I will state each assumption and then briefly indicate the way in which it relates, by agreement or disagreement, to the two views of *Gītā darśana*.

1. *Brahman* alone is ultimately real.

   *Religious View*: Disagrees

*Brahman* is not the only reality, as many passages in the *Gītā* are at some pains to make clear. Thus the Self or *Ātman* is real, and the *Gītā* gives the impression that there are many such Selves that will enjoy eternal, heavenly bliss, happiness, or *śreyas*, once liberation is achieved. All beings possess such a Self, and here is its true nature:

> This Self is never born, nor does It ever die, nor having been can It ever cease to be. Unborn, unending, eternal, this Self is not slain when the body is slain.
>
> Just as a man casts aside worn-out clothes to put on new ones, so the Self casts aside worn-out bodies and enters into others that are new.[58]

Furthermore, not only are Selves multiple and real, but material nature, as *prakṛti*, is also real:

> Know this, that *prakṛti* (material world) and *puruṣa* (spirit) are both beginningless; know also that all changes and transformations, as well as the *guṇas*, are born of *prakṛti*.[59]

Finally, not only are Selves multiple and real, and not only is the material world real, but the Gods are also real, and one God in particular, Lord Viṣṇu. Here Kṛṣṇa speaks of the Gods:

> Neither the many Gods nor the many great sages know My origin, for I am the absolute beginning of all the Gods and all the great sages.[60]

Thus Viṣṇu as Kṛṣṇa is a personal God and identified even by Arjuna as *Brahman*, but a "personal" *Brahman*. Arjuna says:

> You are truly the supreme *Brahman*, the supreme refuge, the supreme purifier, the eternal divine spirit, the first of the Gods, the unborn, the omnipresent Lord.[61]

[58] *Ibid.*, II.20, 22.

[59] *Ibid.*, XIII.19.

[60] *Ibid.*, X.2.

[61] *Ibid.*, X.12.

Therefore, as far as the religious view is concerned, Selves, the world, and God are all real; and *Brahman* alone is not ultimately real. But that is only half of the philosophic story.

*Metaphysical View:* Agrees

*Brahman* is the sole and ultimate reality, the previous quotations from the *Gītā* notwithstanding:

> *Brahman* is the imperishable, the supreme, whose essential nature is called *Ātman*.[62]
>
> I will tell you of that which is the Object of true knowledge, and knowing which eternal life is gained. It is the beginningless holy *Brahman*, which is said to be neither existing nor not existing.[63]

Thus *Brahman* is an impersonal metaphysical principle, beyond all description, beyond all contact, alone and ultimately real. And that is the other half of the philosophic story.

2. There are two forms of *Brahman*, a higher and a lower.

*Religious View*: Disagrees but . . .

This qualified disagreement follows from the previous discussion. The person holding the religious view, the religious man, may agree that *Brahman* can take many forms, but he would hesitate in calling them "higher" and "lower," for in doing so he runs the risk of agreeing with the metaphysician that higher *Brahman* alone is real. Thus, while *Brahman* may have many forms, such as Gods, *Avatārs*, and Viṣṇu, Himself, the religious man would not hold that these forms are ontologically lower—*less real*—than higher *Brahman* Itself. Hence his disagreement is qualified.

*Metaphysical View*: Agrees

But the metaphysician, the person holding the metaphysical view, can point to numerous passages in the *Gītā* in which *Brahman* is described in precisely the terms of the assumption:

> Earth, water, fire, air, ether, mind, and also reason and the ego, such is the eightfold division of My nature.
>
> But this is My lower nature. Now learn My other and higher nature, the *jīva*-being, the Life by which this entire world is maintained.[64]

[62] *Ibid.*, VIII.3.

[63] *Ibid.*, XIII.12.

[64] *Ibid.*, VII.4–5.

The metaphysician means to draw a distinction between these two natures of *Brahman*, and given his agreement with the first assumption, it would follow that only higher *Brahman* is ultimately real while lower *Brahman* is not.

3. *Māyā* is the power of *Brahman* by which lower *Brahman* is manifested.

   *Religious View*: Disagrees but . . . .

For the religious man, *māyā* is simply the power that God uses to create the world and manifest Himself. This does not entail, following his disagreement with the two previous assumptions, that the world or the self is unreal in any sense. Thus, regarding His own divine manifestation as Savior, Kṛṣṇa states:

> Though unborn, for the *Ātman* is eternal, though Lord of all beings, yet using my own *prakṛti*, I come into existence through my own *māyā*.
>
> For whenever there is a decaying of *dharma*, and a rising up of *adharma*, then I send Myself forth into the world.[65]

*Metaphysical View*: Agrees

The metaphysician can account for the existence of lower *Brahman*, the manifested world, from higher *Brahman* in virtue of the power of *māyā* wielded by higher *Brahman*. The *guṇas*, the Gods, the world, every created entity subject to the *guṇas*, is part of created, *saguṇa*, lower *Brahman*, and they all stream forth from the same ultimately real source. The beings caught in *māyā*, the creation, are subject to rebirth again and again, and this includes even the Gods:

> There is no creature on earth nor among the Gods in heaven that is free from the three *guṇas* born from *prakṛti*.[66]

And the source of all of this is higher Brahman:

> Those three natures which are *sattva*, *rajas*, or *tamas*, all these are from Me; not I in them, but they in Me.
>
> All this world is deluded by these three natures which are made by the *guṇas*, and thus the world does not recognize Me Who is beyond these and imperishable.
>
> This divine *māyā* of Mine, made of the *guṇas*, is difficult to penetrate. But those who take refuge in Me alone, they penetrate this illusion.[67]

[65] *Ibid.*, IV.6–7.

[66] *Ibid.*, XVIII.40.

[67] *Ibid.*, VII.12–14.

But the relation of the world and *saguṇa Brahman* to *nirguṇa Brahman* raises some problems for the metaphysician and his monistic philosophy. Not the least of these problems lies simply in explaining how this creation, *saguṇa Brahman*, could be made or constructed from a cause, *nirguṇa Brahman*, which is so metaphysically far removed from its effect—this world, this creation. How could *Brahman* do it and not get all tangled up in the result? To resolve this puzzle one metaphysician, Śaṁkara, resorts to a very exciting theory, one that involves him nicely in the problems of illusion, knowledge, *avidyā*, bondage, and liberation. The theory is meant to get Śaṁkara out of the following nasty puzzle, which will remain to ensnare all those metaphysicians who come tumbling along in Śaṁkara's philosophic wake. Let's call the puzzle "the Creator dilemma"; it goes something like this:

1. If *Brahman* creates the world with some thing outside of and separate from Itself (*asatkāryavāda*), for example with another reality such as matter, then the *advaita* metaphysics is destroyed; that is, if there are two real entities, *Brahman* and another, then *Brahman* is not the only reality.
2. If *Brahman*, however, creates the world with some thing not outside of and separate from Itself but rather from within Itself (*satkārya-vāda*), for example with *Brahman*-matter, then either of two results is possible: (a) either the matter is identical with only a part of *Brahman* (the position called "panentheism"), in which case whenever matter undergoes destruction *Brahman* would too; (b) or the matter is identical with the whole of *Brahman* (the position called "pantheism"), in which case whenever matter undergoes change the whole of *Brahman* would change. Both of these conclusions are absurd, it is claimed.
3. But *Brahman* must create the world from some thing either outside Itself (1) or within Itself (2).
4. Therefore, either *advaita* metaphysics is destroyed, (1); or *Brahman* is subject to destruction (2a), or *Brahman* undergoes change (2b); therefore, either *advaita* is destroyed or an absurdity results.

Śaṁkara avoids the conclusions in item 4 of the Creator dilemma by arguing, in essence, that the type of change involved in the creation of the world is wholly illusory. The theory (*vāda*) he espouses is called *vivartavāda* (from *vivarta*, "manifestation)" or sometimes *adhyāsavāda* (from *adhyāsa*, "projection"), the theory of illusory modification. Both are opposed to another theory, *pariṇāmavāda* (from *pariṇāma*, "transformation"), the theory of real modification. Let us look briefly at *pariṇāmavāda* and the other two theories of change, since they all relate to *Gītā darsana* and our third assumption.

According to *pariṇāmavāda*, a real cause gives rise to a real effect, and cause and effect have the same kind of being; thus butter is as real as the milk from which it comes, and a clay pot is as real as the clay that causes it; for in both the milk and the clay, it is only their secondary or accidental properties that have been altered or changed: But the essential matter of each is still real and still there in the butter and in the pot. The defenders of *pariṇāmavāda* conclude, therefore, by saying that the creation is the same as the Creator; that is, the world is *Brahman*, or matter is God; and this for Śaṁkara simply won't do, as we have seen in the conclusion to the Creator dilemma above: for either *Brahman* is then subject to destruction or else *Brahman* is subject to change.

Śaṁkara ingeniously tries to avoid the absurdities of *pariṇāmavāda* by introducing his *vivartavāda*, the theory that the effect is of a different order of being from the cause, and that change, therefore, is only apparent. His theory says that an illusion or appearance is projected (*adhyāsa*) onto *Brahman* through *avidyā*, ignorance, in the same way, to use Śaṁkara's favorite illustration, that the appearance of a snake is projected through the perceiver's *avidyā* onto a rope when he mistakenly and ignorantly takes a rope for a snake in a case of illusory perception. Using this model of illusory perception, Śaṁkara is able to show that far from having a Creator in *Brahman* we have instead a creator in the viewer. The rope is not the maker of the illusion, but the viewer in his ignorance is. And the analogy applies to the world in precisely the same way: we attribute the world (the snake) to a place (the rope) where it neither exists nor belongs; and yet without the place (*Brahman* or the rope) the illusion (the world or the snake) would not exist: we have met the creator and, in the immortal words of Pogo, he is us.

Now in the same way that one can get over the illusion that the rope is really the snake, so also one can get over the illusion that the world or self is really *Brahman*. Thus one attacks the cause of the illusion from the creator end, and since we are the creator, the problem of overcoming the illusion and breaking the bondage of ignorance that causes it lies wholly and totally with us. The ignorance or *avidyā* is overcome by *jñāna* or the yoga of knowledge. One must discover the nature of reality, and this is accomplished in Śaṁkara's philosophy by the intuitive discovery that the Self within is identical with *Brahman*. With this discovery, that *Ātman* is *Brahman*, one is liberated once and for all from *avidyā*, and liberation or *mokṣa* is the consequence. The Self is thus revealed as *nirguṇa Brahman* and the bewitchment, the enchantment, the illusion, ends. Thus Śaṁkara and the creator dilemma—a dilemma to which we shall return shortly with a solution taken from *Gītā darśana*.

The stage is now set for the fourth assumption and a discussion of bondage, the cause of bondage, and the ways out of bondage according to *Gītā darśana*.

4. Bondage is the result of *avidyā*; hence, *mokṣa* will be a function of *jñāna*.

The situation here is somewhat complicated, since three quite distinct concepts are involved in this fourth assumption: *avidyā*, *mokṣa*, and the yoga of *jñāna*, not to mention bondage, itself. Both the religious and the metaphysical views agree that there is bondage, but that is about as far as the agreement goes. They will disagree on the intension or interpretation as well as the extension or application of all of the other three concepts.

*Religious view:* Disagrees

The assumption regarding bondage, its cause, and the way out of it is stated too narrowly to suit the religious view. There is bondage, true enough, but its cause is not simply ignorance; rather, there may be many causes of bondage. Thus if God's grace is a necessary condition for release, then presumably lack of that grace would be a necessary condition for bondage, and ignorance might have nothing to do with it one way or the other. Kṛṣṇa says:

> Performing all actions, having taken refuge in Me, by My grace My devotee reaches the eternal, indestructible goal.
>
> Focusing all your thought on Me, you will overcome all difficulties by My grace. . . .[68]

Another cause of bondage might be failing to seek shelter and refuge in God through *bhakti*. Other causes of bondage are, of course, the failure to lead an upright and moral life according to the *dharma*. Finally, just plain attachment and desire in general bind the Self to *saṁsāra*:

> *Puruṣa* (Self) seated in *prakṛti* (body) enjoys the *guṇas* born from *prakṛti*. Attachment to these *guṇas* is the cause of its birth in good and evil wombs.[69]

To assume that *avidyā* is the only cause of bondage is much too narrow an interpretation of the nature of bondage, the religious man must feel.

Similarly, just as there are many causes of bondage, so there must be many yogas to overcome those causes. Once again there are at least as many yogas as there are *varṇas* or *guṇa*-natures, and these *guṇa*-natures have been allotted by the law of *karma* in conjunction with the *guṇa*-nature of one's previous existence. And, as we have been at some pains to point out previously (pp. 158–69), there is a specific yoga for each of the three specific *guṇa*-natures, such that "Each man reaches perfection by being devoted to his own

[68] *Ibid.*, XVIII.56, 58.

[69] *Ibid.*, XIII.21.

special innate *guṇa*-nature."[70] The religious view recognizes this pluralism of *guṇa*-natures and yogas and, accordingly, adopts the "something more" attitude of the *dvaitin* or pluralist.

Finally, the religious view interprets *mokṣa, nirvāṇa*, perfection, release, the highest place, *śreyas*, or what-have-you, to mean heaven and heaven alone, the place where the self survives for all eternity. *Mokṣa* for the religious man is simply spending eternity with Lord Kṛṣṇa:

> Merge your mind with Me, be My *bhakta*, sacrifice to Me, prostrate yourself before Me, and you shall come to Me. I promise this to you truly, for you are dear to Me.
>
> Abandoning all *dharma*, come to Me alone for refuge. Be not sorrowed, for I shall give you *mokṣa* from all sins.[71]

This very personal relation to *Brahman* emerges from the pluralistic interpretation that the religious view makes of the yogas, the causes of bondage, and the final goal, itself, however variously they may all be described.

*Metaphysical View*: Agrees

The narrow, nothing-but, *advaita* interpretation of bondage, its cause and the way to release, suits the metaphysician just fine. The *Gītā*, he claims, is quite straightforward in claiming that the cause of bondage is closely related to the enchantment theory discussed previously (pp. 185–88); that is, the cause of bondage is *avidyā*, and the way out of this ignorance would have to be knowledge—*jñāna* yoga:

> Only through the destruction of ignorance by *jñāna* of the *Ātman*, only by that will true knowledge shine forth like the sun, revealing the Highest.
>
> Thinking on That Highest, merging the Self with That, making That the sole aim and object of their devotion, they reach a state from which there is no returning, their sins destroyed by true knowledge.[72]

That state, of course, is *mokṣa*, becoming one with *Brahman*, wherein all traces of personality, *ahaṁkāra*, or *jīva* are lost. Thus *mokṣa* is a state of total absorption in the impersonal absolute of *nirguṇa Brahman*. On the other hand, heaven, for the metaphysician, is simply a temporary halfway house between this world now and this world in a later birth:

> The knowers of the three *Vedas* who drink the *soma* and are purified of sin, worshipping Me with sacrifices they ask the way to heaven. And they finally reach the holy world of Indra; there, in heaven, they taste the divine pleasures of the gods.

[70] *Ibid.*, XVIII.45.

[71] *Ibid.*, XVIII.65–66.

[72] *Ibid.*, V.16–17.

> Having enjoyed the spacious world of heaven, their merit all used up, they return to this world of death.[73]

The key to union or at-one-ment with *Brahman* is through dispelling *avidyā* by *jñāna* yoga: *mokṣa*, unlike heaven or *svarga*, is a permanent and not a temporary state.

The metaphysical view is beset with a difficulty, however, which the metaphysician must be at some pains to treat, and that difficulty emerges with the fourth assumption. The metaphysical view must find a way of explaining away or accounting for all those passages in the *Gītā* that would appear to contradict the fourth assumption, such as those passages previously mentioned in discussing the religious view above. The metaphysician who follows the narrower *advaita* path of interpretation of the *Gītā* must explain why the *Gītā* often seems to support the interpretation that offers a quite contrary and wider, *dvaita* path. The metaphysician must end up either by attacking the interpreters who accept the religious view in the *Gītā*, claiming that those interpreters are misled or biased or ignorant, or by attacking the *Gītā* itself, claiming it doesn't mean what it seems to say or actually does say.

Nor is the religious person in a better or more defensible philosophic position. He has a problem in trying to account for the curiously large number of "nothing-but," *advaita* claims that the *Gītā* seems to make. In trying to give an account of such passages he falls as well into the same either/or choices that faced the metaphysician earlier; he must attack either the *advaita* interpreter or the *Gītā* itself.

The conclusion to all of this is, once again, that *Gītā darśana* is in a far happier position defensibly and philosophically, since it can quite straightforwardly claim that both the religious person and the metaphysician are equally right in their interpretations of the *Gītā*. Which brings us to the fifth and final assumption:

5. Higher *Brahman* is immanent in man as *Ātman*, and *Brahman* is identical with *Ātman*.

   *Religious View*: Agrees but . . . .

Care is needed in interpreting this last assumption, especially for the religious view. The religious man wants to hold that the *Gītā* maintains there is a part of God in every man, that God is *Brahman*, and that that part of *Brahman* in man is *Ātman*. Further, the relation that each man has with *Ātman* is an individual and subjective relation identical with the relation that each man has with God, hence the relation as well as the character of *Ātman* is wholly and deeply personal:

[73] *Ibid.*, IX.20–21.

> Let a man raise his self by his *Ātman*, and let him not lower himself. For only the *Ātman* is the friend of the self, and only the *Ātman* can be the enemy of the self.
>
> The *Ātman* is a friend to him who has conquered the self by that *Ātman*, but for him who has not conquered the self that *Ātman* will be hostile to him, like an enemy.[74]

If we were looking for a new term to describe such a personal, immanent aspect of *Brahman*, then we might call it *saguṇa Ātman*. *Saguṇa Ātman* would possess all the characteristics of a personal God. At times, the *Gītā* refers to what we are calling *saguṇa Ātman* as *puruṣa* and attributes to it all the characteristics of an immanent, personal Spirit:

> The holy *puruṣa* in the body is said to be the Observer, the Permitter, the Supporter, the Experiencer, the great Lord and holy *Ātman*.[75]

But some problems arise for *Gītā darśana* with the introduction of *saguṇa Ātman*. I will mention two such problems, and then we will move on. I don't wish to suggest that the religious man couldn't find a solution to these problems; I suspect he could. I simply raise them here lest anyone think that the religious view is all philosophically clean and undefiled. The problems I mention are those of parsimony and identity:

*The problem of parsimony*. The critic might easily say that having an immanent God, *saguṇa Ātman*, as well as a transcendent God, *saguṇa Brahman*, is just plain theologically wasteful. The lack of economy in multiplying *Ātmans* beyond necessity makes the theory untidy and inelegant. One *Ātman*, whether *saguṇa* or not, one *Brahman*, whether *saguṇa* or not, but not both, is quite sufficient to get the job (getting heaven or *mokṣa*) done; anything beyond that bespeaks a sort of religious greediness that is blushingly inappropriate.

*The problem of identity*. The critic might easily say that the metaphysical relationship between *Brahman* and *saguṇa Ātman* is not at all clear in the religious view of *Gītā darśana*. How are we to take the relation between personal *Ātman* and personal *Brahman*? Either *Ātman* is identical with a part of *Brahman*, or *Ātman* is identical with the whole of *Brahman*. On the first alternative it looks as if chunks or pieces, sparks or aspects, are broken off from God and transplanted like organs into bodies of men and women. This interpretation would seem to make God divisible into parts and reducible to a smaller and smaller size as more and more of Him is broken off. Thus, taken literally, the first alternative leads to a foolish conclusion; therefore, the alternative is foolish.

[74] *Ibid*., VI.5–6.

[75] *Ibid*., XIII.22.

On the second alternative, if *Ātman* were identical with the whole of *Brahman*, then your *Ātman* and my *Ātman* would be identical, since all would be identical with *Brahman*. So when your *Ātman* ceased to be your friend and was angry with you (see p. 213), then my *Ātman* would suddenly have to be unfriendly and angry as well. Thus, taken literally, the second alternative leads to a silly conclusion; therefore, the second alternative is silly.

The critic would conclude that the introduction of *saguṇa Ātman* into *Gītā darśana*, since it leads to such unacceptable conclusions, must itself be both foolish and silly. Undoubtedly, as I said previously, the religious man could find a way out, and I leave the reader to ponder the possibilities.

This completes our discussion of the religious view and the fifth assumption. Let us see what the metaphysician has to say on the same subject.

*Metaphysical View*: Agrees

The metaphysician, of course, will have none of this talk about *saguṇa Ātman*; he regards the fifth assumption simply as a logical conclusion to be drawn from the other assumptions agreed upon previously. *Ātman* and *Brahman* are identical, *Ātman* is, indeed, nontemporally and nonspatially "within" man, but *Ātman* is wholly and totally impersonal; the *Ātman* that is identical with *Brahman* is *nirguṇa* or propertyless *Ātman*:

> The imperishable holy *Ātman*, though seated in the body, being beginningless and *nirguṇa*, It neither acts nor is It acted upon.
>
> Just as the omnipresent spatial ether contains bodies but is not affected by those bodies because of its minuteness, so also *Ātman* though present in every body is not affected by the body.[76]

The metaphysician has his own problems, of course, not the least of which are the problems of parsimony and identity raised earlier with the religious view. Both problems would be formulated in slightly different terms, but they would stand as puzzles waiting for solutions even for the metaphysician. I leave their new formulation as well as their solution for the ambitious reader with metaphysical inclinations.

This completes our discussion of the five assumptions of the two-views interpretation of the *Gītā*. What we have tried to show is that both the religious view and the metaphysical view take quite opposing sides on the assumptions, but that both views have a firm grounding in the *Gītā*. In conclusion, Table IV lists the five assumptions of *Upaniṣadic* philosophy and then compares the stands taken on them by *Gītā* R (the religious view of *Gītā darśana*) and *Gītā* M (the metaphysical view of *Gītā darśana*).

[76] *Ibid.*, XIII.31–32.

TABLE IV. THE FIVE UPANIṢADIC ASSUMPTIONS AND GĪTĀ DARŚANA*

| *Assumptions* | *Gita R* | *Gita M* |
|---|---|---|
| 1. *Brahman* alone is ultimately real. | D | A |
| 2. There are two forms of *Brahman*, a higher and a lower. | d | A |
| 3. *Māyā* is the power of *Brahman* by which lower *Brahman* is manifested. | d | A |
| 4. Bondage is the result of *avidyā*; hence *mokṣa* will be a function of *jñāna*. | D | A |
| 5. Higher *Brahman* is immanent in man as *Ātman*, and *Brahman* is identical with *Ātman*. | a | A |

**Note:* The following abbreviations are used to designate agreement and disagreement:

A—strong agreement
a—weak agreement
d—weak disagreement
D—strong disagreement

It is important to get as clear as possible on the views and what they mean in *Gītā darśana*. To that end we next discuss the two views and the nature of the relation between them in the *Gītā*. Then, in section 4, we shall consider the completeness of *Gītā darśana* and the solution to several interesting problems and curious intellectual puzzles.

### 3. *Gītā Darśana as Progressive Stage Philosophy*

Granted that two entirely distinct philosophies are present in the *Gītā*, what is the point? The point is that the two-views interpretation is the best one for answering that fundamental question with which we began: how can so many philosophers find so many mutually inconsistent metaphysical and religious philosophies in the *Gītā*? The two-views interpretation attempts to answer that question by stating that there are two views of philosophy in the *Gītā*, one religious and the other metaphysical. These two views are quite consistent with one another, however, standing in the same mutual relationship as do, for example, the separate social stages of the *aśramas* ("stages" or "levels"). Just as the *brahmacarya* (student) *aśrama* and the *gṛhastha* (householder) *aśrama* are not inconsistent with one another within Hinduism, and just as the values, goals, duties, and the kind of knowledge found in each are not mutually inconsistent, so in the same way the religious view or stage and the metaphysical view or stage are not inconsistent with one another, nor are the values, goals, duties and the knowledge of the one superior in any way to the other.

*Gītā darśana* wants to maintain that each view, the religious and the metaphysical, is just as good, or right, or true as the other when related to a particular person at a particular level of understanding. We have spoken of the views relationally (p. 204) and as "appropriate to" or "inappropriate to" such persons and their understandings. The two views, therefore, are quite consistent with each other within *Gītā darśana*; that is to say, as far as the side-by-side, mutual existence of the religious view with the metaphysical view is concerned, *Gītā darśana* is consistent. Furthermore, just as one can ripen, mature, grow, and thereby move from the *brahmacarya āśrama* to the *gṛhastha āśrama*, so also one may move, mature, and grow with respect to the religious view and the metaphysical view in *Gītā darśana*.

Maturing and growing in *Gītā darśana* implies mobility, and progressive mobility at that. This progressive mobility, furthermore, is related to a self seen against a metaphysical background consisting of the law of *karma*, the theory of *guṇa* natures, and the doctrine of *saṁsāra*. The usual movement by that self through these two views is generally from the less advanced to the more advanced, relative to a particular self. We tend to call such activity "progressive," as opposed to "regressive," movement. However, if we use the epithets "progressive" and "regressive" to indicate movement from one view to another view, we run the risk of concluding that the former view is not as good, right, or true, in some absolute sense, as the latter view: and that is not what *Gītā darśana* seems to be saying with respect to its two views of religion and metaphysics.

But what is the nature of this movement? Could one, for example, move from "the religious stage," let's call it, to "the metaphysical stage," or *vice versa*? The one-view interpretation (pp. 197–98) would seem to assume that this movement could only be unidirectional, since only one view could be the right one. But *Gītā darśana* wants to argue that both views, both stages, both conceptual frameworks, are "right," because each one stands or exists relative to certain appropriate and specific selves or *guṇa*-natures. The movement that occurs in, as well as between, the stages as each subject finds the stage and the level within it that is most appropriate to his or her *guṇa*-nature is, then, essentially of two kinds: the first kind is bidirectional or interstage movement—movement from the religious stage to the metaphysical stage, or from the metaphysical stage to the religious stage; the second kind is unidirectional or intrastage movement—movement wholly within one stage to higher and more appropriate levels of understanding within it, until heaven or *mokṣa*, the goals of the religious view and the metaphysical view, respectively, are reached. And since both interstage and intrastage movement are goal-oriented, then, insofar as one is moving toward that goal, one is progressing, and insofar as one is moving away from that goal, one is regressing. Thus *Gītā darśana*, insofar as it advocates or prescribes movement toward heaven or *mokṣa*, is in the final analysis a progressive stage philosophy.

One sets out, as Arjuna has, to find the stage appropriate to one's *guṇa*-nature. Lord Kṛṣṇa aids Arjuna in this search until, finally, Arjuna is located at the religious stage. He is tested and examined further by Kṛṣṇa in order to discover whether or not the metaphysical stage would be more appropriate, hence the thrusts and parries around *jñāna* yoga, the principal yoga of the metaphysical stage. In the end, Kṛṣṇa counsels Arjuna on the duties, responsibilities, and ways or yogas of the religious stage—that is, *bhakti* yoga, but also *karma* yoga which can be used at both stages (see pp. 237, 239–40, and especially 271). This leads, then, to Arjuna's progressing further toward the goal of the religious stage, the only goal that he can appropriately pursue given his *rajas guṇa* nature. The *Gītā* stresses the need for a teacher or guide, and the urgent and crucial importance of this *Avatār* or *guru*, whose task it is to set man's foot onto that path which is each man's *svadharma* or own vocation, his *varṇa dharma*, which grows out of each man's *svabhava* or own nature, his *guṇa*-nature.

In concluding this section on progressive stage philosophy in *Gītā darśana*, I would make five points. First, I would contend that the stage philosophy found in *Gītā darśana* is of the type called "progressive stage philosophy." Second, the best evidence that the stage philosophy of the *Gītā* is "progressive" is the fact that Lord Kṛṣṇa, who both represents and himself stands at the metaphysical stage, is the teacher of Arjuna, who stands at the religious stage. And, in the *Gita*, it is Lord Kṛṣṇa, moreover, who invites or exhorts Arjuna to step up to the metaphysical stage or to progress on further in the religious stage; hence the progress by stages in the *Gītā* is both within as well as between the religious stage and the metaphysical stage. Third, and most importantly, when Lord Kṛṣṇa discovers that Arjuna cannot progress to the metaphysical stage, he preaches to him at the religious stage, which is, after all, the appropriate stage for Arjuna given his *guṇa*-nature and his level of knowledge and understanding. Again, there is no question here of one stage's being superior or truer or more real: it is only a question of appropriateness, suitability, and propriety. Fourth, this progressive *stage-relativism* of the two-views interpretation is the essence of *Gītā darśana*:

> Those who worship the gods, they go to the gods;
> those who worship the ancestors, they go to the ancestors
> those who worship devils, they go to the devils,
> but those who worship Me, they come to Me.[77]

The two-views interpretation introduces the two stages, each containing many levels, and with them the invitation to progress toward either of two goals in a way that will eventually leave old levels and the other stage behind.

[77] *Ibid.*, IX.25.

But to find out what stage one is in now takes time, effort, and much self-searching. Hence, as we have seen, the vital need to discover one's *svabhava*, one's *guṇa*-nature.

A fifth and last point emerges from this explanation and defense of *Gītā darśana* as progressive stage philosophy. The *darśana* seems to be couched in ordinary, common-sense language. The language of the two views or stages is clear, the rather traditional language of the five metaphysical assumptions in which *Gītā darśana* stands also seems clear, and the talk about movement between and among the two stages appears clear as well. We can conclude, then, the *Gītā darśana* does not seem to contradict common sense.

We argued earlier that if an interpretation, theory, or philosophy was to be at all "satisfactory," it must meet three standards or criteria of satisfactoriness: it must be common-sensical, consistent, and complete. *Gītā darśana* has met the first two of these standards; now let us consider its completeness.

### 4. *The Completeness of Gītā darśana: Three Problems and their Solution*

In this section we shall try to substantiate the claim that *Gītā darśana* is complete—that it can solve or satisfy certain philosophic problems. *Gītā darśana* cannot solve all philosophic problems. Thus it cannot, as far as I know, solve the problem of induction or the problem of sense data. Nor might *Gītā darśana* be able to solve all of the peripheral problems that are raised in the *Gītā*, at least not to everyone's satisfaction. For example, it might not be able to solve the problem of evil or the problem of human free will, though it may take a stab at them, as we shall do shortly. It can, however, properly handle those puzzles that arose as a result of the development of the two-views interpretation. In our discussions thus far we have isolated and noted six such problems, paradoxes, puzzles, or dilemmas, and I propose to show off the completeness of the theory of *Gītā darśana* by attempting to resolve three of those puzzles. The principle used, which is easily transferred to the remaining three puzzles, is actually quite simple: metaphysical problems arise in the *Bhagavad Gītā* whenever one stands in one stage, the religious or the metaphysical, and projects a theory, an expectation, a conclusion, or a concept from that stage into the other stage. In other words, metaphysical problems develop whenever one makes a category mistake by running the two stages together or by combining them in some philosophic fashion.

For example, return for a moment to the *āśrama* model mentioned previously, and let me argue by analogy from it to the point here. Suppose that someone practices "premature revulsion," as it is called,[78] with respect to

[78]The terminology "premature revulsion" originates with Ananda K. Coomaraswamy and is taken from his paper, "Religious Basis of Indian Society," *East and West and Other Essays* (Colombo: Ola Books, Ltd., n.d.), p. 20.

one of the *āśramas*. That is to say, suppose someone at the *gṛhastha āśrama* suddenly and prematurely renounced that stage and went on to the *vānaprastha* or forest-dweller stage, leaving wife, house, and family heedlessly behind. Such "premature revulsion" carries with it enormous problems and difficulties, psychological as well as social. One attempts to become a solitary anchorite before one is really and naturally ready for that solitude and withdrawal. In forcing oneself artificially into the *vānaprastha* or even the *sannyāsa* stage, before one is ready and before ordinary householder desires and needs have spontaneously fallen away, one can generate psychological problems of a most disturbing and distracting sort. Furthermore, premature revulsion produces the fairly common and infamous phony mystics and fraudulent holy men for which modern India, unfortunately, has become so well known.

Now the same kind of premature revulsion can occur on the philosophic level with respect to *Gītā darśana*, when, for example, a person at the religious stage adopts the assumptions of the metaphysical stage, with the result that, in place of psychological or social problems, we have philosophical or metaphysical problems. Premature revulsion at the philosophic level, rather than at the *āśrama* level, would entail joining, overlapping, or in some fashion combining the assumptions of the religious stage, *Gītā* R, with the assumptions of the metaphysical stage, *Gītā* M. Contradictions result, explicitly, of course, when we try to combine these two inconsistent sets of *Upaniṣadic* assumptions; but what can be implicitly generated are several philosophic paradoxes or puzzles when several of the assumptions are joined together from opposing *Gītā* R and *Gītā* M sides. Thus by combining or overlapping assumption 1 (Table IV, p. 215) as seen by *Gītā* M with assumption 3 as seen by *Gītā* R, we can neatly generate the dilemma of *māyā* (see pp. 109 and 191–92). From combining assumptions 1 and 2 as seen by *Gītā* M with assumptions 2 and 4 as seen by *Gītā* R together with the concept of an *Avatār* or Savior as seen by *Gītā* R, we can generate both the Savior dilemma (p. 164) and the paradox of the *Avatār* (p. 150). It is quite possible that by combining the other assumptions of *Gītā* R and *Gītā* M, entirely new and as yet undreamed of puzzles and problems could be similarly generated.

Now if the problems, paradoxes, and dilemmas that we have noted throughout our investigations of the *Gītā* are generated by this philosophic variety of premature revulsion, by this combining or overlapping of contradictory assumptions, then the solutions to them would simply entail the removal of the overlap, together with a mental note to oneself never again to combine the assumptions and the philosophy of the religious view or stage with those of the metaphysical view or stage. But let's see how *Gītā darśana* fares as a solver of such puzzles.

The three problems that I shall present for solution arise distinctly out of Indian thought but have their parallels in Western thought as well. One of them is all too familiar to us, having been inherited from the *Upaniṣads*, while the other two are peculiar to the *Gītā*. The problems that I have in mind are, first, the dilemma of *māyā*; second, the paradox of the *Avatār*; and finally, closely related to the other two, the Creator dilemma. Let me state each of these puzzles, carefully and clearly, and then show in what way *Gītā darśana* would solve or answer them.

1. *The dilemma of māyā*. This dilemma, which leads to a curious absurdity regarding the metaphysical status of *māyā*, goes something like this:

1) If *māyā* is real, then *Brahman* is not the sole reality, and the *advaita* metaphysics is destroyed.
2) If *māyā* is unreal, then it could not be efficacious in producing the appearance of the world, the Gods, and the self.
3) But *māyā* must be either real or unreal.
4) Therefore, either the *advaita* metaphysics is destroyed or *māyā* is not efficacious.

*Gītā darśana* invites us now to view the puzzle from each of the two separate stages of that *darśana*:

*Religious stage:* There is no problem unless one tries to force a monism into a place where there is a pluralism. Hence, there is no difficulty in letting *advaita* be destroyed. The religious person admits, frankly, that God is real and that *māyā* may also be real and separate from God, or real and the same as God, since a pluralistic metaphysics is at the heart of the religious stage.

*Metaphysical stage:* There need be no problem here either. The problem develops only in trying to have two, *Brahman* and *māyā*, where there is only one, *Brahman*. If *māyā* is real, then it must be *Brahman*, and if *māyā* is unreal, then it cannot be *Brahman*. The problem emerges in our wanting to see the metaphysical stage from the religious stage's point of view—in wanting two where there can be only one. (And Śaṁkara, for example, "solves" the dilemma in his own curious fashion by rejecting the third premise: *māyā*, he says, is neither real nor unreal.)

2. *The paradox of the Avatār*. This paradox leads to another curious absurdity—one about the Savior, such as Lord Kṛṣṇa, who has come to earth to save suffering and demented men, such as Arjuna. The paradox goes something like this:

1) The *Avatār* comes to earth, driven here by love for all suffering creatures.
2) Love, like desire, is an imperfection.

3) The *Avatār* is, therefore, imperfect.
4) The *Avatār* comes to teach man the way to perfection.
5) But how can an imperfect being teach others the way to perfection?

*Religious stage*: There is no problem unless one tries to import a notion or doctrine from the metaphysical stage, that love and desire are qualities, hence imperfect, into the religious stage. For the latter stage, divine love and human love are the highest and most revered qualities possessed by the Savior and his imitative devotees.

*Metaphysical stage*: There is no problem. The *Avatār* is imperfect as *saguṇa Brahman* and there's an end to it. Troubles and problems develop only when one wants a perfect *saguṇa* real Savior (a religious concept) together and simultaneously with a perfect, real, *nirguṇa Brahman* (a metaphysical concept).

3. *The Creator dilemma*. This dilemma is quite similar to the dilemma of *māyā* treated previously, and its solution will follow along similar lines, but with several interesting new features. The Creator dilemma goes something like this:

1) If *Brahman* creates the world with some thing outside of and separate from Itself or Himself—for example, with another reality such as matter—then the *advaita* metaphysics is destroyed.
2) If *Brahman* creates the world from some thing not outside but within Itself or Himself—for example, with some sort of *Brahman*-matter—then either (a) if the matter is identical with a part of *Brahman*, then whenever that matter was destroyed, a part of *Brahman* would be too; or (b) if the matter is identical with the whole of *Brahman*, then whenever matter undergoes change, the whole of *Brahman* would change. But the conclusions to both 2(a) and 2(b) are absurd.
3) But *Brahman* must create the world from some thing either outside or within Itself or Himself, and if from within Itself or Himself, then it must be identical with either a part or a whole of *Brahman*.
4) Therefore, either the *advaita* metaphysics is destroyed; or a part of *Brahman* can be destroyed or the whole of *Brahman* can be changed; and both of the latter are absurd.

*Religious stage:* There is no problem. *Brahman* or God, a Himself and not an Itself, forms the world by His *māyā*, which may be a part of God. The dualism or pluralism does not bother the religious man. Further, the world may quite easily be either a part of *Brahman* or the whole of *Brahman*. When change occurs in one, it may well occur in the other. "Destroyed" is too strong a word for what occurs, here, where only simple change occurs. And since the religious man is not bound to an *advaita* conception of a *nirguṇa Brahman,* he holds that *Brahman* can change and does change as often as He likes.

*Metaphysical stage:* There is no problem. *Brahman* as creator is *saguṇa Brahman* and as a consequence the ontological purity of *nirguṇa Brahman* is saved. Meanwhile, *saguṇa Brahman* creates and carries on, changing or not changing, with matter or without matter, as It pleases. Problems develop, once more, only when we try to import religious concepts, such as God, He, Creator, *saguṇa Brahman,* matter, change, destruction, into the metaphysical monistic realm of *nirguṇa Brahman,* where they clearly do not belong. (See Śaṁkara's *advaita* solution above, pp. 208–9.)

These attempted solutions to three puzzles from the *Gītā* by *Gītā darśana* give us good grounds for holding that *Gītā darśana* is complete. We shall have occasion later, in discussing the ethics of the *Bhagavad Gītā,* to wrestle with still another puzzle, the traditional problem of human free will, and we shall see *Gītā darśana* recalled for service there. For the moment, however, we can tentatively conclude that *Gītā darśana* is very likely a satisfactory interpretation of the *Gītā* because it is common-sensical, consistent, and probably complete, and because it has answered that fundamental question: how can so many philosophers find so many mutually inconsistent metaphysical and religious philosophies in the *Bhagavad Gītā*?

### 5) Conclusion

We began this investigation of the metaphysics and epistemology of the *Bhagavad Gītā* by noting that two *darśanas, Sāṁkhya darśana* and *Upaniṣadic* or *Vedānta darśana,* both influenced the *Gītā*'s philosophy. We argued that the influence on the *Gītā* of these two mutually inconsistent *darśanas,* one metaphysically dualistic or pluralistic (*Sāṁkhya*) and the other generally monistic (*Upaniṣadic* or *Vedānta*), had produced a myriad of interpretations of the *Gītā,* ranging from the several schools of *Vedānta darśana* to the more generalized interpretations dealt with as "the contradictory interpretation," "the subjective interpretation," "the one-view interpretation" and "the two-views interpretation." We argued that only the last, the two-views interpretation, could produce a satisfactory answer to the fundamental question about the *Bhagavad Gītā*: how can so many philosophers find in it so many mutually inconsistent metaphysical and religious philosophies? The answer that we found lay in rejecting the first three of the generalized interpretations of the *Gītā* and in accepting the fourth, the two-views interpretation. We showed the two-views interpretation to be satisfactory by meeting three standards of satisfactoriness: common sense, consistency, and completeness; that is, we were able to state the views in an ordinary though technical vocabulary; we showed that the two views, the metaphysical monistic view and the religious pluralistic view, are harmonious and quite mutually compatible; and we solved several rather curious philosophical puzzles that occur in the *Gītā* by means of the two-views interpretation. The two views, the metaphysical and the religious, can be seen as stages from which change and growth can take place, and we argued that neither stage is superior to or better than the other but only appropriate to particular needs and understandings of persons in those stages.

We have, finally, given the name "*Gītā darśana*" to this philosophic system that has these two views and these two stages as part of its metaphysics and epistemology. Thus, if all of what we have said is true, the *Bhagavad Gītā* has a *darśana* that is not an inconsistent blending of *Sāṁkhya* and *Upaniṣadic* elements, nor is it a hodge-podge, carelessly thrown-together eclecticism wherein every earnest seeker can find whatever suits his fancy. Rather, *Gītā darśana* is a carefully compartmentalized dualism of two quite distinct philosophies, established for at least two quite distinct kinds of persons, each defined, ideally at any rate, by two quite distinct *guṇa* natures.

This completes our discussion of the metaphysics and epistemology of the *Bhagavad Gītā*. We turn next to the last of the fields of philosophy to which the *Gītā* speaks: the ethics of the *Bhagavad Gītā*.

## 4. THE ETHICS OF THE *BHAGAVAD GĪTĀ*

The *Bhagavad Gītā* is primarily a work in ethics. Its essential concern is with man and man's actions in the world and with how those actions affect his future life and progress. This ethical thrust of the *Gītā* will add a new and practical dimension to the stages of the *Gītā darśana* which up to this time we have viewed simply as a metaphysical and epistemological theory. That the *Gītā* is principally ethical in its concern can be most easily seen, I believe, from a reexamination of its story.

The warrior Arjuna, you will recall, is a member of the *kṣatriya* class called upon to fight in a just war to wrest his lost kingdom from an evil usurper. In the first chapter, and on the battlefield before the fighting starts, Arjuna, accompanied by his charioteer-cousin Kṛṣṇa, looks across the field to the ranks of the opposing army. There to his horror he sees men of his own family that he knows and loves. Considering what he is bound by duty to do—to kill to protect the clan—he is suddenly seized by the awful prospect of what he cannot do: to fight against those he loves. The opening chapter of the *Gītā* lands us squarely in the midst of a moral dilemma that we earlier referred to as "Arjuna's dilemma" (p. 151), which led, in turn, to "the dilemma of action" (pp. 151–52). From the beginning it is Arjuna's dilemma that provides the philosophical motivation to the *Gītā*, for it is a moral problem with metaphysical roots and epistemological implications. This dilemma, very simply, is that if Arjuna fights, he's doomed; and if he doesn't fight, he's also doomed; and, since he must either fight or not fight, either way he's doomed. Put more elegantly, Arjuna's dilemma looks like this:

1. If Arjuna fights, then he will be fighting his own family, and then he's doomed.
2. If Arjuna does not fight, then he will have failed to do his duty, and then he's doomed.
3. He must either fight or not fight.
4. Therefore, whatever he does, he's doomed.

The dilemma of action, in turn, is a kind of generalization on Arjuna's dilemma:

1. If one does evil acts (such as fighting one's own family), then this produces evil results that entail rebirth and bondage.
2. If one does good acts (such as doing one's duty and protecting the family), then this produces good results that entail rebirth and bondage.
3. One must either do good acts or do bad acts.
4. Therefore, whatever one does, rebirth and bondage are the results.

The solution to both dilemmas lay, you will recall, in employing *karma* yoga, a technique that effectively attacked the third premise of each of the dilemmas. *Karma* yoga is introduced in Chapter II of the *Gītā* as a way of action that produces no binding results. This technique of *karma* yoga nullifies premise 3 of Arjuna's dilemma by claiming that there is really a third alternative to fighting or not fighting—namely, fighting without producing fighting-consequences. *Karma* yoga nullifies premise 3 of the dilemma of action by slipping between the horns of that alternative and claiming that some actions, those involving *karma* yoga, produce neither good nor bad acts with neither good nor bad consequences. By the time we finish the second chapter of the *Gita*, the moral problems have all been set forth and the chief moral solution has been advanced.

In the concluding chapter of the *Gītā* Kṛṣṇa returns to what we might call "the central problem ot the *Gītā*", the problem that the first two chapters introduce and that all the remaining sixteen chapters are intent on solving: how to get Arjuna to do his duty and fight. That central problem of the *Gītā* has to all intents and purposes been solved by the time we reach the last chapter. There, in his final question to his devoted auditor, Lord Kṛṣṇa asks:

> Has what I have been saying been heard by you with single-minded attention? Has the confusion of ignorance in you been destroyed?

to which the ever-faithful Arjuna replies in his final speech in the *Gītā*:

> My ignorance has been destroyed. I have been reminded of my duty through your grace. I now stand firm with all my doubts removed. I shall act according to your word.[79]

And there the *Gītā* really ends. It began with a moral problem, and it now concludes with that problem having been resolved. That is why I say the *Gītā* is primarily a work in ethics.

But between that beginning and that ending a host of moral issues are raised for the critical philosopher to wrestle with and clarify. Questions arise, and our philosophic confusion often times fails to be removed along with Arjuna's own doubts. Why doesn't Arjuna just run away from it all, leave the world, hide away in a monkery or a cave? Many philosophers have argued that this is precisely what Indian philosophy and religion pushes its devotees into: negating life and the world for the sake of a better future life after death. What role does *Brahman*, God, or Kṛṣṇa play in the carrying out of our human actions? Is there fatalism in the Indian scheme of ethics? As we shall see, several passages in Chapter XVIII of the *Gītā* would lead us to believe that man is fated and not free at all in his moral endeavors. Finally, we are left to wonder just what kind of ethical theory runs through the pages of the *Bhagavad Gītā*. It would have to be a theory, one would suppose, that would prevent man from running off to caves and monkeries, that would eschew fatalism and divine predestination, and that would answer a fundamental ethical question for us: what makes right actions right? This latter question will involve us with two viable contenders for the title of "the ethical theory of the *Bhagavad Gītā*": a so-called "teleological ethical theory" and a so-called "deontological ethical theory."

In part *a* below, I shall take up the question: what makes right actions right in the ethical theory of the *Bhagavad Gītā*? I shall discuss the doctrine of rightness with respect to deontological and teleological ethical theories in order to determine where the doctrine of moral rightness stands in the *Gītā*, In part *b* I shall develop the issue of, and raise some questions about, the putative fatalism and predestination of the *Gītā*, especially with respect to *daiva*, ("fate" or "Providence"). Finally, in part *c* I shall conclude with some general remarks about our two ethical theories and relate them to the religious view and the metaphysical view of *Gītā darśana*.

### *a. What Makes Right Actions Right in the Bhagavad Gītā?*

In the section that follows I want to do two things. First, I will divide what we might call a simple and ordinary action into three constituent parts, somewhat along the line suggested by the *Gītā* (see XVIII.18–19), and then

[79] *Bhagavad Gītā*, XVIII.72–73.

demonstrate the importance and significance of two of these parts to our two ethical theories. Second, I will relate each of these ethical theories to the two views or stages of *Gītā darśana* while offering, at the same time, some remarks and criticisms about the notion of moral rightness in *Gītā darśana*.

**1) Rightness in Actions: Teleological Ethics and Deontological Ethics**

In the *Bhagavad Gītā* two quite distinct theories emerge with respect to ethics: "the teleological theory" and "the deontological theory." Suppose we consider an example and see what these theories come to. Suppose that you are strolling down the street one fine day, approaching a bank. Suddenly, the door of the bank is thrown open and a man in a muffled overcoat and pulled-down hat emerges from the door at great speed. He turns in your direction and comes hurtling down the street toward you, clutching a small black bag. Suddenly out of the bank behind him comes a well-dressed man carrying a revolver. He shouts at you to stop the muffled man, and then starts off in pursuit. Suppose, then, that you heroically throw a magnificent tackle which you learned in soccer, judo, or basketball, bringing the first man to the ground and pinioning him there while he protests and struggles. Suppose then that the man with the pistol approaches, shoots the man that you are restraining, grabs the little black bag, thanks you for your trouble, leaps into a waiting black Mercedes and is off before you can say, Good grief, Charlie Brown! Question: Was your action right?

To answer the question as the teleologist or the deontologist might answer, we need to make some distinctions. I want to divide the "action situation," as I shall call it, into three parts. That is to say, let the "action" be the whole of the activity from your original intention to stop the fleeing man hurtling from the bank door, to your decision to act, to the final shooting and the fleeing of the well-dressed thief. Now let that entire action be divided into "motive," "act," and "consequences." So the first part of the action—the motive—entails your intention for acting; in this case your reason for acting was obviously to prevent a robber from escaping from the scene of his crime and to hold him for the authorities. The second part of the action was the act, itself—your throwing the man to the ground by a well-placed block or tackle and then pinioning him there. The act simply involves a doing of some sort, and the statement of the act is a description of that doing. The third and final part of the action is the result or consequences—the events that occurred after the act.

Thus we have the three parts of the action: motive, act, and consequences. Our original question—was your action right?—is now seen to be rather complex, simply because there are three parts of the action to consider. Should we, for example, weight the rightness or wrongness of each part—of intention, act, and consequences—equally? Or should one of the three parts be weighted more heavily than the other two? Or should the evaluation of one of the three be considered exclusively? In a court of law, for example, evidence of intent in a murder case can mean the difference between a first- and second-degree murder indictment. St. Thomas Aquinas, on the other hand, says that only God can truly know what a man's real intention is and that all knowledge of intention is, consequently, closed to other persons. And we might ask of the second element of action: are certain acts always right, or must consequences always be considered as well?

Teleologists (from the Greek *telos*, "end" or "result") put all of their moral weight for judging rightness on the consequences alone and to the general exclusion of both the nature of the act and the agent's intention; while the deontologists (from the Greek *deontos*, "obligatory" or "necessary") put all of their moral weight for judging rightness on the nature of the act, itself, to the total exclusion of the consequences. Hence, teleological ethics is an ethical theory that defines moral rightness in terms of the fruits, results, or consequences of human acts, while deontological ethics is an ethical theory that defines moral rightness in terms of the recognizably inherent and absolute rightness of certain human acts. The reader is left to decide whether the action in the example was right or wrong. Our immediate task is to find out whether the *Gītā* is promulgating a teleological or a deontological ethical theory or view.

Let's take another example, one that is similar to Arjuna's problem. Suppose you receive a notice from the Federal Government to report for duty in a firing squad. You are an ordinary, morally sensitive but obedient citizen of the country, and besides this, you're curious, so you show up. A legally delegated official announces that you are now an authorized member of the United States Federal Firing Squad (U.S.F.F.S.), since acquiescence to the order to report is tantamount to the acceptance of membership in U.S.F.F.S. The official hands out rifles and ammunition to you and several others. Then he drags out some wretch, stands him up against a wall, and tells you to get ready to shoot this legally tried and lawfully sentenced traitor, murderer, and spy (all three). What would you do? Would you get ready to shoot? Suppose that the official lets it be known that if you fail to comply with this quite legal order, you will be found guilty of treason and cowardice in the face of the enemy, and that the consequences of your refusal will be bad, indeed. Now, what would you do? And, more importantly, why would you make the moral decision that you would make? Would it be right or wrong to obey or disobey? Why? Would it be right to shoot or not? Why?

The teleologist and the deontologist may, in the end, decide to do the same thing, stay and shoot, or go home and not shoot; they may even both decide that staying and shooting is right, or that staying and shooting is wrong. The important point for us to realize here, however, is that they would base their decision about rightness or wrongness, and staying or leaving, on entirely different grounds, and it is in those grounds that we, as critical philosophers, are interested.

Let's analyze the action into its three constituent parts. Suppose the question is simply: should you obey the lawful command of the U.S.F.F.S. and shoot this legally convicted and lawfully sentenced traitor, murderer, and spy? The three parts of the action of shooting would be, first, your *motive*—to obey the Government, to do good, to maximize happiness in the world, to keep from being ridiculed and going to jail yourself, to achieve honor and be recognized as a hero or heroine, and so on; second, the *act*, which may be many things with many parts—to raise a rifle, to aim at a human being, to pull a trigger, to pull a trigger while aiming at a human being, to kill a human being, and so on; third, the *consequences*—the death of a man, the increase of pain in the world, the increase of pleasure in the world, and so on. To mention all the possible elements of motive, act, and consequences would be enormously complex, but in our uncomplicated situation we shall be content to keep the number of the elements low and the example as elementary as possible. Now, if you're a teleologist, you have simply to forget about the motive and the act parts of the action, except insofar as they aid you in focusing on what you consider to be the most important part: the consequences. But what must the nature of the consequences be in order that you can use it or them in determining whether or not shooting would be right? In other words, granted that you are a teleologist, now that you've focused your attention on the consequences and left the motive and the act more or less out of the picture, what next? What's to be looked for in the consequences? At this stage many teleologists answer by calling attention to a particular psychological theory about the nature of man, and they then proceed to ground their teleological ethical theory in that psychological theory. Let me speak for a moment about this theory of man and its relation to teleological ethics.

Think honestly for a moment about the kinds of things you desire and want in this world. Recall our consideration of the *arthas*, the aims or goals of life, in discussing the background to the *Upaniṣads*, where we cited the four traditional goals within Hinduism: *artha* or wealth, *kāma* or love, *dharma* or duty and vocation, and *mokṣa* or liberation. These goals may be all well and good for a Hindu or a follower of the *Upaniṣads* or a devotee of the *Bhagavad Gītā*, but what do they mean to you? And how do they help us to get at man's nature and teleological ethics? Let me begin by asking you several questions about your own *arthas*. Suppose that you're a student and, for a start, suppose I ask you, "Why are you reading this book?" And you answer, "Because it's part of a course assignment" (leaving aside that you may read it for other reasons, too). "Why do you want to complete a course assignment?" "Because then I'll be able to pass the course." "Why do you want to pass the course?" "So I can graduate." "Why do you want to graduate?" "So I can get the degree." "Why do you want the degree?" "Because I'll be able to make more money," you say, intentionally leaving aside all the other myriad reasons for getting a degree, such as impressing your friends by writing "B.A." after your name, having a surprise for relatives who thought you were a deadbeat and would never make it, gaining prestige that enables you to marry into wealth and social position, and so on. But, I persist, "Why do you want more money?" And you reply, "So that I can buy those things that I lack now, such as hi-fi sets, cars, houses, nice clothes, gourmet foods, travel to exotic lands and cities, and so on." "Why do you want these things?", I finally ask you. "Because they make me happy," you finally say.

Beyond this point I really can't ask you any more "Why's." We have reached an ultimate question with an ultimate answer. Happiness, as Aristotle pointed out some several thousand years ago, is an ultimate and final goal in the sense that it would make no sense or would be very odd to ask, "Why do you want to be happy?" At least it is not on the same level as asking, "Why are you reading this book?"—the question that began this rather lengthy inquiry. Thus happiness is an ultimate *artha*, and the other minor goals, such as passing the course, the B.A. degree, money, cars, houses, travel, and the like, are simply instrumental ends or means to that ultimate end, happiness.

But we can ask, "Why do you want to be happy?" for another purpose than seeing whether there is some other goal or end beyond it. And asking that question for this other purpose will steer us back into our psychological ground for teleological ethics. One very good answer to the question, "Why do you want to be happy?" would be to say, "Because that's my nature," or, "Because that's the nature of man"—to seek happiness or pleasure for himself, or for others, or for both. In technical terminology this theory—that man is an animal motivated by the desire for pleasure and the avoidance of pain—is called "psychological hedonism." Psychological hedonism says in essence that man is a pleasure-seeking or happiness-seeking animal.

Now psychological hedonism has a corollary in the moral field called "ethical hedonism," such that the former theory underlies and gives support to the latter. Ethical hedonism is not a psychological theory, therefore, but a moral position that says man ought to do those acts that bring about the greatest amount of pleasuse. And why should he? Why, because that's his nature—to want to maximize his pleasures. Now the latter statement about man's nature rests upon the theory of psychological hedonism. And while psychological hedonism is not a proof or even a valid reason for accepting ethical hedonism, it does serve to give psychological and emotional support to nervous ethical hedonists who want to believe that what they ought to do is what they are probably going to do anyway. So, strictly speaking, while there is no attempt to logically derive an "ought theory" (ethical hedonism) from an "is theory" (psychological hedonism), there is nonetheless a kind of nonlogical support of the former by the latter. At least it seems this way to most ethical hedonists. The only point I wish to focus on here is that ethical hedonism, with its grounding in the nature of man as a pleasure-seeking creature, is precisely what the teleological ethical theory seizes upon in discussing what to look for when you look to the consequences of an act: what you ought to look for in the consequences is the amount of pleasure they produce because that's the way man naturally looks at the world anyway.

### a) TELEOLOGICAL ETHICS

This brings us to the point where we can offer a definition of rightness according to the teleological theory of ethics. (Once we're through with this we can get back to that firing squad.) According to the theory of teleological ethics, now buttressed by ethical hedonism, which is in turn buttressed by psychological hedonism, a right act, any right act, let's call it "*x*", will be defined as follows:

> *x* is right if and only if *x* is done freely or voluntarily and *x* produces more happiness or pleasure (the concepts for the hedonist are interchangeable) for everyone concerned than any other act appropriate to the circumstances.

Some comments are in order regarding this definition. First, we wouldn't want to call your act—shooting with the firing squad, let's say—"right" or "wrong" or even call it "your act," for that matter, if you did it while someone held a pistol to your head. For then the blame for shooting the prisoner would be on the head of the person who forced you to do it against your will by threats of a reasonably serious sort. But we can say (and soon we will elaborate on the point) that for any act to be called "right," it must be done voluntarily, without external physical, or internal psychological, complusion.

Second, for an act to be called "right" it must produce more pleasure, measured quantitatively, than any other act. But for whom? Whose pleasure is to be measured quantitatively? And how does one quantify pleasure? There are three answers to the question about whose future pleasure is to be measured. This teleological doctrine of ethical hedonism can be "egoistic," in which case it is your or the agent's future pleasure, and yours or his alone, that must be quantified and taken into account. Or ethical hedonism can be "altruistic," in which case it is everyone else's pleasure except your own or the agent's that is to be quantified and taken into account. Or ethical hedonism can be "universalistic"; everyone's future pleasure is to be quantified and taken into account—yours and mine, his and hers, or at least that of everyone who would be affected by, or be concerned with, the consequences of your or the agent's act. The only ethical hedonism we shall be concerned with is universalistic ethical hedonism both in our firing-squad example and in the ethics of the *Bhagavad Gītā*.

With respect to the question, "How does one quantify pleasure?" I would suggest that the answer is intuitively obvious, since we do it all the time when we weigh actions that have any bearing on our own future happiness. Thus, you ask, "Should I study for the exam tomorrow or watch TV instead?" "Should I date Smith knowing this will hurt Jones' feelings?" "Should I show up for duty in a firing squad?" The reader ought to have no philosophic doubts about the quantifiability of pleasure, for in fact such quantification is logically possible (it would not be self-contradictory) and empirically possible (it would not violate any known empirical law). For instance, take seriously the following rather silly suggestion and, conforming to universalistic ethical hedonism, assume that you alone are the only person whose pleasure is concerned or affected. Think of the amount of pleasure that you get from eating your favorite variety of pizza pie under normal or standard conditions—when you're not too tired, too hungry, or too thirsty, when the pie is warm, is eaten in pleasant surroundings, and so on. Now compare that amount of pleasure to other things that you like more and that you like less, thereby proving to yourself that comparing pleasures makes sense. This comparing can make sense only where we are dealing with adjectives such as "more" and "less" and "same," which are all relational adjectives dependent on the possibility or actuality of some kind of quantification. Let the pleasure that you get from eating that one pizza pie under normal conditions be quantified and named as $1\pi$ ("one pi"). Now, we have a base with which to compare other pleasures. It is perfectly possible that while some acts, such as pizza pie eating, lead to $1\pi$ pleasure, other acts could lead to lesser or greater $\pi$. The first kiss of young love is notorious for equaling $20\pi$; an "A" on a final exam is guaranteed to produce $25\pi$; listening to the professor's lecture and then detecting a logical fallacy in it invariably produces $50\pi$; and so on.

Suppose we're back at our firing squad with you as a teleologist. The question arises: should you shoot?—and you start doing what all good teleologists ought to do when faced with a moral problem: you start calculating $\pi$'s. If I shoot, you begin, then the man will be killed and that's $-50\pi$ ("minus fifty pi," which means that there are 50 negative units of pleasure, i.e., 50 units of pain, involved). But he's a spy, you might go on, and spies ought to be punished, and so shooting him as a punishment would be good, so that's $10\pi$. And I won't be punished then for not shooting, and that's about $20\pi$. You add up the $\pi$ units for shooting: $(-50\pi) + (10\pi) + (20\pi)$, which equals $-20\pi$. But we aren't through yet. What if you don't shoot? If I don't shoot, you continue, then my conscience won't bother me for not killing him and that's $50\pi$. But a spy might go free (unlikely but possible), and that's $-10\pi$. And I'll probably be punished for not shooting and that's $-10\pi$. You add up the $\pi$ units for not shooting: $50\pi + (-10\pi) + (-10\pi)$, which equals $30\pi$. Now which act, shooting or not shooting, would be the right act? The answer is that not shooting would be the *prima facie* right act, since it would produce more pleasure, $50\pi$ more, to be exact, for everyone concerned, than shooting would. So don't shoot. (I say that not shooting is the "*prima facie*" right act, for there may well be aspects of quantification here that we have not considered.)

But what's to prevent me, a critic might say, from carrying about, up my sleeve, a peanut butter sandwich, the kind of sandwich of which I am extremely fond. In fact, eating peanut butter sandwiches generally produces for me 500$\pi$. So whenever I get into a tight moral dilemma I simply turn to the security of my peanut butter sandwich, dig up my sleeve, haul it out and eat. Since the pleasure of eating the sandwich far outweighs the pleasure of almost any other act, whether shooting or not shooting, it will always be the right act. This sounds silly, but many people have other similar kinds of security and escape mechanisms that they turn to that are just as silly and just as morally outrageous as this turning to peanut butter sandwiches. Some people, when faced with a particularly nasty moral dilemma, turn to alcohol; others turn to drugs, or the TV, or movies, food, sex, sleep, or the radio; our culture abounds in peanut-butter-sandwich substitutes and distractions designed especially for the person seeking to avoid both crucial situations and critical moments where moral decisions must be made. And since the distraction is always more pleasant than either legitimate alternative of the moral situation, the act of distraction would always be the right thing to do. But that would make the teleological definition of rightness absurd. Consequently, we must add to the end of that definition the words "appropriate to the circumstances," so that the range of choices open to us for our moral consideration will be only those which are legitimate or appropriate. For example, consuming peanut butter sandwiches, alcohol, drugs, or a good book would not be appropriate acts for consideration in my determining whether shooting a man is right or wrong. Thus the definition concludes that the right act ". . . produces more happiness or pleasure than any other act appropriate to the circumstances."

### b) DEONTOLOGICAL ETHICS

The deontologist would reject all of the above as stuff and nonsense. The deontologist is an old-fashioned moralist who believes rather strenuously that certain kinds of acts are always right, acts such as promise keeping, truth telling, loving your neighbor, and that, certain kinds of acts are always wrong, such as lying, stealing, and killing. He has little use for talk about the pleasure of consequences or for calculations of pleasures into $\pi$'s. Telling the truth would always be right, he might say, no matter what consequences it happened to lead to. If asked, "How do you know that certain acts are always right?" the deontologist generally falls back on what is technically called "rational intuitionism." Rightness, he says to the critic, is just something that every moral man sees in certain acts or kinds of acts, and if you can't see it yourself then you're just not morally mature. He doesn't mean to turn this defense of deontological ethics and moral intuitionism into an impassioned *ad hominem* attack against the teleological critic, and it shouldn't be seen that way. For when the deontologist says (to take a favorite example), "You're not morally mature, if you don't see that truth telling is always right," he really means, quite literally and coolly, that you can't be a truly moral person unless you have this special mature understanding, or "intuition," as we shall call it, that truth telling and rightness are always and necessarily connected. Nothing personal, he would hasten to add, but it's just that you lack a moral sensitivity. The deontologist argues that whenever we hold these two concepts, truth telling and rightness (or perhaps moral obligation or moral goodness), before our mind, we come to see that they are related in a very special way. In virtue of holding them, juxtaposing them, conceptually and for rational consideration, we suddenly and immediately discover that they are necessarily and *a priori* connected to each other such that the general ethical maxim, "Truth telling is always right," is a synthetic *a priori* judgment (see above, pp. 127–28); that is, the statement, "Truth telling is always right," is always and everywhere factually and necessarily true.

There are problems with this position, some of which relate directly to the nature of all factually necessary judgments and to intuitive knowledge in general (see p. 130) as well as to clashes between two deontologically grounded but hypothetically opposed moral judgments. Such might occur, for example, in a situation where if I tell the truth, I might fail to keep a promise—a situation that we referred to earlier as "the deontological puzzle" (pp. 98–99). Since these problems have been dealt with previously and at some length, I don't wish to repeat them here. Suffice it to say that there are problems that the deontologist must face up to, but they are probably neither insoluble nor insurmountable.

According to the theory of deontological ethics, buttressed by ethical intuitionism and an epistemology of synthetic *a priori* judgments, any right act will be defined in general as follows:

> *x* is right if and only if *x* is an instance of a class of acts, truth telling, promise keeping, or the like, which are recognized certainly and necessarily to be absolutely and inherently right in and of themselves.

Thus, to be a right act—let's say telling my roommate the truth about the person the rommate is engaged to when my roommate asks me for the truth—that act must be an instance of truth telling itself. For if truth telling is alway right, then my doing so now will be right. I know that truth telling is always right by an act of intuition. Hence, if what I tell my roommate about the betrothed (when asked to do so) is the truth, then telling it is right. My act is an instance of a class of acts, all of which are known to be right acts; so my individual act will be right, too.

Some deontologists may, on the other hand, work only with individual acts, in which case separate intuitions would be called for each and every time a moral decision was needed. What binds all deontological decisions together, however, is the intuition, the immediate and certain awareness, of the connection between the act (either as a member of a class of other acts of the same sort or as an individual act, alone and by itself) and the concept or notion of rightness (or moral goodness or moral obligation, perhaps).

There's something psychologically comforting and happily predictable about deontologists. When a deontologist makes a promise to you, and you know that he believes that promise keeping is always right, you know very well that he's going to keep that promise. You can count on deontologists, they are the salt of the earth, they are old-fashioned, fundamentally good and sound people. But take the teleologist—and almost all of us are teleologists: when a teleologist makes a promise, you know that he'll keep it unless there would be more general happiness or pleasure from breaking it. Suppose that you loan two books, one to a deontologist and the other to a teleologist. Suppose that both promise to return them to you on Friday. Suppose that there's a terrible storm on Friday, or your house burns, or an earthquake rips the city to pieces, or the end of the world comes. Who would be there on Friday with your book? That person—the only one with unyielding moral scruples and principles, the only one with true moral feelings, who lives and guides his life in a way that must seem to others too strict, too unbending, too formal and fundamental. But what a human being!—and what a person to loan books to!

Suppose we're back at our firing squad with you as our deontologist. The question arises: should you shoot? Being a good deontologist, you start consulting your list of always-right rules or maxims, a list justified by your rational intuition of a class of moral actions or individual judgments of such actions. We shall have to stop here, however, for anything else we say could be so outrageously hypothetical about how you would act and what you would believe to be right that it would make all moral discussions ludicrous. It may seem a bit odd, but please note that intuition could be used to justify almost any moral stand you'd care to take in the firing squad. It could conceivably justify such diverse judgments as, Killing human beings is wrong, or Killing spies and traitors is right; Killing anything is wrong, or Killing in self-defense is right; Obeying the law is right, or Disobeying certain laws is right; and so on.

So we must leave you at the firing squad, alone with your conscience, which often is another name for moral intuition, and move on. In the next section we attempt to determine what kind of ethics is being promulgated by the *Bhagavad Gītā*. We can do this best by discovering whether our two heroes, Arjuna and Kṛṣṇa, are teleologists or deontologists.

### 2) Rightness in the Gītā

In Chapter I of the *Gītā* Arjuna offers a number of arguments in support of his refusal to fight. Kṛṣṇa counters these arguments with several of his own, exhorting and endeavoring to convince Arjuna that he ought to do his duty, take up his arms, and go into battle. In the course of this moral jousting Kṛṣṇa reveals to Arjuna the technique or method of *karma* yoga, the employment of which will enable Arjuna to fight without incurring sin. In this section we shall do two things: first, classify Arjuna's arguments and Kṛṣṇa's responses to them as teleological or deontological arguments and then deal with the classification of *karma* yoga along the same lines; second, examine the relation of teleological and deontological theories in the *Gītā* to *Gītā darśana*, the philosophical system at work in the *Gītā*. I shall want to argue that the two views of *Gītā darśana*, the religious view and the metaphysical view, relate rather directly to the two ethical theories at work in the *Bhagavad Gītā*.

#### a) TELEOLOGICAL AND DEONTOLOGICAL ARGUMENTS IN THE GĪTĀ

In our previous discussions we have seen a few of Arjuna's arguments for not wanting to fight and several of Kṛṣṇa's arguments to counter them (see pp. 151 and 223–25). I don't wish to drag out the full panoply of these arguments, so let me simply state one of them that is more or less typical of the others and then let it serve as the paradigm of the ethical theory, the teleological theory, as it turns out, that Arjuna employs throughout.

Arjuna begins: He says that if he kills these men, these members of his own family, then the family will be destroyed or at least decimated. With the destruction or decimation of the family, the *dharma*, the religious and social or communal laws, will also perish, for the laws are maintained only by the attentions of the family. Hence, if the *dharma* perishes, then lawlessness will result.[80] In turn, the women of the society will certainly be corrupted, very likely as a consequence of being robbed of suitable and superior male guidance. The corruption (social, sexual, and moral) of the women leads to a confusion of the *varṇas* as a consequence of the helter-skelter production of offspring, outside the proper and legitimate family with its social and sexual boundaries.[81] If the *varṇas* are confused, then, first, the slayers of the family will go to hell; and, second, the ancestors of the family, deprived of the

[80] *Bhagavad Gītā*, I.38–40.

[81] *Ibid.*, I.41.

*śraddhā* or posthumous sacrifices, will also fall into hell.[82] Therefore, Arjuna concludes, if he kills these men, members of his own family, then the entire family will fall into hell.

This is a typical teleological argument; in it Arjuna appeals to Kṛṣṇa to look to the consequences of the action. Given the teleological definition of rightness introduced previously, we need simply fill in *x* with a description of the act being contemplated—killing these men who are members of the family to which Arjuna belongs—in order to see that the amount of pain resulting in the long-run, hellish consequences of the act would be overwhelming, indeed. Hence, the act is not right and it should not be done, as Arjuna quite correctly concludes. Stated more elegantly, the final argument would look like this:

1. Any action that leads to more pain rather than more pleasure is wrong. (The assumption of the universalistic ethical hedonist)
2. Killing these men will carry us all to hell.[83]
3. Hell (*naraka*) is a place of pain not of pleasure. (A common-enough assumption)
4. Therefore, killing these men is wrong.

Having delivered this argument to Kṛṣṇa, Arjuna sits down on the floor of his chariot, dropping his bow and arrows, his heart overcome with grief.

Kṛṣṇa now has his chance and he counters Arjuna's teleological argument, primarily, with a deontological argument that appeals to the concepts of duty, obligation, and inherent rightness. Kṛṣṇa also introduces, as we have seen in our discussion of the religious view in *Gītā darśana* (pp. 200–204), several teleological arguments as well; recall his telling Arjuna that if he fights and wins he will gain the earth; or if he fights and loses he will go to heaven; and that if he fails to fight he will be dishonored.[84] But the principal thrust of Kṛṣṇa's arguments is deontological rather than teleological, and the chief vehicle of this deontological ethical thrust is, of course, *karma* yoga:

> Let your concern be for the act alone and never with its consequences. Do not let the consequences of the act be your concern, and do not be attached to inaction.
>
> Firmly fixed in *karma* yoga, perform your acts, renouncing attachments, indifferent to success and failure. This indifference is called *karma* yoga.[85]

Thus, following our definition of deontological ethics (p. 233), we need simply fill in *x* with a description of the act being contemplated—namely, doing the duty dictated by the *varṇa* to which Arjuna belongs. Teleological

[82] *Ibid.*, I.42.

[83] *Ibid.*, I.38–42.

[84] *Ibid.*, II.32–37.

[85] *Ibid.*, II.47–48.

ethics is rejected by Kṛṣṇa when he tells Arjuna to renounce the consequences: his duty, and the rightness of his act, is not found by calculating consequences, nor by referring to $\pi$'s, pleasures, or pains. The act must be done for its own sake or that of duty and rightness alone, and not for the sake of some future goal, whether that goal entails pleasure and the avoidance of pain or not. The justification is found in the nature of the act itself: rightness is inherent in the act and not after the act. Thus our moral attention comes to be fixed on the act alone and not on any future state, future condition, or future process. And *karma* yoga focuses our attention on those acts which are always right—acts that follow from one's duty, one's *varṇa dharma.* Hence the importance, once again, of finding out what one's own vocation (*svadharma*) really is as a result of discovering one's *guṇa*-nature.

Recall for a moment our discussion of *guṇa*types, *varṇas,* and yogas previously (pp. 156–69); but note that now a new dimension is added to that discussion regarding the yogas and *mokṣa*—an ethical dimension. For the view being espoused here as deontological ethics really entails that one cannot discover what acts are truly right unless one knows ones *svadharma.* And *svadharma* depends on one's *guṇa*-nature or *svabhava.* And *svabhava* can only be discovered by knowing what one's *varṇa* is, or, lacking that in these nontraditional, heterodox, and *varṇa*less times of the *kali yuga,* by knowing through a personality description test or somatotyping (see Appendix I) or some such device what one's *guṇa*type or true nature is. Thus, right acts cannot be determined unless one knows one's *guṇa*-nature or *guṇa*type.

However all this may go, the point is that *karma* yoga is closely, but not exclusively, related to the theory of deontological ethics (see below p. 291).

In the section that follows I want to argue rather tentatively that teleological ethics and deontological ethics as ethical theories tend to belong to the religious view and the metaphysical view, respectively, of *Gītā darśana.* This will necessarily be a brief discourse, since the final and full discussion will not be completed until we have examined the two remaining parts of this chapter, *b* and *c* below, on the ethics of the *Bhagavad Gītā.* But for now let us take a quick and tentative glance at the relation between *Gītā darśana* and our two ethical theories.

### b) GĪTĀ DARŚANA AND TELEOLOGICAL AND DEONTOLOGICAL ETHICS

There are a number of very good reasons for assuming that if teleological as well as deontological ethical theories are in the *Gītā,* and that if *Gītā darśana* is, indeed, *the* speculative philosophy of the *Gītā,* then these two ethical theories must relate to *Gītā darśana* and specifically to the two views of *Gītā darśana.* I want to offer what I consider to be four fairly good reasons for assuming that not only are these two ethical theories part of *Gītā darśana,* but that each ethical theory relates or is tied specifically to one or the other of the two views of *Gītā darśana*. In particular, the central thesis here is that the teleological ethical theory is part of the religious view of *Gītā darśana*, and the deontological ethical theory is part of the metaphysical view of *Gītā darśana*, insofar as the latter view can have an ethical theory (see p. 242). I shall try to prove this central thesis with four arguments. If that thesis is proved, then the previous contention is also proved: that these two ethical theories are probably part of *Gītā darśana*. I shall call the four arguments "the Kṛṣṇa argument," "the stages argument," "the *advaita* argument," and "the yoga argument."

1. *The Kṛṣṇa Argument*

We have seen that Lord Kṛṣṇa is the personification, as it were, of the metaphysical view, and that he is trying to draw Arjuna, who personifies the religious view, up to the metaphysical view. We might assume, therefore, that any doctrine originating with Kṛṣṇa rather than Arjuna is going to be closely related to, if not identified with, the metaphysical rather than the religious view. Further, we have seen that Arjuna was the one who first offered an argument based on the teleological ethical theory of pleasure and pain ("If I kill these men, then the family will fall into hell"), while Lord Kṛṣṇa first offered an argument based on the deontological ethical theory of *karma* yoga ("Do not be concerned with the consequences of your act but only with the act itself"). Hence we can conclude, tentatively, that teleological ethics belongs to the religious view, and that deontological ethics belongs to the metaphysical view, and that deontology and teleology constitute the ethics of *Gītā darśana*. This concludes the Kṛṣṇa argument.

One very large difficulty with this argument might be mentioned. Lord Kṛṣṇa is in fact the source for many elements of the religious view as well as the metaphysical view. It would certainly be incorrect to assume that Lord Kṛṣṇa gives advice about and preaches to the metaphysical view, alone. But, while Kṛṣṇa may indeed speak to and defend both the religious and the metaphysical views throughout the eighteen chapters of the *Gītā*, it seems quite plain that Arjuna speaks only to the religious view. Hence, teleological ethics must surely belong to the religious view. And since this view and its ethics are directly juxtaposed to the metaphysical view in the arguments of the first two chapters of the *Gītā* (see above, pp. 235–37), it is only natural to place the deontological doctrine with the metaphysical view.

But the Kṛṣṇa argument is not meant to stand alone here. It fits in rather well with a second argument, the stages argument:

2. *The Stages Argument*

Lord Kṛṣṇa throughout the *Gītā* is continuously exhorting Arjuna to move up from the religious to the metaphysical stage. His exhortations, however, seem always doomed to failure. Arjuna is a plain man, a plain hard-fighting soldier who thinks plain thoughts in plain ways. But Kṛṣṇa is undaunted even by this advance knowledge of Arjuna's nature, and he begins by trying to drag Arjuna up the metaphysical path. An example of that dragging occurs early in the *Gītā*, where Kṛṣṇa is attempting to make *karma* yoga clear to Arjuna, a task in which Kṛṣṇa is not at all successful judging by the number of times that the doctrine of *karma* yoga must be repeated to Arjuna. Hence we say, tentatively once again, that because Kṛṣṇa is forever exhorting Arjuna to progress from the religious stage to the metaphysical stage, and since he is here exhorting Arjuna to move from teleology to deontology, these exhortings are linked together in such a way as to enable us to argue that teleology belongs to the religious stage and that deontology belongs to the metaphysical stage, and that deontology and teleology consitute the ethics of *Gītā darśana*. This concludes the stages argument.

One problem with this argument is, of course, that Kṛṣṇa may exhort, if it is indeed exhorting, his protégé to do a lot of things. But merely because there are times when Kṛṣṇa exhorts Arjuna to progress from the religious stage to the metaphysical stage doesn't mean that this discussion of *karma* yoga in Chapter II is one of those times. Later in the *Gītā* Kṛṣṇa exhorts Arjuna to be devoted to the personal God that is Lord Kṛṣṇa and to worship him as such at the religious stage. Hence, Kṛṣṇa later exhorts Arjuna to stand firmly in the religious stage. So, early in the *Gītā*, when they are discussing the ethics of Arjuna's problem and Kṛṣṇa introduces *karma* yoga and urges it upon Arjuna, how do we know that this, too, isn't an urging at and for the religious stage as well? The stages argument must seem to come to nothing, therefore.

But in defense of the stages argument I would simply draw the reader's attention to the fact that it focuses only on an event that occurs early in the *Gītā*. And *karma* yoga is introduced in a context of other exhortations, promptings, and urgings that would lend further support to the contention that Kṛṣṇa is, initially at any rate, exhorting Arjuna to progress in understanding from one stage or view to another. And the fact that plain Arjuna seems not to understand what in the world Kṛṣṇa is talking about further strengthens, it seems to me, the stages argument. But the stages argument, like the Kṛṣṇa argument that preceded it, was not meant to stand alone. They both lean for support on yet a third argument, to which we shall turn next:

### 3. *The Yoga Argument*

It is clear from what Arjuna says about the teleological argument that we examined previously ("If I kill these men, then the family will fall into hell"), that what draws him into acting in the world is an envisioned future state of affairs that he desires to bring about. In other words, desire for that state and for the consequences of his acts that make up that state impels him to act. Now the essence of any teleological ethical theory is the desire to maximize pleasure or happiness and to avoid suffering and pain: desire is the essence of teleological ethics. Bur right acts of this sort will lead one to heaven, as the *Gītā* is at some pains to point out—and heaven, as we have seen, is the goal of the religious stage. It is only through desirelessness that *mokṣa*, the "goal" of the metaphysical stage, can be reached, and the "goal" of *karma* yoga is precisely that state of desirelessness. For with nonattachment to the consequences of all actions, the state of desirelessness is achieved. *Karma* yoga is the key to actions that produce no bondage, because such actions are not motivated by desire for future states of affairs: they become actionless, *karmaless* actions. It ought to be pointed out again, however, that *karma* yoga has a proper use in the religious stage as well (see below, p. 271). Kṛṣṇa says regarding *mokṣa* and *karma* yoga:

> For one thus dead to attachments, who has attained *mokṣa*, his thoughts set in true knowledge, doing all of his work as a sacrifice, that man's actions are completely dissolved.[86]

Thus deontology through *karma* yoga falls naturally within the metaphysical stage. Hence, we can conclude that deontology belongs to the metaphysical stage, and that teleology probably belongs to the religious stage, and that deontology and teleology constitute the ethics of *Gītā darśana*.

This concludes the yoga argument. A final argument, however, is dependent on it and follows hard upon its heels. We shall therefore defer any comments on the yoga argument until we have completed that final argument:

### 4. *The Advaita Argument*

The *advaita Vedānta darśana*, we saw, was closely associated with the metaphysical view of *Gītā darśana*. In fact, the rejection of the reality of everything but *Brahman* was the essence of that view. The *advaita* argument depends on this fact in order to demonstrate that deontological ethics comes to a point of close agreement with the metaphysical view on precisely this issue; that is, deontological ethics is monistic in its intentions or ends in a way precisely parallel to that in which teleological ethics is essentially pluralistic in its intentions or ends.

Return for a moment to the passage from the *Gītā* that we quoted just above in connection with the *yoga* argument. That passage had pointed to the fact that *karma* yoga, a deontological ethical enterprise, tended to lead to *mokṣa*, a "goal" of the metaphysical stage, rather than to heaven, a goal of the religious stage of *Gītā darśana*. A passage that immediately follows the

[86] *Ibid.*, IV.23.

above-quoted *śloka* reinforces the point of the *advaita* argument that I am attempting to make now: that deontological ethics is essentially directed toward a monistic rather than a pluralistic view of the world, hence deontological ethics is the most appropriate ethics for the metaphysical stage. Lord Kṛṣṇa says:

> For such a man [the *karma* yogi who has achieved *mokṣa*: a *jīvanmukta*] the act of sacrifice is *Brahman*, the offering is *Brahman*, and into the sacrificial fire of *Brahman* it is poured by *Brahman*. To *Brahman* will he go who thus meditates deeply on *Brahman* in all his actions.[87]

The end is oneness with the impersonal Absolute, highest *Brahman*, and that end is the result of the *Ātman*'s being liberated from personality and from the wants, needs, and desires that constitute the essence of personality. Thus the *advaita* argument concludes that deontological ethics, the ethics of total desirelessness and complete unattachment to consequences, leads one to the ultimate goal of impersonal absorption in the monistic impersonal metaphysical principle of unmanifest *Brahman*.

Teleological ethics, on the other hand, betrays its own groundings in pluralistic metaphysics by the general common-sense commitment that it makes to the ways and means to pleasure and happiness. People must be real in order that I can have an ethical relation to them, a relation in which I attempt, among other things, to maximize their pleasure: if pleasure and happiness are real, then, by heavens, people have got to be real, too, in order to have that pleasure and that happiness. And food, sex, books, cars, horses, dogs, and pianos must be real, too, as sources of that pleasure and happiness for me. Hence, teleological ethics is pluralistic, and it is the ethics that the *Gītā* turns to in order to represent the pluralistic religious view of *Gītā darśana*.

Hence we can conclude, tentatively again, perhaps, that deontology belongs to the metaphysical view, and that teleology belongs to the religious view, and that deontology and teleology constitute, therefore, the ethics of *Gītā darśana*. This concludes the *advaita* argument.

Two difficulties occur as a consequence of the *advaita* argument. Let me mention them and then briefly comment on each. First, a critic might say that the deontological ethics described within the *advaita* argument as well as within the *yoga* argument is surely not the historical deontological ethics that has been attributed in the West to Immanuel Kant, Sir David Ross, and H. A. Prichard. So how can we claim for it here what we do? *Gītā* deontology is plainly not Kantian, nor is it neo-Kantian, and there's an end to it! Now it's quite true that Kant, Ross, and Prichard are not defenders of the metaphysical view of *Gītā darśana*, and none of them appear to satisfy the criteria

[87] *Ibid.*, IV.24.

for being *karma* yogis and *advaita jīvanmuktas*. But so what? The use of "deontology" in our deontological ethics satisfies a familiar and traditional definition we gave earlier in defining "rightness" and "right acts" (p. 233), and that alone justifies its use here. Hence, it seems to me, the use of "deontology" is quite justified, Western terminological proclivities notwithstanding.

But a second objection sounds a more serious note: an ethical theory makes sense only if there is a plurality of real entities among which or around which the ethics can function. An ethics that attempted to operate where there was a subject only or an object only would be no ethics whatsoever, for at the very least we can say that an ethics must prescribe relationships of behavior and action among people or between people and objects. And the critic has only to refer to the *advaita* metaphysics to drive home his contention that no real ethics can exist where there are no people and objects but only *Brahman*. The critic has made a good argument, and I am inclined to agree that the *advaita* metaphysical view is ultimately nonmoral. But the objection misses the point of the relation between ethics and the metaphysical stage: for the ethical rules still apply at the level of *saguṇa Brahman* and to those beings who have not yet reached *mokṣa* and become *jīvanmuktas*. But the actions of the *jīvanmukta*, as we have seen, are desireless, actionless (*karma*less) actions. They are effortless, spontaneous actions like breathing and walking. And the *jīvanmukta*, himself, has really transcended the stages of *Gītā darśana*. He is the realized man who no longer stands in stages, uses philosophy, or delves into metaphysics. He has, to use the old metaphor, crossed over the river of delusion with the boat of the doctrine, and we certainly don't require that he now hoist that boat, the metaphysical view or stage of *Gītā darśana*, onto his back and carry it about with him. The two stages of *Gītā darśana* are meant to be seen as distinct stages of realization. As such they embody different doctrines, yogas, goals, ethics, and all the rest, including separate *darśanas* to be used by those who have not reached realization or *mokṣa*. As a result, the ethics of *Gītā darśana* is similarly meant to be used by those who are on the path and in the two stages. Once the end is reached, once the *jīvanmukta* has been produced, once desire is left behind, once spontaneous action begins, once the world is seen as all Self or *Ātman*, then *Gītā darśana*, the metaphysical view, and deontological ethics are all left behind. Thus the critic's objection is applicable only to those *jīvanmuktas* who have no further use for ethics, views, and stages.

This completes our discussion of the nature of right acts in the ethics of the *Bhagavad Gītā*. We have tried to show that at least two full-blown ethical theories have been set going in the *Gītā*, the teleological and the deontological, and that each theory can be associated with the two views, the religious and the metaphysical, of *Gītā darśana*. We have offered four arguments to bolster this conclusion, and in the course of that bolstering we have suggested and tried to meet several criticisms of the whole venture.

We turn next to an extremely important problem that comes out of the ethics of the *Gītā*, the problem of free will and fatalism. It is important, for it would seem that no ethical theory can make much sense at all unless it allows for "voluntary" acts on the part of its moral agents. And yet the *Gītā* seems to have one strain of ethical thought that runs quite counter to this, even making a kind of fatalism a necessary ingredient in all moral actions. Let us take up this rather puzzling element in the ethics of the *Bhagavad Gītā* and see how the entire issue stands.

### *b. Free Will and Fatalism in the Bhagavad Gītā*

The problem of the freedom of the human will looms large in any ethical system where rightness in actions depends on that freedom (recall our teleological definition above, p. 230) and where such freedom becomes problematical as a result of a lurking, stalking fatalism that threatens to pounce on it and render it nugatory. The *Bhagavad Gītā* is a good example of a text where this freedom and that fatalistic threat meet face to face.

In order to run at this problem as elegantly as possible, we need to clear the ground of certain conceptual misunderstandings and distinguish between the various senses of "*freedom*" and "*fatalism*" with which we shall be concerned. I want to divide our discussion, therefore, into three parts. The first part will introduce the definition of "freedom" with which we shall be concerned throughout our later discussions. In that first part I want to say something about the concept of "compulsion," which is the contradictory of "freedom," by discussing several varieties of compulsion, both internal and external. The second part will present six rather good arguments that support compulsion in human affairs, together with a brief critique of each. In that second part I want to look at a scientific argument, a psychological argument, a law of *karma* argument, and three theological arguments, all supporting compulsion in some fashion or other. The three theological arguments, in turn, will include a predestination argument, a fatalism argument, and a so-called *daiva* argument, all of which attempt the same task: to show that the libertarians (those who believe in free will) are wrong and that some or all of man's actions are compelled. I shall conclude, finally, with several remarks about the relation between free will and compulsion.

#### 1) Clearing the Way

To clear the way for a discussion of the arguments below, it is essential that we get quite straight on the technical vocabulary that we shall be employing in those arguments. We must understand the meaning of "freedom" and "fatalism" as well as several other concepts. In order to work our way as easily as possible into these matters, suppose that we begin with an example of what we would ordinarily take to be a voluntary act—an act done freely and without any sort of noticeable constraint. The analysis of the nature of this ordinary act will serve to launch us into our task of clearing the way.

Take an action (this includes motive, act, and consequences) in which you have only recently engaged, such as reading this book. Let's suppose that you wanted to read it, so you picked it up with the result that you are reading it right now. It is, after all, a self-justifying claim, isn't it, that you're reading this sentence right now? At any rate, our question is: were you free to read this book? That is, is the reading of this book a voluntary action? And didn't you intend to read it (motive)? Didn't you pick it up (act)? And aren't you reading it now (consequence)?

It seems to be the case that the action is quite voluntary. And if someone suddenly rushed into this room, brandished a spear at you and shouted, "Don't read that book!" and if you complied, then we'd probably say that you were acting involuntarily, and that the act of not reading would not be free. We all understand that. And if the spear bearer suddenly shouted "Read the book!" and you picked it up and read, I think we'd ordinarily say, once again, that you were now reading it involuntarily as well. Thus when someone forces someone else to do something by threatening him with some sort of harm or pain, we say that what they do, since it's done under duress, is done involuntarily, under compulsion, and is, therefore, not free.

But this usage is still not sharp enough to clear our way here. We shall want to state the necessary and sufficient conditions under which someone may be said to do an act freely, together with those conditions under which someone may be said to do an act by compulsion. We are laying the conditions for freedom and compulsion in the doing of human acts (not actions now, but only acts, the *doing* part of the action) and also in wanting to do human acts. Let's assume something like this: that a person is acting freely whenever he or she could have chosen or wanted to do differently than he or she actually did choose or want; and that he or she could have done differently than he or she actually did, if he or she had wanted to. If both of these conditions—free wanting and free doing—do not exist, then a person will be said to be acting under compulsion. Put into language that is a bit less tangled and that states the necessary and sufficient conditions for defining freedom of the will, the definition would look something like this, where "*A*" is a person, "*x*" is the act that *A* does or will do, and "choosing" entails both an internal wanting and an external doing:

> *A* is or was free to do *x* if and only if *A* could choose or could have chosen not to do *x*.

I think this is ordinarily what we mean when we say that we did something voluntarily and without constraint, whether internal or external. Thus you were free to pick up and read this book if and only if had wanted to, you could have chosen not to pick up and read this book.

A similar definition can be set up for the case of compelled acts:

> *A* is or was compelled to do *x* if and only if *A* could not choose or could not have chosen not to do *x*.

Again, I think this is ordinarily what we mean when we say that we did something against our will or that we were constrained or compelled, whether internaly or externally. You were compelled to lay down the book when the spear bearer menacingly showed up, because even if you had wanted to you could not have really chosen to keep the book and go on reading (without suffering grievous bodily harm, which is assumed, of course). "Compulsion" has several senses, it would seem, and these senses can be divided into internal compulsion and external compulsion. Internal or psychological compulsion we shall examine shortly, along with several forms of external compulsion. The spear waver is an example of external human compulsion, but there are examples of more interesting external compulsions: the divine or Godly variety and the metaphysical-principle variety, both of which will receive separate treatment below.

These definitions of "free" and "compelled" will be employed in what follows, as we set up six arguments that have been used from time to time to show that man is not free and that in some manner or other his actions, all or some, are compelled. We shall have occasion to make use of these same two notions in the last part of our investigations as well, when we attempt to answer the question: was Arjuna free in choosing (as he eventually did) to fight the enemies of his clan? For the moment, let us push on to our six compelling arguments.

### 2) Six Arguments for Compulsion

The six arguments which can be used to support the case for human compulsion and against human free will I shall call, first, the scientific argument; second, the psychological argument; third, the *karma* argument; and, finally, three theological arguments, a predestination argument, a fatalism argument, and a *daiva* argument. Let me take the arguments in the order indicated, statc each one as clearly as possible, and then offer several comments about it.

#### a) THE SCIENTIFIC ARGUMENT

Geneticists tell us, and I have no reason to doubt them, that physical characteristics such as hair, skin, and eye color are inherited, and that they are the way they are because of our genes rather than because of our environment. Geneticists also say that about 80 percent of what we call intelligence or measured ability is also inherited rather than being due to physical surroundings:

> Using the procedures of quantitative genetics, most experts estimate that I.Q. has a heritability between .7 and .85, but this is based almost entirely on data from whites. We may, therefore, say that 70 to 85 percent of the variation in I.Q. among whites is due to genes.[88]

In the age-old battle between nature and nurture, between the genes and the environment, it is nurture that is losing and nature that seems to be triumphing. But while this may give Marxists and other proenvironment sociologists, reformers, and latter-day philosophic radicals pause, it has simplified a number of scientific testing procedures for determining intelligence and temperament and, as a consequence, gladdened the hearts of a great number of eugenicists, faculty psychologists, and Cartesian philosophers: you are, or about 80 percent of you is, what your parents and ancestors were, and that's that!

The scientific argument against free will, however, really takes a slightly different form, though it may be partially based on the genetic argument described above. Suppose that we want to find out something about your temperament, and suppose that we want to be able to predict your future behavior based on that temperament. In particular, suppose we want to find out if, when you are sufficiently provoked, you will defend yourself and attack your provoker. To discover whether or not you have this propensity we would give you a battery of tests to determine your aggression quotient in the same way, perhaps, that we give you a battery of tests to determine your intelligence quotient. On the basis of these tests, the scientific argument would continue, we could predict how you would behave and what you would do if you were, let's say, standing in a chariot in front of two opposing armies, with weapons in your hands, having recognized your relatives and friends and loved ones in both armies. And we could predict this in the same way that we could predict future occupational success or academic success or social and political success, as a result of several simple tests which any testing center could administer to you right now. The results of the tests would be fed into a computer and the predictive results would be spit out by the machine, and that's that!

The force of "that's that" in both of the above paragraphs is, of course, to sink any libertarian propensities that you might still have. The scientific argument, when put more elegantly, looks like this:

[88]R. J. Herrnstein, *I.Q. in the Meritocracy* (Boston: Little, Brown and Company, 1973), p. 185.

1. Scientific predictions cannot be wrong.
2. Your future behavior can be scientifically predicted.
3. Therefore, scientific predictions about your future behavior cannot be wrong.
4. Therefore, you must do what scientific predictions predict you will do.
5. Therefore, since you cannot do differently than these predictions state you will do, then you are not free.

Comment: Let me be short in my comment on this quite valid but unsound argument: "unsound" because the truth of each of the first two premises can be successfully challenged. Each premise betrays a kind of ignorance of science and scientific method that is worth exposing and laying bare. First, scientific predictions can be wrong even with the best corroborating evidence, and the various revolutions that have occurred in the history of Western science, from the Newtonian to the Einsteinian, underscore this point.

Second, the statements of the laws of science as well as the statements of the hypotheses, theories, and predictive judgments of any scientific discipline are synthetic *a posteriori*, hence nonnecessary, judgments. As a consequence they are always open to doubt, and as long as they are they cannot predict with certainty or absolute necessity what your behavior must be. This lack of certainty is a function, not of the scientist's ignorance, but rather of the very nature of the kind of judgments which empirical scientists must employ: synthetic *a posteriori* judgments (see above, pp. 126f.). Therefore, since there is no certainty with respect to the prediction about your future behavior, there is no necessity in what you will do; that is, the scientific argument cannot be used to establish the denial of free will.

Third, the scientific enterprise and the statements it employs deal only with predictive probabilities and not predictive certainties. All that science can really tell us about your future behavior, following your taking that battery of tests, is that you *might* behave in such and such a way, that you *might* have such and such success, but within the limits of probability. For example, it might say that given your particular temperament, your I.Q., your aggression quotient, and the circumstance of your now standing between two large armies in which you recognize family, friends, and loved ones on both sides, there is a 65 percent chance, based on past correlations with similar persons in similar circumstances, that you will throw down your weapons and sit down on the floor of your chariot, overcome with grief. Science says nothing about what you certainly will do, nor does it say what you must do. The scientific argument cannot be used to establish any kind of fatalism or compulsion with respect to human actions.

A second argument, however, seems to challenge the conclusion to the comment above, by switching the discussion from talk about statements and predictive probabilities to talk about behavior, neuroses, psychoses, and psychological compulsion. Let's see whether or not freedom of the will is successfully challenged by this psychological argument.

### b) THE PSYCHOLOGICAL ARGUMENT

The psychological argument for compulsion and against free will borrows several elements from the scientific argument, as we shall see. The psychological argument says, in effect, something like the following: There are certain kinds of behaviors in our society that we hold to be compulsive. These compulsive behaviors issue from the characters, personalities, or natures of people that we know to be sick in some way. We say, for example, that the musophobe can't help being afraid of mice, that the nyctophobe can't help being afraid of the dark, that the pedophobe, the phonophobe, the gynophobe, the astraphobe and the thanatophobe can't help feeling afraid of children, noise, women, thunderstorms, and death, respectively; that the agoraphobe can't help being afraid of open spaces, that the claustrophobe can't help being afraid of enclosed places; or that the kleptomaniac can't help stealing, and so on.

Let's take the kleptomaniac. When the kleptomaniac steals something and he's caught, we don't throw him in jail; instead, we treat him. It's rather like getting pneumonia; you wouldn't ordinarily lose your job or go to jail for getting pneumonia. Neuroses are the same way. The kleptomaniac, like the other fearful people mentioned above, is sick; like them, he needs treatment, not punishment. The kleptomaniac is not charged with a crime and for the obvious reason that he's not responsible for what he did. Psychologists tell us that the kleptomaniac is driven into doing what he does, is compelled to do what he does, and is not free because he has an uncontrollable and overwhelming desire issuing from an abnormal personality, a malfunctioning character or nature. The kleptomaniac is not responsible for the formation of this kleptomaniac character or personality, for at a previous time in his life when that personality was being molded and formed, and before the age of rational consent, he was denied the kind of normal love and attention that would have prevented this kleptomaniac neurosis. In other words, his personality was really formed for him by his misdirected or misguided parents: and if he's not responsible for his neurotic personality, neither is he responsible for the neurotic behavior which issues from it. And that's what we mean when we say that he's not free but compelled in his behavior.

The psychological argument against free will is built on this model of neurotic, compulsive behavior. The psychological argument states that since all human character, nature, or personality is formed before the age of seven or eight, and that since it is formed by others, by parents or lack of parents, before the age of psychological or intellectual consent, then none of us are responsible for what we are and do; that is, all behavior that issues or comes from that personality in later life is really compelled. Thus, if you're a happy-go-lucky child, you'll probably be a happy-go-lucky adult, since happy-go-luckiness is part of one's basic temperament. And if you're a morose, brooding child, you'll very likely be a morose, brooding adult, since morose-broodingness is part of one's temperament as well. Further, if you're not responsible for the temperament or personality that is thus formed early in your childhood (how could you be? you were only seven years old), then you're not responsible for the behavior that springs from the character in your later life.

But, the psychological argument continues, all human behavior ultimately springs from our character, therefore it follows that we're not responsible for any of it because we're not free to do differently than we do with regard to any of that behavior. We're doomed by our personalities, and therefore we're not free. So there you are, out in front of the two opposing armies, recognizing friends and relatives on both sides. If your temperament is naturally pugnacious or naturally aggressive, then the fighting behavior that would be elicited at the sight of the enemy would not be a behavior that you could really control, unless the ability to control that martial behavior was also built into your personality or character. So no matter what you did, you could not have done differently than your character allowed you to do, and that's that!

The psychological argument, when put more elegantly, looks like this:

1. None of us is responsible for behavior which issues from a nature or character over whose formation we had no control; for such behavior is compelled and not free (recall the kleptomaniac argument).
2. None of us really had control over the formation of any of our personality or character; it is preformed for us.
3. All behavior, more or less, issues from our personality or character.
4. Therefore none of us is really responsible for our behavior.
5. Therefore since none of us is responsible for our behavior, then all of our behavior is, more or less, compelled, and none of us is free.
6. Therefore, you are not free.[89]

Comment: While it is true that we might not hold the kleptomaniac legally responsible for what he does and while we do recognize that his behavior is psychologically compelled rather than free, nonetheless we might still

[89]See also John Hospers, "Free-Will and Psychoanalysis," in Wilfred Sellars and John Hospers, eds., *Readings in Ethical Theory* (New York: Appleton-Century-Crofts, Inc., 1952), pp. 573–574.

discover that the psychological argument is unconvincing. Let me suggest three-counter arguments that might lead us to this conclusion regarding the psychological argument:

First, and most obviously, the language employed to generate the psychological argument is unabashedly vague. What does it mean to say that behavior "issues" from character? What is involved in this sort of "issuing," anyway? What does it mean to say that character is "formed"?—and does this mean that no one can change his character? Who says so and what do they mean? And who says that character is hardened, set, or formed by the age of seven? What does that mean and what kind of evidence is there for it? But notice further that all of the statements that these questions challenge are synthetic *a posteriori* judgments. Hence, once again, any conclusions reached through such statements and by way of the evidence to back them up can only be probable at best and never certain. Hence the conclusion to the psychological argument, provided that some sense could be wrung from such concepts as "issues," "formed," and "set," would be probable only. But more important considerations arise for the psychological argument than the semantic and probability issues raised here.

Second, suppose we have a kleptomaniac before us right now. We can surely distinguish between compelled behaviors that are the result of his sickness and those other normal behaviors that are not. In terms of degrees alone his compulsive stealing is certainly more compulsive than the way he ties his shoes, sneezes, and argues with his boss or friends or teachers, unless, of course, he is sicker in more ways than we thought. And as long as we can distinguish the more compulsive (stealing) from the less compulsive (shoe-tying), we can distinguish the relatively compelled from the relatively free. And if we can distinguish the relatively free in any way—and common sense tells us that we do it all the time—then the libertarian's case is made.

Imagine, if you will, a horizontal line which is to represent a kind of continuum of all possible behaviors. At the left side will be the clearly compelled behaviors and on the right side those behaviors that appear to involve less compulsion. Finally, there will be degrees of more or less psychological compulsion between these two extremes. Now, all that I am suggesting is that there is a midpoint on this compulsion continuum such that to the extreme left there will be behaviors we call "compelled," to the extreme right there will be behaviors we call "free," and between them both are behaviors we call "problematical." In other words, not all behavior is of the kleptomaniac sort, and anyone who thinks otherwise should simply consult our compulsion continuum for evidence to the contrary.

Third, at least one school of contemporary psychology—the school of behaviorism—would completely reject the psychological argument. The behaviorist finds talk about "personality," "character," and "nature" technically meaningless, unless that talk is tied directly to observable behavior.

Therefore he would reject all of the first three premises of the psychological argument as unscientific and so much mumbo-jumbo. Where is the "character," he would ask. Is the "personality" some ghostlike entity which lurks about the brain? Where does it do its lurking? On the top? At the back? Further, is a person's nature really at all different from the way he in fact behaves? In other words, are there two entities here, behavior plus a mysterious substance called "personality" which is a kind of infinite reservoir of possible behaviors? Or is there just that behavior? The behaviorist is too much of an empiricist to linger long on such questions. As far as he's concerned, the only real and testable data worth bothering with at all are the observable behaviors. From his point of view—and he does represent a rather large group of contemporary psychologists—the psychological argument proves absolutely nothing. The very least that any psychological argument could show, perhaps, is that there are sociological constraints on us all. This concludes our discussion of the psychological argument.

A third argument that can be used to challenge the libertarian's free-will thesis comes from the Indian tradition itself. It is the *karma* argument, and we shall look to it next.

### c) THE *KARMA* ARGUMENT

The *karma* argument finds its roots in the law of *karma*, but it appears to have borrowed elements from both the scientific and the psychological arguments, as we shall see. The *karma* argument begins with the law or principle or convenient fiction (see above, pp. 135–36) of *karma* and goes from there into a kind of terrible antilibertarian pessimism. For if the poor get poorer (or the rich get richer) under some kind of banal law of economics, then it is even more true that given the law of *karma* the wicked get wickeder (or the good get better): for under the law of *karma* nothing fails like failure (and nothing succeeds like success).

Let me try to make all of these clichés philosophically sensible. The law of *karma*, whatever it is, insists that wicked people will be punished for the wicked things that they have done and, given the rebirth doctrine, that punishment will come either in this life or the next. But that future punishment has a curious way of guaranteeing that even more wickedness must follow the punishment, and then, after that, more punishment with more wickedness, and then more wickedness, and so on, down, down, down. The *Bhagavad Gītā* reiterates this fate for those of bad conduct when it says that such wicked ones are born into stinking wombs, the wombs of demons, outcastes, and dogs. Lord Kṛṣṇa says:

> These cruel and hateful and most debased of beings I repeatedly hurl back into the wombs of demons in *saṁsāra*.

> Thus fallen into the wombs of demons, these deluded men in birth after birth do not reach Me but they sink instead into the very lowest depths.[90]

Pretty bleak! And the outlook for those of good conduct seems equally predestined, as Lord Kṛṣṇa again says:

> Neither in this life nor in the life to come is there destruction for one who does the right. . . .
>
> Such a one . . . attains to the world of those who do the right, and having lived there for many years he may be born into the house of a pure and prosperous family.

Pretty rosy! But things are guaranteed to get even better once your foot is on the right path:

> Or he may be born into a family of wise yogis. . . .
>
> In such a family he would recover the mental characteristics developed in his previous life, and from there he would start once again his drive to perfection.

It is almost as if the good yogi couldn't help himself, and this, of course, is precisely the point of the *karma* argument, in his ever-spiraling upward rise to success after success: "Thus by his former practices he is irresistibly carried forward and beyond them. . . ."[91] Pretty plush! As we said above, as far as the law of *karma* and human behaviors are concerned, nothing fails like failure, and nothing succeeds like success.

Suppose you are back once again on the battlefield, drawn up in your chariot between the armies of your friends, family, and loved ones. The position you hold in the army, the attitudes you have toward people in general, the sense of duty that you feel right now, the dispositions you have to fight or not to fight are all the result of your previous actions and the law of *karma.* Lord Kṛṣṇa says to Arjuna, consequently,

> If, clinging to egoism, you think, "I will not fight," then that resolve is useless. For your *guṇa*-nature will compel you to fight.[92]

Thus, if you are on the noble upward path, it is set and determined that you will do that noble thing. If, on the other hand, you are on the ignoble downward path, it is just as set and determined that you will do the ignoble thing. Either way you are merely a pawn in the hands of the causal forces of your *guṇa*-nature and the law of *karma*; and, at all events, whatever you do, fight or flee, it's really out of your hands, and that's that!

[90] *Bhagavad Gītā*, XVI. 19–20.

[91] *Ibid.*, VI.40–44.

[92] *Ibid.*, XVIII.59.

The *karma* argument, when put a bit more elegantly, looks like this:

1. All present human decisions and actions are the result of past good and wicked acts and the law of *karma*.
2. Once one begins to be wicked, more wickedness is guaranteed to follow; and once one begins to be good, more goodness is guaranteed to follow.
3. Therefore, there comes a time when one is so deeply enmeshed in wickedness or goodness that it becomes impossible to do the good or to do the wicked, respectively.
4. If it is impossible for you to do the good (because you are too wicked) or to do the wicked (because you are too good), then you are not free.
5. Therefore, you are not free.

Comment: There are several comments we could make about this argument, not the least of which might involve us in an analysis of what kind of "law" the law of *karma* is. But since we have discussed the law in the law of *karma* previously (pp. 134–36), let me confine the discussion to two other matters:

First, imagine if you will a continuum not unlike that mentioned in the second comment to the psychological argument above. At the extreme ends of such a continuum would stand persons with *karmic* natures wholly wicked on the left side and wholly good on the right side. Now it may well be that at these two extremes there would be very little that anyone could do to change the downward or upward slide into hell or heaven, simply because no one would or could do differently than he is going to do. Hence, as mentioned above, there is a problem with free will at the extremes. Recall our definition of free will:

> *A* is or was free to do *x* if and only if *A* could choose or could have chosen not to do *x*.

And here *A*, the wicked person or the good person at the extremes, would not have wanted to do the good or to do the wicked, so steeped is that person in wickedness or goodness, respectively. But this only speaks to those at the extremes on our continuum. For those within the two extremes and, therefore, neither wholly and obdurately wicked nor wholly and obdurately good, there wouldn't seem to be any problem at all. Their *svabhāvas* would be such that desire for the good or for the wicked would still be wholly possible for any of them. No difficulty over free will would arise here either. Thus the *karma* argument would seem to present no real problem for these morally lukewarm creatures.

Second, for those who still feel that the *karma* argument does threaten free will, the *Bhagavad Gītā* appears to offer another way around the difficulty. This other way involves the Lord's *prasāda* or grace. Thus Lord Kṛṣṇa says:

> Performing all actions, having taken refuge in Me, by My grace My devotee reaches the eternal, indestructible goal.
>
> Focusing all your thought on Me, you will overcome all difficulties by My grace. But if you will not heed this advice, then you will be utterly destroyed.[93]

Now it looks as if Lord Kṛṣṇa's grace or favor can overcome even the hard heart of the law of *karma*. But perhaps this is to hope for too much. For if grace were given to the obdurately wicked, willy-nilly and with no preconditions, then at the very least an element of chance and the unexpected would be introduced into the moral life and into the free-will problem. But the *ślokas* just mentioned would seem to rule out this kind of chance and with it all chances that the *karma* argument could be successfully challenged by this second objection. For there are preconditions to receiving grace, as the two *ślokas* indicate: "having taken refuge in Me" and being "My devotee," "focus your thought on Me" and "heeding this advice." Only if these conditions are met—and meeting them would seem to demand that one be not wholly wicked—only then would grace descend and only then would a better life occur and the goal be reached. Again, we are returned to the first suggestion above and to the case of the unchangeably, objurately wicked man who cannot choose to meet the conditions for grace nor a better life nor the imperishable goal.

Third and finally, a note of optimism that sounds throughout Indian thought must be taken into account. All beings will eventually, this optimistic note seems to say, reach the highest goal. There is no doctrine of eternal damnation or everlasting hell or eternal suffering to contend with in the Indian religions. Even the obdurately wicked must sooner or later reach bottom. And having struck the bottom, carried there by the series of inevitabilities that the law of *karma* has guaranteed for this person, the debts of wickedness sooner or later become paid and paid in full. Then begins the slow process of working one's way back up through the ontological chain of being until once again one is a man. For this reason, as Gautama Buddha himself proclaimed, it is a great thing to be born a man.

One can imagine what striking bottom would be like here; for example, in a dog's womb, being born a dog, leading a dog's life. And, it might be argued, one can only be a good dog, for what would a wicked dog be like? Or if you want to claim that there are wicked dogs, compelled by their nature

[93] *Ibid.*, XVIII.56, 58.

to bite and bark and to be in general horrid and loathesome, then we could suppose that in the life following that of the wicked dog a still lower life or body would await one—for example, the body of a slug or worm of some sort. Now that sounds as if one had hit bottom, all right, for it would seem to be rather difficult to be a wicked worm. Hence, the worm's behavior and activities would represent the farthest point of ontological descent for our wicked self. Once bottom is struck, the upward ascent begins, until eventually one reaches the level of man, once again, where a plethora of free choices faces one once more.

However this matter is decided, we do come away with a certain feeling that the thoroughly wicked man is more to be pitied than censured. And we come away, perhaps, with at least two strong feelings from this brief discussion of the *karma* argument. On the one hand, it certainly looks as if, despite the continuum mentioned in the first comment above, the person on the downward path to hell is doomed and predestined to hit bottom and there's nothing he can do about it. On the other hand, I would leave the reader to mull over this puzzle: is such a person doomed because he doesn't want to change or because he can't want to change? If the former—if he chooses to go to the bottom—then he's free, and the *karma* argument doesn't seem to substantiate compulsion. If the latter—if he can't help going to the bottom—then he's not free, and the *karma* argument would seem to substantiate compulsion.

The introduction of *prasāda* or divine grace as one of the powers that Lord Kṛṣṇa has, whether over the law of *karma* or not (the point is moot in the history of Indian thought), brings us to a discussion of God's other powers and the final set of arguments for compulsion, the theological arguments.

### d) THREE THEOLOGICAL ARGUMENTS

There are three theological arguments. Two of them relate directly to two of God's powers, his omnipotence and his omniscience, and lead to the conclusion that all of man's actions are compelled. I shall call these "the predestination argument" and "the fatalism argument." The third is a curious argument that is built up in the *Gītā* and seems to involve God, Providence, or what is called *daiva*, as a necessary condition to all human actions. As a result, this argument, like the others, threatens man's autonomy and freedom in acting. It, too, leads to the conclusion that man's will is not free and that all of his actions are compelled. This third and unique theological argument I shall call "the *daiva* argument."

Let me take these three arguments in order, now, state them as clearly as possible, and then comment briefly on each one.

1) *The Predestination Argument*

The predestination argument says, in effect, that all events are foreordained by God. It rests on one power of God and one alone: omnipotence. God has the power to foreordain that all events happen the way that they do; therefore, you cannot do differently than God has foreordained that you do. In other words, it would be logically impossible for you to do differently than God has foreordained even if you wanted to, for that would mean that omnipotent God was not omnipotent. Consequently, you are not free.

It seems, however, that there might be several types of foreordination, and it might be well to spell these out. Let's distinguish between total predestination and selective predestination (for a previous parallel see selective and total omnipotence, pp. 80–81). For selective predestinarians, God simply foreordains certain big events in a person's life; but the rest, the little events, are left pretty much up to each individual to do with as he or she sees fit. The big events foreordained by God in your life might include, for example, where you will spend eternity, in heaven or in hell. Other big events that God might have selected to foreordain might include your death date, and this would follow from God's ordination that you will go straight to heaven or hell at a certain time after a life spent on earth. But if both your death date and the length of your life on earth are foreordained, then it would logically follow that the exact time of your birth would also have been foreordained. Big events, important events in one's life—initiation into the tribe or church, marriage, birth of one's sons and daughters, and so on—might also be selected to be foreordained; but not all the events in one's life would be thus predestined. For it sounds theologically silly to argue that God with his majestic and infinite power has foreordained every sneeze and every burp for every gnat, sloth, and bacterium. But that's only because the selective-predestination doctrine itself is shortsighted, the total predestinarian might say. God with his infinite majesty and power has foreordained everything, for gnats, sloths, and bacteria as well as for man. And "everything" means everything; the motive, the act, and the consequences are fated in your action, along with your birth, your death, your afterlife, and every act and action in between. Everything is all solidly locked up by divine fiat and it cannot happen differently than it has, does, or will.

The *Gītā* gives a hint of the working of this power when it suggests that man is a puppet or a marionette that dangles or dances from strings which God manipulates. Since marionettes don't move at all unless the strings are pulled, this must be an instance of the sort of total compulsion spoken of above. Lord Kṛṣṇa says to Arjuna:

> The Lord lives in the hearts of all beings, Arjuna. By his power [*māyā*] he causes all beings to turn about as if they were dangling on a string.[94]

[94] *Ibid.*, XVIII.61.

Now this type of manipulative foreordination would be complete in the case of total predestination but only partial in the case of selective predestination. Thus, concerning those actions that both kinds of predestinarians agree are foreordained, man is not free because, even if he wanted to, he could not choose to do differently than he does. But concerning those actions that both disagree about as being or not being foreordained, man is either compelled or not compelled, respectively, by God, and for the reasons already mentioned.

Return for a moment to the battlefield where we have been so many times in the past. Suppose you suddenly leap from the chariot, grab your bow and arrows, and shout, "I'll fight!" Standing with me off to one side, witnessing this act on your part, are two theologians, one from the total predestination school and another from the selective predestination school. If I asked them whether they thought that you could have done differently than you did, these theologians might agree or disagree, depending on how selective the selective predestinarian is. Suppose, first, that they agree: then both say (in answer to my question), "No, God ordains events (all or some)," and we agree that this event on the battlefield is one such ordained event (either because it's an event or because its a big event), and that the person out there (you) leaping up and down (fighting) was not free precisely in the way that we defined "free" previously. That is to say, you could not have done or chosen to do differently than you did. To argue otherwise, they might continue, would be to turn God into a probability-calculating scientist, which God isn't. Suppose, next, that they disagree: then one, the selective predestinarian, would say, "God isn't concerned about ordaining little events like your fighting or not fighting in this battle; God has bigger fish to fry." So the choice, here, is up to you. The other one, the total predestinarian, would say precisely what he said before: "God is all-powerful, and He has ordained through that power that everything will happen the way that it does, and no one could have done differently than he has already done, even if he had wanted to, and that's that!"

Our interest here, since we are testing those arguments which tend to support the argument for compulsion in human actions, is only in the argument that leads to agreement between the selective and the total predestinarians. That predestination argument, when put more elegantly, looks like this:

1. God is omnipotent.
2. Therefore, God has foreordained that events (all or some) must happen as they do, and they cannot, logically, occur differently than they do.
3. Therefore, you could not, logically, have done differently than you did do in the past, nor can you do differently than you will do in the future.
4. Therefore, you are not free.

Comment: I shall confine the comment to the total-predestination argument. The foreordination by God, as we have said, is with regard to actions—with wanting or willing (using motive or intent), with the act and with the consequences of the act. In the first place, the *Gītā* lends strong support to aspects of this total predestination accounting for actions when, as we've seen, Lord Kṛṣṇa says that he causes all beings to turn as if they were dangled from a string. The reference is to a puppet or marionette—God pulls the strings and man moves accordingly. The fact that the Lord does this from within rather than from without would seem to indicate that it's not merely man's acts that are thus fated, but man's intentions as well.

Let me digress for a moment and relate these results to *Gītā darśana.* Notice that total predestination produces some very curious consequences for the religious view of *Gītā darśana.* For example, *bhakta* religions must give a modicum of freedom to the devotees, else the turning to God, the repentance, the faith, the conversion, and so on would make no moral or religious sense. I'm going to suggest, therefore, that selective predestination, together with certain limitations on God, is an element of the religious view of *Gītā darśana*; and I'm also going to suggest that total predestination, which we are facing here, is an element of the metaphysical view of *Gītā darśana.* I want simply to indicate, but without argument at this point, that freedom and compulsion are important ingredients in the religious view and the metaphysical view, respectively, of *Gītā darśana.* I will reserve further comments on this ethical aspect of *Gītā darśana* till later (pp. 266–67 and 269–71).

This single comment on the predestination argument is unashamedly brief, but I shall have more to say on all three of the theological arguments for compulsion when we finish the two arguments that remain.

2) *The Fatalism Argument*

The fatalism argument says, in effect, that all events are foreknown by God, and it rests on one power of God and one alone: omniscience. We could use the same dichotomy here that we used with predestination above; that is to say, we could concern ourselves with both total foreknowledge and selective foreknowledge (for a previous parallel see selective and total omniscience, pp. 79–80). But I want to forego such a move, both because it might be familiarly repetitious and also because it's not really what we're involved with here in the fatalism argument. The fatalism argument is generated because of the theological assumption that God is omniscient—all-knowing—hence we must be concerned only with what we might call "total foreknowledge" and not with "selective foreknowledge." For while God could be omnipotent and still be selective in what he manipulates and foreordains, God could not be omniscient and still be selective in what he knows: if God is omniscient (*all-*knowing), then God knows everything. The fatalism argument concludes that since man cannot do differently than God knows he will do, then man has no real choices, no open alternatives to what he did do, will do, or is doing. Hence, man could not have done differently than he did, so man is not free.

Suppose, once again, that you're on that ever-present battlefield, sitting dejectedly on the floor of your chariot, when suddenly you leap to your feet, grab your weapons, mount your chariot, and charge off into the fray. Later, after the carnage, I ask you if you could have done differently than you did. Could you, for example, have stayed on the floor of your chariot and not leaped to your feet? Or if you had leaped to your feet, could you have not grabbed your weapons? Or if you had grabbed your weapons, could you have not mounted your chariot? And even if, finally, you had mounted your chariot, could you have driven off in the opposite direction for chapatis and tea behind the battle lines? If you accept the omniscience of God as an assumption to this entire discussion, then I contend that you would have to answer "No!" to each of these questions. Thus, if God is omniscient, then he knows all events in the past, the present, and the future. And so God knows your future events. But if God knows that you are indeed going to grab your weapons, mount your chariot, and charge off into the fray, then you cannot not grab your weapons, not mount your chariot, and not charge off into the fray without contradicting the original assumption. That assumption is precisely as Lord Kṛṣṇa tells Arjuna:

> I know the beings that are past, those that are present, and those that are yet to come, Oh Arjuna . . . .[95]

Hence, because you cannot really do differently than God knows you will do, you are not free, and that's that!

When put more elegantly, the fatalism argument to support the argument for compulsion in human actions goes something like this:

1. God is omniscient.
2. Therefore, God knows all events, past, present, and future.
3. If God knows human events as they will occur in the future, then human beings must act as God knows they will act.
4. If human beings must act as God knows they will act, then they cannot do differently than they in fact do whether in the past or the future.
5. Therefore, you could not have done differently than you did in the past, nor can you do differently than you will do in the future.
6. Therefore, you are not free.

Comments. First, one might object to the fatalism argument by saying that God also knows that you are exercising your own free choice when you

[95] *Ibid.*, VII.26.

choose to grab your weapons, mount your battle wagon, and dash off to battle. In other words, God knows how you will act, but He also knows the motive and choice by which you freely elect to do the act: He knows the whole action—each and every motive, act, and consequence. But then He knows that it was your free choice that brought it about. Thus the objection. But the objection is nonsense, as a little thought should reveal. The point is what it has always been: could you have chosen differently than you did? And the answer, once again, is that no, you could not have chosen or willed differently without putting limitations on God's foreknowledge. The conclusion is simply that even if you had wanted to you could not, logically (without contradiction), have willed or done differently than in fact you did do. And that's that!

Someone else might object that as long as we don't know what God knows, then we can continue to act as if we were free, and that's sufficient for establishing free will. So, this objection concludes, what real difference can it make to our lives as long as we stay ignorant of God's foreknowledge? But this objection misses one of the salient features of the fatalism argument: if that argument leads to the conclusion that all human actions are compelled and not free, then either we must give up the myth of free will or we must give up the belief in the omniscience of God. In other words, if free will and divine omniscience are inconsistent concepts, then the issue of human awareness or human ignorance of the divine mind is quite beside the point, and that's an end to the matter.

Let me digress again and relate these results to *Gītā darśana*. On this entire issue of free will and compulsion, *Gītā darśana* has made a place for both views by attributing free will with limited divine foreknowledge to the religious stage, and fatalism with unlimited divine omniscience to the metaphysical stage. There are sufficient historical examples of *advaita* philosophers and religious mystics who seem willing, when they speak about God at all, to accept the fatalistic route and the compulsion that it entails, to lead us to this tentative conclusion. I would suggest that the reader simply consider what we said earlier about the connection between teleological ethics and the religious view of *Gītā darśana*, and the connection between deontological ethics and the metaphysical view of *Gītā darśana* (see above, pp. 237–42 and below, pp. 269–71), and then attempt to relate talk about ethics with the talk about free will and compulsion going on here. It seems to be the case that there might be a linking bridge between the two sets of talk and that the link lies in the yogas, especially *karma* yoga with its stress on unwilled or spontaneous action. Let me conclude, rather darkly, perhaps, by saying that a proper analysis of "spontaneous action" might allow all of these concepts to fall into their proper place within *Gītā darśana*. If they could thus fall, then we might have an ethics that could live consistently with a compulsion of the sort described in the fatalistic argument above. And it may well be, as Bertrand Russell once said, that free will is quite superfluous to ethics, anyway:

> I conclude that free will is not essential to any rational ethic, but only to the vindictive ethic that justifies hell and holds that "sin" should be punished regardless of any good that punishment may do.[96]

For those philosophies that have transcended rational ethics, Russell's remark would seem quite apt.

A final objection to the fatalistic argument is this: since God only knows the things that you will do and doesn't really make you do them—for we're not assuming that God is omnipotent in this argument but only that He's omniscient—then you and you alone do them. Since you do them, they must be your acts; if they're your acts, then you're responsible for them; and if you're responsible for them, then they must have been done freely. Thus the objection.

But this objection is couched in a messy and confusing manner. It tempts us into an analysis of "responsible" and "your acts" that I'm going to leave for the reader to undertake at his own risk and in his own time, for there are at least two senses of each of those two concepts floating through the objection. Instead of pursuing the final objection along that route, let me offer an agreement and an objection of my own and let it go at that.

The final objection is quite right in suggesting that God does not compel you to do what you're going to do; neither by His knowledge nor by His doing is God responsible for your act. If God were omnipotent and could, as a consequence, either prevent or compel your act, then we might hold Him responsible; but given our sole assumption of omniscience we cannot ascribe responsibility for your act to God—nor, curiously enough, to you either, and here lies my objection. Given the limited information that we have in the fatalistic argument (for we are told nothing, for example, about *Ṛta*, the Fates, *karma*, Devils, Gods and the rest), we have no justification for assigning responsibility, an assignment that could only come about under conditions of free will, to any one or any thing or any process or any being or any entity. But that you are not responsible is clear, for you have to do what someone (God), who never makes mistakes, knows that you will do. And God's not responsible, and that's equally clear; for all we know He's just a superwise, impotent but innocent spectator. God can no more be held responsible for what He knows must happen than could Cassandra of Troy for what she knew would happen. Hence there is no ground for the final objection: merely because you must do what you do doesn't make *what* you do *your* responsible act. No one is responsible for this act, since, as far as we know, no one has the power (the freedom) to do differently than he does—not God, not you, not anyone; and that's that!

We turn next to the third and final theological argument that denies the existence of human free will.

[96] Bertrand Russell, *Human Society in Ethics and Politics* (London: George Allen & Unwin, Ltd., 1954), pp. 97–98.

3) *The Daiva Argument*

The *daiva* argument holds that God must necessarily be a part of every action and that, as a result, nothing happens or could happen unless God was somehow involved in the happening. The issue of free will enters precisely because it would seem that events could not have happened differently than they did; that is, God gave His assent to the action that occurred and He withheld it from all the other actions that didn't occur. The passages in the *Gītā* that give rise to this very important but perhaps curious argument are the following, where, once again, Lord Kṛṣṇa counsels Arjuna:

> Learn from Me now the five causes for the accomplishment of all actions as taught in *Sāṁkhya*:
>
> The body, the agent in the body, the various organs of action, the many kinds of efforts or energies, and *daiva* as the fifth.

Lord Kṛṣṇa concludes by saying:

> Whatever action a man performs by his body, speech or mind, whether right action or wrong action, these five causes are its necessary conditions.[97]

The argument is reminiscent of similar pronouncements by Western philosophers such as Descartes and the Continental Occasionalists, the latter being those seventeenth-century Cartesians who followed after their master, Descartes, on the point at issue above. The Occasionalist philosophers had argued that God was a necessary part of the causal chain of events leading from physical objects to my ideas of them. For instance, here is a comment by the great German philosopher, Gottfried Wilhelm von Leibniz, taken from his famous "*Journal des Savans*" of June 27, 1695, summarizing the views of these Cartesian Occasionalists:

> [B]ut [Descartes'] disciples . . . judged that we feel the qualities of bodies because God causes thoughts to arise in the soul on the occasion of the movements of matter, and when our soul wishes in its turn to move the body they judged that it is God who moves it for the soul. . . . [T]hey believed that God gives movement to a body on the occasion of the movement of another body.[98]

Descartes, himself, had argued some years earlier that God implicates himself in human actions as the direct cause of all of our clear and distinct ideas:

> Since all clear and distinct awareness is undoubtedly something, it cannot owe its origin to nothing, and must of necessity have God as its author—God, I say, who being supremely perfect, cannot be the cause of error.[99]

[97] *Bhagavad Gītā*, XVIII.13–15.

[98] Quoted in *The Philosophy of the Sixteenth and Seventeenth Centuries* Richard H. Popkin, ed., (New York: The Free Press, 1966), p. 328.

[99] *Meditation IV* in *The European Philosophers From Descartes to Nietzsche* Monroe C. Beardsley, ed., (New York: The Modern Library, 1960), p. 60.

This same kind of Cartesian theistic epistemology is picked up and reiterated further by the famous British idealist philosopher of the eighteenth century, Bishop George Berkeley, when he says:

> But, whatever power I may have over my own thoughts, I find the ideas actually perceived by sense have not a like dependence on my will. When in broad daylight I open my eyes, it is not in my power to choose whether I shall see or no, or to determine what particular objects shall present themselves to my view; and so likewise as to the hearing and other senses, the ideas imprinted on them are not creatures of my will. There is therefore some other will or spirit that produces them.[100]

And this "other will or spirit" is, of course, God.

When we turn from theistic epistemology, the belief that God is a necessary condition for all human knowledge, to theistic ethics, the belief that God is a necessary condition for all human action, we see that these two beliefs are not really different at all. In each belief God is a direct and necessary causal agent in both knowledge and action. God, in fact, dominates both the epistemological as well as the ethical scene, such that man becomes superfluous in the former and of mere secondary importance in the latter.

But it is theistic ethics that concerns us here. The *ślokas* that are of direct moment for us indicate that *daiva*[101] is one of the five causes of all actions, right as well as wrong actions. The use of *daiva* in the Indian epic period of about 400 B.C.E., the time in which the *Gītā* falls, generally guides translators into rendering the world as "divine," "fate," or "providence," and usually with honorific, upper-case initial letters. Following that practice here, the significant phrase in the above *ślokas* from the *Gītā* would then be translated to mean something like this: "and divine Fate or Providence is the fifth necessary condition of all the actions that a man performs." As a result of accepting this interpretation of the *śloka*, and with the addition of several other related concepts, two rather familiar philosophic problems can be generated, one of which, again, is of direct concern to us here. If we assume that *daiva* is also all-good in some sense, then the goodness of the Divine is directly and necessarily involved in all human actions. Furthermore, if those human actions involve wickedness or evil, then *daiva* is responsible, as an assumed necessary cause, for all evil or wicked actions: thus the theological problem of evil. On the other hand, and more to the point here, if *daiva* must be present in all human actions, and if those actions cannot occur without

[100] *Of the Principles of Human Knowledge*, ¶29 in *The English Philosophers From Bacon to Mill*, E.A. Burtt, ed., (The Modern Library, 1939), p. 532.

[101] The word *daiva* is related to *deva* (Latin *deus*, and Greek *dios*), which means "divine," "God," and "Goddess" in Sanskrit. And *deva*, in turn, comes from *div* (Latin *Jovis*, Greek *dios*, which are related to the Sanskrit *dyaus*, which in turn is cognate with the Greek *Zeus* and the Latin *Jupiter*; these two latter names mean "Heaven" and "Father"), and *div* means "sky," "heaven," and, as the personification of Heaven, "Father."

*daiva*, and if those actions cannot be different than they are because of these two reasons, then those actions cannot be called "free": thus the problem of free will.

But the *daiva* argument for human compulsion needs some further explanation, for it is simply not clear yet how *daiva*'s presence in action works so that I am compelled to do what I do. It seems clear, first of all, that nothing gets done without *daiva*. Let's assume, therefore, that some kind of *daiva* assent is necessary for any human action. If we interpret *daiva* as an all-powerful "Fate," on the one hand, then we are back to the fatalism argument (see above, pp. 258–61). If we interpret *daiva* as an all-knowing "Providence," on the other hand, then we are back to the predestination argument (see above, pp. 256–58). But if we can slip beyond or between these two interpretations and see *daiva* instead as some kind of divine or Fatherly assent, then we'll not only be on a new and interesting track of interpretation but perhaps we can find a new and interesting kind of theological compulsion at work here in the *Gītā*.

This interpretation of the *daiva* argument would seem to come to the following-divine assent is necessary for the performance of any and all human action. And since human action consists of the motive or desire, the act or doing, and the consequences or results, it would seem that divine assent must enter at all three stages of human action. This triple-assent doctrine is not as far-fetched as it sounds, for "checking with God" at all three stages of human action is a religious practice familiar to theists the world over who talk and converse with their Gods through prayer. One plans an event and checks with an ever-present God in the desiring; if there are no negative signs, one goes on to the next stage. One does the act and checks with God in the doing; if there are, once again, no negative signs, then one goes on to the next stage. One reaps or enjoys the fruits or consequences of one's planned act and checks with God in the enjoying; if there are, again, no negative signs, then one continues to enjoy the results of one's planned act. If God does not assent to the first stage, then one cannot go on to the second. If God does not assent to the second, then one cannot go on to the third. Further, God cannot assent to the second or third unless he has at least assented to the first.

Thus the rules of assent can get to be extremely complex. A negative sign at any stage halts the game, as it were, and no sign, or the absence of any sign, signals assent. Further, a positive sign—for example, a voice, a dove, a rainbow, a miracle, a conversation with Lord Kṛṣṇa, and so on—would also signal assent; and the world's theistic literature, at what is comparable to the religious stage in *Gītā darśana*, is shot through with rich and moving examples of such assent stories.

But in what sense are human actions compelled and in what sense are man's actions really not free, if the divine-assent assumption of the *daiva* argument is accepted?

Suppose that we go back to the battlefield once more. Suppose, once again (and for the last time now), that you suddenly leap to your feet from the chariot, grab your bow and arrows, and shout, "I'll fight!" Whereupon you act on this intention by rushing off at top speed into the fray. Later you return and we sit down for a chat. I ask you whether you were free. Yes, you answer, I was free. But, I remind you, God assented at every stage of your action. Yes, you understand and agree that that happened, else you could not have done all that you did. And, furthermore, you confess that at one moment during the battle God even withheld his assent, for there was one act in particular that you were not able to carry out. I ask what you mean. And you tell me how you wanted to rescue a friend who was outnumbered and being attacked by the enemy, but you were unable to because God didn't assent. I ask how you know this. Why, because your legs froze, your arrows stuck to your hand, you were suddenly beset with the numerous enemy yourself, and then you saw your friend cut down. All of which proves, you conclude, that God withheld his assent. But then I point out that the withholding of assent meant you could not have done what you wanted to do. You agree. But then you were not free, I conclude, and I point to the definition of "free will" with which this whole long and sometimes dreary account began (see above, p. 244).

Perhaps you demur and protest at this first suggested conclusion. But then I remind you that you went into battle to begin with only because God assented. You agree. And, I continue, you could not have not gone into battle, because the assent was given to go into battle. In other words, unless *daiva* assents to everything *carte blanche*—which is extremely unlikely, given the fact that he did not give his assent to your saving your friend—we must assume that if *daiva* assents to your choosing to fight, he wouldn't assent to your choosing not to fight. Therefore, I conclude, you could not really have chosen not to go into battle. Therefore, you could not have done differently than you did. Therefore, you're not free, and that's that.

The *daiva* argument, when put more elegantly, looks like this:

1. God's assent is a necessary condition of all human action.
2. Therefore, without this assent no action is done, and with it any action can be done.
3. When God gives you his assent to do $x$, he withholds his assent from your doing not-$x$, where $x$ is any action whatever.
4. Therefore, if you did $x$, then you could not have done not-$x$.
5. Therefore, you could not have done differently than you did in the past, nor can you do differently than you will do in the future.
6. Therefore, you are not free.

Comments. First, one might object that what I did was chosen by me, and that if I wanted to I could have done differently because I could have chosen differently. But this objection overlooks the fact that the entire action, all three elements of it, needs God's assent, including the motive or choice that gets the act going to begin with. The *daiva* argument tends to see God as the wielder of the big sticks of assent and dissent that keep all human actions within extremely narrow bounds. Seen in this way, the *daiva* argument can only lead to divine compulsion in all human actions.

Second, one might object that the *daiva* argument implicates God in all wicked as well as all good human action, and this implication is theologically absurd; and any argument that leads to an absurdity must itself be absurd. Hence, the *daiva* argument is absurd. To this objection we might simply say, "Well, so what?" Absurd or not, the argument would seem to stand. The objection does not attack the argument itself but simply points to another unhappy result of this putatively sound argument—a second unwanted, because absurd, implication of assuming that divine assent is needed in all human actions. I leave the reader to mull over these possible disturbing results.

### 3) Conclusion

The arguments that we have examined in exploring the issue of free will and fatalism in the *Bhagavad Gītā* may or may not destroy ethics as the West knows that discipline. It seems to me, however, and primarily because of the two-views doctrine in *Gītā darśana* that philosophic room can be made for both free will and fatalism. The reasons are similar to those we discussed previously in examining teleological and deontological ethics and their relation to the religious and the metaphysical views, respectively, of *Gītā darśana* (pp. 237–42). At the very least a theory involving a fatalism or compulsion could exist consistently with the metaphysical view. The only proviso would be that there would be but one reality in such a theory and that it would be this one reality that was compelled or fated in its activities; that is, it compelled itself. And the defenders of the metaphysical view seem to speak in precisely this fashion when they proclaim, for example, their own unreality, their own illusoriness, unworthiness, and lack of value, in relation to the Supreme. One of the great Muslim poets of the mystical Sufi tradition, Jalāl Al-Dīn Rūmī (672–738 A.H.), spoke directly to this issue and out of the metaphysical view within Islam when he said:

> If we let fly an arrow, the action is not ours; we are only
> the bow, the shooter of the arrow is God.
> This is not compulsion (*jabr*): It is almightiness (*jabbārī*)
> proclaimed for the purpose of making us humble.[102]

[102]See A. L. Herman, "Sufism, Fatalism and Evil in the Mathnawī of Jalāl Al-Dīn Rūmī," in *Iqbal Review*, Vol. 12, No. 3 (October 1971), p. 8.

Just as Rūmī takes the metaphysical view in his own tradition, so also does the Christian who is like Meister Eckhart's "truly poor man" (pp. 161–62), the man who wills nothing, knows nothing, and has nothing. Such a person is emptied of self and filled with the only reality there is, Godhead. Realizing this truth, that all action is ultimately God acting on God, that God's will is always done, is the essence of divine fatalism and the *sine qua non* of the metaphysical view.

Further, an ethical theory dependent on a free and separate human will existing side by side with God is the *sine qua non* of the religious view. The pluralism of this view, a pluralism of selves with wills and of Gods with wills or a God with a will, is not without its problems, as we've seen. The defenders of the religious view, however, are not intimidated by these problems. They speak unashamedly about doing God's will, or making their will conform to God's will, and so on. But, consistent with the pluralism of the religious view, there are always two wills, and two quite distinct and separate wills at that; and there are two wills because there are at least two real beings: God and man.

We might say that a *prima facie* case has been made for fitting both free will and compulsion into *Gītā darśana*. It remains to say a final word about the ethics of the *Gītā* in terms of the rules and patterns of behavior in Indian culture that are provided for by both Indian and *Gītā* ethics. In the conclusion that follows I want to bring the doctrine of the *āśramas* (stages of life) once more to the front of our discussions, relating through them what have been called "the ordinary and the extraordinary norms of the Indian cultural pattern"[103] to the religious and metaphysical views, respectively, of *Gītā darśana*. I will then summarize *Gītā darśana* and the nature of the two views with which it is essentially concerned.

## c. *Conclusion: Gītā Darśana and Indian Thought*

### 1) Some Preliminaries

The time has come to draw together the several threads that have run through this philosophical narrative on the *Bhagavad Gītā* and to make good on certain promises made with respect to *Gītā darśana*. The reader will recall that we began with a fundamental question (p. 194): how can so many philosophers find so many mutually inconsistent metaphysical and religious philosophies in the *Gita*? The answer that we gave and then defended we

[103]The terminology "ordinary norm" and "extraordinary norm" originates with Franklin Edgerton and is taken from his fascinating paper, "Dominant Ideas in the Formation of Indian Culture," *Journal of the American Oriental Society*, Vol. 61, pp. 151–156.

called "the two-views interpretation" or *Gītā darśana*. The model that we used (pp. 215–16) for the construction of the two-views interpretation was that of the *āśramas*. We argued that the two views in the *Gītā*, the metaphysical view and the religious view, bear the same relationship to one another as do the four *āśramas* to one another. Thus, just as the *brahmacarya* (student) *āśrama* (stage) and the *gṛhastha* (householder) *āśrama* are not inconsistent with one another, unless possibly one tried to be in both stages at once, so in the same way, if we can now accept the two views as philosophical stages for growth and development, the religious stage and the metaphysical stage are not inconsistent with one other, unless one tried to be in both stages at once. On this latter point, however, it is quite possible that as one moves from one stage to the other, whether in the *āśramas* or within *Gītā darśana*, there will be an overlap and a running together of the two *āśramas* or stages: and then there will be inconsistency. This overlap, we suggested, produced the inconsistencies in *Gītā* interpretation by both *Sāṁkhya darśana* (see pp. 187–88) and *Vedānta darśana* (pp. 193–94) and is responsible for the several philosophical and theological problems and puzzles that we managed to conjure up and then treat with *Gītā darśana* (pp. 218–22).

The two-views or two-stages interpretation, then, is precisely what its name suggests: a doctrine wherein one moves from lower to higher levels within a stage, or from one stage to another stage, in the course of one's own philosophical and spiritual development. The two stages of religion and metaphysics, like the *āśramas* before them, are indicative, furthermore, of levels of understanding or knowledge that relate to the values, goals, and duties inherent in each. This understanding, in turn, is closely and causally related to the *varṇas*, yogas, and *guṇas* of those stages. Thus, three things can be said about the two-views interpretation as it relates to these three other concepts:

First, given the law of *karma* and the doctrine of *saṁsāra*, it is no accident that one is born with the intellectual, religious, and metaphysical abilities that one possesses. One's previous life, after all, determines one's *guṇa*-nature in this life, and together with that *guṇa*-nature goes one's *varṇa* and the yoga appropriate to that *varṇa* (see pp. 156ff., "*Guṇa*types, *Varṇas*, and Yogas").

Second, the type or kind of intellectual or philosophic *guṇa*-nature one has will be reflected specifically in the way one interprets the *Gītā*, and we have seen that two such interpretations are possible—interpretations from either the religious view or the metaphysical view.

Third, it must follow that these interpretations and these views are related causally to the *guṇas*, the *varṇas*, and the yogas in exactly the same way that all other human attributes, activities, and proclivities are related (see pp. 169ff., "*Guṇa*types and Somatotypes"): and this is precisely what we learned from examining the personalities and beliefs of Kṛṣṇa and Arjuna and their attitudes toward the five metaphysical assumptions of the *Vedānta.* Recall that Kṛṣṇa and *advaitins* such as Śaṁkara emerge as the chief representatives of the metaphysical view, while Arjuna and *dvaitins* such as Madhvācarya emerge as the chief representatives of the religious view. They represent those views precisely because of the determinism inherent in both the law of *karma* and the doctrine of *saṁsāra,* which, along with the *guṇa*-natures of these individuals, has locked them, so to speak, into the stages of development at which we find them.

Let me now conclude this long study of the *Bhagavad Gītā* by briefly summarizing our findings with respect to the two views of *Gītā darśana.*

### 2) Ordinary and Extraordinary Norms

One key to understanding the two views of *Gītā darśana* is found in the existential distinction between what are referred to as "the ordinary and the extraordinary norms of the Indian cultural pattern." This distinction is "existential" for two reasons. First, it relates to two authentic ways of living—in the world, following *dharma*, *artha*, and *kāma*, and all that those concepts entail; and outside of the world, following *mokṣa* and rising above all that the ordinary norm offers. Second, the distinction depends upon two quite separate understandings and valuings regarding the self in relation to those ways of living. Thus these norms are ways of living that depend on one's understanding or realizing or knowing something-or-other in virtue of which a valuing or disvaluing of something-else-or-other then occurs. In other words, what makes these two kinds of existences possible, the ordinary and the extraordinary, is an understanding at the metaphysical-epistemological level, followed by an accepting at the ethical level, of certain truths and values. It is here, at the levels of understanding and accepting of what is taken to be real and valuable, that the two-views interpretation and *Gītā darśana* begin to make their appearance. That is why the distinction between the ordinary and the extraordinary norms is the key to *Gītā darśana,* for it is at the level of authentic, honest living, living actively and reflectively rather than slothfully and passively, that the religious stage and the metaphysical stage are first made manifest.

### 3) The Religious Stage and the Metaphysical Stage of *Gītā Darśana*

The religious stage is the heart of the ordinary norm of the Indian cultural pattern. The religious stage is characterized by a pluralistic metaphysics, by religious rites and sacrifices, and by prayers to a personal but Holy Other, a transcendent Divine Being. The religious stage holds to a belief in the reality of heavens, hells, and Gods. Its ethics, furthermore, is teleological—that is, goal-oriented and purposive, wherein rightness and goodness are defined in terms of the values inherent in realizing and achieving those goals and purposes. The ethics of the religious stage, moreover, believes in the reality and the necessity of human free will, and its ethics as well as its social philosophy are built around this belief.

The metaphysical stage, depending as it does on a new understanding followed by a new set of values, stands in sharp distinction, but not contradiction, to the religious stage. The metaphysical stage is the heart of the extraordinary norm of the Indian cultural pattern. Furthermore, the extraordinary norm makes metaphysical and ethical demands on its practitioners that carry them far beyond the demands of the ordinary norm and the religious stage. The life style of a person in the metaphysical stage is beautifully characterized as that of "the abandoner." The philosophy of abandonment is essentially negative; but the negative life style, following from the abandonment of the old Adam, the old ways of living, the old beliefs and practices, is the direct result of a metaphysical understanding. What the abandoner has done is simply to draw the existential consequences of this metaphysical understanding. The result of that understanding has, therefore, ethical or practical consequences—namely, abandonment; and what is abandoned is, of course, the religious stage, the ordinary norm of the cultural pattern.

The metaphysical stage is characterized by a monistic metaphysics and by a rejection or a transcending of the pluralisms of the religious stage. While the person in the metaphysical stage may pay lip service to God or the Gods, to religion and ethics in general, or to the "reality" of other beings, whatever or whoever they are, this apparent reference to plurality is not metaphysically grounded and it should not, therefore, be taken seriously where it looks *as if* real others were being referred to. There is only one ultimate reality for the metaphysical stage, and all else that appears real is merely that: appearance. There is no survival of a personal self, complete with consciousness and memory, after liberation or *mokṣa*; there is only the Wholly Other, the One, the Real, Godhead, *Brahman*, or the Unmanifest. The ethics, or the theory of behavior toward others, is beset with difficulties for the person in the extraordinary norm, for there are no "others," strictly speaking. Where an ethics does exist, or where it is spoken of at all, it remains deontological and fatalistic; behavior at this metaphysical stage is oriented to duty, and such behavior is "divinely" or metaphysically compelled or necessitated in virtue of the necessity that pervades the manifested world of appearance.

The yogas and the goals of the two stages are also different, as might be expected. The religious stage is heaven- and God-oriented, hence *bhakti* plays a large role in the accomplishment of that goal. There are, after all, for the religious stage real others toward whom one can have a religious relationship, just as there are real others toward whom one can have a moral relationship. In the religious relationship these others are the Gods who have, or God who has, the power whereby one's goal or goals can be achieved. Hence, *bhakti* yoga must seem the most appropriate way of securing that power and that goal or goals.

The metaphysical stage, on the other hand, is *mokṣa-* or freedom- or release-oriented and not heaven- or earth-oriented. There are no transcendent and real Gods to help in the search for freedom; hence, prayer, sacrifices, and devotions, while they may be of psychological benefit to the aspirant, are of no ultimate legitimate use. As a consequence, the yoga that characterizes the metaphysical stage is, of course, *jñāna* yoga, the yoga of knowledge or metaphysical realization. But I would reaffirm my contention that *dhyāna* yoga, the yoga of meditation, is a necessary preliminary for calming the mind and making *bhakti* yoga as well as *jñāna* yoga possible. Hence, *dhyāna* yoga is found at both the religious stage and the metaphysical stage of *Gītā darśana.*

Like *dhyāna* yoga, *karma* yoga may also be a useful adjunct to either the religious or the metaphysical stage. Its stress on selfless and unselfish activity, on the one hand, or its stress on spontaneous, compelled, and even necessary activity, on the other, makes it a natural and easy choice for religious yogis and metaphysical yogis, respectively. As the self becomes less and less a barrier to action or selfless action as a result of the practice of *karma* yoga, God becomes more and more important as the guide and the very doer of the action: thus the religious stage. And as the self is seen to be less and less real as it comes to figure less and less in action as a result of the practice of *karma* yoga, action is seen to do itself of necessity and not by the choice of a self: thus the metaphysical stage. As a result, *karma* yoga can be used by yogis in the religious stage as well as the metaphysical stage.

Numerous problems and questions arise with this interpretation of the philosophy of the *Gītā* as *Gītā darśana.* Several have already been treated in our discussion of the two-views interpretation (pp. 215–18); others we shall consider below.

### 4) Comments on *Gītā Darśana*

My comments, questions, and observations regarding *Gītā darśana* are rather simple and straightforward.

First, who is on or in the two stages called the religious and the metaphysical? The question is easily answered: people are at or in these stages; people such as Arjuna are at the religious stage, and beings such as Kṛṣṇa are at the metaphysical stage. Further, the people at the two stages will all have something in common. In particular, they will share a common knowledge or understanding, whether explicit or implicit, about the nature of the real and its manifestations in the visible universe. Further, they will share, whether they can articulate this sharing or not, in the duties, means, and goals entailed by the metaphysics as those duties, means, and goals are expressed in the two stages. But this answer naturally leads to another question, more bothersome and more important. For if it is people and beings such as Arjuna and Kṛṣṇa who are in the stages, then how does one get into the stages? How many stages are there in actuality? How does one move from one to another?

Let's look at our second question: how many stages are there in actuality? For there must be some kind of a preparatory stage before one even gets into the religious stage; and presumably there is another stage or superstage beyond the metaphysical stage for those beings who transcend the stages altogether; and presumably there is some kind of intermediate stage between the religious stage and the metaphysical stage, noticeable if one is moving from one stage to the other. If all of this talk makes any sense, then it would follow that there are many more stages of human existence than are dreamed of in *Gītā darśana.* I would respond by saying that there are many other levels of human awareness and activity that include the two stages under discussion here. *Gītā darśana* merely draws attention to the two ideal stages without making any judgments regarding the actuality of pre-stage, inter-stage, and post-stage levels. The existence of such extra-stage levels is not essential to the argument that *Gītā darśana* with its two stages does in fact exist, that it is common-sensical, consistent, and complete, and that it has its grounding in the *Bhagavad Gītā.*

Third, does one move or progress from one stage to another? If so, how? The answer is "yes" to the first question; that's why the two views can be called "stages," and that's why we earlier referred to the movement between the stages as "progressive" (see pp. 215–18). The answer to the second question is not quite so simple. Suppose that Arjuna will progress from the religious stage that he is now on to the metaphysical stage that Kṛṣṇa is now on. But if this is so, an objector might respond, then doesn't it imply that Kṛṣṇa's metaphysical stage is superior to Arjuna's? And doesn't that mean, then, that a metaphysical monism such as *advaita Vedānta* is the correct interpretation of the *Gītā* after all? And if that is the case, then isn't the *Gītā* an *advaita* text after all, and mustn't everyone who says differently be wrong?

As we noted earlier, questions such as these can occur only where one sees relations such as "superior to" or "more progressive than" as if they entailed relations such as "more correct than" and "more real than." And they don't. The argument that assumes they do rests on a not-so-subtle ambiguity that begins with the concept of "superior." For there are two senses of "superior" at work here. One—the only sense intended in talking about the stages,—is purely descriptive; the other, unintended sense is purely prescriptive or normative. The descriptive sense of "superior" merely intends that the metaphysical stage is ordinally or serially above or beyond the religious stage, and that's all. The normative sense of "superior" intends that the metaphysical stage is valuatively better than the religious stage. Confusing these two senses of "superior" introduces the ambiguity, and the unintended interpretation is the result: the metaphysical stage should be seen as serially superior but not valuatively superior to the religious stage. It would be just as inappropriate, for example, to argue that the *vānaprastha āśrama* is normatively superior to the *gṛhastha āśrama*: and that's the whole point in calling them all *āśramas*—"stages"—rather than "doctrines," "beliefs," or "philosophies."

An identical ambiguity rests with the concept of "progress," and similar *caveats* should be offered regarding it. For while it is true that one can progress from the religious stage to the metaphysical stage (or *vice versa* for that matter!) in serial order, one ought not, once again, to read normative connotations into the concept of "progress," which, like "superior," is purely descriptive in this context and entirely value-neutral.

This concludes our discussion of the ethics and the speculative philosophy of the *Bhagavad Gītā*. Let me turn in closing to a summary of the nature of Indian thought and restate what this book has been attempting to do.

# G.
# *Some Conclusions*

It was St. Augustine who first said, "Life is a predicament and not a spectacle." As we saw in the Introduction to this book, the responses that men have made to the predicament of life are the chief reasons for the existence of speculative philosophies and religions; in truth, those speculative philosophies and religions are the responses. Initially, man finds himself alone in a world he never made, imprisoned in a body that is ill-equipped for the rugged tasks that nature has set for it, doomed to spend his earthly time in suffering and pain only to be finally and ignobly trampled into the earth by indifferent death. In his anguish and agony he wonders: Why did it all happen? Why am I here? What's the sense of it? So he begins to speculate; and armed, then, with the explanations and answers that only his speculations can give, man endeavors to end the agony and the pain, and he attempts to make the small hour that he has on earth bearable and meaningful. The *darśanas*—the philosophic and religious speculations and responses to the predicament—serve a double purpose, really, for not only do they answer certain fundamental questions about the universe, man, and life, but in the very answering they bring a peace and tranquillity that surmounts the uncertainties and terrors of life. In the Introduction we referred to this philosophic undertaking as "speculative philosophy." In it lie the answers, in Augustine's terminology, to the predicament of life.

But man has set standards of adequacy that any answer to the predicament must meet. For not only do several *darśanas* compete with each other as the best answer to these questions about the universe, man, and life, but within each *darśana* there are standards to be met as well. The standards that man sets for his *darśanas* are embodied in the activity of another aspect of philosophy that we have referred to as "critical philosophy." Critical philosophy assures the speculative philosopher that the *darśana* he constructs—if it meets those standards—will be a satisfactory or adequate *darśana*. But just as people change, grow, and develop, so do their standards. As time passes, a Santa Claus or a tooth fairy *darśana* inevitably fails to satisfy the three essential standards of common sense, consistency, and completeness; and the questions that those *darśanas* answered have ceased to be significant ("Who brought the presents on Christmas Eve?" "Who put the money under my pillow and took my tooth?"). The problems and the questions of life begin to be far more complicated, and the need for a more sophisticated but satisfactory speculative philosophy is inevitable.

Hence, a *darśana* embodies both a speculative and a critical aspect. Generally, the speculative aspect of a *darśana* is the outcome of both its metaphysical and its religious outlook on the universe, man, and life, while the critical aspect of a *darśana* is the outcome of its epistemological struggles with what is said in the metaphysics and religion. Looking back on our endeavors in this book, we can see that we have really been investigating three *darśanas*, for the *Vedas*, the *Upaniṣads*, and the *Bhagavad Gītā* each possess the speculative characteristics (metaphysical and religious) as well as the critical characteristics (epistemological) of a *darśana*. All three were responses to life as a predicament, and all three attempted to give adequate or satisfactory answers to that predicament.

I would like to conclude our investigation of Indian thought by briefly reviewing all three of these *darśanas* from a vantage point within *Gītā darśana*. More specifically, I propose to try to see *Veda darśana* and *Upaniṣad darśana* as the two views, the religious and the metaphysical, respectively, of *Gītā darśana*. There are two reasons for doing so. First, *Veda darśana* with its pluralistic tendencies and *Upaniṣad darśana* with its monistic tendencies seem so plainly to represent the religious view and the metaphysical view, respectively, that not to draw attention to this fairly obvious parallel would be foolish if not careless. Second, it would be equally foolish and careless not to return to the earlier *darśanas* of Indian thought armed with the insights garnered from later Indian thought. *Gītā darśana* has taught us something about views and stages and about their appropriateness to people in the stages that may have application to *darśanas* and their appropriateness to historical periods. And it seems to dispose of any question about superior and inferior *darśanas*, or about more true or more real *darśanas*; the question, rather, once certain standards have been met, is whether a *darśana* is appropriate or relevant or proper not only to people but, perhaps, to cultures and to historical periods as well.

In what follows, I want to look once more at the philosophies of the *Vedas* (the *Ṛg Veda*, really), the *Upaniṣads* (the early *Upaniṣads*, really) and the *Bhagavad Gītā*, seeing them now as *darśanas*, organized systems of speculative and critical thought, attempting to answer, solve, or ameliorate the predicament of life, and, from the vantage point of our later discussions, see them as religious views, metaphysical views, or both.

But in order to do this elegantly let me recast a problem that we met early in our discussions of the *Vedas* and then refer that same problem to the *darśanas*. We talked of the problem that the self faces in confronting a threatening and hostile world, and we spoke of the anxiety, the pain, and the sheer terror that can come from such a confrontation between this small self and the great nonself world. Thus, in place of talking about "the predicament of life" or "the problem of the universe, man, and life," let's speak instead about "the problem of the self and the world." The problem we are seeking to solve, in other words, is generated when the individual, a self, is suddenly confronted by that which is not-self, what we are calling "the world," where that world threatens that self in some sense or other. This threat produces the fear and anxiety which lead to, or are part of, the suffering and pain that the self then experiences. Any solution to this problem must involve relieving the fear and anxiety by manipulating either the self or the world or both.

In other words, we are faced with a causal sequence that involves the self and the world in confrontation with each other, which causes anxiety, which in turn causes suffering. To treat the suffering involves treating the anxiety, which in turn involves treating the relation that the self has to the world. So the solution to this problem of self-WORLD, as we might graphically render it, lies in somehow manipulating the two relata. Now let's turn to our three *darśanas* and see, once again, how each manipulates the elements of the relation and brings about a solution to this fundamental and most perplexing problem, the problem of self-WORLD.

## 1. VEDA DARŚANA

*Veda darśana* is characterized, generally, by a pluralistic metaphysics (God, man, plants, animals, and rocks are real) and a realistic epistemology (they can all be known). In attempting to answer the questions about the universe, man, and life, it turns to what we have called "the religious view." Through its metaphysics and epistemology it adopts the way of the ordinary norm of the Indian cultural pattern. The problem of self-WORLD was solved by *Vedic brahminism* through the office of the ritual sacrifice and all that it entailed. Thus by manipulating the WORLD rather than the self, *brahminism* as a speculative philosophy recast the relationship between the self and the WORLD that had led to the problem in the first place. This recasting was done in two ways, really, and both depended on a reinterpretation of the WORLD through the sacred sacrifice.

In the first place, the *Vedic* seers seem to have argued, there is no need to worry about the WORLD, for through the sacred rites the Gods can be contacted and they will give you whatever you want and need in order to make the WORLD bearable and enjoyable. After all, WORLD is a threat in the first place because it refuses to be amenable to your needs and desires; it stands outside your control. But now, through the sacrifice, the priests will force the Gods to yield the goods of life, such as sons, cattle, wealth, victory, and happiness. So, on this first interpretation, the threatening WORLD is shrunk to a wholly accommodating world, and the threat, anxiety, and suffering vanish. Thus the first solution to the problem of self-WORLD by *Veda darśana*.

In the second place, the *Vedic* seers seem to have argued, there is no need to worry about the WORLD, because standing beyond it, waiting to receive you when you die, is another world, heaven. So, the argument continues, why be fearful of this WORLD when, compared to heaven, it doesn't really matter at all. Thus, when *Vedic* man cries out in the *Ṛg Veda*, "Make me immortal in that realm of eager wish and strong desire," the promise of a future world, where all wishes will be satisfied, has the effect of reducing the significance, the importance, the threat and suffering of this WORLD. So, on this second interpretation, the threatening WORLD is shrunk once again to a wholly manageable world, and the threat, anxiety, and suffering vanish. Thus the second solution to the problem of self-WORLD by *Veda darśana*.

These solutions presuppose, as we have seen in our discussion of the *Bhagavad Gītā*, all of the speculative paraphernalia of the religious view. There is a pluralism and a realism throughout the *darśana*, a down-to-earth common sense that Arjuna, the human warrior hero of the *Bhagavad Gītā*, would have understood all too well. The *Vedic* religion can be seen as Arjuna the religious man probably saw his own religion—that is, as he saw it before Lord Kṛṣṇa began to disturb and unhinge him with all that talk about metaphysics, the Unmanifested One, becoming one with *Brahman*, and so forth. *Vedic* religion believed in the Gods who had the power to make man happy and relieve the problem of self-WORLD. The way to that power lay, for *Vedic* man, in the religious rites of the sacrifice and a certain devotion to the Gods who attended that sacrifice. If we can further interpolate the religious view from the *Gītā* back into the *Vedas*, we might add that *Vedic* man very likely believed in the freedom of the human will, rather than fatalism; and, by analogy, we might even conjecture further and state that *Vedic* man was a teleologist in his ethics. But we are now on slippery philosophical ground in the realm of retrodictive probabilities, as we always are in attempting to reconstruct the religion and the philosophic views of the *Vedas*.

Let's turn to the second system of thought that we have dealt with in this book, see it, too, from the later vantage point of the *Gītā*, and recall its approach to the problem of self-WORLD.

## 2. UPANIṢAD DARŚANA

*Upaniṣad darśana* is characterized generally by a monistic metaphysics (*Brahman* alone is real, all else is vain appearance) and an idealistic or spiritualistic epistemology (but *Brahman* can be known). In attempting to answer the questions about the universe, man, and life it turns to what we have called, "the metaphysical view." Through its metaphysics and epistemology it adopts the extraordinary norm of the Indian cultural pattern. The problem of self-WORLD is solved by the *Upaniṣads*, or by the *advaita Vedānta* interpretation we gave to the *Upaniṣads*, by rejecting the *Vedic* religious view and adopting, instead, a solution distinctively characteristic of the metaphysical view. In place of manipulating the WORLD, the *Upaniṣad* solution lay in manipulating the concept of the self. Under this *Upaniṣadic* way to human happiness, the WORLD ceases to be a threat to the self, for the self is no longer the pipsqueak ego that formerly groveled in terror at the approach of the WORLD. The great discovery of the *Upaniṣads*, of course, was *Ātman*, the true Self, the all-powerful, holy Power of the universe, immanent in man: and *Ātman* really turned self into SELF. So how can I ever be afraid of the WORLD again, the *Upaniṣadic ṛṣi* cries, when I know now who I really am? How can anything ever hurt or threaten me again? Thus the solution of *Upaniṣad darśana* to the problem of the self-WORLD.

This solution presupposes, as we have seen in our discussion of the *Bhagavad Gītā*, all of the speculative paraphernalia of the metaphysical view. There is a discoverable monism and idealism or spiritualism throughout the *darśana*, a more or less uncommon-sense, other-wordly point of view that Lord Kṛṣṇa, the Savior hero of the *Bhagavad Gītā*, understands all too well. The *Upaniṣadic* religion leads, not to heaven and a life of eternal comfort and bliss, but to self-absorption and self-annihilation in *Brahman*. This religious goal follows logically from the monistic metaphysics that says: only *Brahman* is real and nothing else can survive anywhere for eternity. The way to this discovery of the overlying Oneness of reality is through knowledge, mystical intuition. The *bhakti yoga* to heaven is replaced by the *jñāna yoga* to *mokṣa*. The problem of self-WORLD dissolves, as all illusions should, in the discovery that only SELF is real, and that both self and world are *māyā*, a concoction of our own foolishness and ignorance. If we could also interpolate an ethical theory back into the *Upaniṣads* from the vantage point of our knowledge of the *Gītā*, then we would have to say that, to be consistent, the *Upaniṣads* probably ought to have opted for both an ethical fatalism, if that makes sense, and a deontological ethics to boot. But once again we are on slippery ground, for the *Upaniṣads* quite plainly do not seem to adopt either a fatalism or an out-and-out deontological ethics.

Let's turn now to the third system of thought we have dealt with in this book and see how it manages to deal with the problem of self-WORLD.

## 3. GĪTĀ DARŚANA

Indian thought culminates in *Gītā darśana*. The *Gītā* is the philosophical and religious product of three earlier and major influences on Hindu thought: the Indus Valley civilization (its influences now incorporated into post-*Vedic* culture), the *Vedas*, and the *Upaniṣads*. It should not be surprising, therefore, if the *Gītā* attempts to bring together under one *darśana* the major trends and doctrines that were part of that earlier philosophic heritage. We called the two principal trends or doctrines of the *Gītā* "the religious view" and "the metaphysical view," and we contended that together they formed the speculative system of thought called "*Gītā darśana*." We further indicated that the religious view is very likely *Vedic* in origin and the metaphysical view very likely *Upaniṣadic*. Both views exist side by side in the *Gītā*, each answering to two quite distinct philosophic and religious needs of man. Each view is *dharma* specific; that is, each is appropriate to particular human *dharmas* and conditions, hence each is relative to a level or stage of human development. Since we have already discussed movement between as well as within each stage, there is no need to repeat that discussion here, except to say once again that such interstage or intrastage movement reinforces the point that neither view is valuatively superior to the other.

*Gītā darśana* advocates, therefore, both the ordinary as well as the extraordinary norms of the cultural pattern. *Gītā darśana* includes an ethics and a doctrine about human free will that, we have tried to argue, are radically different for each of the two views in *Gītā darśana*. The religious view entails a teleological ethics and a solid belief in human free will; while the metaphysical view entails a deontological ethics and a solid belief in human fatalism. Finally the problem of self-WORLD is solved by *Gītā darśana* through adopting the separate solutions advocated by the *Vedas*, on the one hand, using the solution of the religious view (making the WORLD less important), and by the *Upaniṣads*, on the other, using the solution of the metaphysical view (making the self more significant). Again, neither solution is better than the other; instead, each solution advocated by *Gītā darsana* is simply more appropriate or less appropriate to the individual men and women caught up in the world's suffering, pain, and agony.

# *Appendix I: The Personality Description Test**

Please complete the following statements by writing into the blank spaces that follow each statement *any* three of the nine words that are listed immediately below each statement. Choose those words that seem to you to fit the statements most clearly and most closely. *Please feel free to repeat any words that have the same meaning in each selection,* as long as the words seem appropriate to you.

1. Much of the time I really feel rather ________________, ____________, and ________________.

| | | | | |
|---|---|---|---|---|
| calm | detached | shy | reflective | friendly |
| forceful | competitive | soft-tempered | energetic | |

2. I would like people to think of me as ____________________________, ________________, and ________________.

| | | | |
|---|---|---|---|
| gentle but aloof | calm | warm-affectionate | contented |
| active | intellectual | forceful | reflective |
| | | | commanding |

3. My parents consider me most often to be rather ________________, ________________, and ________________.

| | | | |
|---|---|---|---|
| extra-sensitive | soft-tempered | shy | never hungry |
| impetuous | dependent | hot-tempered | domineering |
| | | | always hungry |

*See p. 156, fn. 11.

4. My close friends look upon me generally as ____________________, ________________, and ________________.

| | | | |
|---|---|---|---|
| never hungry | talkative | competitive | intellectual |
| assertive | lazy | cool-detached | soft-tempered |
| | | | warm-affectionate |

5. My greatest faults are that I am sort of ____________________, ________________, and ________________.

| | | | |
|---|---|---|---|
| impetuous | hot-tempered | lazy | shy |
| domineering | contented | slow | extra-sensitive |
| | | | withdrawn |

6. In social situations I think I am generally ____________________, ________________, and ________________.

| | | | |
|---|---|---|---|
| relaxed | cool-detached | talkative | extra-sensitive |
| assertive | withdrawn | warm-affectionate | energetic |
| | | | friendly |

7. In working and studying I guess I am generally ________________, ________________, and ________________.

| | | | |
|---|---|---|---|
| competitive | always hungry | reflective | dependent |
| precise | forceful | slow | assertive |
| | | | never hungry |

8. When I am depressed and sad I think I usually tend to be ________________, ________________, and ________________.

| | | | |
|---|---|---|---|
| active | always hungry | dependent | impetuous |
| never hungry | introspective | hot tempered | withdrawn |
| | | | warm-affectionate |

9. When I am happy and joyful I think I tend to feel ________________, ________________, and ________________.

| | | | |
|---|---|---|---|
| active | introspective | always hungry | cool-detached |
| friendly | gentle but aloof | hot-tempered | contented |
| | | | energetic |

10. All in all, I hope that I could become even more ________________, ________________, and ________________.

| | | | |
|---|---|---|---|
| contented | precise | gentle but aloof | relaxed |
| competitive | calm | intellectual | forceful |
| | | | commanding |

Now that you have finished the *Personality Description Test*, please turn next to the *Key to Personality Description Test* and follow the accompanying directions.

## KEY TO PERSONALITY DESCRIPTION TEST

| *Endomorphic* | *Mesomorphic* | *Ectomorphic* |
|---|---|---|
| lazy | energetic | cool-detached |
| dependent | impetuous | withdrawn |
| relaxed | hot-tempered | reflective |
| contented | domineering | precise |
| calm | assertive | intellectual |
| always hungry | competitive | introspective |
| warm-affectionate | talkative | shy |
| soft-tempered | forceful | extra-sensitive |
| friendly | active | never hungry |
| slow | commanding | gentle but aloof |

*Directions:* Take the words that you have written in the test blanks and check them against the three lists above. Count the number of times each word you wrote appears in the lists. Then total the numbers of these times at the bottom of each of the three lists. You should have a grand total of 30 words. Now, whichever one of the three totaled numbers is highest should indicate, hypothetically, your somatotype. If your totals run 25 and 5 and 0, then you have a strong tendency to endomorphy. If your totals run 10 and 15 and 5, then you have a tendency to meso-endomorphy. And if your totals run 10 and 5 and 15, then you have a tendency to ecto-endomorphy. And so on.

# *Appendix II: The Table of Predicates**

Please relate your somatotype (from Appendix I) to the two sets of predicates below; then refer to the accompanying Directions for the Use of The Table of Predicates.

| *Your Somatotype* | *Your Personality Predicates* | *Your Guṇa-Nature Predicates* | *Your Appropriate Yoga* |
|---|---|---|---|
| | | (*Tamas*) | |
| 1. *Endomorphy* | 1. lazy | 1. laziness | *Bhakti* yoga |
| | 2. dependent | 2. procrastinating | |
| | 3. relaxed | 3. sleepiness | |
| | 4. contented | 4. lethargic | |
| | 5. calm | 5. negligent-stagnant | |
| | 6. always hungry | 6. stupid-ignorant | |
| | 7. warm-affectionate | 7. serving | |
| | 8. soft-tempered | 8. sluggish | |
| | 9. friendly | 9. subservient | |
| | 10. slow | 10. deceitful-malicious | |

*See pp. 174–75.

| | | | |
|---|---|---|---|
| | | (*Rajas*) | |
| 2. *Mesomorphy* | 11. energetic | 11. passion | *Karma* yoga |
| | 12. impetuous | 12. restless | |
| | 13. hot-tempered | 13. attachment | |
| | 14. domineering | 14. hatred | |
| | 15. assertive | 15. vigor | |
| | 16. competitive | 16. envy | |
| | 17. talkative | 17. firmness | |
| | 18. forceful | 18. violence | |
| | 19. active | 19. action | |
| | 20. commanding | 20. ambition | |
| | | (*Sattva*) | |
| 3. *Ectomorphy* | 21. cool-detached | 21. indifference to success and failure | *Jñāna* yoga |
| | 22. withdrawn | 22. mindful of moral duty | |
| | 23. reflective | 23. illuminating | |
| | 24. precise | 24. unwavering | |
| | 25. intellectual | 25. attached to knowledge | |
| | 26. introspective | 26. self-control | |
| | 27. shy | 27. acting without love or hate | |
| | 28. extra-sensitive | 28. purity | |
| | 29. never hungry | 29. firmness in control of mind and senses | |
| | 30. gentle but aloof | 30. serenity, patience | |

## DIRECTIONS FOR THE USE OF THE TABLE OF PREDICATES

1. *Endomorphy*: If you have the somatotype of endomorphy with a predominance of personality predicates 1–10, then you also have *tamas guṇa* predicates 1–10, and the yoga appropriate for you is *bhakti* yoga.

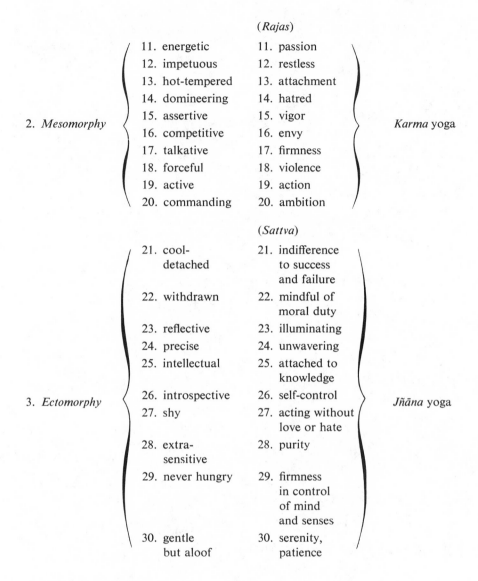

2. *Mesomorphy*: If you have the somatotype of mesomorphy with a predominance of personality predicates 11–20, then you also have *rajas guṇa* predicates 11–20, and the yoga appropriate for you is *karma* yoga.
3. *Ectomorphy*: If you have the somatotype of ectomorphy with a predominance of personality predicates 21–30, then you also have *sattva guṇa* predicates 21–30, and the yoga appropriate for you is *jñāna* yoga.

# *Bibliography: Indian Thought*

The books listed in the four categories below are all in English. They are generally introductory in nature and have been selected for their scholarly readability.

## GENERAL

A. L. Basham, *The Wonder That Was India* (London: Sidgwick & Jackson, Ltd., 1954). A grand survey of Indian culture from the Indus Valley civilization to the coming of the Muslims in the twelfth century.

Satischandra Chatterjee and Dhirendramohan Datta, *An Introduction to Indian Philosophy* (Calcutta: University of Calcutta, 1960). A fine introduction to the subject by two eminent Indian philosophers.

S. N. Dasgupta, *A History of Indian Philosophy*, 5 Vols. (New York: Cambridge University Press, 1951–54). A brilliant and exhaustive investigation of the history of Indian philosophy.

M. Hiriyanna, *The Essentials of Indian Philosophy* (London: George Allen & Unwin, Ltd., 1932). One of the best, short, modern accounts of Indian philosophy.

Karl H. Potter, *Presuppositions of India's Philosophies* (Englewood Cliffs, N.J.: Prentice-Hall, Inc., 1963). A splendid account of the assumptions of Indian philosophy by one of its foremost modern scholars.

S. Radhakrishnan, *Indian Philosophy*, 2 Vols. (London: George Allen & Unwin, 1923 and 1927). Still one of the best *advaita Vedānta* approaches to the history of Indian philosophy.

S. Radhakrishnan and Charles A. Moore, eds., *A Source Book in Indian Philosophy* (Princeton, N.J.: Princeton University Press, 1957). Basic philosophic materials in translation from the *Vedas* through the *darśanas* and the modern period with sound introductions written by the editors.

CHANDRADHAR SHARMA, *Indian Philosophy: A Critical Survey* (New York: Barnes & Noble, Inc., 1962). A critical appraisal of Indian philosophy by a modern teacher and scholar.

## THE VEDAS

M. BLOOMFIELD, *The Religion of the Veda* (New York: AMS Press, 1908, 1969). A classic introduction to Vedic studies, dated but great.

J. GONDA, *The Vision of the Vedic Poets* (The Hague: Mouton & Co., 1963). A sympathetic and authoritative account of *Vedism* by a first rate *Vedic* scholar.

R. T. H. GRIFFITH, trans., *The Rig Veda*, 2 Vols. (Benares: Chowkhamba Sanskrit Series Office, 1963). A reprint of the 1896–97 translation of the *Ṛg Veda.* Dated but useful.

A. B. KEITH, *The Religion and Philosophy of the Veda and Upanishads*, 2 Vols. (Cambridge, Mass.: Harvard University Press, 1925). Still one of the best introductions to early Indian thought as found in these texts.

D. D. KOSAMBI, *Ancient India* (New York: Pantheon Books, Inc., 1965). A fine study of the ancient period by a brillant Indian historian and scholar.

## THE UPANIṢADS

R. E. HUME, *The Thirteen Principal Upanishads* (Fair Lawn, N.J.: Oxford University Press, 1931, 1954) A well-written introduction with an uneven but readable translation of the essential *Upaniṣads.*

JUAN MASCARO, *The Upaniṣhads* (Baltimore: Penguin Books, 1965). Seven complete *Upaniṣads* and parts of five others are translated clearly and well, and there is a good introduction on the significance of the *Upaniṣads*.

S. RADHAKRISHNAN, *The Philosophy of the Upanisads* (London: George Allen & Unwin, Ltd., 1924). A good *advaita Vedānta* interpretation of the *Upaniṣads* by India's most famous modern philosopher.

S. RADHAKRISHNAN, *The Principal Upaniṣads* (London: George Allen & Unwin, Ltd., 1953). The major *Upaniṣads* with the Sanskrit, an English translation, and a commentary on almost every verse by India's most famous twentieth-century philosopher.

## THE BHAGAVAD GĪTĀ

FRANKLIN EDGERTON, *The Bhagavad Gītā* (Cambridge, Mass.: Harvard University Press, 1944). Reprinted in paperback (New York: Harper & Row, 1965). Literal and authoritative translation by one of the great Sanskritists of this century.

MOHANDA K. GANDHI, *The Gītā According to Gandhi* (Ahmedabad: Navajivan Publishing House, 1946). This is Mahadev Desai's English translation of Gandhi's Sanskrit translation; it shows what the *Gītā* meant to Gandhi; a good introduction and a verse-by-verse commentary written by Gandhi.

A. L. HERMAN, *The Bhagavad Gītā* (Springfield, Ill.: Charles C Thomas, Publishers, 1973). A critical commentary pointing to the myriad philosophical problems and puzzles of the *Gītā* highlights the translation.

R. C. ZAEHNER, *The Bhagavad Gītā* (Fair Lawn, N.J.: Oxford University Press, 1969). A translation with a verse-by-verse commentary together with a literate and readable introduction by a fine scholar.

# *Glossary–Index*

*A*

Action (activity composed of intention, act and consequences), 224, 225–226, 228, 244
Adam (*see* Eve)
*adharma* (lawlessness, moral confusion), 146, 147–149, 150, 175, 185, 207
*adhyāsavāda* (*see vivartavāda*)
*advaita, advaitin* (nondualistic, monistic; the person holding this view) (*see also* Metaphysical monism, *Vedānta*), 107, 120, 187, 194, 195, 198, 208, 211, 212, 220, 221, 242
*advaita* argument, the, 238, 240–242
*advaita Vedānta* (*see Vedānta*)
Afterlife in the *Vedas*, 35
Agni (*Vedic* God of fire), 34, 45, 52
*ahaṁkāra* (ego-maker, the ego, consciousness, an evolute or evolved entity in *Sāṁkhya* cosmology) (*see also Sāṁkhya darśana*), 180–181, 211
Altruistic ethical hedonism (*see* Ethical hedonism)
Analytic *apriori* judgments (*see also* Analytic judgments, *Apriori* evidence), 127
Analytic judgments (statements that are necessarily, or logically, true [or false]) (*see also Apriori* evidence, *Aposteriori* evidence, Synthetic judgments), 126–127
*anātman* doctrine (the view that there is no self), 186
Andronicus of Rhodes (1st century B.C.E. editor of the works of Aristotle), 4
Anxiety (the fear of the future), 36–38
*aparā Brahman* (*see Brahman*)
*Āpas* (*Vedic* Lord of waters), 35
*Aposteriori* evidence (justification that is dependent on the senses) (*see also Apriori* evidence), 127
*Apriori* evidence (justification that is not dependent on the senses) (*see also Aposteriori* evidence), 127, 233
*Āraṇyakas* ("forest texts," used for meditation by those who retire to a solitary life), 23, 24, 25
Argument from silence, the, 55–56, 196
Aristotle (384–322 B.C.E.), 1, 4
Arjuna (the human warrior-hero of the *Bhagavad Gītā*), 143, 144, 145, 148, 150, 151, 156, 158, 159, 163, 165, 168, 169, 175, 187, 200, 201, 202, 203, 205, 217, 220, 223, 224, 225, 235, 236, 237, 238, 239, 252, 259, 268, 269, 271, 272, 277
Arjuna's dilemma (*see also* Dilemma of action), 151, 152, 158, 200–201, 223–224
Art in Harappān culture, 11–15
*arthas* (the four traditional aims or goals of life) (*see also* individual *arthas* elsewhere), 85, 89–100, 138, 139, 148, 228, 229
  *artha* (wealth), 89–90, 99, 228
  *kāma* (sexual pleasure), 90–91, 99, 228

## *H*



## *I*

## *T*



## *U*

## *W*



## *Y*



## *Z*